The Morality of Revolution

NEW AFRICAN HISTORIES

SERIES EDITORS: ALLEN ISAACMAN, DEREK R. PETERSON, AND CARINA RAY

David William Cohen and E. S. Atieno Odhiambo, *The Risks of Knowledge*
Belinda Bozzoli, *Theatres of Struggle and the End of Apartheid*
Gary Kynoch, *We Are Fighting the World*
Stephanie Newell, *The Forger's Tale*
Jacob A. Tropp, *Natures of Colonial Change*
Jan Bender Shetler, *Imagining Serengeti*
Cheikh Anta Babou, *Fighting the Greater Jihad*
Marc Epprecht, *Heterosexual Africa?*
Marissa J. Moorman, *Intonations*
Karen E. Flint, *Healing Traditions*
Derek R. Peterson and Giacomo Macola, editors, *Recasting the Past*
Moses E. Ochonu, *Colonial Meltdown*
Emily S. Burrill, Richard L. Roberts, and Elizabeth Thornberry, editors, *Domestic Violence and the Law in Colonial and Postcolonial Africa*
Daniel R. Magaziner, *The Law and the Prophets*
Emily Lynn Osborn, *Our New Husbands Are Here*
Robert Trent Vinson, *The Americans Are Coming!*
James R. Brennan, *Taifa*
Benjamin N. Lawrance and Richard L. Roberts, editors, *Trafficking in Slavery's Wake*
David M. Gordon, *Invisible Agents*
Allen F. Isaacman and Barbara S. Isaacman, *Dams, Displacement, and the Delusion of Development*
Stephanie Newell, *The Power to Name*
Gibril R. Cole, *The Krio of West Africa*
Matthew M. Heaton, *Black Skin, White Coats*
Meredith Terretta, *Nation of Outlaws, State of Violence*
Paolo Israel, *In Step with the Times*
Michelle R. Moyd, *Violent Intermediaries*
Abosede A. George, *Making Modern Girls*
Alicia C. Decker, *In Idi Amin's Shadow*
Rachel Jean-Baptiste, *Conjugal Rights*
Shobana Shankar, *Who Shall Enter Paradise?*
Emily S. Burrill, *States of Marriage*
Todd Cleveland, *Diamonds in the Rough*
Carina E. Ray, *Crossing the Color Line*
Sarah Van Beurden, *Authentically African*
Giacomo Macola, *The Gun in Central Africa*
Lynn Schler, *Nation on Board*
Julie MacArthur, *Cartography and the Political Imagination*
Abou B. Bamba, *African Miracle, African Mirage*
Daniel Magaziner, *The Art of Life in South Africa*
Paul Ocobock, *An Uncertain Age*
Keren Weitzberg, *We Do Not Have Borders*
Nuno Domingos, *Football and Colonialism*
Jeffrey S. Ahlman, *Living with Nkrumahism*
Bianca Murillo, *Market Encounters*
Laura Fair, *Reel Pleasures*
Thomas F. McDow, *Buying Time*
Jon Soske, *Internal Frontiers*
Elizabeth W. Giorgis, *Modernist Art in Ethiopia*
Matthew V. Bender, *Water Brings No Harm*
David Morton, *Age of Concrete*
Marissa J. Moorman, *Powerful Frequencies*
Ndubueze L. Mbah, *Emergent Masculinities*
Judith A. Byfield, *The Great Upheaval*
Patricia Hayes and Gary Minkley, editors, *Ambivalent*
Mari K. Webel, *The Politics of Disease Control*
Kara Moskowitz, *Seeing Like a Citizen*
Jacob Dlamini, *Safari Nation*
Alice Wiemers, *Village Work*
Cheikh Anta Babou, *The Muridiyya on the Move*
Laura Ann Twagira, *Embodied Engineering*
Marissa Mika, *Africanizing Oncology*
Holly Hanson, *To Speak and Be Heard*
Paul S. Landau, *Spear*
Saheed Aderinto, *Animality and Colonial Subjecthood in Africa*
Katherine Bruce-Lockhart, *Carceral Afterlives*
Natasha Erlank, *Convening Black Intimacy in Early Twentieth-Century South Africa*
Morgan J. Robinson, *A Language for the World*
Faeeza Ballim, *Apartheid's Leviathan*
Nicole Eggers, *Unruly Ideas*
Mark W. Deets, *A Country of Defiance*
Ademide Adelusi-Adeluyi, *Imagine Lagos*
Jody Benjamin, *The Texture of Change*
Patrick William Otim, *Acholi Intellectuals*
Daniel Magaziner, *Available Light*
Admire Mseba, *Society, Power, and Land in Northeastern Zimbabwe ca. 1560–1960*
Benedito Luís Machava, *The Morality of Revolution*

The Morality of Revolution

Reeducation Camps and the Politics of Punishment in Socialist Mozambique, 1968–1990

Benedito Luís Machava

OHIO UNIVERSITY PRESS

ATHENS, OHIO

Ohio University Press, Athens, Ohio 45701
ohioswallow.com

Printed in the United States of America
Ohio University Press books are printed on acid-free paper ∞ ™

Hardcover ISBN: 978-0-8214-2582-4
Paperback ISBN: 978-0-8214-2583-1
Electronic ISBN: 978-0-8214-2584-8

Library of Congress Cataloging-in-Publication Data available upon request.

The Morality of Revolution is the recipient of the Ohio University Press First Book Fund, established by Gillian Berchowitz in 2018.

First-time authors are often pioneers in their fields, and their writing and research are crucial to understanding the critical issues of our time. The Ohio University Press First Book Fund sets out to make the process more equitable for African and Appalachian scholars as they seek to publish their first books.

For more information, please see ohioswallow.com/first-book-fund/.

Contents

Illustrations

MAPS

FIGURES

TABLES

Acknowledgments

This book is the product of a chance encounter with a forbidden story and a difficult-to-explain call to bear witness on behalf of those who lived through it. As a fresh college graduate in Maputo, Mozambique, I got hired as a research assistant to anthropologist Helene Kyed. Part of my job was to run a survey on community policing in the labyrinthine neighborhood of Chamanculo, only a few miles from downtown Maputo. To my bemusement, several of my interlocutors insisted that community policing was a continuation of *vigilância popular*, or "popular surveillance," one of the key tenets of Mozambique's socialist experiment in the 1970s and 1980s. Commanded by the ruling party to guard against so-called internal enemies seeking to undermine the revolution, citizens were organized into neighborhood vigilante groups and helped security forces rid the country of threats to the socialist order. Prostitutes and vagrants were among their main targets. Tales about how my Chamanculo respondents identified internal enemies and got them sent away to remote internment camps in the far north led me to search for more information. How could prostitutes and vagrants, I asked myself, constitute a serious threat to the revolution? My curiosity increased after my mother, who was worried about my declining mood every time I returned home from Chamanculo, told me to stay away from that story. *Campos de reeducação*—as the internment camps were known—were taboo and seemed to unsettle people whenever mentioned. People in Chamanculo lowered their voices when talking about the camps. My mother did not like what I was getting myself into. Her attempt to save me from something potentially dangerous only spurred my interest, and I became even more immersed in my research.

The stories I heard in Chamanculo and the cases I read in newspapers at the archive were depressing. They could well have scared me away from dedicating several years of my life uncovering this story. But my point of no return was when my mother told me that, many years earlier, she nearly got detained and could have ended up in a camp somewhere in the north. This was her reason for me not to pursue my searches. Her near detention occurred precisely in front of the hospital in Chamanculo, where she had gone for her monthly checkups. She could not remember if she was pregnant with me or one of my six siblings, but she was halfway through the pregnancy. As she stepped out of the hospital, she saw an army truck filled with detained people—including women with babies in their arms—and soldiers rounding up pedestrians. One came after her, demanding to see her papers. Did she have any employment? If not, did she have any written authorization to be in the city? As an uneducated housewife, she did not fulfill his requirements for urban citizenship and was about to be manhandled into the truck when two nurses, who had just seen her, rushed out to her aid. Their uniforms might have persuaded the soldier to let her go. Although my mother's story had a happy ending, several similar cases had tragic outcomes. The more I read about them, the more their voices haunted me, as if urging me to bear witness to their silent—and silenced—tragedy. I did my best to honor their memory in these pages.

One does not embark on the journey of writing a book without collecting debts along the way. I have too many to count, and it gives me great pleasure to acknowledge some of them here. This book would not have been possible without the energy and commitment from Simeão Mazuze (a.k.a. Salimo Mohamed), the late Ché Mafuiane, and Felizardo Chaguala. This trio of former detainees went from informants to dear friends. Much of what I know about reeducation camps comes from our countless gatherings at Mazuze's home, where a lot was said about camp life amid good music, delicious food, and laughter. Their immense sense of humor made my research a lot easier, and their embrace of this project opened many doors. I am extremely thankful for their friendship and support. In Maputo and Niassa Provinces, where I conducted most of my research, archivists and administrators opened the doors of archives and private collections to me unreservedly, at times at their own peril given the reluctance of Mozambique's government to provide access to information. I bow to the bravery and professionalism of Natércia Massango, who held the keys of the archive of the defunct *Tempo* magazine, and Artimiza Machel of the archive of *Jornal notícias* in Maputo. Ivan Mazula, Deolinda Ernesto, Rosa Augusto, Joaquina Assaia, and Armando Rosário welcomed me into the administration building in Lichinga, Niassa, and were never bothered by my presence in their workplace. Benvindo, Amélia, Dona Felícitas, and Manuel Vene made my time in Niassa as productive as it was memorable. Fernando Machava translated my interviews and was always ready to respond to my requests for further archival material. I thank him for his hard work. I am forever in debt to all the former detainees who were brave to reopen the crust of the wound to share their stories with me.

This project took shape at the University of Michigan in Ann Arbor. I could not have asked for a better place to nurture my ideas and become a historian. My co-advisers, Anne Pitcher and Derek Peterson, created the right environment for me to flourish as a graduate student and to trust my own instincts. I am forever grateful for their mentorship, boundless support, and friendship. I owe them more than words can express. At Michigan I had the privilege to engage with stimulating scholars and generous readers who pushed me to think beyond my narrow interests. I thank the late Fernando Arenas (a rare soul who death took away from us too soon), Rudolph "Butch" Ware III, Martin Murray, Christine Feak, Gabrielle Hecht, Mike McGovern, Kelly Askew, Omolade Adumbi, Adam Ashforth, Howard Stein, Nancy Hunt, Christian de Pee, Geoff Eley, Rebecca Scott, John Carson, Joshua Cole, and Par Cassel. Kathleen King, Diana Denney, and Terre Fisher were a special trio in the history department's staff and pulled some heroic tricks to support international students. They are my heroes! A special thank-you to my colleagues and friends in the history and anthropology programs and in the Institute for the Humanities: Doreen Kembabazi, George Njung, Hillina Seife, Sara Katz, Emma Park, Jon Shaw, Robyn D'Avignon, Edgar Taylor, Baruani Mshale, Christopher Tounsel, Hiroaki Matsusaka, Pedro Cantisano, Leslie Hempson, Tara Weinberg, Pedro Monavile, Nana Quarshie, and James Hammond.

I received inspiring ideas and mentorship from many people in various stages of this project. I discussed and refined most of my thoughts with my mentor and dear friend David Hedges, a master of the historian's craft and teacher of many generations of Mozambican scholars. João Paulo Borges Coelho, a refined historian and storyteller, inspired me beyond academia. Among other things, he is responsible for my love of jazz and gave me the soundtrack that carried me through the ups and downs of writing this book. I conducted part of the research for this project with Maria Paula Meneses, a gracious and very generous friend. I learned a great deal about academic field work with Helena Kyed and Anne Pitcher. Barbara and Allen Isaacman offered important advice in different stages of my research and provided key contacts in Maputo. Kathleen Sheldon pointed me to sources and answered my queries. Colin Darch has been a true treasure. His splendid online database, Mozambique History Net, is my favorite source of material on postcolonial Mozambique. I have benefited enormously from his friendship and his ample collection of documents. Teresa Cruz e Silva, Jocelyn Alexander,

James Brennan, Eric Allina, Lars Buur, David Morton, Maria-Benedita Basto, Eric Morier-Genoud, Marissa Moorman, Didier Péclard, Michael Panzer, Euclides Gonçalves, Victor Igreja, João Cabrita, Pedro Comissário, Paolo Israel, Barbané Ncomo, Omar Ribeiro Thomaz, João de Regina, Yussuf Adam, Alda Saúte Saide, and the late Amélia Souto offered insights in various stages of this project. I thank them wholeheartedly.

The Society of Fellows at Princeton University was the perfect place for me to transition from graduate student to scholar. Here I found the intellectual stimuli to challenge my own assumptions and speak to a much larger audience. I thank the mentorship of Simon Gikandi, Michael Gordin, Emanuel Kreike, Wendy Belcher, João Biehl, Filip Nord, Michael Laffan, Gavin Steingo, Donald Vence Smith, Thomas Levin, and Jacob Dlamini. My colleagues and friends Miqueias Mugge, Rudo Mudiwa, Changue Chachague, Guangchen Chen, Joshua Freeman, Matthew Larsen, Serena Stein, and Themba Mbatha read and commented on different parts of the manuscript. Beate Witzler, the power engine behind the Society of Fellows, made sure my time and work at Princeton went as smoothly as possible.

It was at Princeton that I had the privilege to know Jonathan Ort, a brilliant mind and generous soul. Our connection started in the classroom and blossomed into a beautiful friendship. Jon read through and edited my manuscript with that rare ability to make a text more readable without scratching the author's cadence and addressivity. I was lucky to continue to benefit from his skillful editorship and friendship at Yale University, where we both moved at around the same time. I cannot thank him enough for his hard work on this book. I also thank Nina Gaither, a generous interlocutor, for commenting on parts of the book.

I joined the faculty of Yale University's history department at a very difficult moment. We are yet to fully assess the profound impact of the COVID-19 pandemic on our lives and the world we knew. Starting a new job and writing a book when all was uncertain was a daunting task. Although we all adapted to it eventually, remote work from afar and no access to archives, libraries, and the stimuli of corridor chats and coffee meetings with colleagues made academic life a nightmare at first. It could have been an impossible job if I had not benefited from the warm welcome and support from wonderful colleagues: Marcela Muñoz, Robert Harms, Dan Magaziner, Rohit De, Arne Westad, Valerie Hansen, Alan Mikhail, David Engerman, Fabian Drixler, Paul Freedman, Sunil Amrith, Joseph Manning, Isaac Nakhimovsky, and David Sorkin. At the Yale MacMillan Center Council on African Studies, I found a wonderful intellectual community with Cajetan Iheka, a dear friend, Stephanie Newell, Louisa Lombard, Kiare Wa'Njogu,

Michael Cappello, Cecile Fromont, Jill Jarvis, Kyama Mugambi, Veronica Waweru, and Jonathan Wyrtzen. Aside from being an inspiring colleague, Arne Westad opened the doors of the International Security Studies institute at the Jackson School of Global Affairs for me and supported my idea of an Africa Security Program, a promising initiative to think about Africa's security challenges in a volatile world. Thanks to Arne and Ted Wittenstein, the initiative has taught me the benefits of collaboration. My ongoing work with Vivien Chang is the product of the generative environment of ISS.

The research for this book was made possible by funding from the Social Science Research Council, the Guggenheim Foundation Dissertation Fellowship, and fellowships at the University of Michigan, namely the Rackham International Research Award, the International Institute Individual Fellowship, the Humanities Institute Graduate Student Fellowship, and several grants in the Department of History and the Department of Afroamerican and African Studies. I conducted further research from grants from the Humanities Council at Princeton University. The Whitney Humanities Center at Yale University contributed to book production costs through the Frederick W. Hilles Publication Fund. It was a privilege to work with Ohio University Press and the editors of the New African Histories series to bring this book to fruition.

My academic journey started at Eduardo Mondlane University, where I was given wings to fly by Solange Macamo and the late Gerhard Liesegang. António Manso, Napoleão Gaspar, Luisa Chicamisse, Sérgio Cabá, Marlino Mubai, Cláudio Mandlate, Adérito Machava, Arnaldo Caliche, Júlio Machel, Denise Malauene, Carlos Quembo, and Eulésio Viegas were supportive colleagues and mentors.

My time in the US was and continues to be sustained by wonderful people. Historians Jeanne Penvenne and Norman Bennet have welcomed me with wide open arms and hearts into their beautiful home in Duxbury, Massachusetts. They have supported me in indescribable ways. A trip to Duxbury is like going home. Wes, Jamie, and Margie Pein—proud Marylanders—have been a family to me and I will forever be grateful for their support and friendship. Wes was a close witness to the ups and downs of this journey. Thank you, *mein bruder.*

I welcomed my son, Ives, while working on this project. He and his mother, Clinarete Munguambe, are the loves of my life and I thank them for being there for me. May the joy of finally having this book in print help repair the wounds of many years of sacrifice, absence, and longing.

I finished the book a few months after my father passed away. My hope that he would see the fruit of his sacrifice of many years was dashed, leaving me with a hollow feeling of an undelivered present. My mother does not read English, not even much Portuguese. To be accessible to her, the book will have to be translated into Ronga, her native language, in which she is as literate and proficient as very few people can be. I thought about her when I included many illustrations in the book. She loves pictures. The thought of her flipping through these pages and gazing pensively for several minutes at each illustration gives me great satisfaction. This book and my unbelievable journey would not have been possible without her unconditional love and boundless care. It is to her and my late father that I dedicate this book. *Incomo pswinene.*

Abbreviations

AGGPM	Arquivo do Gabinete do Governador da Província de Maputo (archive)
AGGPN	Arquivo do Gabinete do Governador da Província do Niassa (archive)
AHM	Arquivo Histórico de Moçambique (archive)
AJN	Arquivo do Jornal Notícias (archive)
APIE	Administração do Parque Imobiliário do Estado (real estate agency)
ART	Arquivo da Revista Tempo (archive)
CAN	Centro Associativo dos Negros da Colónia de Moçambique / Negroes Association of Mozambique
CDSM	Centro de Documentação Samora Machel (archive)
COC	Comando Operativo Central / Central Operative Command
COD	Comando Operativo Distrital / District Operative Command
COP	Comando Operativo Provincial / Provincial Operative Command
CPPM	Centro de Preparação Político-Militar / Center for Political and Military Training
CRL	Center of Research Libraries
DNSR	Direcção Nacional dos Serviços de Reeducação / National Directorate of Reeducation Services
DPSR	Departamento Provincial dos Serviços de Reeducação / Provincial Department of Reeducation Services
DPSRN	Direcção Provincial dos Serviços de Reeducação do Niassa / Provincial Directorate of Reeducation Services of Niassa

FEN	Feira de Exposição do Niassa / Niassa Trade Fair
Frelimo	Frente de Libertação de Moçambique / Mozambique Liberation Front
GCP	Grupo Cultural Polivalente / Multipurpose Cultural Group
GD	Grupo Dinamizador / Dynamizing Group
GVP	Grupo de Vigilância Popular / People's Vigilance Group
MHN	Mozambique History Net
MINT	Ministério do Interior / Ministry of the Interior
NESAM	Núcleo dos Estudantes Secundários Africanos de Moçambique (student union)
OJM	Organização da Juventude Moçambicana / Organization of Mozambican Youth
OMM	Organização da Mulher Moçambicana / Organization of Mozambican Women
PIDE	Polícia Internacional e de Defesa do Estado (Portuguese secret police)
PPI	Plano Prospectivo Indicativo / Indicative Prospective Plan (development plan)
Renamo	Resistência Nacional Moçambicana / Mozambique National Resistance
SNASP	Serviço Nacional de Segurança Popular / National People's Security Service
TMR	Tribunal Militar Revolucionário / Revolutionary Military Tribunal

Introduction

> We must launch an unyielding struggle against the vestiges of colonialism, decadent values, erroneous ideas, the attitude of uncritically imitating foreigners, and against immorality. . . . In this respect, we must bear in mind that the city is one of the centers of vice and corruption and of alienating foreign influences. The blood of our people was not shed only to free the land from foreign domination, but also to re-conquer our Mozambican personality, to bring about the resurgence of our culture and to create a new mentality, a new society. . . . We are engaged in a Revolution whose advance depends on the creation of the New Man, with a new mentality.
>
> —Samora Machel, "FRELIMO's Tasks in the Struggle Ahead," 1974

THE ABOVE statement was part of a long speech delivered by Samora Machel on September 20, 1974. As president of the Mozambique Liberation Front (Frelimo)[1]—the movement that fought for Mozambique's independence from Portugal through a ten-year armed struggle and emerged victorious—it was his responsibility to instruct the incoming government on how to transition toward complete independence. From the headquarters of Frelimo in Dar es Salaam, Tanzania, Machel listed the tasks ahead while the Frelimo-dominated transitional government was taking power in Mozambique's capital, Lourenço Marques (soon to be renamed Maputo). The transitional government included three Portuguese officials and six Frelimo nominees and resulted from the peace agreement reached in the Zambian capital, Lusaka, between Frelimo and the new Portuguese government, which was formed after a military coup brought down the colonial regime in Lisbon five months before. In addition to ending the war in Mozambique, the bloodless coup ended the wars of liberation that had begun in Angola and Guinea-Bissau in the early 1960s.[2] In Mozambique, racial violence marked the transition because conservative sections of the settler population saw the unilateral handing over of power to Frelimo as a betrayal of their political aspirations.[3] It took a joint effort by Portuguese soldiers and Frelimo guerrillas to bring peace and prevent further violence.[4] The main task of the transitional government was to pacify the country and prepare the conditions for the declaration of national independence, which was scheduled for June 25, 1975. One of the conditions was the elimination of the "decadent vestiges of colonialism," chief among them prostitution, alcoholism, vagrancy, and all sorts of wayward lifestyles. This was part of an ambitious effort to eradicate "bourgeois morality" and replace it with the "revolutionary morality" that Frelimo developed during the liberation struggle.[5]

Machel's call for an "unyielding struggle" against immorality directed the government to focus its efforts on the cities, especially the capital, where the mental damage of colonialism was allegedly most intense. Machel reasoned that Mozambique's city dwellers, having lived in the center of colonial society, had been exposed to and influenced by the most degrading aspects of bourgeois culture. The evidence of the deep wounds that colonialism had created was in the social fabric itself. Prostitution, drunkenness, vagrancy, drug addiction, familial instability, indecent dress, crime, and cultural tastes imported from the West ran rampant. These social pathologies needed immediate redress because they were an obstacle to nation building and the socialist revolution that Frelimo was about to launch in Mozambique. The revolution entailed cultural and mental decolonization, aimed at changing the moral behavior of the people, especially those most psychologically harmed by colonialism. Implicit in Machel's directive was a belief in the contrast between the urban and the rural. Whereas the former was a space of social degradation and, as such, a political threat, the latter was uncontaminated by the decadence of bourgeois culture. Despite the persistence of oppressive traditions such as polygamy and superstition, the countryside was where the work of transforming wayward urbanites had to take place. This dichotomy between urban decadence and rural decency places Frelimo's project within a long history, traversing space and time, of anxiety over city life.[6]

The party cadres in charge of the unyielding struggle to bring about a new mentality were thirty-five-year-old prime minister Joaquim Chissano and thirty-year-old minister of internal affairs and national political commissar Armando Guebuza. Under their command, in October 1974, Frelimo guerrillas launched several campaigns to round up so-called anti-socials and anyone who exhibited the visual signs of moral decadence: short skirts, wigs, Afro hairstyles, hippie fashion, and the like. They targeted places of leisure: brothels, dance clubs, and beer halls.[7] The roundups continued well beyond the formal declaration of independence. As one newspaper reported in November

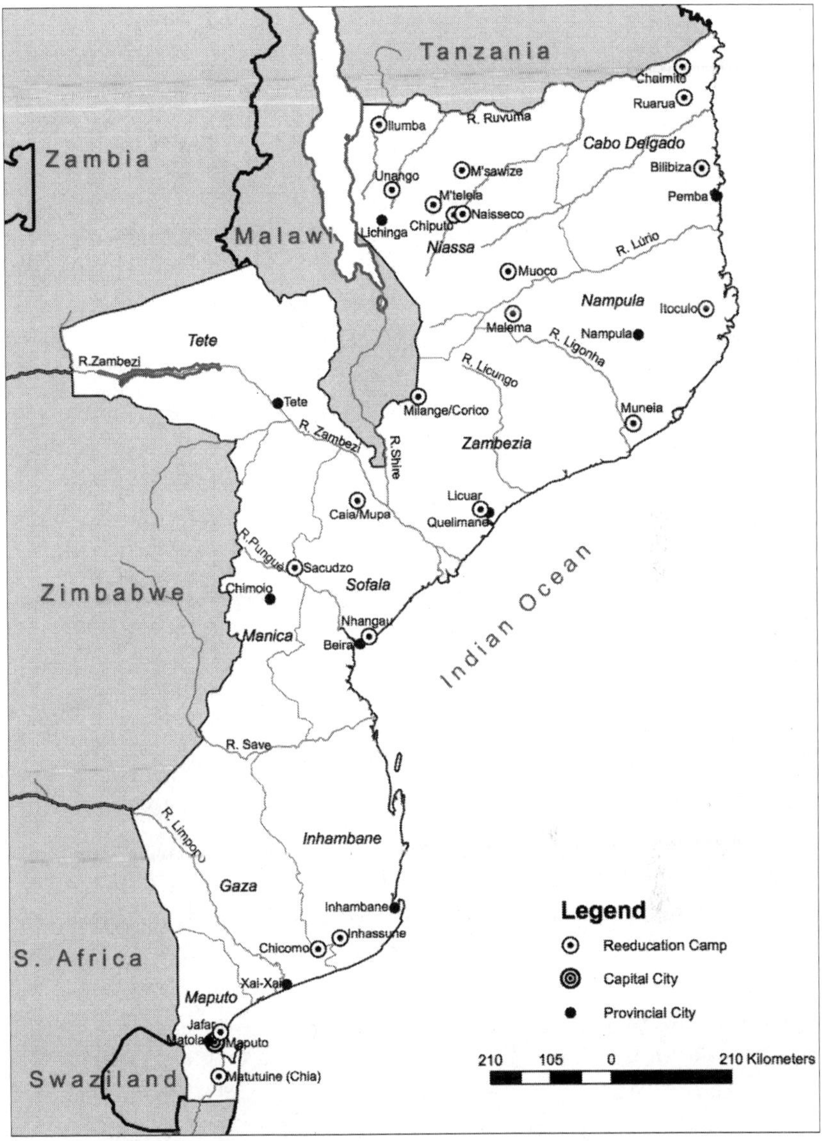

MAP 0.1. Mozambique and the reeducation camp complex. Courtesy of Clark Library, University of Michigan

1975, "Over 3,000 men and women were rounded up in five of Mozambique's major towns during an operation aimed at the rehabilitation of thieves, prostitutes, drug pushers, and vagrants."[8] In announcing the campaigns, Guebuza told the press that these individuals would be interned in reeducation camps, where their degeneracy would be washed away through manual labor and political education. "We are now installing camps," he said, "where we seek to raise their awareness so that they can learn a new life in conformity with the society that we will build."[9] He justified the campaigns by claiming that "the presence of such people in the country would corrupt the society into crime and immorality."[10] By January 1976, the government had established more than twenty reeducation camps in remote rural sites throughout the country. Analysts estimated that there were ten thousand detainees in that year alone.[11] Until the campaigns were halted in 1988, more than one hundred thousand people (about 1 percent of the country's population) passed through the pipeline of reeducation and labor camps in Mozambique.[12]

This book offers the first historical examination of the ideological architecture of urban cleanup campaigns and reeducation camps and of the central role they played in Mozambique's socialist experiment. The book presents the reeducation camps as the template of independent Mozambique's punitive society—that is, of the ways Mozambican society under Frelimo dealt with those who transgressed the law and who violated normative codes of individual and collective behavior that the party obsessively pursued in its efforts to build a new society from the ruins of Portuguese colonialism.[13] Along with ushering in a new era of economic development and social progress, the socialist experiment, I argue, also sought to remake the moral fabric of Mozambican society. The camps and the cleanup campaigns were an essential component of this ambition to remold the people of Mozambique according to new moral aesthetics. At play were two contradictory impulses: on one hand, high-modernist aspirations that sought to radically transform Mozambique into a rational and technologically advanced country under socialist principles; and on the other, conservative anxieties rooted in a moralistic reading of society. Although nearly all twentieth-century socialist experiments, with varying degrees of intensity and violence, suffered from the same contradiction, the Mozambican case presents some intriguing and, in the African context, unique features.

Scholars of postcolonial Mozambique have examined Frelimo's politics of punishment from various angles. In his search for the root causes of the civil war, Christian Geffray pioneered the study of Frelimo's role in creating the conditions for its own opposition.[14] Michel Cahen picked up the critique to further highlight the implosion of Frelimo's revolution due to its oppressive policies (at times questioning the credibility of the party's socialism).[15] One by one, Frelimo's policies and discursive apparatus were dissected from several disciplinary approaches. From a historical and anthropological viewpoint, João Paulo Borges Coelho and Harry West examined the project of communal villages and the way they allowed the state to exert its power over reluctant and often rebellious subject populations.[16] Bertil Egerö, Merle Bowen, Kathleen Sheldon, Anne Pitcher, Yussuf Adam, Éric Morier-Genoud, and many others critiqued Frelimo's developmentalist choices, religious and gender policies, and their impact on peasants, women, and workers.[17] More recently, Maria-Benedita Basto, Paolo Israel, Drew Thompson, and David Hedges and Colin Darch explored the various political dimensions of Frelimo's cultural production, visuality, rhetoric, and performativity, often hinting at their exclusivist character.[18] Lars Buur and Maria Paula Meneses analyzed from a discursive perspective the construction of internal enemies and traitors, whereas João Cabrita, Barnabé Ncomo, and Victor Igreja illustrated how Frelimo dealt with such persons through public trials, incarceration, and execution.[19] More to the heart of the object of study in this book, Omar Thomaz and Carlos Quembo looked at the implementation of Operação Produção, Frelimo's largest cleanup campaign in 1983, as a failed attempt at socialist modernization.[20] Recent biographies of Samora Machel by Sarah LeFanu and Allen and Barbara Isaacman have also alluded to his severe personality, which led Frelimo to adopt draconian measures to enforce social and behavioral change in Mozambican society.[21]

Despite these pioneering scholarly works, few have examined reeducation camps as the single most important punitive measure deployed by Frelimo in its efforts to remake Mozambique. Reference to the camps have been brief and fall into two opposing views. In most accounts, the camps figure only in the margins of Frelimo's socialist project and are often dismissed as simple policy error. Under this view, the camps seem to reveal something about Frelimo's quest for political hegemony and authoritarianism and why the revolution ultimately failed.[22] For scholars with little sympathy for Frelimo, the camps were a grotesque imitation of Soviet extermination camps and betrayed the ruling party's bloody thrust and purposeless violence against innocent citizens.[23]

This book demonstrates that far from being marginal institutions and aimless imitations of external models of mass incarceration, reeducation camps in fact constituted an important component of Frelimo's project of nation building and socialist revolution. At the heart of this political agenda, the book posits, lies a deep-seated ambition to transform the moral outlook of Mozambican society and to produce an ascetic citizenry by enforcing ethical configurations of how people conducted themselves in public and private domains. Labeling and purging social groups and punishing them through internment served a pedagogical purpose: to delimit the boundaries of permissible behavior that circumscribed Mozambican citizenship. The "New Man with a new mentality" that the advance of the revolution depended on could only be produced by reeducation camps because they set the parameters of citizenship—of national belonging and exclusion.[24] The categories of deviance that the reeducation program targeted gave substance to the socialist revolution and the social order that it sought to produce. They served as reference points that allowed the party to unite the public around a set of ethical principles that could guide the country in its transition from colonial modernity to socialist modernity. The reeducation program materialized the discourse of the Homem Novo (New Man) that infused Frelimo's socialist rhetoric because this elusive entity was defined by its opposite or antithesis. As Lars Buur puts it, "The work of defining who belongs to the nation-state and what characterizes its members is often achieved by way of a negative procedure, that is, through the creation of an exemplary Other." Frelimo leaders defined Mozambican citizens by what they ought *not* to be. This explains why the party's talented Department of Information and Propaganda never produced a visual representation of the Homem Novo or the Mulher Nova (New Woman), whereas the images of their antithesis, the anti-socials, littered the iconography of the socialist period in the form of a cartoon figure named Xiconhoca (see figure 2.4). While the "new socialist man remained stable in his unachievability," Xiconhoca, the embodiment of moral decay, "took specific forms that could be acted upon."[25] In framing the opposite of the Homem Novo as an enemy—the obstacle that impeded the realization of the revolution—Frelimo leaders produced the exemplary subjects on whom power could be concretely exercised.[26] This point is made clear in the statement that the architects of the campaigns issued during the first national conference on the reeducation program held in November 1976. "The Revolution demanded that, in order to advance rapidly and correctly," they claimed, "certain measures had to be taken to 'cleanse' the cities of pernicious elements to society, elements that constitute an obstacle to a society of a new type."[27] The urban cleanup campaigns and reeducation camps were essential dispositives for the instantiation of state power; without them, the "New Man with a new mentality"—the central pillar of Frelimo's socialism—would have remained an abstraction.

By peeling off the discursive archetypes of Frelimo's socialism, this book brings to light a chapter of contemporary history that has remained underexplored. If scholars have mentioned the camps in passing, the organic functioning of the camps and the everyday life of internment has remained terra incognita. Building on uncharted archival records and interviews, *The Morality of Revolution* foregrounds the contradictions of Frelimo's ambitions and the gap between the party's ideals of moral reform and the reality of the carceral regime. Conceived of as disciplinary institutions to rehabilitate putative wayward members of society and produce the idyllic Homem Novo, the camps were spaces of social abandonment where detainees were laid bare at the hands of camp overseers and the wretched conditions of remote rural sites.[28] From its inception in 1974 to its demise in the late 1980s, the reeducation program was a do-it-yourself enterprise, operating under conditions of extreme scarcity. The nature of the carceral regime reflected these conditions as the Frelimo government, unable to finance and support the program, expected its agents and the detainees to carry out the ambitious project with limited resources.[29] Not only did the weight of establishing and running the camps fall on the backs of detainees, but the daily regimen of camp life was largely left to the discretion of each camp commander and, in some cases, of detainees themselves. These organic features of the camps, I argue, did not stem from any marginal place that the camps may have occupied in the whole effort to build a socialist modernity in Mozambique.[30] Rather, they stemmed from the constraints under which the camps operated. Without material and human resources to run the program, state officials compelled detainees to build their own detention facilities, grow their own food, carry out political education on their own, and, in many ways, watch over their own incarceration. The state's inability to transmute the salvationist ideas of reeducation into planned action—a general feature of the socialist experiment in Mozambique—produced spaces of social neglect and castigation that affected both the inmates and the personnel tasked with disciplining and reeducating them. In documenting the urban cleanup campaigns and reeducation camps in Mozambique, this book sheds new light on the history of socialism in Africa and the Global South at large.

AFRICAN SOCIALISM AND THE POLITICS OF MORALITY

The anxieties that animated Frelimo's campaigns against urban decadence have a distinctly African trajectory. While they resonate with various twentieth-century examples of social engineering on both sides of the global Cold War divide, they are situated within the specific context of experiments with socialist alternatives in postcolonial Africa.[31] Between the late 1950s and mid-1980s, thirty-five out of fifty-three states in Africa declared themselves socialist at some point in their short history as independent nations.[32] Although the brands of socialism they adopted varied considerably, with some more nominal than others, most states pursued schemes to reengineer their societies in the name of cultural renascence, nation building, and modernity.[33] They dedicated inordinate amounts of time and resources to reorganizing rural settlements, sending unwanted urbanites to rural villages, and regimenting even the most intimate aspects of social life, from marriages and styles of dress to various modes of self-fashioning.[34] In fairness, these reformist efforts were not confined to socialist regimes. The *authenticité* movement of Mobutu Sese Soko in Zaire and the anti-miniskirts and anti-prostitution campaigns across the continent—from Hastings Banda's Malawi to Idi Amin's Uganda—were all part of a general concern for social and moral reform in postcolonial Africa.[35] While their architects may have disagreed over the scale of their polities (ethnic versus national), they were in accord that public comportment, modest dress, temperance, and asceticism in one's personal conduct were key components for building political constituencies, for composing civil societies, and for upholding respectable citizenries.[36] This is an aspect of modern African history that social scientists, obsessed with the pathologies of African bureaucracies and the politics of extraversion of some African statesmen, have by and large failed to see.[37] Among many other facets of twentieth-century African history, moralistic efforts to reform societies marked the political landscape of late colonial and early postcolonial Africa far more than belly politics.[38]

While historians of Africa have mapped these reformist efforts within the politics of postcolonial cultural nationalism (or ethno-nationalism), students of African socialist experiments have largely confined social reforms within the pragmatic role of socialism as an economic alternative for development.[39] However, on closer inspection, the power of socialism in Africa did not arise exclusively from the political and economic alternatives it offered African politicians in the age of decolonization. Its power rested on allowing its advocates to synthetize and reconcile these pragmatic alternatives with ethical principles they viewed as equally urgent for building new nations and their corresponding citizenries. Scholars of African socialist experiments have explored at great length the different degrees to which African politicians adopted socialism for political and economic ends. They have, for example, distinguished first wave African socialism of the 1960s from second wave Afro-Marxism of the 1970s and 1980s. While the first wave advocated for a non-Marxist understanding of socialism and located the roots of socialism in precolonial African traditions of communalism and humanism (and was hence devoid of class differentiation and social conflict), the second wave claimed that there was but one socialism—the scientific socialism of Marx and Lenin.[40] The assumption is that, in rejecting the "unscientific" African socialism of the first wave, Afro-Marxists also discarded the moral and religious undertones that characterized it. A closer look at Mozambique's socialism—one of the most radical Afro-Marxist regimes, alongside Angola and Ethiopia—reveals more continuities than changes in Africa's conception of socialism and its role in remolding the ethical and cultural fabric of African societies.

The first place to examine these continuities is Tanzania, the actual mecca of revolution in southern Africa and where Mozambican nationalists lived for more than ten years while waging their liberation struggle against the Portuguese regime.[41] Here, Julius Nyerere outlined the main tenets of his socialist philosophy by defining socialism as "an attitude of the mind"—that is, a system in which people devote their energies to materializing self-reliance by avoiding selfish greed and by engaging in collective production, sharing, and mutual care. Despite the focus on the village and the proverbial extended family, or *ujamaa,* as the unit from which socialist development would spring, Nyerere was less concerned with economic productivity and more with people's attitude in relation to material wealth and their relation to one another. Rather than the creation of wealth, it was its distribution that was at the core of ujamaa. As Nyerere postulated in various edicts, anyone who sought wealth or private material gain was a capitalist, a parasite who sucks the blood of society. A product of European colonialism and its "acquisitive society," individualistic materialism could only be transcended if Africans "re-educate[d]" themselves and "regain[ed] [their] former attitude of mind," which is key for a socialist society, a society in which everyone looks out for one another, where everyone is part of the extended family. In such a society, virtue lies in sharing with others what one gains from one's labors. As he warned his audience, "We have to establish the kind of social organization which reduces personal temptations above that level to a minimum."[42] For those who listened to Nyerere's Arusha Declaration of 1967 (which launched the socialist experiment in Tanzania), the religious and moralistic orientation of ujamaa was not lost. "How can any well-informed man fail to see, even from the Bible alone, that socialism in the true sense is inseparable from Christianity?" asked A. S. Bukenya, president of the Dar es Salaam University Catholic Students' Association, soon after the Arusha Declaration. "For, above all," he concluded, "socialism, if it is to work at all, presupposes a perfect *charity and faultless moral integrity and responsibility* [his emphasis]."[43] Reverend John Lavoie, one of the speakers at the symposium organized at the university to reflect on Nyerere's declaration, concluded that "*ujamaa* is not politics, it is a philosophy of life, a philosophy which comes so very near to the foundation of Christianity itself"; therefore, "it is not enough that the Church approves of the Arusha Declaration—it must preach it."[44]

Other prominent African intellectuals and political leaders shared the religious and moralistic dimensions of African socialism by equating them with emancipation and decolonization. For Sékou Touré of Guinea, the ethical values of socialism and religion (Christianity and Islam) were not only the same but also complemented each other in helping African countries transcend the legacies of colonialism. As he put it, "Both [socialist] Revolution and Religion demand of its militants, its adepts, a pugnacious attitude in the course of life: struggle within oneself, struggle against selfishness, shortcomings, and against all defects." He insisted that "real independence, complete decolonization, requires first of all a decolonization of mentalities" and that victory depends on the "constant fidelity to the revolutionary morality, the regular practice of self-criticism and constructive criticism" and the cultivation of the "character of incorruptibility." Like Nyerere, Sékou Touré was certain that "without a revolutionary mentality, there is no socialism."[45] This obsession with moral incorruptibility, at times bordering to Jacobinism, ran through the political thinking of most African socialists.

There could be no political personalities more different than Sékou Touré's and Senegal's Léopold Senghor's. Yet, substantively, they shared the same understanding of African socialism and its liberating power in both ethical and spiritual dimensions. Despite his secular erudition, Senghor did not hesitate in identifying the founders of Christianity and Islam as revolutionaries who sought to guide humanity toward the same destiny as socialism. If "Jesus was a revolutionary" who "took a sympathetic interest in the fate of the poor and oppressed of all races," Senghor reasoned, "Mohammed proposes first to perfect the Arab community by making it overcome its anarchy and tribalism." Both figures aimed to elevate humanity from its alienation. Like Jesus, Mohammed "labors for the establishment of a new society, for the birth of a new man."[46] Even Joe Slovo, the hard-liner Orthodox Marxist and military leader of the South African Communist Party and the African National Congress's Spear, conceded to the shared values of socialism and Christianity, not only in their egalitarian principles but also in their aspiration of bringing about a mental and spiritual transformation in society.[47]

Afro-Marxist movements like Frelimo did not dispense with the ethical role of socialism in bringing about a new social order. While they criticized African socialism for its undialectical traditionalism, they clung to the rhetorical power of its messianic message. Frelimo was founded in Tanzania by Mozambican political exiles in 1962. This was an exhilarating time in East Africa—and in Africa in general. It was, in Adom Getachew's apt formulation, a time of "worldmaking after empire."[48] One after another, most British, French, and Belgian colonies achieved self-determination and joined the concert of nations as independent countries. Algerian revolutionaries emerged victorious against imperial France in a show of force that reverberated across the continent and immediately welcomed freedom fighters from all corners of the world. Frelimo's first guerrillas, including Samora Machel, were trained in Algeria and picked up their formative Pan-Africanist and leftist outlook.

They read Marxist pamphlets and learned to associate their struggle with larger Pan-African and Third World struggles for emancipation. Yet, in Tanzania, Pan-African and nationalist politics were deeply enmeshed with moralistic campaigns to reform people's behavior in the name of socialism. It was from Tanzania that, for more than a decade (1964–75), Frelimo carried out the liberation struggle against the intransigent Portuguese colonial regime. Frelimo's training camps were sites of pilgrimage for young African activists eager to learn the art of revolutionary warfare.[49] Leaders of the Youth League of the Tanganyika African National Union (TANU) and students from the University of Dar es Salaam (among them Yoweri Museveni, the future president of Uganda) were frequent guests in Nachingwea, Frelimo's main rear base in southern Tanzania.[50] The intellectual exchanges that took place during these visits encouraged the cross-fertilization of ideas about how to build new societies out of the ruins of colonial rule. As Frelimo leaders pondered the future of Mozambique at the party's headquarters in Dar es Salaam and in Nachingwea, they closely followed the debates around the Arusha Declaration, the ujamaa villagization scheme, and Operation Vijana (a campaign against urban decadence and indecent dress launched in Dar es Salaam in 1968).[51] In fact, throughout the 1960s, Dar es Salaam was a center of both Pan-African activism and socialist-inspired campaigns of moral reform. It is therefore not surprising that the words that TANU activists employed to label their purge targets (e.g., *bloodsuckers, parasites,* or *anti-socials*) permeated Frelimo's anti-urban discourse in independent Mozambique.[52]

However, Frelimo took its reformist project to the extreme. As Jocelyn Alexander and Gary Kynoch observed, within southern Africa, Frelimo "stands out for the ideological fervor of its early years of rule."[53] In a recent short survey on Mozambique's history, historian Malyn Newitt was puzzled by Samora Machel's puritanical speeches in the first years of Mozambique's independence. Newitt struggled to understand why Machel devoted much of his energy exhorting party cadres and citizens in general to detach themselves from material indulgence and aim for a higher existence of self-denial and moral rectitude. Newitt posited that "Machel's speeches read like *evangelical sermons,* representing Mozambique's quest for independence as a *moral crusade* as well as a political revolution" (my emphasis).[54] Newitt concluded that while Machel's political discourse echoed that of other nationalist leaders like Amílcar Cabral of Guinea-Bissau, his speeches were dominated by "moral, somewhat puritanical, exhortations."[55] In fact, a close examination of Frelimo's political writings since 1968, particularly Samora Machel's speeches from 1970 onward, reveal the revolutionary's obsession with moral improvement. Like most of his closest mission-educated comrades, Machel saw and projected himself as the moral paragon of the society he envisioned.[56] After his ascension as president of Frelimo in May 1970, Machel became an energetic preacher of the catechism of self-improvement and moral purification. For him, self-improvement and moral purification were a necessary path for the emancipation of the people from colonialism and for the full realization of the revolution. His tireless exhortations for Mozambicans to wage an internal struggle for self-perfection and self-discipline were not disconnected from his broader socialist politics. Anthropologist and Frelimo veteran José Luís Cabaço notes in his study of Mozambique's national identity formation that, under Machel, Frelimo's ideological struggle, with a strong emphasis on moral values, was elevated to the consciousness of each militant in an internal dialectics between the present and the past. Cabaço argues that this moralistic ideology was "not so distant from some protestant missions that opened the doors of modernity and nationalism" to Frelimo leading cadres.[57]

Pinpointing the ideological roots of Frelimo's reformism is a difficult task given the panoply of political influences, morality systems, and revolutionary models that the movement accrued over the years. A list of possible influences would include the premises of Portugal's civilizing mission and European modernity; the evangelical and conservative pedagogy of Christian missions where most prominent leaders of Frelimo were educated; the nativist politics of African elites who, as far back as the turn of the twentieth century, viewed ethical reform as a route to civil recognition in a particularly oppressive colonial regime; and, of course, the various brands of socialism to which Frelimo cadres were exposed in the 1960s, from the Arab socialism of Algeria and Egypt, the orthodox Soviet Marxism-Leninism, and the neo-Confucian Marxism of Mao Zedong and Vietnamese leaders Ho Chi Minh and Vo Nguyen Giap to the communalism of Tanzania's socialism. Tracing these influences and the way they shaped Frelimo's ideological makeup falls outside of the scope of this book.[58] What is evident is that their combined cogency among Frelimo top leaders resulted in a markedly messianic vision of revolution and social transformation loaded with contradictions.

To fully appreciate the contradictions and violent modes of Frelimo's governmentality during the socialist experiment in Mozambique, we need to consider the messianic, salvationist predisposition of the party's ideology and political culture.[59] More importantly, we need to examine the ways Frelimo leaders viewed and conceptualized the social composition of Mozambique. While various texts and political tracts from Frelimo's Central Committee address these questions, the most illuminating source is a 1978 address to the press by Samora Machel. In it, the supreme leader of the revolution classified

Mozambican society into three hierarchical social groups—namely, the party leadership, the peasantry, and the townspeople. For Machel, the party leadership represented "the most advanced model of the New Man." Coming out of the struggle against the Portuguese, they were politically conscious, industrious, frugal, temperate, and pure. The years of struggle had allowed them to transcend the backwardness of precolonial African traditions and their cultural localisms as well as the immoral trappings of colonial modernity. In this sense, they were above the peasantry and the townspeople. If the former, Machel asserted, were still trapped in "backward feudal-traditional costumes and religious obscurantism," the latter were "still mentally colonized, they reveal a mentality of bondage to foreign society." If feudal structures still governed the countryside, where chiefly authority, polygamy, and witchcraft prevailed, "in the urban society resides the vices of civilization which offend the traditions and morality of the people of Mozambique."[60]

This classification of society followed the template that Mao Zedong formulated when the Chinese Communist Party took power in 1949.[61] It informed Frelimo's major socialist policies (economic and others) and provided the constitutive elements for the definition of Mozambican citizenship. The New Men and New Women forged in the struggle were the genuine revolutionary citizens on whom no demands were made other than the permanent vigilance against moral relapse.[62] They had to guard against material temptations and keep faith in the revolution by being first in the line of duty and last in collecting rewards. The rest of the people had to elevate themselves to achieve such a status by undergoing a process of mental, political, and ideological reeducation. Thus, revolutionary citizenship entailed social renewal and purification. For the majority peasant population to break away from backward feudal culture and obscurantism, they needed to abandon their scattered settlements and live in communal, socialist villages where education and other services could be provided by the state. Although Tanzania's ujamaa inspired Frelimo, the party's villagization scheme followed the schematic principles that Machel outlined in his classification of Mozambican society and citizenry.

The path toward revolutionary citizenship was more strenuous for townspeople. Their mental and cultural decolonization required a total rejection of the habits and values that four centuries of Portuguese colonial exploitation had imparted on them. Their transformation would occur through intense ideological and political education as well as through their earnest engagement in revolutionary tasks under the guidance of local party committees. Urban people would transform their mental structure and undo the damage of colonial rule by joining local party cells and vigilante groups; by participating in weekly meetings in their neighborhoods to discuss issues of public concern, study the political orientations of the party, and subject themselves to honest criticism and self-criticism; and by carrying out collective works such as cleaning the streets, reorganizing neighborhoods, or painting murals containing party slogans. Revolutionary tasks like these, performed under the tutelage of those tempered in the liberation struggle, would free urbanites from the degrading influences of bourgeois culture and turn them into Homens Novos and Mulheres Novas.[63] Failure in this process of change would breed anti-socials, reactionaries, and internal enemies ready to bring the revolution down.[64]

Largely overlooked in the vast literature of postcolonial Mozambique, the messianic overtones of Frelimo's socialism were remarkable.[65] Rather than as public servants, Frelimo leaders held themselves out as saviors who would deliver the masses from darkness, social degeneracy, and cultural alienation.[66] As vanguards pursuing an "inner-worldly political kingdom"—the idyllic classless society free from the exploitation of men by men—Frelimo leaders, like the Bolsheviks and Chinese revolutionaries before them, "defined themselves as a *moral élite*."[67] For them, political leadership was not a professional field of governance but a position from which the ontological problem of human existence and salvation could be realized.[68] They saw the revolution as a moral crusade to elevate society from darkness. In their estimation, before Portuguese conquest, people lived under the mantle of feudalism and superstition. Under Portuguese rule, they were all oppressed and humiliated. After centuries of gloom, the party brought enlightenment, political awakening, and self-awareness.[69] Historian Igal Halfin has characterized this rendering of historical time by socialist revolutionaries as Marxist eschatology, which he defines as "a narrative that structured historical time as an odyssey of human consciousness." The endpoint of this odyssey, he writes, is the "bright light of Communism, a symbol of human metamorphosis into the New Man."[70]

Under Frelimo, Marxist eschatology took the form of a fable or, as João Paulo Borges Coelho puts it, a liberation script.[71] The party became more than just a political organization: it was a sacred congregation to which all Mozambicans had to dedicate their devotion and loyalty. To be Mozambican was to blindly obey the party. The opposite was to side with the enemy to undermine the revolution. As Margaret Hall and Tom Young put it, Frelimo identified the enemy "according to a taxonomy of moral failings—laziness, corruption, and self-indulgence."[72] Led by the party and enlightened by the experience of the liberation struggle, the masses had to wage a permanent battle with themselves in order to cleanse their mentalities of the damage imparted by years of darkness and degeneration under the old society.[73]

The edification of a Homem Novo and a new society depended on purifying the people and elevating them to a new moral plane.[74] Frelimo conceived the reeducation camps for those who resisted change and failed to elevate themselves to the standard of the Homem Novo. Reeducation was meant for those who still had not emerged from darkness and cultural alienation, despite the liberating effect of the revolution. For such unworthy individuals, membership in the national fraternity was only possible through the ascetic and purifying ritual of public repentance, moral renewal, collective manual labor, and the hardship of taming nature in remote labor camps. The party expected people to emerge from reeducation camps as reformed citizens, "politically conscious, physically apt, and mentally sound."[75]

However, as this book demonstrates, the gap between aspiration and reality was abysmally wide. Rather than delivering ethical transformation, Frelimo's idealistic vision produced new forms of oppression and the rustication of thousands of urban citizens. The party's promise of salvation and liberation came with new chains.[76]

THE CARCERAL REGIME

If Frelimo's moral anxieties have a particular African trail, the punitive institutions that rendered them consequential belong to a global history of mass incarceration and penal regimes of reform through labor that characterized much of the twentieth century. Regardless of ideological persuasions, authoritarian states used internment camps to broadcast their power, to confine dissent, to exploit unpaid labor in order to speed their developmentalist ambitions, and to enforce high-minded visions of social transformation.[77] This book situates Mozambique's penal regime of reeducation within the larger context of state-led mass internment of subject populations in the pursuit of grand ideals of decolonization, development, social reform, and nation building. In attempting to reveal the inadequacy of prisons in today's legal landscape—especially in light of the crisis of mass incarceration in the United States—recent carceral studies have largely focused on the punitive, capitalistic, and racial origins of the carceral industrial complex, often forgetting its reformatory roots. The consensus seems to be that, passed down from their nineteenth-century iteration, carceral institutions (in all their forms and shapes) are obsolete, serving only to advance exclusionary and exploitative agendas.[78] A case needs to be made for revisiting the ideals of reform and emancipation that informed carceral projects without eschewing their inadequacy in fulfilling the aims for which they were devised.

The scholarship on carcerality in Africa has primarily revolved around the question of the colonial structural continuum and the limits of European modern penality. While there has been little to dispute in the colonial origins of modern punitive confinement in Africa (including their architectural apparatus), the extent to which their organic functions and the cultures and practices of confinement they produced mirrored European models has elicited much debate. On one end of the spectrum, some scholars have seen Africa's punitive institutions in the colonial and postcolonial eras as simple extensions of European disciplinary violence and social degradation.[79] On the other, scholars have shown the limits of European carcerality by highlighting prisons and camps as sites of resistance, cultural creativity, political imaginations, and struggles for freedom.[80] If some endorse Michel Foucault's model of the carceral archipelago and its panoptic totalitarianism, others dispute its applicability in Africa, given the porosity of penal institutions and the predominance of physical punishment and public shaming.[81] Despite these enriching discussions, there has been little effort to parse the different modalities of carceral punishment (for example, prisons and detention camps) and to illuminate the creative ways in which they have been deployed to advance projects of nation building and citizenship. Katherine Bruce-Lockhart's recent monograph on the history of the prison in postcolonial Uganda tackles this very topic by highlighting both the variety of colonial penal practices and their mobilization by successive Ugandan postcolonial regimes.[82] Another good example is Andrea Purdeková's study of Ingando camps in postgenocide Rwanda and how they have been deployed to change the fabric of Rwandan society after the traumatic events it faced.[83]

While I agree with the argument about the colonial legacy and continuum in postcolonial African carceral regimes, I see carcerality more as a field of innovation rather than a simple punitive template inherited from colonial rule. More importantly, its embrace by postcolonial revolutionaries like Frelimo derived not from oppressive frameworks but liberatory ones. Frelimo may have drawn from colonial repertoires of confinement and punishment, but its reeducation camps stemmed from a genuine belief in the redemptive, reformatory, and emancipatory power of confinement. The camps were meant to replace conventional penitentiaries, which Frelimo believed were only focused on punishment and not rehabilitation. Their attack on prisons would have pleased American prison abolitionists. Yet Frelimo's carceral alternative proved equally punitive and dysfunctional.

Like prisons, internment camps have a very recent history. They are an amalgamation of interrelated systems of punishment—the prison, the juvenile reform school, and the counterinsurgency camp—all of which developed in the nineteenth century. With its barbed wire and security rim of armed guards and attack dogs, the counterinsurgency camp transmitted the physical shape that we now associate with internment camps. The juvenile reform school and the prison offered their reformist and disciplinary regime as well as their organizing principle based on the ethos of rehabilitation and redemptive labor. This amalgamation of systems of punishment did not follow any chronological or schematic order, nor did it produce a uniform type of camp. Rather, the result was a motley of carceral institutions employed for a variety of goals. Camps in Nazi-occupied Europe during the Second World War were different from the Soviet Gulag. The Gulag was different from the Chinese *laogai* and its Vietnamese offspring. And the laogai was different from Cuba's Unidades Militares de Ayuda a la Producción.[84] Yet, whether we call them extermination, concentration, labor, refugee, or reeducation camps, these institutions became a ubiquitous presence whenever states sought to mass manage subject populations viewed as a threat to perceived notions of order.[85]

Building on Michel Foucault's notion of biopolitics, on Carl Schmitt's idea of the state of exception, and on Hannah Arendt's understanding of totalitarianism, Giorgio Agamben suggested a more capacious definition of the internment camp. For Agamben, the camp is a delimited space "in which the normal order is de facto suspended and in which whether or not atrocities are committed depends not on law but on the civility and ethical sense of the police who temporarily acts as sovereign."[86] The camp is thus a "zone of anomie," a gray area between law and the absence of law. It is a zone of suspension, the ultimate space where the state of exception and sovereign power reach their absolute manifestation. The notion of abandonment is central to Agamben's understanding of exception and sovereign power. The camp is a space of exception in that detainees are in a state of abandonment by law, left in the hands of those who have the power to decide whether they live or die.[87]

In conceiving the reeducation camps, Frelimo leaders had in mind a sophisticated pedagogical penitentiary. Speaking to his cabinet members in 1976, Samora Machel instructed the Council of Ministers "to give further attention" to the reeducation program. He told them that the camps should be organized in categories where reeducatees should be classified and interned according to their offenses. There should be specific camps for drug addicts, for prostitutes, for drunkards, for vagrants, for the undisciplined, for thieves, and so on. "Our general concern," he said, "is to transform the old man into the new man, to transform society. Now, all we need is to find the adequate means to achieve this goal."[88] To succeed in transforming "old men" into "new men," camp overseers were to be diligent knowledge gatherers, observing the behavior of each detainee and recording their improvement. "The reeducation center should be a school where professional knowledge should be passed on and made use of," Machel urged. "It is the fundamental task of officials in charge of reeducation centers to know the history of each one of the people being reeducated—his life history and his origin, in order to understand why he committed his crimes. Who is his father, mother, and sibling, who are his grandfathers, what type of life did they lead?" For Machel, "these are essential things that should be taken into account in order to understand why this or that one committed a crime."[89]

Machel imagined the camp as an agricultural penal colony that would function as a moral filter through which the "dangerous mixtures" of society would be purified and reinserted as useful members of the nation. For him, camp supervisors were to be what Michel Foucault called technicians of behavior, agents of moral change with panoptical powers. According to Foucault, it is in penal institutions that the panoptic mechanisms of power reach their finest shape. Unlike the spectacular and degrading forms of punishment of old times, the panoptic institution functions "as a kind of laboratory of power" that meticulously surveils human subjects down to the most minute, intimate aspects of their lives, producing new forms of subjecthood. In the prison, the elusive and insidious panopticon is permanently vigilant. It is endowed with effective techniques of discipline through the architectural arrangement of the space of confinement and a central watch tower. The panopticon was thus devised to induce in the incarcerated individual the sense of self-discipline and penance while allowing for the extraction of knowledge about the individual's "behavior, his deeper states of mind, his gradual improvement." No longer conductors of public theatrics of brutality, prison supervisors are "technicians of behavior: engineers of conduct, orthopaedists of individuality" tasked with producing docile, obedient, and physically apt subjects.[90]

Machel's reeducation program in Mozambique had panoptic ambitions. But the ambition was never realized. The gap between aspiration and reality stretched wide. Scholars who have studied other interventionist programs with panoptic ambitions like the ujamaa-inspired communal villages in socialist Mozambique fail to appreciate the dissonance between what Frelimo aimed for and what it was able to achieve. Anthropologist Harry West assumes that "in fundamental ways," Mozambique's communal villages "worked like Jeremy Bentham's panopticon" and that "the spatial concentration of the village rendered subjects directly susceptible to a monitoring eye—embodied in the Frelimo-appointed village president—that could pass unobstructed through surveillance corridors in a matter of hours."[91] Like the villages, the reeducation camps were only panoptical on paper or in Machel's imagination. In reality, they mirrored the thing that created them—an aspirational state with big ambitions that was working within the constraints of austerity.[92] The carceral regime of reeducation in socialist Mozambique, I argue, was not an archipelago endowed with biopolitical mechanisms of surveillance but an extension of the society in which it existed. Given the shortage of personnel, the bureaucratic and policing apparatus of Mozambique's camps were very shallow. They lacked the iconic elements of internment camps: barbed wire fences, watch towers, and armies of well-equipped security forces. Consequently, the camps were not strictly regimented, and detainees were not subject to permanent surveillance. There was no separation and individualization of bodies, no pedantic annotation of individualized observations about their criminal antecedents and progress, and no classification of inmates (they had no identification numbers and no plates). Meticulous surveillance requires bureaucratic capabilities and material resources that the Frelimo government did not possess.

Unlike most African countries that gained political independence in the golden years of the global economic boom of the early 1960s, Mozambique came of age during the oil-induced depressions of the 1970s that eroded African economies, wrapping them in the ropes of permanent crisis until the last years of the century.[93] Austerity was the order of the day throughout the fifteen years of the socialist experiment, and it conditioned and defined the organic functioning of the reeducation program. Established in remote corners of the country, the camps had no electricity and no lights (the insidious backlight from the tower was thus an impossibility). Basic implements of bureaucracy and professional observation were not available. Camps had no typewriters. Paper and ink were scarce. Camp overseers, who were meant to be technicians of behavior and diligent collectors of knowledge, could hardly read or write. As one supervisor of Niassa's Department of Reeducation Services observed in one of his reports in 1976, the "level of literacy among camp overseers is minute."[94] Most camp commanders were former guerrillas with no more than a primary school level of literacy. Much of their work consisted of enforcing military discipline on detainees and compelling them to till the land not for economic or developmental goals but simply for their own subsistence. Moreover, the camps were porous. Although they were located in remote sites, there was no complete separation of the "dangerous mixtures" from society. In the rural areas where the camps were established, detainees were often in contact with local communities where they exchanged their meager belongings for food, alcoholic drinks, hemp, and sex. The work of surveillance was not done by the architectural apparatus and the monitoring eye of camp supervisors but by the remote location of the camps and the wilderness that surrounded them. Rather than armed guards with dogs or the backlighting effect of a tower, it was the roar of lions and other wild beasts that kept detainees in line. Authorities assumed that the remote location of the camps—often in the middle of the forest to which inmates were transported in the dark cover of the night—was enough to curb escapes. Here was a different kind of panopticon, one that was regulated not by a modern seeing machine, with its abstract mechanisms of biopolitical power, but instead by the very nature that defied modernity. This was a panopticon that had no regard for bodily legibility, not because it was unwilling to do so but because it had no capacity given the conditions of austerity in which it had to operate.

Mozambique's reeducation camps were panoptic in aspiration and sites of social abandonment in reality. The few scholars and commentators who have discussed the camps were tempted to portray them as spaces of social death on par with the Nazi camps or the Soviet Gulag.[95] Although many people perished in the camps—either due to covert executions or the harsh conditions of internment—Mozambique's camps were not like German camps or Stalin's Gulag. If one takes the death toll and the number of people who revolved through the pipeline as a valid comparative metric, Mozambique's camps would rank as the least severe in a long list that may include camps in Eastern Europe, China, Cuba, Vietnam, and North Korea, to mention only those communist regimes with which Mozambique authorities had close ties and from which they gathered expertise on mass internment. Nevertheless, the less bleak character of Mozambique's camps compared to their more sinister counterparts does not set them completely apart from the larger family of modern institutions of mass internment, which derive—for better or worse—from the mechanism of social control that consists of concentrating many people in one place against their will. This observation must inform a comparative examination of Mozambique's camps with camps elsewhere. In my estimation, such a comparative exercise should not be oriented toward assessing the extent of the austerity of Mozambique's camps in relation to other camps. To those who experienced reeducation, such a quest is meaningless because it presupposes that suffering can be measured.[96] Rather, the central questions are what kind of carceral regime the inmates were subjected to in Mozambique and how that regime relates to the larger field of mass encampments to which the history of Mozambique's camps belongs.

Although the Portuguese colonial regime had always combined carceral penalty with compulsory labor, including the employment of agricultural penal colonies in its counterinsurgency measures in the 1960s,[97] Frelimo drew its model of reeducation camps from the Chinese *laogai* (reform through labor) and *laojiao* (reeducation through labor)—the former reserved for the enemies of communist society and the latter intended for the lumpenproletariat.[98] Chinese military and political instructors introduced the practice in Frelimo's major training camp and military headquarters of Nachingwea in southern Tanzania as early as 1965. By 1970, reeducation was an established mechanism to correct indiscipline and the dissolute ways of cadres as well as of civilian populations under guerrilla authority.[99] After assuming power in 1974, Frelimo institutionalized the pedagogy of revolution tried out during the struggle and transferred the punitive mechanisms of reeducation to independent Mozambique. As a significant part of decolonization, the camps were meant to replace colonial prisons and introduce a more humane form of dealing with social deviance and crime. By focusing on rehabilitation rather than punishment, the architects of the reeducation program in Mozambique believed that the camps were an important contribution to a global socialist revolution and, as such, a contribution to the "scientific theory" of Marxism-Leninism.[100] The reality of the camps never matched their ambitions.

ARCHIVAL JOURNEYS

In 2012, Mozambican filmmaker Licínio Azevedo released a much-acclaimed feature film called *Virgem Margarida*. Based on an earlier documentary on prostitution and reeducation in Mozambique, the film tells the story of a rural virgin teenager named Margarida who is arrested as a prostitute in Maputo in the early days of independence.[101] The young girl had gone to the city to purchase her trousseau and was caught in a police roundup against anti-socials. Margarida, along with hundreds of other women, is sent to an internment camp. For several days, the detainees travel north on a packed bus without knowing *why* they were arrested and *where* they are being taken. An armed convoy accompanies them throughout the journey. In Nampula Province, the bus stops, and the detainees are transferred to a military truck. Several other women—presumably arrested in towns in central and northern Mozambique—have also been assembled at the transit spot. Like their fellow detainees from the south, the only possessions these women have are the light clothes they were wearing when they were arrested. Clumsily, they all climb aboard waiting trucks, and the cars fume for several hours until the destination. The reeducation camp is in the middle of the jungle, without a single building in sight. The camp commissar is a woman who is also assisted by female guards. Although a few men armed with AK-47s can be spotted here and there, women in military garb run the camp. They distribute hoes and axes to all the *reeducandas* (reeducatees) and instruct them to start building their huts and prepare the fields to grow their food. A while later, they receive their black uniforms (trousers, shirts, and boots for some) and the ordeal of camp life begins. The film reaches its climax when a reeducatee is devoured by a lion during a failed escape attempt, and the male political commissar responsible for overseeing all camps in the area rapes Margarida after learning that she is a virgin. In the end, the reeducatees convince the female camp commander to release them, and they all march out of the camp in defiant triumph.

I began the research for this book when *Virgem Margarida* premiered. I envisioned my work as a scholarly reproduction of what Licínio Azevedo had achieved. I aimed for a simple narrative of what these camps looked like, of the injustice and violence that many innocent people like Margarida were subjected to. I had few illusions about the limitations of my project given the sensitivity of the subject. The story of the camps is not only very recent but also still contentious in present-day Mozambique, where evocation of the violence of the camps has political currency for opposition politics.[102] I also did not expect to find any official archival records about the camps. This is both a sensitive topic and a part of a chapter of Mozambique's recent history that the ruling party would rather have erased from public and historical memory.[103] Therefore, I imagined that the project would be entirely based on oral sources, newspapers, and the only fictional representations of the camps available (Azevedo's films and the gripping novel *Campo de trânsito* by João Paulo Borges Coelho).[104] As I made my field research plans, I hoped the film would prepare the ground for my work. But the film had little circulation in Mozambique, and in Maputo, where I started the research, few people knew about it.

Nevertheless, I carried a copy of the film with me during my fieldwork in 2014 and 2015.[105] I also carried a copy of a special edition of the illustrated weekly magazine *Tempo,* which covered the first visit that Machel made to Niassa's reeducation camps in October and November 1979. The magazine includes illustrations of the camps and photos of Machel delivering speeches and interacting with detainees. These materials not only facilitated my initial interactions with my informants, but they also enriched the content of my interviews and opened unanticipated angles for my research. Although I did not show the film to all my interviewees, whenever the conditions were suitable, I projected it from my laptop. One such occasion happened in December 2014. After our first interview, Ché Mafuiane insisted that I should see his friend Ana Maria. Ché was a former reeducando at the Chaimite and Ruarua camps in Cabo Delgado Province. I knew him through Simeão Mazuze (a.k.a. Salimo Muhamed), a renowned pop singer who immortalized the camps in his song "Bilibiza," named after one of the camps where he served time in Cabo Delgado. Mafuiane and Mazuze had been together in Chaimite in 1979 and remained friends after reeducation. For my pool of informants, I relied on these networks of social ties that had developed inside the camps and endured for many years after detention. Ana Maria was part of that social network of ex-detainees. She was a former reeducanda at the M'sawize camp in Niassa, one of the only two camps established exclusively for women. Although Azevedo does not mention the name of the camp in his film, the events on which he based the film certainly took place in M'sawize or in Ilumba (both in Niassa). The circumstances under which Ana Maria was arrested were not totally different from those of the fictional protagonist of the film. But unlike Margarida, Ana Maria was a sophisticated and outgoing urban girl. In 1977, she was eighteen years old and a student at one of Maputo's best high schools. One night, she went to dance with her boyfriend at the famous nightclub Búzio (today, Coconuts). When the police appeared unannounced, she was one of the many women arrested for prostitution. The outfit she was wearing earned her two years of detention without trial. Having Ana Maria and Ché Mafuiane see the film and talk about their experiences made it possible for me to sift fact from fiction.

"This film is very beautiful compared to what really happened in reeducation camps," she said when the film was over.[106] I had observed her reactions as the film rolled on my laptop in the veranda of her unfinished house, taking note whenever a scene caused her to shake her head in disapproval or nod in approbation. At times, she would utter a comment, not to me, but to Ché Mafuiane. I sat in the back, notebook and pen in my hands, as the two old friends watched the moving picture attentively, puffing hemp and sipping iced brandy. They both pointed out several flaws or misrepresentations in the film while acknowledging that many aspects of camp life depicted in the piece were accurate. The most revealing moment of our conversation was when Ana Maria told me that one of her close friends at the camp was a woman named Flora, who she claimed was Samora Machel's younger sister. She insisted that many of Machel's comrades in the party's Central Committee also had relatives detained in Niassa.

These were not just astonishing revelations. They changed my whole conception of the reeducation program. Influenced by Lynne Viola's monograph *The Unknown Gulag*, I began this project to search for evidence to make a scholarly case for Mozambique's unknown gulag.[107] Viola's well-researched description of Stalin's special settlements, along with Azevedo's *Virgem Margarida*, put me on a very specific and strictly defined path. If the top leaders of Mozambique's socialist revolution really had their close relatives detained in reeducation camps, then there was more to the reeducation program than the story of the unknown gulag. The very socialist experiment in Mozambique had to be seen through a different lens. I was determined to lay my hands on

FIGURE 0.1. Archive room in Niassa, 2015. Photo by author.

archival sources, if only to confront and confirm Ana Maria's revelations. A four-day trip to the heartland of the reeducation program in Niassa, where I was allowed access to the local government archives, gave me the answers.

The Niassa archive was a treasure trove despite the dire conditions in which it was kept. Like the "accidental" archives of postcolonial Africa that have been neglected and remain largely uncatalogued, the Niassa archive was dispersed in humid basements, dusty verandas, and leaky attics, where the bureaucratic paperwork produced since independence was dumped together with outmoded equipment and all kinds of bureaucratic debris (see figure 0.1).[108] *Arquivo morto,* or "dead archive," is the common designation in Mozambique for these archival dumping sites.[109] Handed the keys and left on my own to handle the arquivo morto of Niassa, I found confidential circulars, meeting minutes, party-state resolutions on the cleanup campaigns and the reeducation program, reports on the administration of the camps, lists of camp inmates and their supposed crimes, and much more. While flipping through one of the reports that the commissar of the M'sawize camp sent to the local department of reeducation services, I confirmed Ana Maria's revealing story. The file was a list of all the children and their mothers living in detention in the camp. An *x* marked in blue ink (the only handwritten mark on the document) highlighted number 62. The entry noted: "Child: Boaventura Aurora / Age: 12 months / Mother: Flora Moisés

Machel."[110] This was indeed the sister of the president and the person with whom Ana Maria had shared the wretched camp barracks between 1977 and 1979. Yet, as more files revealed, in addition to detaining his sister, President Machel also sent his seventeen-year-old daughter and a teenage niece to Niassa for reeducation. They were all held under charges of *corrupção moral* (moral corruption), more specifically self-indulgence, hedonism, and pregnancy out of wedlock.[111]

Although these were high-profile cases, people accused of all kinds of moral offenses populated the reeducation camps of Niassa. Very few people were there for murder, robbery, or political opposition to the regime. Most of the cases were related to the most mundane and intimate aspects of social life, such as adultery, fornication, debauchery, and styles of dress viewed as representations of bourgeois decadence. Although the archival record is fragmentary, it became clear to me that the camps were not simple imitations of the Soviet Gulag. It was evident that, in their pursuit of a socialist modernity, Frelimo leaders were engaged in a moral crusade to produce ethical transformation in society. They targeted what they considered to be moral challenges, whether those challenges manifested in public or in the secluded, intimate domains of domestic life. They did not see intimacy and domesticity as dissociated from the public exigencies of nation building, even if those matters involved their own family members. To borrow from an elegant phrase and argument from Ann Stoler, in socialist Mozambique, "matters of intimacy were matters of state," or as Jean Allman put it in reverse, "matters of state" were "also matters of intimacy."[112] Attempts to build Mozambique as a modern and developed socialist nation went together with efforts to regiment people's behavior. Anxieties over moral laxity and the policing and criminalization of carnal relations and dress codes were not marginal aspects of politics and policies in socialist Mozambique.[113] These efforts were the very ways in which Frelimo leaders sought to constitute a reputable citizenry, the Homem Novo.

In telling this story, *The Morality of Revolution* takes inspiration from Frank Ankersmit's manifesto that the "historian always has obligations towards both the past and the present."[114] This methodological cue is particularly important to bear in mind considering that the subject matter of this study has not cooled down completely.[115] More significantly, I take the call from Ankersmit to produce a history that is meaningful in the present. A few years ago, as I was beginning to formulate the first questions for this research, Frelimo veteran and former president Joaquim Chissano told reporters that "it is a pity that we no longer have reeducation camps" in Mozambique. He claimed that the camps were established to rehabilitate criminals, not to torture people. "We created the camps for assassins and criminals," he said; "the camps were a place where people farmed, they had their income, were educated, and learned crafts."[116] Aires Ali, his former prime minister, had also told members of the parliament in Maputo that the experience of reeducation camps should "inspire" the reformation of the country's prison system.[117] These comments do not speak only to the lack of objective knowledge about the past; they also indicate the dangers of silencing the past.[118] One of the dangers is the veneration of an unrealized ideal. As I demonstrate in the last three chapters of the book, few detainees were interned for the kinds of criminal offenses that Chissano alluded to. The majority were punished for moral deviancies that bordered on petty trivialities. In present-day Mozambique, both the politicians who engineered the camps and the general public have distorted ideas about what these camps were. It is my hope to set the record straight because many victims of the camps are still battling with the trauma of reeducation.

Apart from addressing what Dipesh Chakrabarty calls historical wounds, this book also attempts to remind people of the human cost of high-minded schemes of social engineering.[119] The book grew out of my deep commitment to rescue the voices, faces, names, and trials of the "defeated of history" in Mozambique's recent past. Although historians of Africa have grown wary of histories from below and the tribulations of everyday life, and even more skeptical of giving voice to subaltern subjects, as a social historian I am committed to sharpening "our sights for history's victims and the multiple contours of their suffering."[120] This book explores the cultural and material conditions of life, and importantly, it gives voice to marginalized and silenced historical actors. My interrogation of the ideology and political thought that produced the material conditions that victimized the hitherto nameless mass of people sent to reeducation and labor camps led me to explore the production, circulation, and debate of discourses and actionable ideas.[121] Over the course of this project, I recorded more than 140 interviews in Mozambique, Portugal, Eswatini, and Amsterdam with former detainees, journalists who covered political events in the 1970s and 1980s, and former government officers involved in the reeducation program. I consulted five different archives in Maputo and Niassa Provinces, including the private papers of Samora Machel, and the extensive media coverage of the events under study here. All these sources enabled me to rescue the names, faces, and voices of those who paid the highest price for Mozambique's socialist utopia. For those who did not survive the camps to tell their stories, this book is, if anything, a modest attempt to make sure they will not die a second death.[122]

1 ~ Revolutionary Morality and the Struggle for Mozambique, 1968–1974

In September 1970, the Mozambique Liberation Front (Frelimo) held its second conference on education and culture at its headquarters in Dar es Salaam, Tanzania. This was a triumphalist meeting that marked eight years since the organization had launched Mozambique's armed struggle for independence. Thirty-seven-year-old Samora Machel, president of the liberation front since the February 1969 assassination of Frelimo's founder, Eduardo Mondlane, opened the event with a meandering speech on the role education was to play in the creation of a "new society with a new mentality"—the most important goal of Mozambique's revolution.[1] Machel told his audience that, before liberation, two detestable systems of education competed for the hearts and minds of Mozambique's youth. The first and most dominant was "traditional," precolonial education. "Irrational, unscientific, and superstitious," he claimed, such a system froze society in a permanent state of backwardness. It aimed to keep the youth trapped within *ideias velhas* (old ideas) and to induce them to reject all that was new and foreign. It fostered patriarchy and the subjugation of women as second-rate human beings through the "humiliating practice of polygamy."[2] Here, Machel was articulating a century-old discourse championed by Christian missionaries across colonial Africa and largely embraced by mission-educated African elites like himself. Such was the gospel of progress and emancipation that informed and shaped African politics in the twentieth century.[3]

Colonial education constituted the second system of education. Though Machel conceded that pedagogical innovation informed colonial education, he reasoned that the European system perpetuated the exploitation of the "masses." In addition to preserving the bourgeoisie's dominant position, colonial education served as a dangerous tool in the state's repressive arsenal, which sought to "depersonalize the Mozambican people." Under this system, Machel asserted, the student "is corrupted by the decadent tastes of the colonial society, and must become a black-skinned petty bourgeois, a docile instrument of colonialism, and his highest ambition is to live as the colonizer, in whose image he was educated."[4] Here, Machel spoke in the fashionable language of socialist revolutionaries, combining Marxist-Leninist dicta with Fanonian inflections on the psychological and cultural impact of colonialism on educated Africans.[5] This was also a self-reflexive assertion, not unusual among radical thinkers. An *assimilado* and a graduate of mission schools, Machel—like all his comrades in the party leadership—was the product of Portuguese colonial education.

In the same way that Frantz Fanon had prophesized "a dying colonialism," Machel declared that the two systems of education in Mozambique were destined to collapse.[6] In their place would rise the revolutionary education already being realized in areas under Frelimo control (the so-called liberated zones in northern Mozambique as well as in military training camps in southern Tanzania). This revolutionary system would create a New Man, a new mentality, and a new society in independent Mozambique. This society was to be founded on a wholly new "revolutionary morality," an ethic that would promote the "emancipation of women" and create "a generation with a sense of collective responsibility." This was to be a society of scientific and rational thought—a society of politically conscious and collectively industrious citizens who cherished "manual labor," who did not seek material gain and personal benefit but strived to "serve the people." The New Man was to be virtuous in his behavior, in his mentality, and in his physical outlook. Self-denial, temperance, and frugality were to be his guiding principles. Above all, the New Man was to be devoted to the party (the vanguard of the Mozambican people), honor the one and indivisible Mozambican nation, and be blind to all other identity colors (ethnic, racial, or otherwise). Achieving this ideal, Machel remarked, "demands the destruction of old ideas and inherited corrupt tastes."[7]

This chapter examines the intellectual architecture of Frelimo's revolutionary morality as well as the pedagogical and punitive mechanisms that the party employed to produce the idyllic New Man during the last phase of armed struggle (1968–74). Machel's vision of Mozambican society comprised the substance of Frelimo's socialist manifesto and became foundational to the party's revolutionary ideology. The socioeconomic and cultural policies that Frelimo pursued in the years after Mozambican independence—among them, reeducation camps and campaigns against urban social ills—sought to realize the goal outlined in this manifesto: to transform the cultural, mental, and moral infrastructure of Mozambican society. Altogether, Frelimo undertook a nationalist, modernist, and conservative project, one that blended Christian asceticism with a Marxist vision of social transcendence predicated on personal struggle, criticism, and self-criticism. This apparently oxymoronic combination of both a progressive (anticolonial) and conservative vision of society was the trademark of Mozambique's socialist experiment and the country's politics of punishment.

In the rich historiography of contemporary Mozambique, scholars have dissected the nationalistic and modernist stances of Frelimo's socialist ideology before and after independence.[8] However, this corpus of scholarship largely overlooks the party's Christian-Marxist reformism, without which it is difficult to understand Frelimo's obsession with moral decrepitude in postcolonial Mozambique or the carceral and punitive policies that arose from such moral fervor. Elsewhere in Africa, especially in those territories where independence also came only after long and bloody struggles, the story of how guerrillas received and perceived anticolonial ideologies is just beginning to be told.[9] Across the continent, young political activists with modest education became ardent socialists—ideologues who inspired thousands of men and women to take up arms. To understand how these revolutionaries appealed to their respective populaces, we must turn to the shape that socialism took in the remote camps where nationalist armies trained their soldiers and tended to the needs of populations under their control. Does the Marxist idiom of revolution capture the goals that these anticolonial nationalists set for themselves, for those under their command, and for their societies at large? When they described their cause as revolutionary, what did they mean?

I argue that, under Samora Machel, Frelimo's liberation struggle became an experiment in moral reform—or, as he called it, a "laboratory" where the foundations of Mozambican society could be devised, tested, and refined. The challenges of military insurgency provided Frelimo's leaders the opportunity to calibrate techniques of social reform and normative rules of identification in guerrilla sanctuaries, which represented Mozambique in a microcosm.[10] After independence, such projects were to be replicated at a national scale. At the heart of this historical development was the rise to power of a younger cohort of mission-educated southerners who embraced socialism and assumed leadership of Frelimo in 1968–70. Their embrace of various brands of Marxism-Leninism gave rise to a hybrid ideology, *samorismo,* which combined the many political and social aspirations of their generation. With conflicting aspirations of nationalism and modernity and conservative ideas of moral reform, this young cohort of revolutionaries found in Marxism a powerful lexicon with which to articulate an old, Christian-inspired project of social transformation. Revolution meant both outward political change and an inner, personal struggle for moral betterment. During these years of internecine struggle, Frelimo cultivated the notion and practice of reeducation, both at the politico-military and psycho-cultural levels.

FROM THE GOSPEL OF PROGRESS TO MARXISM

When Frelimo was founded in Dar es Salaam in 1962, a heterogeneous mixture of exiled people with diverse ethnolinguistic origins and cultural and educational backgrounds comprised the party leadership. While they shared strong anticolonial sentiments, Frelimo's founders adopted divergent philosophies about how to liberate their country. More importantly, they had no clear or coherent vision of what kind of nation independent Mozambique ought to be after the fall of the Portuguese.[11] Within a few months, crisis engulfed the party, which nearly dissolved after almost half of the founding members withdrew (or were forced to leave). Frelimo's official history recognizes this internal turmoil as "the crisis of the two lines," which putatively divided revolutionaries from counterrevolutionaries.[12] Of course, the political and ideological disputes that fueled the crisis were far more complicated than the party claimed. Power struggles rooted in ethnic rivalries and class asymmetries nearly doomed the nascent organization. At the same time, these struggles reflected the challenges of insurgency, which transformed Frelimo from a simple nationalist coalition into a liberation army. The party's contested politics reached a boiling point at its Second Congress in 1968 and following the assassination of the founding president, Eduardo Mondlane, shortly afterward. This succession of events proved consequential in Frelimo's ideological trajectory and paved the way to power for a younger and more ideologically fervent leadership with a socialist orientation. Under Samora Machel's charismatic leadership, the liberation struggle became a vehicle to carry out a more ambitious goal than simply defeating the Portuguese and declaring independence. Rather, Frelimo aspired to build a wholly new society, imbued with a new mentality and rooted upon a new morality.[13]

While most twentieth-century revolutionary movements spoke of creating a New Man, Frelimo was exceptional in its rather Promethean ideal. Inspired by the gospel of progress of Mozambique's nativist politics under Portuguese colonial rule and by various brands of socialism that circulated among their ranks, Frelimo leaders understood political liberation through a strong messianic lens, in which their struggle gained a new salvationist meaning. Liberation would no longer only free Mozambicans from the shackles of colonial bondage. Liberation required saving the people from their own iniquity and elevating them to a new life of moral righteousness. By *revolution,* Frelimo meant profound reformation, not only of the economic and political structures that governed the people but also of the ethical principles that undergirded society. This rather ontological understanding of revolution bears its own localized history, the details of which have been explored elsewhere.[14] Here, a summary will suffice.

Since the first decade of the twentieth century, educated African elites debated vigorously about the cultural and aesthetic values that ought to guide their society, a particularly fraught question under Portuguese colonialism. Their discursive archetypes revealed much about their religious orientation and educational experience.[15] Scholars have rightly classified their political activism from the turn of the century until the Second World War as nativism.[16] The term refers to a stage of African political consciousness restricted by regional (sometimes ethnic) identity, the base from which later nationalist sentiments developed. Also termed proto-nationalists, nativists were essentially reformists. They did not call for the end of colonialism but rather sought to materialize the European ideals of civilization and progress to the benefit of the majority native population. They struggled above all for the extension of the Portuguese civil franchise to all Africans through access to education and the elimination of forced labor and all other racial laws that kept them as subordinate. By virtue of their education and close contact with European modernity, their religious, cultural, and political associations served as intermediaries between the dominant White settler population and the disenfranchised majority Black population. They were confined to their regions, with very little territorial representation. In southern Mozambique, where most political activism revolved around the colony's capital, Lourenço Marques, the pioneer and most active association was the Grêmio Africano and its offspring Negroes Association of Mozambique (CAN).[17]

The politics of these organizations paired the gospel of progress—that is, industry, frugality, and cleanliness (some of the pillars of Protestant worldly asceticism)—with aspirations of civil recognition within the realm of Portuguese civilizational and assimilationist modernity.[18] Their main objective was to "promote the material, intellectual, and moral development of their associates" under the Portuguese flag.[19] Unlike the British practice of indirect rule in force in the colonial territories surrounding Mozambique, Portuguese colonialism established limits within which African elites formulated and developed their modernist aspirations. These limits were clearly inscribed in the chief instrument of Portuguese colonial rule in Africa, the infamous *indigenato* regime. Drawing from the French doctrine of assimilation and association, the indigenato differentiated and policed the boundaries of citizenship according to race and, to a lesser degree, class. Yet, unlike the bifurcated French system that differentiated citizens (*evolués*) from subjects (*sujets*), the Portuguese created a multilayered regime of racial stratification whose legal parallelism could only be found in apartheid South Africa. In force until its abolition in 1961, the regime of indigenato was subject to several modifications, but its ultimate goal remained intact: to reduce and maintain the majority Black population as cheap laborers for colonial enterprises.[20]

Elite Africans in Mozambique decried the regime of indigenato and the humiliations associated with assimilation. They vigorously contested the regime until the Estado Novo clamped down on any form of dissent in the mid-1930s. Nevertheless, they shared the evolutionist molds of assimilation and the European values that underpinned them. Although their subscription to European values was always in conflict with African values and cosmologies (such as the persistence of polygamy and the reliance on spirit mediums during life predicaments), African elites aspired to achieve the Portuguese civilizational standard—that is, they longed to be recognized as civilized and culturally refined and thus meritorious of Portuguese citizenship on par with White colonists.[21] Unlike their contemporaries in British colonial Africa, they asked neither "Why am I fit to rule?" nor "What have I done to deserve subjection?"[22] At least until the 1950s, their central preoccupation remained "Why am I not a Portuguese citizen?"[23] At the same time, they assumed their aspiration would only be possible if—among other things—all Africans conducted themselves according to the disciplinary norms of the gospel of progress. In their estimation, by leading ascetic and morally upstanding lives, the African people would not only prosper and become virtuous before God but would also convince the Portuguese to recognize them as worthy citizens.[24] Their vision of how to achieve unqualified citizenship was not a fully formed, comprehensive road map. It was neither homogeneous nor consensual. But their hopes informed and shaped the aspirations of the generation that came to political maturity in the 1950s and 1960s.

Despite the socioeconomic changes that swept Mozambique in the interwar years and immediately after, African elites (loyalists and anticolonialists alike) believed that a well-educated, industrious, temperate, and well-mannered African populace was necessary to achieving civil recognition and political participation. They viewed with great alarm the dangers of modern city living and their accompanying social ills, such as alcoholism, prostitution, vagrancy, and other socially deviant practices. These choices not only represented sins, but they also harmed the motherland's prestige and respectability. In this regard, Mozambican elites closely resembled their *amarespectable* contemporaries in neighboring British colonies in their efforts to promote proper Victorian manners and civic virtue. The newspapers that Mozambican elites published pursued moralistic agendas, which enjoined their compatriots to elevate their own ethical standards and serve as models for others, especially the noneducated, to follow. *O brado africano,* the most vocal and long-running Black newspaper (1918–74) in Mozambique, was what Hlonipha Mokoena calls an "almanac of African letters."[25] A bilingual (and sometimes multilingual) newspaper, *O brado africano* was one of the main forums in which the educated elite of southern Mozambique imagined and sought to construe a moral community.[26] The paper addressed different audiences simultaneously. Whereas the pages in Portuguese addressed the colonial regime and were a space for political contestation against indigenato and other humiliations of colonial rule, the *secção landina* (vernacular section in Ronga) was a platform for self-criticism, self-promotion, and Christian proselytization. It had little content concerning grievances with the colonial regime and was filled instead with exhortatory messages and preachifying articles addressed to the African community. The editorials and readers' letters in Ronga exhorted people to avoid inebriation and to battle the shame of prostitution. They also urged readers to modernize their farming techniques, increase productivity in the countryside, work for wages in the city, and educate themselves and their children.[27] In addition to the promotion of *ndóndro* (instruction or education), concerns about the destructive effects of *psakunwa* (drinking) and the proliferation of *businge* (depravity) in the city of Lourenço Marques were the most common themes of *O brado africano*'s vernacular section in the interwar years and beyond.[28] Their message was unequivocal: by ending alcoholism and its immoral by-products (adultery, the breakdown of families, prostitution, and vagrancy), the path was open for the rise of a civilized, respectable, God-loving, and industrious society in Mozambique.[29]

The gospel of progress and the nativist politics of Lourenço Marques's African elites molded the cohort of mission-educated cadres who rose to power within Frelimo in the late 1960s. Coming of age in the convoluted postwar years dominated by African nationalist agitation and subsequent

FIGURE 1.1. An illustration of the gospel of progress and the work of moral exhortation. The cartoon contrasts "a worker on a resting day" with "a vagrant on a working day." The worker, in his modern and clean attire, poses confidently and proudly in front of a tidy farmhouse, while the vagrant walks in the wild in tatters and in shame, with his head bent down. The note in Xironga exhorts urban residents to follow God's commandments, to seek waged work, live honestly, and avoid the social ills that lead to vagrancy and an impious life. Illustration from *O brado africano* (Lourenço Marques), 21 May 1966.

decolonization, they grew up listening to and believing that urban social ills like prostitution, drunkenness, and idleness were not only a sin but a serious harm to the motherland and its future prospects as a civilized and prosperous nation. Forums such as CAN's youth league and the Núcleo de Estudantes Secundários Africanos de Moçambique (NESAM), where they gained political awareness, marked the generational transition from reformist nativism to anticolonial nationalism.[30] The structure and organic function of these organizations followed the pedagogical footprint of Protestant missions from where their members came. As a prospective leader of the Swiss-Presbyterian Church in Mozambique, Eduardo Mondlane founded NESAM with members of his church's Juventude (youth group).[31] While the organization aimed to represent the interests of Black secondary students in the spirit of student unionism that Mondlane learned during his time as a student in South Africa, its main activities took inspiration from the gospel of progress and educational efforts of Protestant missions.[32]

It took more than a decade for NESAM to evolve from self-promotional and elitist concerns (like its parent organization, CAN) to anticolonial contestation. When Joaquim Chissano and Pascoal Mocumbi led the student union in 1959, this transformation was not yet apparent. It was under their successors in the early 1960s that NESAM became the beating heart of nationalist agitation in southern Mozambique, especially under the leadership of Armando Guebuza, Luís Bernardo Honwana, the siblings Lina and Albino Magaia, and Samora Machel's future wife Josina Muthemba, to mention but a few individuals. Many of the organizational principles of Protestantism that animated NESAM were transplanted into Frelimo's pedagogical methods and codes of conduct.[33] The liberation struggle and Frelimo's embrace of socialism—with its emphasis on individual virtue, collective renewal, and social transformation—reinforced the party's belief that, to become citizens in an independent, socialist nation, the people of Mozambique had to undergo a profound reformation in values, attitudes, and behavior.[34]

The people who made the tortuous journey from Mozambique to Tanzania to join Frelimo had little if any idea about socialism. The encounter with socialism came in the context of exile in highly cosmopolitan Dar es Salaam, where they rubbed shoulders with activists of various leftist persuasions, and from their many travels for military training and financial aid in Algeria, Egypt, the Soviet Union, and China. Some Marxist influence was exerted by a few members who joined the movement from Europe and who regarded themselves as bona fide Marxists.[35] However, Frelimo's embrace of socialism was slow and uneasy. It was not until 1968 that the party began to acknowledge its ideological alignment.[36] Until then, various brands of socialism had circulated within the movement. Those trained in Algeria and Egypt came with bits of Arab socialism and some ideas of Casablanca Pan-Africanism.[37] Those who went to the Soviet Union assimilated chunks of Marxism-Leninism. And those who went to China came back with Maoist lessons. Tanzania, their main host, was home to non-Marxist African socialism and ujamaa. All these leftist tendencies coexisted within Frelimo, often in contentious ways. The ascendant military commanders, among whom Machel was certainly the most important figure, affirmed and cemented Frelimo's socialist philosophy. Since he founded the training camp of Nachingwea in late 1965, Machel had benefited from the assistance of Tanzanian and Chinese military instructors.[38] According to Hélder Martins (Machel's personal physician between 1965 and 1968), the Chinese instructors at Nachingwea were the single most influential factor in Machel's ideological evolution. The Chinese, Martins wrote, "were not only military instructors, [they were] also political instructors. They suggested readings for Samora, and through their suggestion, Samora read almost all the 'Complete Works of Mao Tse-Tung.'"[39] Whether Machel did in fact read all of Mao's works cannot be determined with certainty. But an examination of all his speeches from 1970 onward reveals that he did indeed borrow from Mao, sometimes repeating entire sentences from the chairman in his own writings.

Given the military predicament in which Frelimo found itself in 1965–66 after Portugal's insidious counterinsurgency campaigns, the appeal of Mao's call for Third World revolutionaries to adapt Marxism-Leninism to their own circumstances cannot be overstated.[40] In asserting that the peasantry is naturally predisposed to revolution, Mao diverged sharply from the Soviet Union's approach to Third World struggles. Under Stalin, Moscow believed that conditions were not yet ready in Africa for socialist transformation. Yet, the Kremlin also understood that nationalist anticolonialism, which could fit within an anti-Western narrative and serve the cause of world revolution, represented a promising force. Therefore, the Soviets concluded, African nations should not rush to advance from the first phase of the struggle (national emancipation) to the second (class struggle).[41] Initially, the Chinese subscribed to this perspective. But as the gulf between Beijing and Moscow widened (especially after the 1955 Bandung Conference), Chinese policy toward Africa gained a new dimension, signaling Beijing's desire to strike its own course on the international stage. Eager to pioneer their own revolutionary model, the Chinese argued that a revolution could take place even if conditions were not ripe. In contrast to their Soviet counterparts, they assured African nationalists that they did not have to wait for the conclusion of the struggle's first phase to launch the second (the social-revolutionary phase). Indeed, the seeds of the

FIGURE 1.2. Chinese military instructors train Frelimo guerrillas in Nachingwea, ca. 1960s. Photo courtesy of Centro de Pesquisa da História da Luta de Libertação Nacional (CPHLLN).

second phase were to be sowed while the first was being fought.[42] The Soviet Union under Khrushchev would come to the same conclusion.[43]

The Maoist mantra belied the fact that Mozambique, a territorial unit, was nothing close to a nation. In fact, many of the groups that converged in Tanzania to fight for independence did not even consider the prospect of Mozambican citizenship. A protracted people's war thus represented a perfect opportunity not only to inaugurate the social-revolutionary phase but also to build the nation. Commanders such as Machel were the first to realize the urgency of this task. In the training camps, ethnic, cultural, linguistic, and ethical differences fractured the militants, who often fought one another. Before soldiers could be sent to the battlefield, they had to become Mozambicans. To cultivate patriotic unity, Frelimo instilled in its members a sense of national belonging and a common code of conduct.

As early as 1965, Machel had implemented Maoist methods to train Frelimo soldiers at Nachingwea. Although soldiers were sent for training in friendly socialist countries, Nachingwea soon became the most important training camp, and nearly all future military instructors were trained there under Machel and Chinese personnel (figure 1.2).[44] When he assumed the important post of chief army commander in 1967, Machel persuaded other commanders and instructors to follow his techniques.[45] By this time, Machel and his closest comrades in the Department of Defense were convinced that the Chinese model of protracted guerrilla warfare offered the best chance for Frelimo to regain the initiative in the war against the Portuguese.[46] The strategy emphasized political mobilization of the peasantry and socioeconomic transformation in the areas that the guerrillas already occupied. The party was to transform production, commerce, and education as well as campaign against traditional education. Under this revolutionary model, political objectives prevailed over military or tactical strategy. In other words, the military commanders had begun to understand the liberation struggle as a socialist revolution.[47]

Since Mondlane's assassination, scholars have continuously, and as yet inconclusively, debated whether he came to embrace socialism.[48] Until Frelimo makes its archives public, this question will remain open. Given his proximity to both military commanders and bona fide Marxists in Dar es Salaam, it seems likely that Mondlane was not indifferent to the party's ideological fervency. He might very well have moved toward socialism. He visited Nachingwea frequently to discuss all aspects of the party's life and to address the military instructors there. The party's center of gravity shifted from the political infrastructure in Dar es Salaam to the military headquarters in Nachingwea.[49] Mondlane did not escape the draw of his juniors' revolutionary fervor. In his address to the party's Second Congress, he recognized the importance of the Chinese method in shaping the disciplinary and political lives of party cadres led by Machel. His recognition testifies to Machel's role in shaping the liberation army's character as well as to the militaristic culture that would define Frelimo over the years to come. By 1968, Nachingwea had become the revolution's beating heart. Unlike his deputy, Reverend Uria Simango, Mondlane realized that the balance of power had shifted from Dar es Salaam to Nachingwea and so-called liberated zones, where young guerrilla commanders had taken up the struggle. Their backing secured Mondlane a second mandate at the Congress. Unsurprisingly, his victory precipitated the party's formal adoption of the Chine military strategy of a protracted people's war instead of an all-out assault on the Portuguese forces or focusing on liberating the district of Cabo Delgado, options defended by sections of Frelimo's leadership opposed to Mondlane. After his reelection, Mondlane conceded that "Frelimo is now really far more socialist, revolutionary, and progressive than ever before, and now tends more and more in the direction of socialism of the Marxist-Leninist variety."[50]

The party leadership saw no contradiction in Frelimo's decisive embrace of socialism and its previous Christian orientation. Mondlane could not have made this point clearer. "The training of politico-military cadres includes instruction about socialism," he said in an interview soon after the Congress, "so that those who come to the movement with a Catholic religious background continue to be Catholics but Marxist Catholics. It is possible!"[51] In his remark, Mondlane alluded to the fact that most Frelimo guerrillas recruited in the Mueda Plateau in northern Mozambique practiced Catholicism. On a personal level, his words indicate his attempt to reconcile socialism with his own Christian and sociodemocratic convictions.[52] As Nelson Mandela observed in his autobiography, "Communism and Christianity, at least in Africa, were not mutually exclusive."[53] This was as true for Frelimo leaders as for all other socialist-leaning politicians across the continent.[54] Mondlane was certain that "the principles and teachings of Christianity, applied to the political and social world, could form the basis for the ultimate liberation of his people."[55] History will never know the ideological synthesis Mondlane might have produced had he lived to see through the liberation struggle that he inspired and spearheaded. Whatever occupied his attention vanished on that fateful day—February 3, 1969—when a parcel bomb planted by the Portuguese secret police in a book by Georgi Plekhanov exploded, killing him. Now it was incumbent on his juniors to forge that ideological synthesis. And so they did. In scholarly circles, their response is often called Marxismo de Samora (Samora's Marxism), or samorismo.[56]

SAMORISMO AND FRELIMO'S REVOLUTIONARY MORALITY

The term *samorismo* was coined by Frelimo's diplomatic broker, Aquino de Bragança, and by Machel's first biographer, Ian Christie, who saw in Machel's writings and public discourses a cunning and original rendering of Marxism. In my analysis, the essence of Machel's Marxism lays in his doctrinaire, quasi-evangelical harangues, which exhorted the people to moral comportment and revolutionary asceticism.

Machel succeeded Mondlane after a contentious and very tense transition. For some time, Simango had been alienated from the organization's political decisions, and he stood little chance of assuming the reins of power. At the Second Congress, the party expanded the number of Central Committee members from twenty to forty—its most consequential decision, excepting the official adoption of a protracted military strategy.[57] The cohort of young militants who held bureaucratic and military positions filled most of the new high-ranking posts. They not only distrusted Simango because of his ethnic origin and detachment from the struggle's military aspects, but they also saw in him an absence of the ideological fervor that they now shared. For his part, Simango did not see any sense in the ideological craze that had all but consumed many of his junior colleagues. In late 1969, he angrily wrote in his famous and equally fateful pamphlet, *Gloomy Situation in Frelimo:* "The question of scientific socialism and capitalism in Mozambique should not be allowed to divide us."[58] Simango's disgruntled and denunciatory polemic sealed his fate. He was linked with the assassination of Mondlane and with maneuvers to take power. In May 1970, the Central Committee decided to expel him from the party and elected Machel as Frelimo's new president. The Central Committee published a brief note on Simango's expulsion. The note said nothing about Simango's alleged crime. Instead, it focused on his apparent turpitude: "Having analyzed the political and moral behavior of Uria Simango, characterized by counterrevolutionary action, opportunism, ambition, corruption and irresponsibility, the Central Committee concluded that he does not have the qualities to be a member of Frelimo and decided to expel him from our organization."[59]

At that moment, Frelimo framed crime, deviation, and dissidence within the liberation movement in a new light. Morality and moral behavior became central to the party's ideology—the line that separated those who belonged to the revolutionary clique ("the brotherhood of the elect") from those who did not. From that point, faults punishable by expulsion or other forms of castigation reflected militants' moral failings. Simango's guilt arose not from his traitorous acts or even the party's suspicion that he had connived in Mondlane's assassination. His guilt lay in his moral character. This type of condemnation, which was to become standard in the party's lexicon and political culture, portended Frelimo's new penal morality. Heavily moralistic, puritanical, belittling, and often ambiguous rhetoric soon replaced Mondlane's careful and largely conciliatory language (particularly his tendency to remain politically correct). Much of this lexical change can be attributed to Machel's penchant for combat. Yet, though he embodied the revolutionaries' new, aggressive spirit, his views resonated within the young, radical, and vanguardist Central Committee.[60]

Upon assuming power, Machel combined his work as a military commander, political leader, and vigorous moral crusader. In communiqués, directives, editorials, and speeches delivered to Frelimo cadres and civilian populations between 1970 and 1974, Machel condemned the moral decay he perceived within the liberation front and society at large. He urged Frelimo militants to cleanse their inner selves from decadent habits allegedly inherited from feudalism and colonialism, including intrigue, individualism, drinking, sexual promiscuity, idleness, and carelessness. He defined these habits as moral enemies living inside Mozambicans' minds, bred by colonial hierarchies and traditional societies. If party cadres and guerrillas were to truly become Mozambican citizens, they had to exemplify a revolutionary probity, which fused both Christian and socialist values, such as solidarity, collectivism, self-discipline, self-denial, sobriety, and thrift. These qualities, Machel believed, could only be attained through revolutionary education and reeducation, through criticism and self-criticism, and through the emulation of leaders' exemplary conduct.[61] As he warned his subordinates in Nachingwea in September 1970: "If we do not engage in a serious fight against the decay in our minds, against the putridness that exists in our zone, the representatives of the enemy in our midst, sooner or later, shall disunite and destroy us. *We must fight the moral enemy* through the lessons from our leaders, from the meetings, from the sessions of criticism and self-criticism, and above all, from the effort that each one of us does to liquidate the internal enemy" (emphasis mine).[62]

Brazen though they were, the messianic and moralistic overtones woven within samorismo were not without precedent. Nearly a century before, moralistic condemnations of capitalism and social decay had given rise to the very doctrine of Marxism.[63] Machel's political thought was shaped by his upbringing in rural southern Mozambique, the humiliations he suffered under Portuguese colonialism, the various sources of socialist inspiration in exile, and the experience of war.[64] But the imprint of Mao Zedong's writings on Machel was quite salient. Mao not only taught Machel how to use sheer discipline and strict verticality to command a guerrilla army of largely illiterate peasants but the chairman also offered a powerful moral lexicon to critique the Portuguese colonial endeavor—part of the "hateful" global capitalist system. Mao furnished Machel with a seductive interpretation of the liberation struggle, which came to entail individual self-betterment. In the face of pervasive human corruption, Mao insisted that individual self-reform was as an integral, essential element of socialist revolution.[65]

Although Soviet literature, including pamphlet summaries of Marx, Engels, Lenin, and even the writings of Vietnamese leaders Ho Chi Minh and Vo Nguyen Giap, were prevalent in Frelimo camps, Mao Zedong's writings far exceeded them in influence. Machel possessed a complete collection of Mao's books, particularly the volumes of his *Selected Works*.[66] Mao's catechisms on moral rectitude, unity, collective labor, and self-sacrifice for the cause of liberation resonated deeply with the ascendant commander. Machel read Mao's praise of peasants—hardworking and modest in contrast to the urban bourgeoisie and Western society at large, who had succumbed to the "corrupting effects of material well-being"—with care and admiration.[67] Such rhetoric conformed to the Protestant morality in which Machel and his closest mission-educated comrades had been raised. Throughout his political career, Machel pursued these revolutionary virtues with obsessive fervor. He sought to instill them in every militant—and, after independence, in every Mozambican citizen.

In a 1970 pamphlet entitled *Qualidades de um membro do Comité Central* (Qualities of a member of the Central Committee), Frelimo enumerated the virtues that informed its conception of Mozambican citizenship.[68] Of all the literature produced by the party, none was more evangelical and Maoist than *Qualidades de um membro* in its outline of the virtues of the New Man. After independence, the moral criteria established in the pamphlet demarcated the line between citizens and noncitizens. In Frelimo's view, noncitizens—those who lacked the New Man's qualities—had to be redeemed through reeducation.

THE ATTRIBUTES OF FRELIMO'S NEW MAN

Two years after assuming power, Machel convened the military instructors and guerrilla cadres at the Center for Political and Military Training (CPPM) in Nachingwea. The meeting took place in the heat of the Gordian Knot Operation, by far the largest counterinsurgency campaign that the Portuguese undertook in Africa.[69] Machel told his subordinates that soldiers should be at the forefront of transforming Mozambican society, a body politic that would be free from the moral corruption and degradation inherited from colonial and feudal ways of life. The soldiers' task, he asserted, was not merely to "eliminate the enemy physically" but also to wage an internal battle against the moral enemy, "the enemy in our own minds." For Machel, not military action against the Portuguese but "the fight against the enemy that lives in the mind is the toughest." Therefore, the CPPM, as the "laboratory where we create this agent of change, the New Man," demanded of militants and trainees a "radical change in values, attitudes and behavior."[70]

It is perhaps surprising that a commander facing such a massive assault should have been so preoccupied with the moral behavior of his troops. But this was precisely the radical transformation that Machel envisioned for the liberation front. He understood political power to be a vehicle for fostering a moral community, even in the most heated moments of struggle. He believed that Frelimo's most daunting challenge lay in transforming the hearts and minds of the Mozambican people. To that end, soldiers were to be trained not principally as killers but rather as agents of moral change. The training camps were to be the "laboratory where we create this agent of change, the New Man."[71]

Archaic though the notion of moral reinvigoration may be, Machel's New Man was quintessentially modern, the product of European Enlightenment.

In modern history, radical reformers have often sought to deliver a "new (sublime) Man from the corruption of previous history," as a matter of both vocation and duty.[72] The "extraction of the sublime, pure object from the corrupted body," Slavoj Žižek explains, necessarily entails moral purification.[73] According to Yinghong Cheng, the idea of the New Man originated in Enlightenment thought about human nature. Many Enlightenment thinkers held that human beings could be perfected into virtuous creatures. Champions of socialist and communist ideology, from Robert Owen to Karl Marx, and Vladimir Lenin to Mao Zedong, inherited this aspiration to "remold the mind, psychology, and even character of individuals."[74] At the core of the Marxist precepts that inspired and informed twentieth-century socialist revolutions lay a conviction that individuals could be transformed from evil to virtuous, given appropriate work, education, and egalitarian social relations. Only under such conditions could revolution's ultimate objective—the rise of "a new model of human being, morally and psychologically superior to all other types hitherto known in world civilization"—be achieved.[75] Thus, the Bolsheviks strove to create the Soviet Man. Chinese Communists cultivated Mao's good soldiers. And Cuban revolutionaries cried, "Let them all become Che."[76]

In all iterations, however, the New Man embodied a paradox. If such a being must be extracted from an existing society, from which model is his character to be carved? Žižek puts this question more poignantly: "How can somebody who does not exist deputize the mission to create himself?"[77] Radical social reformers have often presented themselves as *the* exemplary model of the New Man. Their faultless being and moral exhortation provide the model by which followers must remold themselves. The leader's example ensures the birth of a new society. Žižek formulates this principle elegantly: "By conceiving himself as an agency through which the People gives birth to itself, the Leader assumes the role of a deputy form (of) the future; he acts as a medium through which the future, not yet existing People organizes its own conception."[78]

Frelimo first articulated its conception of the New Man in *Qualidades de um membro do Comité Central*, the pamphlet published in 1970.[79] The party official who compiled the most recent collection of Frelimo's key texts attributes Machel as the pamphlet's author.[80] Earlier collections do not mention any individual author. The text seems to have been originally written and circulated among top cadres in late 1968 or early 1969. It is possible that Mondlane's aides authored the document, and Machel or one of his assistants revised it (possibly Sérgio Vieira). While Mondlane was still alive, the party sponsored workshops for members to study and debate the contents of the pamphlet.[81] The original title seems to have been *Qualidades de um membro da Frelimo,* which was later amended to focus more explicitly on the Central Committee, a body all the more important after Simango's expulsion. Despite the final title, which refers only to the highest-ranking officials, the text was concerned with the personal qualities of *all* members of the liberation front. The pamphlet served as a pedagogical text par excellence. Within the document, symbiotic imprints of the gospel of progress and socialism are very pronounced. While distinct in format, Frelimo's pamphlet shares striking similarities with Mao Zedong's *Three Main Rules of Discipline and Eight Points for Attention,* a set of rules that Mao enacted to discipline his army.[82]

Put simply, Frelimo's pamphlet instructed party members on how they ought to behave; it offered them a moral compass. The party militant was expected to constantly struggle for his ethical improvement, to be conscious of his mistakes, to always strive to acquire new qualities, and to distinguish himself by "revolutionary virtues."[83] A Frelimo militant was expected to model the Mozambican New Man. He had to "sacrifice private interests for the benefit of the people" and be "disciplined and respectful to his hierarchical superiors." He had to "stand against *ideias velhas* (old ideas and values: tribalism, individualism, racism, and intrigue)." The pamphlet also stressed the need for party matters to be addressed internally through criticism and self-criticism within the *estruturas* (party structures), until members reached consensus.[84] And, finally, as a disciplined, self-denying, and self-reliant individual, the Frelimo militant was expected to cherish collective manual labor and rely on his own gumption for shelter and food.[85] The stakes were very high. After all, from the example of their reformed selves an entire nation was to "organize its own conception." As the embodiment of the New Man, Machel was the master crusader of this struggle for internal renewal, for personal and collective purification, and for social transcendence. He waged this battle through his exhortatory power and personal example.

EXEMPLARY PEDAGOGY

Frelimo's new leaders presented themselves as the image of the New Man they so vociferously lauded in party literature. All militants—and, after independence, all citizens—were to follow their exemplary lives. Indeed, the leadership's moral standing was the standard against which the people were to measure their reformation. Accordingly, Frelimo adopted exemplary pedagogy as its chief method in inculcating behavioral change among militants. True to their missionary upbringing, party officials believed that change could only occur when people looked toward visible and positive examples.

In Frelimo's view, exemplary pedagogy inspired the people and set the reference point against which to evaluate efforts for self-improvement. The party abided by the missionary creed that "neat dress, personal cleanliness, and a healthy body [speak] of a worthy heart and an alert mind" and that "melioration, therefore, [ought] to be visible in everyday comportment."[86]

Machel championed exemplary morality. He projected himself as the personification of the ideal New Man more than as a commander of a guerrilla army. He cultivated the gardens, read extensively, and maintained a superb physique (he was said to be displeased at seeing his companions with protruded bellies).[87] He urged party cadres, teachers, military instructors, and guerrilla trainees to follow suit. They had no choice but to embrace the new mentality, given that it was their responsibility to pass that ethic on to others. They had to be the driving example of righteousness upon which the entire society was to be predicated. Their exemplary moral outfit was to be on display and in action at all times and under every circumstance. More than on military tactics, most of Machel's lectures to his subordinates in Nachingwea focused on this necessity for ethical self-betterment and the example that instructors set for others.[88]

Like all Frelimo sanctuaries, Nachingwea was situated in rural surroundings. To accommodate its growing army, the party built many housing facilities and small farming operations from scratch, adding to those infrastructures inherited from the colonial plantation that existed in the location. By clearing land, building their own lodging, and growing their own food, trainees learned from the moment they arrived to be self-sufficient and self-reliant.[89] As chief commander of Nachingwea and later as president of Frelimo, Machel had free rein to mold (or attempt to mold) the young military cadres in his own image—quite literally, the prototype of the sublime, incorruptible Jacobin. He combined military training with manual labor, a great deal of moral exhortation, and what he termed "political education and reeducation."[90] He did not just dictate what trainees were to do. He was often the first to perform domestic chores or to pick up the hoe to prepare the gardens.[91] As we know from one of his biographers, in Nachingwea, Machel would often ask trainees to show their hands because "he wanted to see callused palms, signs of honest work and open hearts."[92]

Apart from shaping people's moral outlooks, Frelimo's project of social engineering also sought to excise difference and to foster homogeneity. The diverse cultural and linguistic backgrounds of trainees, whom Frelimo recruited from regions across Mozambique, posed a serious challenge to the instructors tasked with creating unified New Men and New Women. But that diversity also furnished Frelimo with a unique opportunity to experiment with instilling notions of national unity. In Frelimo's discourse and praxis, nationalism figured as a virtue, a personal quality, such as honesty or courage, that individuals could attain by waging an internal battle against their "tribal" allegiances.[93] In the same way that Frelimo exhorted militants to be sincere and kind, it urged them to acquire a nationalist spirit. But cultivating nationalist sentiment required building strong bonds among people of different ethnic origins. To that end, Frelimo compelled all incoming militants to undergo a common ceremony, largely akin to a rite of passage or an oath. Frelimo called this practice *narração de sofrimentos* (narratives of bitterness or suffering).[94]

In confession-like ceremonies, chaired by a political commissar and held before a small but ethnically diverse group of veteran guerrillas, newcomers narrated the suffering and humiliation they had endured under colonialism. Following this account, the narrators were subjected to questioning, as the commissar sought to extract accurate details about their origins and motivations for joining the struggle. Before the ceremony concluded, the veteran guerrillas recounted their own narratives of bitterness. This ceremony served several purposes. First, it helped to "liberate the individual from personal rancor" against those who had caused humiliation.[95] By transferring the struggle from the level of the individual (the White man) to a malignant system (colonialism), the ceremony transformed the struggle's psychological contours. Second, Frelimo used the ceremony to screen new recruits for secret agents deployed by the Portuguese. By asking guerrillas to name their places of origin and explain how they came to the party, Frelimo employed an ingenious security strategy, which largely precluded enemy infiltration. But the ritual's most important role was to forge group solidarity. The narratives of bitterness fostered a sense of sharing a common cause and underscored that the suffering inflicted by colonialism was limited neither to individual nor to region but rather extended across the whole of Mozambique. Thus, the ceremonies included guerrillas from villages and towns scattered across the country. To recruits, the point was clear: colonialism constituted a crime collective in nature and national in scope.[96]

These ceremonies were often followed by debates about virtuous and revolutionary behavior. As LeFanu informs us, Machel "watched, judged, [and] intervened as groups and individuals within groups struggled to learn new ways of seeing themselves . . . and new ways of seeing each other."[97] The ritual represented a second birth, from which each candidate emerged as a new individual, free from the burdens of impurity imposed by colonial society. When Machel inaugurated the first conference on Mozambican women in March 1973, he explained the significance of shared suffering: "We are united through the discovery of common wounds and scars, but above all unity is realized through common effort, links are forged through collective work and study, through collective internal struggle, through criticism and self-criticism, and through action against colonialism."[98]

The narratives of bitterness illustrate the models of social engineering that Frelimo interwove in its revolutionary praxis. The ceremony drew upon Chinese antecedents. Mao Zedong employed a similar ritual, which fell within his wider vision of ideological education during his prolonged insurgency against Chiang Kai-shek's Nationalist forces.[99] Frelimo commanders, who learned of the ritual through their exhaustive reading and from the Chinese instructors at Nachingwea, assimilated it into the party's pedagogy. For mission-educated revolutionaries, however, such ceremonies mapped onto the familiar practices of self-revelation and collective exercises of self-scrutiny much in vogue among Christian congregations in Mozambique.[100] In fact, as Frantz Fanon once contended, self-criticism was "first of all an African institution."[101] Frelimo's narratives of bitterness, criticism, and self-criticism were symbiotic pedagogies that combined elements of socialism and African Christian praxis. Like their missionary teachers, Frelimo's leaders "envisioned the human career as a cumulative moral voyage, unrelieved by the possibility of confession, atonement, or absolution."[102] For missionaries, public self-revelation was the first step into a world of righteousness. By giving accounts of their lives, converts exposed themselves to scrutiny, allowing others to commend or condemn their deeds. Only after the convert had acknowledged his sins was his heart ready to receive the "Light which is Jesus."[103]

The new cohort of Frelimo leaders not only imbued the struggle with religious practices; they also presented the liberation movement as a sacred entity and the militants as missionaries. "The comrade who likes material wealth will be easily separated from the people and from its organization, FRELIMO," Machel wrote in one of his didactic essays. "This must become the current preoccupation of all of us here. And each one of us must realize and accept in his heart that wherever he may be, he is on a mission for FRELIMO. We are all on a mission for FRELIMO."[104] The mission to which Machel referred was not the military and administrative activities that the cadres—his audience—were to undertake. Rather, the ceaseless struggle for self-betterment comprised the mission. "Through criticism and self-criticism each one of us vowed to correct our conceptions and behavior that do not conform to the exigencies of the Revolution," Machel asserted. "Our experience has shown us that it takes an endless process of criticism and self-criticism to eliminate the residue of the colonial system that persists in us, for us to place ourselves decisively on the right side of history, for us to discover and implement the necessity of the Revolution."[105]

Like ardent believers, Frelimo militants were expected to embark on a permanent process of moral improvement, dialectically revealed through criticism and self-criticism. Machel and his comrades were convinced that exercises of collective scrutiny would puncture old ideas and implant new codes of conduct. Frelimo never produced a manual that detailed how to achieve this desired state of purity. Instead, the party compelled its members to narrate their backgrounds and reveal their own ways of life, to listen to their colleagues' experiences, and to take note. In these sessions, meritorious aspects received praise while deplorable behavior elicited rebuke. Diligent and honest guerrillas—men of recognized probity—were duly exalted. Those given to frequent inebriation or disrespectful advances toward women faced public censure and warnings to mend their ways.[106] In the years to come, Frelimo's program of reeducation was to rest upon the same logic of self-revelation and acceptance of past missteps.

After issuing the first version of its pamphlet on the qualities of the New Man, the party organized workshops and group study sessions to disseminate the message among militants. In these convocations, leaders armed with blackboards listed the virtuous qualities of the militant on one side and deviant behavior on the other. They urged their listeners to strive for the former and reminded them that those who failed to do so could be expelled from the liberation front. In January 1969, Joaquim Chissano, then Secretary for Security, conducted one of these sessions. With his finger pointed at the list behind him, Chissano told his subordinates: "If you do not have these qualities listed here, you are enemies of Frelimo. It is necessary to have these qualities to be a militant."[107] He then stressed a point that he found deeply meaningful. "If a woman behaves well here but there outside she sells her body," he enjoined, "then she is not a militant, she does not have the required qualities."[108]

Chissano's remarks are of particular salience. His warnings, like all of Frelimo's moral prescriptions, looked toward the future. Six years before independence, Chissano helped demarcate the line that would later define not merely who possessed the qualities of a party member but also who deserved citizenship in independent Mozambique. In the following chapter, we shall see how Frelimo reformulated and extended these qualities to define citizenship after independence and how those found lacking in the New Man's moral attributes were labeled enemies and condemned to reeducation. It is not surprising, then, that the urban cleanup campaigns that Chissano launched as prime minister of the transitional government first targeted women perceived to be "sellers of their bodies." Independent women and prostitutes—who until then had only been a source of shame and allegedly

FIGURE 1.3. Joaquim Chissano instructs guerrillas on the moral qualities required of Frelimo's militants, 1969. Photo courtesy of Centro de Documentação Samora Machel (CDSM)

impeded attempts to lift the African people to respectability—were now cast as enemies. Frelimo now waged the armed struggle on two fronts: one against Portuguese colonial rule and the other against the enemy within.

THE ENEMY WITHIN, REEDUCATION, AND PUNISHMENT

Political change, revolutionary or otherwise, often validates its legitimacy by construing and condemning an allegedly traitorous enemy.[109] When the goals of a given movement extend beyond overthrowing an oppressive regime and instead aim at profound social reformation, the enemy encompasses more than the revolutionaries' ostensible opponent. The enemy becomes a broad category. It includes all obstacles—tangible and intangible, visible and invisible, the very embodiment of evil—that are thought to impede such transformation.[110] These roadblocks, radical reformers are often convinced, originate within the movement seeking change. Traitorous enemies, be they physical agents or generalized behaviors, constitute moral impurities that the movement must purge.[111] Thus, even before seizing power, radical activists may attempt to ideologically define and catalog their enemies, so as to facilitate subsequent purification.[112] Eliminating enemies, whether through rehabilitation or excision, allows the leaders to present themselves as the "sublime, pure object"—the paragon of purity against which followers can measure their own ways of life.[113]

For Frelimo leaders, moral conduct distinguished revolutionaries from enemies. The enemy was not limited to agents of the Portuguese. Rather, the enemy encompassed everything from direct collaboration to daily routine. In 1970, Machel told a group of military instructors: "We came to the Revolution loaded with vices and defects. Some came impelled by ambition, to get high positions in independent Mozambique. Others came because they like easy life, drinking, and women."[114] In Machel's view, Frelimo's proverbial enemy, the one which undercut the liberation movement and gave rise to real acts of treachery, was to be found—and destroyed—in militants' behavior. Personal ambition, moral corruption, individual ambition, elite pretension, disrespect and abuse of women, idleness and robbery, superstition, and religious fanaticism: these were the enemy characteristics that could destroy Frelimo from within.

In several publications between 1970 and 1974, Machel urged militants to heed the boundary between what he called the "zone of the revolutionaries" (or "our zone") and the "zone of the enemy." He exhorted cadres to recognize the latter's telltale signs—its economic system, lifestyle, and ideology. Once again, Machel's rhetoric alluded to the future. Identifying the zone of the enemy during the liberation struggle sowed the seeds for a new system, a new moral community for a future independent nation.[115] Living within a liberated area did not mean that a militant belonged or contributed to Frelimo's nascent progressive system. Machel urged militants to constantly separate themselves from the enemy and to decry what the insidious zone of the enemy represented. Membership in the liberation front required a permanent battle, fought on mental and behavioral terrain. He reminded soldiers to "combat the idea that the simple fact of living in the liberated areas is a guarantee to have a revolutionary consciousness." In fact, he reasoned, "the demarcation between the enemy and us is not merely physical; it is at the level of consciousness, and it manifests in all aspects of life and behavior." For Machel, "moral slackness and liberalism destroy the demarcation between the enemy and us. And when the boundary line is destroyed, the physical agents of the enemy can spring unrecognized, for nothing else would distinguish their life and actions from ours."[116]

Military instructors and teachers in guerrilla-run schools worked on the frontlines of Frelimo's campaign to construct the New Man. The young Mozambicans growing up in Frelimo-controlled areas (especially the trainees at CPPMs) represented a pristine generation. In Machel's words, they comprised the "first generation to rise in the heat of the revolution."[117] Collectively, they were a tabula rasa on which Frelimo could inscribe new forms of being and behaving. Within them lay the revolution's future. "It is this generation," Machel held in a 1970 essay, "that in the next 20 years shall be called to continue the task we have started. They are the nursery whence the selected plant will rise, and which will make the revolution triumph."[118] Frelimo was to protect this new and pristine generation from moral corruption at all costs. Raised and educated in the old system, teachers and instructors were thought to carry with them the defects and addictions inherent to prerevolutionary society: individualism, ambition, corruption, and superstition. Teachers and instructors were to sanitize their inner selves before so much as communicating with members of the new generation. "Teachers and education staff must act like the medical doctor," Machel asserted, "who, before approaching the patient in the operation room, disinfects and sterilizes himself to avoid infecting the patient."[119]

A renowned orator and trained nurse, Machel often resorted to clinical analogies and medical allegories to convey his message. In several meetings and lectures in Nachingwea, Machel reminded instructors that their work was akin to that of a medical doctor. The golden generation tasked with carrying on the revolution and founding Mozambique's new society could not be infected or contaminated. Failure to observe proper precautions warranted harsh punishment. "How do we classify the doctor or nurse who comes and contaminate the patients? Who, instead of protecting and saving them, transmits disease?" Machel asked his audience. An unclean instructor was a counterrevolutionary. Deviancy was an act of the enemy within, a dangerous pathogen lurking inside the movement. "We must manifest the maximum of severity against all that among teachers and education staff indicates subjectivism, individualism, tribalism, arrogance, superstition, and ignorance," Machel declared.[120] The making of the New Man was a clinical endeavor. Impurities had to be surgically excised.

Within Frelimo, enforcing a common code of conduct complemented what Émile Durkheim called "punitive sanctions."[121] The party often resorted to disciplinary measures to ensure that the cleansing processes produced the desired results. Traces of archaic values and decadent behavior, blatant manifestations of the enemy, were to be expunged with what Machel called "revolutionary violence." Indeed, thorns lined the path toward the virtuous New Man. Public buttock floggings (*chamboco*), underground prison cells, forced labor, and firing squads—abuses that resembled the grimly familiar tapestry of Portuguese colonial violence—constituted the most common punishments meted out to party members.[122] The Chinese endorsed similarly punitive techniques. The tactics of laogai and laojiao were known to the Chinese military instructors at Nachingwea.[123] Frelimo commanders harnessed all of these punitive techniques to keep their soldiers, as well as civilians, in line.

The party did not administer punishment for the sake of inflicting pain. Rather, punishment became a pedagogical tool. It was necessarily employed in public, where everyone could see and heed the gruesome example.[124] Punishing so-called enemies before cheering crowds became routine in guerrilla bases and sanctuaries such as Nachingwea. The *rassemblement*—the open square and center of the camp's collective life—was a privileged space for punitive spectacles.[125] Frelimo's notion and praxis of reeducation encompassed all of these disciplinary measures.

At least until 1966, party leadership refused to give guerrilla officers permission to administer justice. Soldiers often felt powerless and disillusioned in the face of unruliness among their ranks, which they saw as an enormous impediment to the struggle. Cases of indiscipline plagued guerrilla units. Women in guerrilla bases were sometimes victims of sexual harassment and rape. The very presence of women in camps often caused internecine fights among competing soldiers, occasionally resulting in death. The most common infractions included drinking, theft of property (usually food and clothing) belonging to local communities, and mass desertion. Soldiers often deserted out of hunger, for family reasons (most locally recruited soldiers could not withstand long periods away from their wives and children), or from fear of war. As one guerrilla commander lamented of new recruits, "Many drop their weapons and run away at the first sound of gunshots."[126]

Frelimo had no uniform punitive sanctions. Field commanders often employed arbitrary criteria to assess alleged wrongdoings—or, in the party's rhetoric, "manifestations of the enemy." Within the liberated areas and training camps, chamboco and forced labor in local gardens or fields (*machamba*) were most commonly used to discipline errant militants. These punishments were often combined with political reeducation, which entailed little more than moral exhortation.[127] Several of Frelimo's primary guerrilla bases, such as Base Central, Moçambique D, and Chaimite in the Mueda Plateau featured prison cells, which were reserved for recalcitrant wrongdoers. In one case, a soldier was incarcerated for fifteen days for killing a wild boar without having first sought permission from his commander at Base Central.[128] How the soldier's actions might have contravened Frelimo's moral standards is not immediately clear. Similarly, deviant soldiers could receive up to thirty lashes in front of their colleagues in the rassemblement, after which they were asked to repent.[129]

For guerrilla commanders who had received formal military training in the Soviet Union or in China, such as Sebastião Mabote, these measures were far too mild. They had no doubt that sterner discipline was integral to the struggle's success and that, due to the political leadership's pacifism, a corrosive liberalism was spreading within the liberation movement.[130] The issue of how to discipline party members caused friction between the Department of Defense and the Department of Security (the most radical wings of the liberation movement) as well as among the political leadership in Dar es Salaam.[131] It is therefore unsurprising that as military commanders rose to prominence in the Central Committee, the party adopted—or at least allowed—more severe disciplinary measures to address deviations from the guerrillas' code of conduct. The party thereafter introduced an array of unprecedented punishment techniques, which ranged from building huts, felling trees, digging holes, and laboring for hours under the scorching sun to death by firing squad.

Once guerrillas were given free rein to adjudicate cases within their own units, even the smallest of faults became a manifestation of the enemy, and the cadres applied the harshest of penalties in response. Although some guerrillas deserted, spied, or committed grave crimes, such as rape, most infractions arose when emaciated soldiers invaded local communities to steal a hen or to harvest a few ears of maize. The party considered acts of theft, even if insignificant, as indicative of inner selfishness and a lack of endurance. As Machel put it, "The struggle against stealing, waste and avarice is part of developing a collective spirit. To steal is a selfish act, an act of disregard for the interests of one's comrades." Drawing from Mao's *Three Main Rules of Discipline*, he added, "Fighters should be taught to return even a needle they find."[132] Once again, how Frelimo instilled such a lesson varied widely from unit to unit. Many soldiers were publicly disciplined for minor faults. Others received death sentences. The line that ran between the zone of the revolution and the zone of the enemy was razor-sharp. As Mariano Matsinhe, the Central Committee's former secretary, told journalists in an interview, "All those who crossed to the zone of the enemy were seen as enemies and were shot by firing squad."[133]

Shocking though they must have been, theatrics of violence soon became routine across Frelimo bases. Such practices affirmed the party's supreme authority and warned spectators against moral treachery. They also revealed, in concrete, tangible ways, how the party's discourse about the enemy within developed over time. From 1970 onward, Frelimo increasingly predicated its legitimacy on identifying, condemning, and, whenever possible, punishing the alleged enemy within. The liberation movement pursued this endeavor with every medium it could harness. Apart from the party's ubiquitous coverage of traitorous acts—for example, those allegedly committed by Simango—in its bulletins and other papers, internal enemies figured centrally in revolutionary cultural work, such as choir songs, anthems, and plays. "Frelimo aina mwisho" (Frelimo has no end) was perhaps the most iconic anthem in this category. In just one song, Frelimo lyricists referred to eighteen "traitorous" enemies.[134] The specter of internal enemies inspired guerrilla poetry and furnished Frelimo cartoonists with endless satirical material.[135]

As the liberation struggle concluded in September 1974, Frelimo began to adapt the pedagogical punishments it had instituted in guerrilla units. The party's stern but provisional practices of the previous decade would ultimately translate into reeducation camps in independent Mozambique. Guerrilla cadres who had trained in the austere laboratory of the New Man at Nachingwea were placed in command of the camps. They faced their assignments in the same zealous fashion with which they operated Frelimo training camps and military bases during the armed struggle. Accordingly, the first inmates in reeducation camps were Frelimo militants who had erred during the struggle.[136] In coordination with Portuguese, Tanzanian, Zambian, and Malawian authorities, Frelimo's secret service hunted down and arrested the most notorious enemies, including former vice president Simango. Frelimo subjected these alleged internal enemies to a public reckoning in the spring of 1975 in what came to be known as the Nachingwea show trial.[137] As we shall see in the next chapter, the trial laid bare the blueprint for Mozambique's penal system under Frelimo's socialist experiment.

2 ⁓ Political Transition and the Birth of the Reeducation Pipeline, 1974–1976

IF FRELIMO had experimented with disciplinary pedagogies to produce a new moral order in its training camps and so-called liberated areas during the armed struggle, the party cemented the pillars of Mozambique's punitive society during the tumultuous and exhilarating months that followed the military coup in Lisbon and the colonial government's sudden fall in 1974. That Frelimo held the upper hand in the deliberations that led to the transfer of power on September 7, 1974, is apparent from its majority status in the transitional government and reflected the coup plotters' eagerness to rid Portugal of its colonial burden. To secure its hegemonic position as heir to the colonial regime, Frelimo detained political dissidents and others who could challenge the new establishment. With listless and sporadic cooperation from the Portuguese authorities (the high commissioner and police corps, in particular), Frelimo's punitive measures also targeted people whose moral outlook seemed to contravene the ethical norms of Frelimo's New Man. In a long list of revolutionary tasks to be carried out before the independence ceremony, the Frelimo-dominated transitional government prioritized a series of campaigns to rid the cities of social degeneracy (prostitution, alcoholism, and vagrancy) and compel citizens to conduct themselves according to new moral aesthetics.[1] Frelimo would soon open its first reeducation camps and subject hundreds of alleged dissidents to show trials at Nachingwea.

This chapter presents the Nachingwea show trial as the foundation that undergirded socialist Mozambique's punitive apparatus—that is, of the ways in which Frelimo disciplined those who transgressed the law and the obsessively propagandized normative codes of individual and collective behavior. The trial offers crucial clues into the psychology of Frelimo's politics of punishment and the party's subsequent conception and definition of reeducation. Nachingwea and Frelimo's reeducation program, I argue, amalgamated morality, legality, and salvationist jurisprudence into a single but fractured corpus of punitive sanctions. This combination produced irreparable contradictions in Mozambique's penal system, contradictions that the party leadership was quick to recognize but was unable to mend. Punitive societies determine the forms of punishment according to their professed conceptions of crime.[2] Frelimo conceived of crime as an act of enmity against the moral order that the socialist revolution was meant to precipitate in Mozambique. This conception of crime accounted for neither factual causation nor degree of criminal behavior. Deviancy was a propensity that existed in people's biographies, fostered in the social environment they inhabited before the revolution. That environment was colonial rule and its corrupting, decadent bourgeois culture. By collapsing all kinds of criminal activity and any departure from normative codes into one category—moral failure—Frelimo leaders conceived of punishment as a moralizing technique, as a way of salvaging the people from their improbity and elevating them to the righteous standard of the New Man. Therefore, reeducation camps were spaces of salvation, repentance, and ethical renewal. They aimed to produce New Men and New Women from the mass of urban social misfits who could not, on their own, shed the lingering vices that colonialism had implanted within them. On paper, this penal system would culminate in returning the reeducated deviants to society. In reality, it entailed permanent banishment from the putative corrupting environment—that is, the urban space where the denigrating influence of colonialism was most intense.

In addition to utilizing press material, my analysis draws on an intriguing collection of legal documents that the Ministry of the Interior—the state organ that oversaw the reeducation program—prepared in early 1976 in a failed attempt to pass legislation that would systematize the reeducation camps. The documents' contents, the discussions that took place around them, and the reasons the legislation failed offer a unique window into Frelimo's governmentality and the competing forces within the party (salvationists and technocrats) that were ultimately responsible for the reeducation program's makeshift character and shortcomings.

Ad hoc state projects characterized Frelimo's socialist experiment from the very start of its reign. Decisions and actions came first. The rationale behind them came later. Therefore, those charged with implementing government programs often misapprehended their ostensible goals. Policy contradictions and chaos ensued. While austerity and shortage of qualified personnel were partly responsible for this extemporary predisposition, Frelimo leaders' eagerness to effect immediate change left little room for acuity and preparation. This was surely the case when Frelimo established the reeducation camp pipeline—its first major act of governance upon assuming power. Long before Frelimo held the Nachingwea trial in early 1975 and outlined the objectives of reeducation in early 1976, the party created camps in the country's far reaches. The transitional government labeled the first inmates as urban anti-socials whose outlook and behavior harmed society and could hinder the revolution's advance by infecting the social fabric with their depravity. As Armando Guebuza, the interior minister and national political commissar, put it in a press conference, "The presence of such people in the country would corrupt the society into crime and immorality."[3]

The first camp was established on October 29, 1974—only nine days after the transitional government took power. Party agents situated the camp in a remote area of Inhassune District in Inhambane Province, about 450 kilometers (280 miles) north of Lourenço Marques-Maputo. The camp held a group of "unoccupied and marginal individuals" who were detained in a joint operation undertaken by Frelimo guerrillas and the remaining Portuguese police corps following the wave of racial violence and rioting that took place in the capital city on October 21.[4] Of the initial 1,200 people that the joint security corps detained, about 200 failed to provide evidence of formal occupation in town.[5] The first group of 90 detainees arrived in Inhassune ten days after Jorge Tembe, the state secretary for agriculture, surveyed the site. They were placed under the care of Amós Mahanjane, the camp commissar and one of the many former NESAM (Núcleo de Estudantes Secundários Africanos de Moçambique) activists who did not manage to reach Tanzania in the 1960s. He counted on the aid of thirty guerrillas turned warders.[6] The number of warders remained constant, but the inmates soared to nearly a thousand.

Frelimo began the reeducation pipeline at a tense and vulnerable time. The threat of military invasion from apartheid South Africa or the White minority regime of Rhodesia loomed. Mozambique's transitional authorities tightened security in the capital city and areas that bordered the two hostile states. Internally, the country risked dissolution. Frightened Portuguese settlers abandoned their homes in a whirlwind, taking with them everything they could and destroying what they could not. Acts of economic and infrastructural sabotage were rampant.[7] The economy stagnated, and the understaffed government rushed to fill the voids that departing colonial settlers left in the public and private sectors.[8] The young government, therefore, faced urgent demands. But Frelimo viewed the reeducation program as a matter of equal urgency.[9] Its zest for reform left no space for considering the technicalities necessary for implementing the program. Such a large undertaking required a considerable amount of human and material resources: camp supervisors, warders, educators, transportation, building materials, equipment for communications, bureaucracy and security, uniforms, and food and medicines, to mention the most basic. The government was never able to provide even a quarter of the elementary resources needed to run the program until the end of the socialist experiment in the late 1980s.

The government was always several steps behind the party's decisions. While the government was getting ahold of the proverbial horses, the party had already thrust the cart into motion. Rank-and-file officers charged with establishing and running the camps expected the camps to function as disciplinary institutions, where they could institute appropriate conditions to rehabilitate the anti-socials and reinsert them into society as useful citizens. The government created Inhassune with this vision in mind. When he surveyed the camp site, Secretary Tembe told the press that the camp was temporary. A permanent one was to be established near the Save River, and each reeducatee would receive two hectares of land and be provided with seeds, equipment, and technical assistance from the Department of Agricultural Services.[10] Tembe envisioned the reeducation camp as an agricultural settlement that government support would transform, in the long run, into a productive village for the urban unemployed. This long-term vision contrasted with the demand for immediate results asserted by salvationist party leaders at Nachingwea. Their obsessive drive for rapid social reform trampled any consideration for calculated preparations, much less for factual evidence about the social ills they sought to vanquish. Frelimo's alarmist views on crime and inimical behavior often betrayed perception divorced from facts. The initial campaigns against moral decadence during this transitional period indicated the dissonance between reality and Frelimo's salvationist renderings of society.

In launching the first cleanup campaign on November 3, 1974, Armando Guebuza claimed that there were 75,000 prostitutes in Lourenço Marques alone. He announced to the press that the government had initiated a campaign to cleanse the cities of prostitutes and anti-socials and created a reeducation program in the countryside to reform them.[11] Guebuza drew this astronomical figure from an article authored by an old friend of his from his NESAM days, the journalist Albino Magaia. The piece, published in the weekly magazine *Tempo* the previous month, featured illustrations of bawdy houses by the famous photographer Ricardo Rangel. Magaia claimed that Lourenço Marques was the "capital of prostitution."[12] He affirmed, without any reliable statistical evidence, that 600,000 people, of which half were women, lived in the unplanned suburban areas (*caniço*).[13] He stressed that more women than men lived in the city. In his calculation, of the more than 300,000 African women living in Lourenço Marques, "150,000 earn their living from semi-prostitution and 75,000 are declared prostitutes." He concluded that "fifty percent of Lourenço Marques women live under one of the most shameless forms of exploitation."[14] For Guebuza and his colleagues in the transitional government, this alarming observation offered a convincing confirmation of their own long-held assumptions about urban decadence.

There was little truth in Albino Magaia's article. The astronomical numbers that he provided were unfounded, if not fabricated. The journalist did not explain what he meant by *prostitution* and *semiprostitution,* nor did he provide the source for his staggering figures. By *semiprostitution,* he might have had in mind single women who maintained nonconventional relationships with men—somewhere between the *malaya* and *wazi-wazi* forms of prostitution that historian Luise White identified in her seminal study of women's comfort economies in colonial Nairobi.[15] Magaia distorted what was a rather less alarming situation. A survey that the municipality of Lourenço Marques conducted in 1971 indicated that 360,000 people inhabited the caniço area of the city. By 1974, that number had slightly risen to 400,000.[16] Given the gender imbalance and measures that restricted women's mobility in urban areas—a phenomenon common in colonial cities across Southern and Eastern Africa—the gender ratio in Lourenço Marques was around 140 men for every 100 women.[17] Although these figures changed after independence, until 1980, the capital city (and all major cities in Mozambique) remained predominantly male. If Magaia's presumptions were correct, all women in the capital city would have been prostitutes. In his 1968 survey of Lourenço Marques's African residents, anthropologist and colonial civil servant António Rita-Ferreira estimated that the number of professional prostitutes was less than 500 and that there were a few thousand more who combined prostitution with other trades, such as beer brewing, to get by in the city.[18] The city's social structure could not have changed so radically in just six years.[19]

Moral reformers such as Magaia had little regard for exact statistics and objective assessments of social reality. Magaia's views about the decadent life of his native city were set long before Frelimo took power. His essay echoed the conservative and chauvinistic anxieties that dominated the nativist politics practiced by earlier generations of African elites in colonial Mozambique. Magaia, like Guebuza, descended from Lourenço Marques's nativists and sounded the same old alarms about the moral decay gripping urban society. The idea of women "selling their bodies"—which Joaquim Chissano lectured his subordinates about in Nachingwea back in 1969—was a dreadful image that, more than any other social ill, threatened their modernist and reformist aspirations. As was true elsewhere in colonial and early postcolonial Africa, the presence of independent women in urban milieus disconcerted men. This was not merely because some women engaged in prostitution—which men found deeply troubling—but because their very presence in a space that had long been assumed to be a male space challenged the patriarchal foundations of nativist politics and the moral order that African men sought to inculcate. Independent women imperiled a moral community that men imagined as their prerogative. In an environment fraught with masculine anxiety, women were confined to the private, domestic sphere—their "natural" domain, where they were to behave as docile wives, caring mothers, and obedient daughters.[20] In the heyday of decolonization and in the time that followed, exercising domestic control over women rendered nativist men socially and politically consequential, which offered proof of their capacity for self-mastery and maturity for self-government.[21]

Although independence achieved the aspiration of Mozambique's nativists for civil recognition and self-government, reformists such as Magaia clung to the notion that loose women—like vagrants or intemperate and idle men—hindered their political ambitions and brought disrepute to the nation. The only difference was that, now, they expressed their misogynistic anxieties in the language of socialism, of exploitation of men by men. The grim picture that Magaia painted of Lourenço Marques's women did not call the city's social pathologies to the transitional government's attention. It simply reinforced the party's dogma of urban degeneracy and the need for a sweeping campaign and a state-led program of social reform.

Guebuza named the first campaign Operação Limpeza (Operation Cleaning). Applying militaristic and clinical vocabularies to state policies became a trademark of Frelimo's governance, a direct influence of Tanzanian politics. The act of governing was a *battle* carried out through *campaigns, operations,* and *offensives.* The reformist program was a clinical endeavor to *cleanse, disinfect, heal,* and *purify.*[22] Guebuza's choice of the word *limpeza* conveys exactly the understanding that he and his comrades shared of the task at hand. The cities were full of human dirt that needed urgent cleansing to avoid contaminating the social fabric. The campaign began on November 7, 1974. In just one day, authorities detained two hundred women.[23] In June 1975, several weeks before the declaration of national independence, the transitional government decided to launch a "decisive blow" against prostitution.[24] The capital city had to be "clean" before the important day. The city authorities closed all cabarets and brothels in the downtown red-light district, the notorious Rua Major Araújo. Rather than operating overnight, from then on, bars were to serve customers from seven in the morning to seven in the evening. The mayor, Alberto Massavanhane, congratulated the government's vigorous "blow on the immoral business" of prostitution: "The city council can only be pleased that the city is cleaner," he told reporters.[25]

The campaign extended to other cities: Beira, Nampula, Quelimane, Tete, and Chimoio. By November 1975, newspapers were reporting more than "3,000 men and women" rounded up in only a few days in the country's major towns.[26] One source indicates that "some 15,000 people were detained in the first month" of Mozambique's independence alone.[27] As soldiers and police officers invaded preselected places of leisure late at night, they took into custody everyone inside, women and men alike. Men found in those places without identification papers (IDs or passports issued by the colonial government) were taken into detention as vagrants, alcoholics, drug addicts, and promoters of moral corruption. But women were the main target, at least initially. Authorities regarded women in miniskirts, high heels, painted nails, makeup, wigs, and Afro hairstyles—the modern fashion of the time—as *mulheres de má vida,* "women of low life."[28] Historians of Africa have aptly demonstrated how, throughout the twentieth century, social reformers took signs of modernity mapped onto free-moving female bodies as signifying women's disrepute, as an affront to efforts to build honorable civil societies in Africa. Such efforts often ignored the multiple positions that women held as urban workers, single mothers, divorcées, or, in the case of Mozambique, *amancebadas* (women who entered common-law relationships with men out of wedlock).[29] Frelimo authorities were particularly anxious about—even incensed at—the free mobility apparently enjoyed by young women and single mothers, especially when such mobility connoted play and fun. The party's military wing for women, the Female Detachment (DF), and the national organization for women's affairs, the Organization of Mozambican Women (OMM), were not immune to paranoia about urban women. The cadres of the Female Detachment and OMM often worked closely with security forces in the cleanup campaigns.[30] It was as if they, as fellow women, could better spot the signs of decadence in their

FIGURE 2.1. Frelimo guerrillas escort an alleged prostitute in downtown Lourenço Marques, 1975. The proof of her crime was mapped onto her body and outlook: her Afro hairstyle, short dress, and makeup. Photo by Ricardo Rangel, *The Last Stray Sister.* Photo courtesy of Centro de Formação Fotográfica (CDFF).

female compatriots than could male cadres. Yet, more often than not, they simply followed orders from the dominant male party leaders.[31]

Along with administering Operação Limpeza, the transitional government conducted a campaign against vagrancy and alcoholism. The triumph of the socialist revolution depended on the temperance, self-denial, and industriousness of the nation's citizens. Authorities often conflated drinking with vagrancy, prostitution, adultery, drug addiction, crime, and antirevolutionary plotting. They made little effort to distinguish the pastime of drinking from the pathology of alcohol abuse or dependency. As long as people gathered in a beer hall, authorities saw alarming signs of alcoholism. "We know that in the cities there is alcoholism," Machel told thousands of eager listeners in his first rally shortly after Independence Day in 1975; "where there is alcoholism, there is backwardness, illiteracy, ignorance, crime, immorality, and disrespect."[32] At his instruction, the government prohibited any new brewing or distillation facilities and introduced regulations for the sale of alcoholic drinks.[33] At the same time, the party instructed local party cells, or Grupos Dinamizadores, to combat alcoholism in residential areas, to dismantle informal brewing installments, and to denounce sellers and consumers of alcohol.[34] Through Mozambique's Presbyterian Church, the government requested the help of the International Blue Cross to assist the country in the fight against alcoholism.[35]

In their role as self-appointed mouthpieces of government campaigns, newspapers published several articles exhorting the masses to obey the new dry commandments. For months on end, they dedicated an exclusive page to the "struggle against alcohol," which included readers' statements and editorials about the ongoing campaign. Their message was clear: the country's future depended on having a sober citizenry. Local party committees held long meetings with residents, calling their attention to the perils of alcohol and enjoining people to part with their drinking habits. Jossefa Macie, who lived in Bairro Hulene in Lourenço Marques, informed *A tribuna* that residents of his *bairro* (neighborhood) met every Saturday "to be lectured on the dangers of drinking alcohol." He told the reporter that the committee of his bairro prohibited all residents from selling drinks. "Those who continue to sell in secret are being discovered," he said, "because the committee gave orders to denounce all individuals who sell alcoholic drinks in the *bairro*."[36]

The party's all-out struggle against prostitution and intemperance thus turned residents into stool pigeons. These campaigns were not isolated acts by party agents or security forces. Newspaper editors, reporters, and ordinary citizens furnished authorities with information as to which places they should target.[37] While the campaigns were running, *Tempo* and *Notícias* published several articles and letters to the editor by readers alerting the authorities that, after the initial swoops, "prostitutes" were devising more creative ways to continue their trade by frequenting "respectable" places, such as restaurants, cinemas, and theaters, while brewers and consumers of alcohol were setting up new drinking dens.[38] The declaration of independence spurred tremendous civil energy, public vigilance, and voluntarism, which shaped Mozambique over the two years that followed. The government worked with an army of collaborators who denounced prostitutes, brewers, and drinkers all around. In his report to the president, the governor of Maputo Province indicated that there were "500 collaborators in the district of Matola [alone], helping in the fight against drunkenness and prostitution."[39] It was as if the entire country was busy supporting the call to remain sober and chaste.

Rather than factual data, an overstated, alarmist perception justified the dry campaign. Colonial authorities in Mozambique and elsewhere had always agonized over Africans' alleged predisposition toward drunkenness. The problem was no more troubling than in any other modern society. But in colonial Africa, drunkenness was just one of many behaviors that rendered colonial subjects susceptible to state intervention, either by being

FIGURE 2.2. Producers and sellers of alcohol apprehended with the tools of their alleged criminal activity in Maputo, December 1978. A man who was possibly a client may have been caught red-handed. Reeducation camps were filled with detainees accused of selling and consuming alcohol. Photo courtesy of Arquivo do Jornal Notícias (AJN).

racially segregated or incarcerated and forced to provide cheap convict labor for public and private enterprises.[40] Postcolonial governments such as Mozambique's inherited and reproduced the same practices, not necessarily to segregate or extract cheap labor but to genuinely reform society. Like the battle against prostitution, Frelimo's campaign against alcohol amounted to a military operation, undertaken by those whose characters had been forged in the austere laboratory of the New Man in Nachingwea. Armed with AK-47s, security forces and members of Grupos Dinamizadores and OMM invaded homes known for producing and selling alcoholic drinks. As figure 2.2 illustrates, in most cases, the patrols destroyed brewing implements, poured out the inebriating liquids, and rebuked the offenders and their clients. In other cases, depending on the agent leading the operation, the raids resulted in arrests and the apprehension of criminal evidence.[41] The campaign's architects made no distinction between distilled, highly intoxicating spirits (*tontonto* or *sope*) and low-alcohol grain- and fruit-based drinks (*uputsu, bukanyi,* or *xicaju*—which were, as Jeanne Penvenne has observed, "an important part of social renewal and the pleasures of summertime" in Mozambique).[42] These "agents of moral change" reproduced the violent scenes of colonial days: Portuguese authorities, mounted on horseback, raiding

African neighborhoods to enforce the prohibition on producing and selling alcohol among Africans.[43] As in colonial days, women were the primary victims, since they were most often the brewers, distillers, and sellers of drinks. Many ended up in reeducation camps.

Frelimo's cleanup crusade was not restricted to rounding up and sending people to reeducation camps. The party was also invested in transforming the very sites of ill repute into dignified locales for public works. As Operação Limpeza was underway in November 1974, Frelimo militants were busy transforming the prominent bar Vasco da Gama into the party's provincial headquarters. President Machel, who was still in Tanzania, financed the bar's conversion into an office building.[44] When he first visited the site in 1975, he told the press that "the selection of that place was not mere chance." The party's goal was to transform the "bastion of corruption" into a "center for the diffusion of new ideas."[45] Like most of his peers, Machel had lived in the labyrinthine bairro of Mafalala, only a few yards from Vasco da Gama and not far from the Matlhotlhomane brothels, before joining Frelimo. "Troubling" memories of the buzzing noise of drinking and dancing, which often lasted all night, played in the president's mind when he returned home.[46] He professed relief to see Vasco da Gama converted into a center of political and social transformation. Likewise, the infamous sin street of Lourenço Marques, Rua Araújo, was renamed Bagamoyo after one of Frelimo's former training camps in Tanzania. Frelimo replicated the work of cleansing Mozambique from the yoke of colonial, bourgeois depravity in the country's infrastructures, their taxonomy, and their purpose.

The roundup operations and mass arrests inundated the small prisons left by the Portuguese. It was here that detainees were kept temporarily before being transported to the camps. By 1976, Frelimo was running close to twenty camps scattered throughout the country (map 0.1). The total inmate population was estimated at ten thousand.[47] Although the police sometimes triaged individual cases before sending victims away to the camps, there were virtually no hearings before a court of law. As H. G. Adler noted more than six decades ago, mass incarceration in detention camps is impossible under the normal rule of law, "impossible in a formal sense and because of the great number of persons affected."[48] Even if Frelimo possessed a well-staffed judiciary—which was not the case—the party could not have processed detainees in a timely and effective way. The entire process was fraught with irregularities and arbitrariness. Yet, as Tzvetan Todorov puts it, in autocratic regimes, the arbitrariness of power is never a perversion of well-intentioned policies but rather their "fundamental trait."[49] Indeed, the impromptu character of the cleanup campaigns expanded the reeducation pipeline far beyond the government's capacity to control the process. As if to prove the point, reports from camp authorities in Niassa Province informed the Ministry of the Interior that many detainees were arrested "mistakenly" and "arbitrarily."[50]

In addition to the challenges from Mozambique's incipient judiciary and the campaign's makeshift character, the reeducation program's arbitrariness reflected a moralistic jurisprudence, which put a premium on appearances of moral failure. Detainees did not need to be factually guilty. Their physical demeanor—style of dress, for example—and the place where they were apprehended—a beer hall or a night club—were enough to incriminate them. It was not in the police station or in the courtroom that Frelimo authorities determined whether moral offenders were culpable. They assessed culpability in the reeducation camps, where they forced detainees to depict themselves in biographical narratives and confessions of guilt. This judicial method drew its blueprint from the dissuasive example of the four hundred detainees put on trial in Nachingwea and whose moral downfall the party publicized widely.

THE NACHINGWEA SHOW TRIAL

Along with Operação Limpeza, the trial of Frelimo's dissidents in Nachingwea marked the end of one revolutionary circle (the liberation struggle) and the beginning of another (the socialist experiment). In intermittent sessions from March to May 1975, Frelimo showcased four hundred alleged traitors to thousands of cadres, journalists, and eminent guests (among them Julius Nyerere and Kenneth Kaunda, presidents of Tanzania and Zambia, respectively). Frelimo compelled the accused to read their biographical narratives and to confess their duplicity. At the trial's end, the party relocated all of the detainees to the newly established reeducation camps in the northern provinces of Niassa and Cabo Delgado. As a public exercise in soul-searching and penance, the trial inaugurated a punitive culture that would dominate Mozambique's criminology, jurisprudence, and carcerality for the following fifteen years.

The Nachingwea trial is a compelling case of what historian Igal Halfin has called the juridical hermeneutics of the soul, the public trial of intimate enemies through judicial proceedings that do not center—or do not seek—factual evidence of betrayal or crime but rather implicate moral failure, the weakness of the spirit that leads the individual to traitorous and illicit acts.[51] As Barrington Moore once noted, for revolutionary movements animated by puritan and salvationist ideals, political disagreements are "moral differences and opponents moral outlaws—lepers and menaces all at once."[52] In such movements, enemies must not only be denounced and expurgated. They must also face public reckoning, in which their crimes are exposed for all to see. In such cases, it is vital to the proceedings that the enemies themselves provide an unsparing account of their actions through biographical narration and confession of guilt. As Halfin concluded from the case of Soviet show trials during Lenin's tenure, "Culpability was determined according to the accused's personal record: the intention behind the crime was key, and the object of investigation was the soul of the accused, its moral inclination, its hopes and designs." Rather than detail actual misdeeds, Soviet investigators concentrated their zealous quest on the life history of the accused. "Motives grew out of biography; without biography no verdict could be rendered."[53] The agonizing process of self-revelation, personal struggle, and confession of duplicity that characterized Chinese reeducation and thought reform as narrated by psychologist Robert Lifton and sociologist Martin Whyte followed the same inquisitorial script. Here, too, party cadres and reeducatees produced countless files of biographical narratives that traced the roots of their guilt to their ancestors' class background, sometimes stretching back three generations.[54]

Frelimo leaders never developed their inquisitorial hermeneutics to the same level of perfection as their more senior revolutionary counterparts in the Soviet Union and China. Nevertheless, they produced similar ritualized theatrics of public confessions with their own revivalist flair. Although radio and video recordings of the trial and transcripts of the proceedings exist in local archives in Mozambique, I was denied permission to consult them. I therefore rely on fascinating and detailed coverage by Marcelino Komba, a Tanzanian reporter who covered the events. I also have a rare documentary on Nachingwea produced by Frelimo's Department of Information and Propaganda, which portrayed a few minutes from the trial. Fortunately, the most important material for my analysis is Uria Simango's confession, which Mozambican newspapers published in full at the time.[55]

Komba described the trial's audience as "a sea of militants, young and old, black and white," all of whom "sat on the ground, legs crossed and looking alike in their green combat uniforms, complete with jungle hats."[56] Samora Machel was now the supreme leader of the "brotherhood of the elect" and took center stage as presiding judge, "clad in Frelimo military gear and walking up and down as he spoke."[57] It was before such an intimidating mass that the detainees were commanded to stand and narrate their histories of betrayal.

In repetitive, ritualized sessions of self-disclosure and narration of their shortcomings, detainees were to show their awareness and recognize the moment of failure, the moment in which their faith in the revolutionary cause faltered and led them to treachery.[58] President Machel singled out detainees at random as they filed past the watching crowds and he gave the histories of "how they teamed up with the enemy." Komba observed that the crowd frequently interrupted the biographical narrations with uproarious song. "At times [the singing] was to praise the struggle. At others, it was to laugh at the traitors," he wrote. The following lyrics typified the latter: "You are reactionaries, agents of the Portuguese. We shall show you what you deserve. We thank you Mondlane for leading us into the struggle."[59] The supreme judge was never bothered by such interruptions. Hymns composed by militants who had trained in Protestant church choirs had always underpinned the revolutionary struggle's cultural ensemble.[60] At Nachingwea, several choral groups entertained the crowds and, importantly, endowed the event with the appropriate sacramental solemnity. Machel was a passionate chorister himself, at times leading the choirs in his favorite number, "Khanimambo, khanimambo Frelimo" (Thank you, thank you Frelimo). As the amazed Tanzanian newsman observed, "Before the group came on stage, *ndungu* Samora broke out singing. His militants joined him with alacrity."[61] When Uria Simango and Joana Simeão entered—the two most notorious alleged traitors—the singing grew even louder. Simango's introduction "had to be spoken very loudly because the militants were singing: 'Simango is a traitor.'"[62] When Machel brought Simeão "to face the militants, holding her by the arm," the crowd broke into song: "Joana you are a reactionary. Frelimo has no end!"[63] Despite her apparently defiant demeanor as Machel dragged her by the arm, as if she were a trophy the excited crowd had won, she could not escape these theatrics of power. The trial footage does not show her breaking down into tears. But many others who confessed their guilt did lose their composure while the presiding judge smiled and gesticulated triumphantly.[64] Similarly theatrical scenes of public justice and penance became routine in socialist Mozambique, often with President Machel at the helm.

Reverend Uria Simango's "marathon confession statement" lasted for several hours, during which "he had to drink water thrice."[65] His confession was unique. It was written and read aloud. Over twenty pages long, the confession included a chronology of Simango's political biography since Frelimo's founding in 1962. The opening, which I translate from Portuguese, is particularly illuminating: "I, Uria Timóteo Simango, declare that: before the documentation that FRELIMO possesses, have concluded that it is vain to deny the facts. . . . To make this document public is one way of beginning to pay the debt that I have with the people, a way of beginning to depict myself."

In disarming fashion, nearly baring his soul to all, the former vice president admitted that ambition for power had blinded him, leading him to oppose the revolutionary line and ultimately betray the revolution. He assumed blame for the crisis that befell Frelimo in the mid-1960s, including the plot that led to Eduardo Mondlane's assassination. It is irresistible to quote this rather long passage from the confession:

> Throughout my life, I have been a very ambitious man. In all the organizations in which I was a member I always desired to be the first. Appointed or not, I always worked to achieve that ambition. Ambition blinded me; it led me to join FRELIMO and to commit many mistakes. My 1969 pamphlet "Gloomy Situation in FRELIMO" was elaborated amid this blindness for ambition, because I wanted to be president of the Party. . . . It was impossible for me to see what was going on until I reached the abyss. Many students lost their way and turned against FRELIMO because of me, an errant man. . . . Therefore, I accept my mistakes and invite all those who have defected from FRELIMO because of me to return, because I am confident that FRELIMO will have mercy on them. . . . Since my arrival [in Nachingwea] I have received wonderful treatment. . . . Why does FRELIMO act this way? I have two answers for this question: a) because FRELIMO has assumed the responsibility for the well-being of the Mozambican people; b) because FRELIMO wants to educate and it educates the errant and wants to lead them in the righteous way. A request to the people: Although I arrived at this decadence owing to my blindness, I acknowledge the paths that I took; I acknowledge my mistakes and their magnitude for the people of Mozambique. I beg for three things: that they forgive me; that they educate me; that my example is used to educate future generations.[66]

According to his biographer, Reverend Simango never could have written this statement.[67] A comparative textual analysis of the confession with Simango's previous writings, particularly his pamphlet *Gloomy Situation in Frelimo,* also leads me to the firm conclusion that Simango did not author the confession.[68] Simango wrote in a less vigorous, less commanding manner. His textual cadence—or, as Karin Barber would have it, addressivity—was halting, denoting the writer's effort to persuade rather than to prescribe or to urge.[69] The confession's vigorous and exhortatory tone, particularly its messianic and salvationist message, is closer to the normative valence and rhetorical meter of Frelimo's Central Committee. The line of argumentation, particularly the presentation of the facts about Frelimo's internal crisis, exactly reproduces the official perspective that the Central Committee provided on the subject immediately after Simango's

FIGURE 2.3. A group of alleged traitors on exhibit in the Nachingwea trial, 1975. Photo courtesy of Mozambique History Net (MHN).

expulsion in 1970.[70] Moreover, no evidence has ever linked Simango with Mondlane's assassination; in fact, Polícia Internacional e de Defesa do Estado (PIDE), the Portuguese state police that committed the assassination, sent a parcel bomb to Simango a few days later, which the newly alert Tanzanian police disarmed.[71]

The significance of the conclusion that Simango did not write the text he was forced to read rests not in the travesty of the confession—on which scholars have concentrated their analytical efforts.[72] Rather, it rests on the nature of Frelimo's hermeneutics of the soul, on the ways in which Frelimo revolutionaries sought to establish Simango's culpability. His guilt did not necessarily lie in the traitorous crimes that he putatively committed; it was found in his unethical character. His ultimate crime was personal ambition, lack of faith in the revolution, and the wickedness of his soul, which lingered in the dark abyss whence his companions had been elevated by the revolutionary struggle's awakening and purifying light. The theological imprint in the confession is apparent. Frelimo transformed a political misdeed into a sinful failure, which carried consequences for the whole of Mozambique's people. And it was from the wronged people that the sinner had to ask for forgiveness, while highlighting the merciful character of the brotherhood of the elect, that missionary congregation with whom he had parted ways. That a Frelimo cadre wrote the text and Simango was forced to read it aloud reinforces the trial's liturgical goal of producing a linear, sanitized narrative of the liberation struggle's righteousness. Triumph was not limited to military victory over the Portuguese but rather entailed transcending the perils of internal treachery.

The confession's significance extended to its utility for Frelimo's project of nation building, inscribed in the opening sentence: "To make this document public is one way of beginning to pay the debt that I have with the people, a way of beginning to depict myself." Simango was cast as the ultimate traitor. Titled "The Confession of Simango," his statement was printed in the local press, which held his words to epitomize the moral lesson regarding reactionary behavior and treachery.[73] The defamatory song "Frelimo aina mwisho," which depicted Simango and others as traitors, became standard fare at schools and party meetings. His self-depiction, like that of other alleged traitors, served as a model for similar exercises of autobiography and self-revelation required of every individual who in one way or another betrayed the revolution or, at the very least, was in league with the enemy. The case of the *comprometidos,* who were compelled to showcase their photographs and autobiographies in public spaces in 1978, is the most illustrative example of the party producing and identifying sinful enemies—a key component of Frelimo's jurisprudence and nation building. The term *comprometido* means "compromised" or "the compromised one," and it referred to all Mozambicans who were part of the Portuguese army and other repressive institutions of the colonial regime, such as the Portuguese fascist party Acção Nacional Popular (People's National Action) and PIDE. As journalist Jay Ross observed in 1980:

> Reeducation is not confined to the camps in Mozambique. Displayed outside every government office is a row of pictures of people working there who cooperated with the colonial government, with their "crimes" listed. The theory, [the minister of information José Luís Cabaço] said, is that people who worked against Frelimo should confess so they are not vulnerable to blackmail either by the fellow workers or dissident elements, formerly based in Rhodesia but now shifted to South Africa [Renamo]. The "rogues gallery" of photos was first put up in 1978 and the government intends to end the practice later this year [1980].[74]

Like reeducation camps, the rogues' gallery epitomized Frelimo's hermeneutics of the soul. As the party assumed power, concrete examples of antirevolutionary behavior became increasingly important to rally the masses behind the common cause of building a new nation.[75] Thus, Frelimo's project became intrinsically related to and dependent on a never-ending struggle against internal enemies. That notion vindicated the need to purify the party ranks and the social fabric at large—namely, by demanding that suspects depict themselves in biographical accounts. Such biographies—printed in newspapers, plastered on walls in public buildings, and filed in the party-state security and administrative offices—provided the Frelimo regime with a hermeneutic archive that validated the never-ending struggle against internal enemies, which is embedded in the party's revolutionary maxim, "A luta continua" (The struggle goes on).

The trial's end revealed what was to come in Mozambique's penal system. In his closing remarks, Machel said: "We will not kill them. They are our educators. They are fertilizer for us. We shall always use this pain [of treason] to enrich our struggle."[76] All the accused pleaded for forgiveness and asked to be reeducated. Although the party instructed them to ask for forgiveness from the wronged people, only President Machel had the power to absolve them. In November 1975, they were divided into three groups and moved to the reeducation camps of Ruarua in Cabo Delgado Province and Chiputo in Niassa Province. The most notorious detainees—including Simango and Simeão—went to M'telela, the most heavily guarded camp in Niassa. They joined thousands of urban anti-socials who already populated a punitive network of camps that combined multiple modalities of punishment, including public and spectacular humiliation, banishment, exclusion, redemption, and confinement, into a single system. The party, however, had yet to define and regulate the system of reeducation already in place.

THE DEFINITION OF REEDUCATION AND THE ICONOGRAPHY OF MORAL DECAY

The Nachingwea trial inaugurated the reeducation program's redemptive tenets. The trial proceedings outlined the salvationist and pedagogical ideology that underlay Frelimo's definition of reeducation and its reformist objectives. In January 1976, several months after the show trial and more than a year after the party established the first reeducation camps, the interior minister Armando Guebuza drafted a bill and a memorandum on proposed legislation to regulate the reeducation program.[77] He sought to resolve the arbitrary detentions, among other contradictions, that permeated Frelimo's program of reeducation. Until then, police roundups and arrests followed no procedural criteria. Another goal was to integrate the conventional prisons (which continued to operate in parallel to the camps) within the reeducation complex, thus instituting the camps as the matrix of Mozambique's penal system. The two documents articulated a formal definition of reeducation, laid out the program's objectives, and provided a long list of social ills and categories of people who should be subjected to reeducation. Although the bill's main points and the preamble to the memorandum appeared in local newspapers, the two files were confidential.[78] The memorandum was sent to provincial governors, police departments, and camp overseers, who were to follow the new rules to avoid "more arbitrariness" in the revolutionary task of cleaning the cities. Members of the Council of Ministers also received the bill for commentary. Before we look at the legalist commentary, let us examine the two documents and Frelimo's conception of reeducation and how the party visualized the anti-socials' supposedly immoral traits.

Puritan inflections and salvationist vows recur throughout the bill and memorandum. They exemplify Frelimo's Marxist eschatology—that is, the party's understanding of "historical time as an odyssey of human consciousness" whose end point is the New Man's rise from the old regime's darkness, while the socialist revolution's "bright light" reveals a new world.[79] In the memorandum's preamble, which outlined the objectives of reeducation, the legislator claimed that five hundred years of "colonial domination" under the Portuguese "left deep wounds" in the physical and psychological fabric of Mozambican society.[80] These wounds ranged from "prostitution to alcoholism, vagrancy to drug abuse, and banditry to idleness." In addition, colonialism "subverted some mentalities, initiating them in the subtle game of the decadent tastes of the bourgeoisie." All these "abject social ills" (*males sociais abjectos*) stood in stark opposition to the new society that Frelimo was building. Consequently, the party needed a new "battlefront against the vices of the bourgeoisie, against the social evils, against ideological deviations." This battle involved the creation of a New Man who, according to the legislator, was to be "politically conscious, physically apt, and mentally sound." Thus, the camps sought to rehabilitate the "elements of the population of our country that are affected by any of the above ailments, both physical and ideological."[81] To accomplish these goals, the legislator determined that reeducation camps were to have "appropriate political conditions" to help reeducatees "rediscover themselves as valid elements" and "gain proper political consciousness and the physical vigor that they lack." The following passage is illuminating in its definition of *reeducatees:* "All reeducatees are individuals who by their ideology, by their addictions or health condition, undermine the advancement of the revolutionary process. Therefore, it is necessary to transform them into elements that can make a contribution to the cause of the revolution, by reeducating them, by healing them from the evils that affect them."[82]

Beneath the memorandum's reformist message is an eschatological interpretation of Mozambique's social reality. Before Frelimo, darkness and depravity reigned supreme. Social evils such as intemperance, indulgence, idleness, and all kinds of wayward behaviors afflicted the mental and physical composition of urban populations. Having lived under the direct spell of the Portuguese colonial bourgeoisie and its vices, Mozambican urbanites carried with them the old regime's immoralities. Frelimo brought light, awareness, and salvation. Gone were the long years of suffering and alienation. The party and its revolution would heal all the social wounds and wash away all the evils that harmed society. For those most severely affected by the old regime's decadence, the reeducation program offered salvation, healing, purification, and redemption. The bill laid out this vow in unequivocal terms: "Reeducation aims, essentially, to offer the reeducatee an environment and conditions of life and work that allow him or her to become conscious of the erroneous in his or her pervious conduct, and then be reintegrated into society as an element with a new consciousness, capable of participating in the construction of Mozambican society."[83]

The salvationist ethos of reeducation is starker in the list of "erroneous behaviors" (*comportamentos desviantes*) that, according to the bill, harmed society and impeded the revolution's advance. The legislator listed eighteen offenses that warranted reeducation, including "lack of discipline in the work place," "impairing social harmony," "intrigue," "domestic violence and disharmony," "rumor mongering," "buying or consuming stolen products," "economic sabotage," "vices against nature," "disobeying the orders of the Party," "discouraging people from participating in revolutionary tasks," "practicing sorcery," and "producing, selling and consuming alcoholic drinks."[84] These social ills and the definitions that the bill offered were elastic and amorphous. One wonders how law enforcement officers and citizens were to recognize a "vice against nature" or which acts "impaired social harmony." The line in the memorandum regarding people whose health condition undermined the revolution is particularly striking. The document did not specify what the legislator meant by *health condition.* It seems to indicate drug addicts and alcoholics. But another possible reading suggests that the legislator regarded urban decadence as a social pathology. Prostitutes, alcoholics, drug users, and vagrants—whose numbers government statistics inflated astronomically—were sociopaths who needed the government's full attention to avoid further public contamination.

Of all the *males sociais* listed in the bill, the legislator provided a definition for only vagrancy and prostitution. Prostitutes, he claimed, are "women above 16 years of age who habitually dedicate themselves to the practice of sexual relations with the purpose of obtaining remuneration or economic advantage." The legislator did not mention prostitutes' male clients. Although he referred to individuals who "consciously promote, facilitate and foster the practice of prostitution or who intervene in prostitution for profit-making," he gave a pass to men who procured prostitutes' services. In general, the label *prostitute* was rarely associated with the johns, unless one was—as the bill indicated—an owner of a cabaret or any house of "ill repute" where prostitution was promoted or practiced. The chief offense for men was vagrancy. The legislator defined *vagrants* as "those individuals without any means to secure their sustenance, who do not perform any profession or craft in which to earn a living, who avoid work and instead dedicate themselves to the habit of idleness and show no serious and honest effort to improve their condition, without any evidence of the unavoidable circumstances that justify their situation."[85]

In singling out prostitution and vagrancy, the legislator relayed what Frelimo believed to be the matrix of all social ills. Vagabonds and prostitutes formed but one underclass of enemies who threatened Mozambique's new society. Prostitution brought the nation into disrepute and also distracted men from those noble acts of industry and thrift that ensured the material reproduction of families and the economic well-being of society. Likewise, vagrants forsook the obligation incumbent upon all to work and produce for the nation. Their idle, parasitic conduct harmed Mozambique's prospects for economic independence. This moralistic understanding of vagrancy carries a long history in Mozambique. From the very beginning of colonial rule in the late nineteenth century, the Portuguese administration enacted a corpus of legislation that, on the basis of Africans' purported moral obligation to society, compelled them to sell their labor. The Portuguese made no attempt to hide the direct relation between the productive imperatives of their nascent capitalist economy and the new set of illegal behaviors that the legislation sought to police.[86] On paper, Frelimo also employed the same economic logic—that those who did not work were harming the national economy. But Frelimo went further. The party conflated vagrancy and unemployment, framing both as a deliberate refusal to work. In the party's estimation, the urban unemployed were jobless not because they lacked waged work but rather because they were lazy and enjoyed living in towns as parasites, indulging in leisure and pleasure. One way to identify them was through their lack of documentation—identification attesting to their professional occupation and civil status.[87] The other was to associate them with a particular visual representation that could combine all the features of moral decay.

While Ministério do Interior (MINT) legislators were listing the kinds of people who should be subjected to reeducation, a creative group of Chinese-trained graphic designers at Frelimo's Department of Information and Propaganda was producing a cartoon figure to typify all the features assigned to anti-socials. Widely published in newspapers, magazines, and painted in public murals, Xiconhoca, o Inimigo (Xiconhoca, the enemy) made his debut in 1976 as the definitive image of moral decay. As William Mitchel argues, "Images are not just a particular kind of sign, but something like an actor on the historical stage, a presence or character endowed with legendary status."[88] Xiconhoca was an actor whose status became legendary in the iconography of Mozambique's socialism. His easygoing and comic persona was both charming and menacing. His personality conveyed all the wicked deeds that contrasted with the ideal citizen. According to Lars Buur, "The cartoon character came to stand for a host of negative figures undermining the new state and nation through ideological and moral decay." An omnipresent threat to Frelimo's project, Xiconhoca "represented everything that the Party's equally elusive, modern, and rational 'New Man' must reject."[89]

It was easier for Frelimo propagandists to produce a visual representation of what people ought not to be than the virtuous opposite. Whereas the party published booklets codifying the virtues of the Homem Novo, no effort was ever undertaken to produce a cartoon figure of the ideal citizen. As a biographer of Samora Machel has suggested, one may assume that the ostensive representations of the revolution's supreme leader were meant to indicate that *he* was the living image of the New Man, the moral paragon that all Mozambicans ought to follow.[90] It is not surprising, then, that both Samora Machel and Xiconhoca have remained the two most recognizable iconographic symbols of Mozambique's socialist experiment.[91]

The extensive defamatory features that Xiconhoca represented included drunkenness, always portrayed by a bottle of liquor in his pocket. He was also a drug addict, a condition visualized by the cannabis leaves clasped in his hands and mouth or hanging out of his pockets. He was dressed either in dirty slippers and short trousers or Made in USA hippie garments, symbolizing his attachment to capitalism and a decadent bourgeois life. His dislike of African folklore and penchant for Western music (rock and roll—especially Jimi Hendrix) added to his rootlessness and cultural alienation. In some of his most iconic depictions, he is featured hosting boisterous, funky parties in which drugs, drinks, and pornography are sold to the youth, contributing to their degradation (figure 2.4). Xiconhoca was a criminal, a bandit, a rumormonger, a black marketeer, a religious fanatic, a polygamist, an adulterer; he was sexually corrupt (*corrupto sexual*). His

FIGURE 2.4. Xiconhoca, the Enemy, was the definitive image of moral decay. Here, he is depicted celebrating bourgeois culture and promoting "freak parties" to corrupt the youth. Illustration from *Xiconhoca, o Inimigo* (Maputo: Departamento do Trabalho Ideológico [DTI], 1979).

female partner (*pita,* or "girlfriend") typified the iconography of prostitution and independent urban women. She not only led a licentious life but also fell pregnant and gave birth to fatherless children who would in turn become social degenerates because they lacked the support of a nuclear family. As sociologist James Aho once noted, "Defamatory language rarely, if ever, simply describes things; it also rhetorically 'accomplishes' them. And what it accomplishes is an enemy ready for violation."[92]

Anyone with the visual characteristics of Xiconhoca's moral attributes was an enemy who needed internment and reeducation. Unworthy of Mozambican citizenship, Xiconhoca's place was in the reeducation camp. In theory, reeducation was designed to reconcile social misfits with the society they harmed through their moral failings. Reeducation was meant to reinsert the "moral deserters" into society as productive, useful members. As the bill underscored, contrary to the "vindictive" penal system in the "capitalist world," Frelimo's model was "uniquely" based on the "principle of rehabilitation, recovery, and reintegration of the individual back to society."[93]

Reeducation camps were to replace Mozambique's prisons both as a rejection of Western vindictive penality (in its disregard for genuine rehabilitation of the deviant) and as an assertion of Frelimo's messianic role in society. Party leadership thought of reeducation as a form of caritas, a method for bringing those who had lost their way back into the fold of national brotherhood. They believed reeducation was an act of benevolence and proof of Frelimo's concern for those with wicked souls. Through it, the party could show "concrete love" and provide a path to salvation for those who were still trapped in the dark, for those who had not been touched by the revolution's awakening light. Guebuza's bill lays out this creed. But President Machel articulated it more poignantly in the following terms:

> Religious people talk of love for our neighbors. But our love cannot be abstract. It must be concrete. . . . One can only love what he knows in substance. . . . However, if some of us are vagabonds, are lazy, how can we love each other? . . . To jail indiscriminately those who fell under the scope of the law is to disbelieve that some of them can, here and now, be transformed. . . . This is where reeducation takes place. It is about fulfilling the principle that we never reject a man. It is a great achievement of our Party: a policy of clemency and believing in the transformation of man. . . . Just like Christ, we have this halo that sometimes we are not aware of.[94]

Notwithstanding Machel's outward secular rhetoric, Christianity—as practice, symbol, or theme—was never far from his political work. He saw himself as a carrier of a messianic mandate to elevate the Mozambican people onto a new moral plane. The deviants ought not be abandoned but "reconstructed and liberated." Unlike the vindictive Western penality, which incarcerated people or killed them, Frelimo's leaders believed their system to be merciful. Rather than "shooting them," Frelimo offered to the moral deserters a school in which they could absorb the New Man's virtues, inculcated through manual labor and self-reliance. Only by earning a living from the fruits of the land through their own labor could the anti-socials salvage themselves from social alienation.[95] Such reconstructive work required meticulous oversight from those who ran the camps. The stakes were high. After all, their work was to transform people who had fallen from grace and guide them toward a virtuous existence as worthy citizens. This was a noble task that resembled sacrificial holiness, of the sort exemplified by Jesus Christ. "As Jesus never realized he had a halo," remarked Machel, "we too, crushed by everyday concerns, we are not aware of the changes we have effected."[96] Camp officials were to be diligent teachers who knew each of their pupils well enough to be able to help them improve as new social beings. They had to know the "life history" of each social misfit and also the type of life that their grandparents, parents, and siblings led so that they could "understand why this or that person committed a crime."[97]

Under Machel's directive, camp authorities were to employ a hermeneutic reading of inmates' souls by digging into their past lives, the lives of their ancestors, and the environment in which they grew up. The motives for detainees' crimes were to be found in their biographies. Forensic investigation by police was of no use in explaining the cause of the crime or in determining inmates' guilt. Culpability lay in people's personal stories. Machel and his fellow ardent reformers in the party, however, found it difficult to reconcile the moralistic penal system with the ideals of civil liberty enshrined in Mozambique's constitutional law. The crimes listed in Guebuza's bill and their visual concretization in the figure of Xiconhoca could not be inscribed in the country's legal apparatus. Reformism and legalism found themselves at odds.

REFORMISTS, TECHNOCRATS, AND THE LIMITS OF THE LAW

In Mozambique and elsewhere, morality and jurisprudence were no strange bedfellows. But reconciling the rule of law with a salvationist program of social reform was a difficult, if not impossible, undertaking. The debate and commentaries that followed the bill's submission to the Council of Ministers exposed the two competing forces within the ruling party and the legalistic tension inherent in the reeducation program. If Frelimo's ranks were on the same page as to the salvationist principle behind reeducation, they did not agree on how to legislate vis-à-vis this punitive system. As journalist Joseph Hanlon observed in 1984, whenever the party failed to come to an agreement, "no action [was] taken," which meant that the "problems remain[ed] unresolved for long periods of time."[98] This was one of the costs of Frelimo's culture of *pensamento único*, or "political consensus." Unable to reach agreement, the Council found it difficult to pass the bill.

The debate revolved around two main issues. The first was that the members of the Council knew that shortages in human and material resources created a bottleneck in the reeducation program. They were also aware that most people went from the police station directly to a reeducation camp, without any formal hearing. At the time of the debate, the Ministry of Justice was still working on adapting the judicial system to the dictates of the socialist state. The few jurists and law students in the country—fewer than a dozen—were racing against time to reestablish the courts (the first "people's courts" did not open until late 1978).[99] Without judges to interpret the law and pronounce sentences, there seemed to be no pressing need for legislation on the camps. Any attempt to solve the problem of reeducation required those in detention to first be tried and sentenced. Such a task demanded human resources that were not available. Moreover, if the need for clear rules was justifiably necessary, the program's fundamental principle and salvationist character were incompatible with normal legislation. Reeducation camps were born extralegally—not even a decree was issued when the program began. Legislation for the program required objective definitions of offense, which had to be inscribed in the larger body of law in force in the country. Guebuza's bill conceptualized the reeducation program as an exceptional penal system. Therefore, he proposed producing an exceptional law, which could not be reconciled with Mozambique's constitution.

The first constitution of Mozambique was a closed document, written almost in secret, with no debate outside the small task force appointed by Frelimo. Its approval and adoption by the party's Central Committee in June 1975 (five days before Independence Day) was quick and unceremonious. It was hardly a liberal or democratic document. It provided no separation of powers, made no distinction between the party and the state, and granted absolute powers to the figure of the president. It was written in the messianic overtones typical of samorismo: grand normative vows to "eliminate the structures of oppression and colonial and traditional exploitation and the mentality that underlies them." Yet, it provided for basic civil liberties, such as individual freedom, the inviolability of domestic privacy, and, more importantly, the "guarantee" that "nobody can be detained and put on trial unless under the law" and without defense.[100] These promises remained a dead letter for the most part. There is little indication that the document became a people's constitution.[101] In fact, party leadership gave the constitution little thought. They rarely mentioned it in public meetings, mass rallies, or press conferences. Unlike other party documents, which were ostensibly publicized and commented upon, the constitution made little appearance in newspapers. It is therefore probable that, in drafting the bill on the reeducation program, Guebuza and his team did not think of the constitution and the limits it imposed on his legislation.

The bill's main commentator was the then minister for labor, Teodato Hunguana.[102] A jurist by training, Hunguana did not disagree with the principle of reeducation. He was, however, opposed to the bill's exceptionality. In his estimation, any attempt to legislate on reeducation camps had to consider the whole body of legislation and reformation of the entire penal system to avoid the contradictory end of two carceral regimes. He contended that the bill's basic principle—reeducation through labor—ran counter to the International Convention against Forced Labor that Mozambique had just signed. He rightly noted that, once ratified, international laws automatically took effect internally. Therefore, legislation on the reeducation program had to account for all the laws in force in Mozambique—or else face "profound contradictions." He also observed that the legislator could neither narrow reeducation's objective targets nor distinguish behaviors that needed redress from trivialities. As he put it, the bill "is very ambiguous" and some articles "are too vague," leaving ample room for "arbitrariness."[103] On the article on vagrancy, for example, he commented that the definition of *vagrants* was "so wide that it can easily include the unemployed," who, under the civil liberties guaranteed in the constitution, could not be "deprived of freedom" simply because of their unemployed status. "Because this is about granting the power to maintain or suspend the freedom of a person," he wrote, "the criteria for the exercise of that power needs to be defined with clarity, rigor, and precision."[104]

The boldness of these remarks does not need to be emphasized. Hunguana did not just highlight the deficiencies of the bill. He hinted at the limits of power in a constitutional system of governance that Frelimo leaders could not ignore. For him, one of the bill's main problems was the lack of objectivity in indicating who should be subjected to reeducation and, more importantly, for how long. The bill suggested that people could be held between twenty-four hours to three years. Hunguana called for the settlement (*fixação*) of a specific period of detention according to individual crimes. The bill suggested that "undisciplined" or "reckless" workers should be subjected to reeducation. Hunguana disagreed. He commented that problems related to discipline in the workplace should not be included in the list of deviant behaviors that warranted reeducation. He noted that such cases fell "off the purview of the penal system" and should be resolved through dismissal or other measures, such as deprivation of remuneration, but never incarceration. At most, he suggested, fired workers could be persuaded to "voluntarily accept" reeducation. On the intriguing section on health conditions, Hunguana commented: "This is not a matter of penal legislation or reeducation, but of specialized sanatoriums." He held that the government should assist alcoholics and drug addicts in medical facilities rather than intern them in labor camps.

By writing in a persuasive but confrontational tone and with great attention to detail, Hunguana might have convinced the Council's members of the impracticality of legislating on reeducation. He disagreed, for example, with the claim that the Ministry of the Interior was responsible for reforming people. He claimed that this responsibility should be granted to institutions of justice, not to the police. His overall claim was that Mozambique's independent government should preserve respect for individual liberties; he stressed that objective criteria about *who* the program should target were necessary to avoid abuses of power and arbitrariness.[105] His concluding remarks placed individual rights and civil liberties at the pinnacle of any credible constitutional system of governance: "Only in this way we can effectively guarantee the individual rights and freedoms enshrined in our Constitution," he concluded, "and position ourselves in a correct perspective of the function and implementation of justice in our country."[106]

Hunguana's comments undermined the very pillars of the reeducation program by laying bare its fundamental contradictions. His work also revealed something important about Frelimo, namely the divide between the salvationists who joined during the liberation struggle (and who also drafted the bill) and the technocrats who joined the party after independence. Armando Guebuza and Teodato Hunguana shared the same social background. The two men knew each other before the liberation struggle, having rubbed shoulders in the activist days of NESAM in the early 1960s. They both agreed about the need to address Mozambique's urban decadence. But Hunguana had not joined Frelimo cadres in Tanzania. While Guebuza, who never finished his high school education, learned the Maoist pedagogy of revolution in Tanzania, Hunguana was studying law in Lisbon. Guebuza was one of the self-proclaimed prototypes of the New Man produced in the struggle. Like President Machel, he wanted to see immediate results in reforming society. The revolution had to produce a new social order regardless of where social iniquity existed: it could be in the public space or in the secluded world of domesticity. The mental and physical wounds that the old regime imparted on society had to be addressed, whether they manifested in a woman's short dress and what happened behind closed doors with her partner(s), or in the lack of temperance and thrift by those who spent their time in beer halls and dance clubs, indulging in pleasures. In contrast, Hunguana was not steeped in Maoism and its reformist puritanism. He was a technocrat, a man of law. He assessed the structural impediments to legislation on the camps based on objective analysis of what was possible and what was not. Considering his political context and his ministerial roles, one could hardly call him a liberal. But he was not an autocrat, and he had a clear sense of the limits of power and the law. His comments indicate that his major concern with Guebuza's bill was its autocratic breadth and its disregard for the rule of law. Guebuza was an ardent moral reformer, a salvationist who believed the law should be at the party's absolute disposal. Hunguana regarded his political work as a technical, professional exercise within the parameters of legal jurisprudence.

These fundamental differences in the conception of politics and the rule of law within Frelimo are important for understanding not only the reeducation program's makeshift character but also other aspects of the socialist experiment in Mozambique. When Teodato Hunguana was appointed minister of justice in 1978, he presided over legislative decisions with which he did not agree, including capital punishment by firing squad.[107] Such was the first rule of pensamento único consecrated in the pamphlet that defined the qualities of Frelimo's Central Committee. According to this rule, disagreements were to be kept inside the party. Outside the party, all members spoke in a single voice. As we shall see in the next chapter, as the party moved toward Operação Produção—the single largest cleanup campaign in 1983—the very technocrats who did not agree with the campaign on technical grounds were compelled to execute it. On the public stage, they donned the persona of the New Man and hailed the campaign as a revolutionary battle to advance socialism. Because the salvationists held the reins of power, technocrats knew well the price of veering from the unanimous script: one was either with the revolution or the enemy.

3 ~ "These Moral Deserters Must Be Reeducated"

Political Consolidation, Development, and the Punitive State, 1977–1983

> All these enemies will go to the Revolutionary Military Tribunal. They swarm the city like flies, infesting our society. . . . This is a liberated city; we must defend it vigorously. There can be no room for these thugs who violate the revolutionary morality, the socialist morality.
>
> —Samora Machel, 1982

In October 1981, members of Mozambique's Parliament gathered to hear President Machel present the much-awaited Plano Prospectivo Indicativo (PPI), a ten-year development program devised to propel the country into rapid economic growth in the following decade (1981–90). Designed according to the dictates of Soviet-style central planning, the party's development of PPI was partly animated by the prospect of Zimbabwean independence, which President Machel was directly involved in negotiating. The president was confident that independent Zimbabwe's emergence in 1980 would bring the Rhodesian-backed Mozambique National Resistance (MNR) / Renamo insurgency to an end and, with it, the commercial loss and deprivation that Mozambique had suffered since Frelimo first imposed economic sanctions on the pariah state of Rhodesia in 1976. The fall of Rhodesia's White minority regime would usher in a period of prosperity for both countries.[1] But for PPI to succeed, Mozambique had to overcome a series of obstacles that stood in the path to development. The main obstacles, Machel remarked, were the anti-socials, the parasitic mass of people who fled the countryside and swarmed the cities, eating what others produced, occupying houses where only workers should have lived, and spreading their depraved ways across the fabric of Mozambican society. These idle, self-indulgent urbanites, the president asserted, were "moral deserters" who skirted work and "ought to be reeducated."[2] The initial campaigns such as Operação Limpeza had not done the job, and the cities were still filled with human dirt. Vagrants, prostitutes, and the unemployed at large were to be flushed out from the cities and relocated to the countryside, where they would produce food and assist in the country's economic reconstruction.

Here was a dramatic change in the discursive archetype that sustained Frelimo's reformist policies and their correlated punitive measures. From the purely salvationist vows that justified the reeducation program during the transitional period, we land at a developmental discourse in the name of which the party unleashed the state's power against those who, voluntarily or involuntarily, fell outside the bounds of Frelimo's moral citizenship. This change, I argue in this chapter, corresponded with a new phase of the revolution. The party's consolidation of its socialist experiment characterized the years between 1977 and 1983. This period concluded the voluntarist phase of transition and yielded an overconfident, developmentalist party-state. In February 1977, Frelimo held its Third Congress, which established the party in the vanguard Marxist-Leninist vein and set the socialist experiment's guiding principles. Although the Third Congress conceived of the state as a mere instrument of the party, the two entities became indistinguishably intertwined. At the formal level of party-state reorganization, Frelimo followed a Soviet template, thus moving away from the Chinese model that it had deemed detrimental to the liberation struggle. The party welcomed a stream of experts (*cooperantes*) from Eastern European countries (the German Democratic Republic, Romania, Bulgaria, and the USSR) and, to a lesser extent, Latin America (particularly Cuba) to serve as economic advisers, technical engineers, military and police instructors, and in several other such advisory positions. Their ranks included enthusiastic leftists from the West. Most pushed Frelimo toward the Leninist-Soviet style of socialism to which they subscribed.[3] The bloody tumult of the Cultural Revolution overshadowed China, which was reassessing its own socialist model and recalibrating its position in the international arena. From Frelimo's viewpoint, the Leninist-Soviet model seemed more promising, particularly given the possibility of joining the Soviet-led Council for Mutual Economic Assistance (COMECON).[4] Frelimo's development projects, most importantly PPI, came to hinge on the prospect of COMECON membership.[5] Rather than fading away, Frelimo's salvationist yearning to reengineer Mozambican society according to new moral aesthetics changed form. The moral project lost its voluntarist, ad hoc character and instead informed an overarching and ambitious plan to lift the country from poverty in just a decade. Production became the main watchword and the defining metric of citizenship. In urban areas, only those with formal wage employment retained the right to residence. The regime's politics of punishment during this period betrayed the party's ambition to develop and modernize the country.

While scholars of postindependence Mozambique argue that the 1977 Congress shaped this period of socialist consolidation, in my view the period's most important driving force was the rather peculiar political campaign that President Machel launched in late 1979, Ofensiva Política e Organizacional, or the Political and Organizational Offensive (hereinafter Ofensiva). Ofensiva was a Maoist-style campaign that sought to tackle the internal problems of state bureaucracy, which, in President Machel's understanding, hindered the revolution's advance. President Machel and his cadres devised the campaign to create the conditions that would allow for PPI's implementation. It sought to address structural impediments to development, which ranged from rampant illegalities and corruption in the security and judicial branches to contradictions in the reeducation program. They also included rural-to-urban migration, urban shortages of consumer goods, and the wayward lifestyle of indulgent urbanites. Ofensiva sharpened the state's punitive apparatus in the name of expeditious development. Xiconhoca, the cartoon figure that Frelimo's Department of Information and Propaganda created as a visual representation of the anti-social and ubiquitous enemy within, became a household name.

The cartoon evoked the satirical side of Mozambique's punitive state, but it also inhabited the same space as the most draconian and theatrical penalties that the party introduced during this period in its attempts to exterminate the internal enemy. These measures included the reimposition of transit passes (*guias de marcha*) and urban curfews, restrictions on rural-to-urban migration, criminalization of unemployment, mass trials, public floggings, and executions by firing squad. The party administered punishment in an overdramatized, spectacular fashion, which brought together archaic and modern penalties. The civil war, which entered what Borges Coelho has aptly described as the South African phase of the conflict (1980–84), dashed Frelimo's hopes for a peaceful and prosperous decade and prompted the state to intensify its punitive measures against the enemy within, including through the sweeping militarization of Mozambican society.[6] During this period, Frelimo's theatrics of power crescendoed with Operação Produção.

Unlike previous campaigns, which the party invariably halted after a few weeks, Operação Produção ran uninterrupted for the year that stretched from June 1983 to May 1984 and then continued intermittently until May 1988. Although the exact number of people rounded up and expelled from the cities remains unknown, higher estimates place the number around a hundred thousand. Half the victims were expelled from the capital city of Maputo alone.[7]

OFENSIVA AND THE WAR ON THE ENEMY WITHIN

Understanding how President Machel concluded that the successful implementation of PPI hinged on reorganizing the state—and that such efforts demanded his personal energy—requires a detailed narration of events that have escaped scholars of postindependence Mozambique. These events make clear the central place that the reeducation program occupied in Frelimo's development initiatives in this period of socialist consolidation. As early as 1975, the Catholic Church and ordinary citizens inundated the president with letters in which they raised complaints about the security forces' rampant abuses of power and indefinite detention of innocent civilians in reeducation camps.[8] Many citizens decried additional failures: corruption in the real estate agency Administração do Parque Imobiliário do Estado (APIE); illegal schemes within the security forces, including the secret service agency Serviço Nacional de Segurança Popular (SNASP); and the malfunction of public services in general. These complaints alerted the president to the political crisis of the party's declining popularity and the populace's waning enthusiasm, and they also reinforced his salvationist fervor. President Machel took matters into his own hands and sought to correct structural problems with moralistic exhortations and a beating stick. In response to public complaints, the president's first move was to create the Department of State Inspection, which operated under his direct command. Bypassing the Council of Ministers (where party officials seemed unable to reach agreement), he instructed the head of State Inspection, liberation war veteran Raimundo Pachinuapa, to conduct thorough investigations into the problems that citizens denounced in their missives.[9]

The reports that Pachinuapa's State Inspection task force produced yielded a series of reforms, which transformed the Mozambican state and its punitive instruments. Although the reforms aimed to address the arbitrariness that plagued the initial cleanup campaigns and to rectify the contradictions that pervaded the reeducation program, thus paving the way for PPI, they instead fueled a more repressive state apparatus. Of the numerous teams that the inspection department created, four stood out. Headed by the chief inspector himself, the first team investigated the conditions of reeducation camps in Niassa and Cabo Delgado Provinces. Pachinuapa instructed the second team to investigate illegalities within the security forces, especially within SNASP. The third team surveyed the state housing agency. The fourth team assessed living conditions in the capital city. All these task forces were in operation until 1981.[10] In Niassa and Cabo Delgado, Pachinuapa's team conducted surveys in several reeducation camps. Unsurprisingly, they were confronted with a series of unjust detentions. In the Chiputo Reeducation Camp, for example, the team found soldiers serving sentences since 1975 for failing to salute their hierarchical superiors, for adultery, and for similar trivialities. Most detainees in Chiputo, however, were former Frelimo guerrillas who had deserted during the liberation struggle, including some who had been defendants in the Nachingwea show trial. The conditions of detention were pitiful, and no path to freedom was foreseeable.[11] Theirs was a state of abandonment. The inspection team impressed the same conclusion upon the revolution's supreme leader, who had never set foot in a reeducation camp until then. With the reports of Pachinuapa's task force in hand, President Machel journeyed to Niassa in October 1979 to see the conditions for himself.

Machel's eventful trip to Niassa marked the beginning of the Ofensiva. *Tempo* magazine devoted a special edition to the president's travels. Teodato Hunguana's earlier objections to reeducation legislation might not have persuaded the president, instead only bringing to light the tensions between Frelimo's doctrine of moral reform and professed constitutionalism, but this trip allowed Machel to see in person the contradictions of Frelimo's reformist programs and to reckon with the party's failure to reconcile its extralegal carceral institution with the rule of law. In several meetings with Niassa reeducatees, Machel reenacted the Nachingwea show trial by singling out individual detainees to narrate their past betrayal and confess their wrongdoing.[12] After seeing firsthand the harsh conditions in which detainees lived and the pretense of a functioning reeducation program, the president granted amnesty to detainees in two reeducation camps, Unango and Chiputo, presaging the closure of all camps south of the Zambezi River by 1981–82.[13] It is true that the intensifying civil war factored into the president's calculus. Across central and southern Mozambique, Renamo rebels had targeted camps since launching their insurgency. Nonetheless, the president's decision to close roughly 80 percent of the camp complex directly pertained to PPI, and amnestied detainees were compelled to remain in Niassa and participate in the development projects that the PPI package designated for their province.

Following Machel's return from Niassa, the remaining three task forces gave the president a grim picture of government institutions and living conditions in Maputo. Their reports confirmed Machel's long-held belief that the recklessness plaguing the reeducation camps in the country's far reaches also ran rampant in the capital city. The reports on SNASP and APIE concluded that both institutions had been infiltrated by enemies who abused their power in order to undermine the socialist project. Security agents harassed innocent civilians, and APIE functionaries practiced nepotism and arranged corrupt schemes in the allocation of public housing simply to discredit the ruling party and the revolution.[14] Earlier in February 1979, the party brigade that surveyed the living conditions in Maputo reported that the city was the "bastion of the enemy" and the "center of the decadent values of bourgeois society."[15] The report garnered attention in the First National Meeting on Cities and Neighborhoods, which was held in February and March 1979 and attended by four hundred delegates, including guests from the German Democratic Republic and Vietnam.[16] The surveyors observed that most residents in Maputo lived "cheek by jowl along narrow, labyrinthine streets in unsanitary conditions" in the forty-three bairros in the caniço area. In bairros such as Chamanculo and Mafalala, unemployment was "endemic," and most people led "idle," "parasitic" lives. These locales housed rural migrants "who come to the city to aggravate crime, vagrancy, and disorganization in the rationing [of consumer goods] and transports." The surveyors noted with alarm that women frequented bars and the informal brewing houses that dotted the shantytowns. "This situation," they wrote, "causes many social conflicts such as prostitution, corruption of minors, beatings, and divorce." The anti-revolutionary activities of religious congregations, particularly independent and born-again evangelicals, exacerbated this "lamentable" state of affairs. These congregations were said to "hold meetings and prayers while the *Grupos Dinamizadores* had their meetings with the people," thus hindering participation in revolutionary activities. Congregations such as the God's Assembly, Zion, and the Twelve Apostles performed their "loud masses" late at night, "which prevent the working people from getting enough rest." The survey estimated that, in the caniço area, some two hundred religious sects pursued "the sole objective of alienating the population, particularly the youth, and deterring them from the main goals of the revolution."[17]

If infrastructural and mental decrepitude afflicted the capital's caniço areas, the concrete core (*cimento*) presented a different set of challenges. Here, most residents were said to have occupied nationalized houses without paying rent to APIE. For the surveyors, the residents' failure to meet rent betrayed their unemployment, and they occupied houses that should have been allocated to the working people.[18] In fact, the president's chief of staff, Óscar Monteiro (who chaired the Meeting on Cities), had announced when the seminar opened that only a quarter of the more than one million inhabitants in Maputo were part of the active work force. The mass of out-of-work residents, he claimed, "results in chronic unemployment, underemployment, banditry, prostitution, alcoholism, idleness, and other ills that we must combat."[19]

Like the alarmist and inflated findings of journalist Albino Magaia, the party's surveys were not meant to reveal an objective social reality but rather to confirm an ideological conviction. Party cadres with no research experience took just two weeks to conduct the survey on Maputo's living conditions, which drew upon a very modest sample. They went to the field to substantiate the perceptions of Maputo's living conditions already outlined in party directives and widely publicized in media outlets since Frelimo came to power.[20] Theirs was a work of bureaucratic bricolage that fabricated evidence to justify and vindicate a political decision that had already been made. Nevertheless, it was with these reports in hand that President Machel called for an Ofensiva Política e Organizacional to mend the bureaucratic dysfunction that hamstrung public institutions and to root out all forms of corruption, unlawfulness, and immorality within party-state ranks and society at large.[21] He was convinced that the government alone could not solve the problems of the people and prepare the ground for PPI. It was incumbent upon him, the supreme leader, to make both happen. This mantle called for Machel to publicly turn against his own bureaucracy and to begin what he called an "internal purification" in an open war against the enemy within.[22]

Framed as a battle to "restore the rule of law," the Ofensiva exemplified the Weberian dilemma between charismatic authority and bureaucratic routinization so well documented in other socialist experiments. When the leader's charismatic authority far outpaces that of the government and the combined branches of state bureaucracy, an interdependent imbalance of power and instability ensues. Such was the case in Mao's China.[23] But unlike Chairman Mao, Samora Machel did not stay within the comforts and relative security of his presidential quarters; instead, he took matters of bureaucratic and social reform into his own hands. From late 1979 to 1982, the president carried out the Ofensiva campaign, thus transforming the face of government and its punitive measures against internal enemies.

Initially, the campaign consisted of Machel's unannounced visits to detention centers, government institutions, and state enterprises. In overdramatized acts of public menace, the president stormed into working sites and offices, interrogating and remonstrating managers and workers about this or that problem. The media, tasked with educating the public, invariably covered the events.[24] Machel's unannounced visits to public institutions resulted in hundreds of officers being arrested for corruption, recklessness, negligence, and abuse of power—all of which the party labeled as acts of an internal enemy seeking to undermine the revolution.[25] By early 1982, Machel had purged more than four hundred agents from SNASP alone; many received the sentence of reeducation.[26]

If these theatrical displays of charismatic authority remain emblematic of Machel's ruling style—nostalgically celebrated in the postsocialist era—at the Ofensiva's heart were mass rallies in which Machel prescribed surveillance and outlined punitive measures against ubiquitous enemies, particularly urbanites. He held his first rally at Ponto Final, one of Maputo's principal intersections, on March 18, 1980. "Today we shall have a conversation which will be disagreeable," he warned the audience at the outset. He had a consequential announcement to make: he was "launching war against the enemy within" through a sweeping campaign, the magnitude of which the country had never seen. As he put it in his usual clinical language, the battle would require self-excision. "When we have a jigger in our foot, we must grab it and take it out," he said, "but that hurts and draws blood too."[27] Pain and blood were the due that Maputo residents would receive.

Machel's declaration, like all such statements in the Ofensiva's subsequent rallies, conveyed the tenets of Frelimo's reformist discourse and illuminated the road map of punitive policies that the party would follow for the next three years, culminating in Operação Produção. Machel's words—*flush out, clean up, sweep out, steamroll,* and *crush*—were not simple political rhetoric.[28] These words held power, commanding action and upended the lives of thousands of people. The force of Machel's passion can be gleaned from his listeners' countenances, which the photojournalist Carlos Calado captured (figure 3.1). Machel was renowned for keeping crowds at ease and for eliciting cheerful laughter at his rallies. But the crowd photographed by Calado on that day was somber and pensive. Some members seemed to frown as they heard Machel indict Maputo as the example of all that was wrong in Mozambique's urban society and the site where reform was needed most urgently. "When Frelimo took power, we found Lourenço Marques the model of all our country's cities: a city of patronage, orgies, bacchanalia, corruption, favors," Machel accused. "It was the city where the Portuguese colonial soldier arrived and departed, bringing and leaving the seeds of vice, degradation, immorality, drunkenness, venereal disease and

FIGURE 3.1. President Machel addresses Maputo residents during the launch of the Ofensiva at Ponto Final, March 18, 1980. Note the somber countenances of the audience members as they listen to the president's vitriolic attack on urban decadence and to his warnings about the bloody battle ahead. Photo by Carlos Calado. Courtesy of Centro de Formação Fotográfica (CDFF).

crime," he continued.[29] The residents of Maputo assembled to hear their president tell them that theirs was a city of adulterers, of concubines and prostitutes; a city of loafers and drunkards; a city of drug pushers and criminals; a city of rootless and alienated youth. In all these shortcomings, the capital represented the reality of the entire country.

For two years, the president toured the country, holding mass rallies and mesmerizing listeners with harangues about internal enemies, public comportment, and urbanites' moral lapses. The country's prompt development, he asserted, hinged on people mending their depraved ways and upholding proper civility. While the reformist work in the countryside required a particular set of measures (for example, the fight against obscurantism, efforts to subdue traditional backwardness, and the collectivization of rural settlements), the cities figured as the critical battlefield in this new phase of revolution. The task to which Machel exhorted all city dwellers would transform cities into "liberated areas," in the same way that the liberation struggle had freed the countryside from the degrading yoke of colonialism and its alienating bourgeois culture.[30] As he concluded the Ofensiva campaign in Maputo on June 22, 1982, Machel reminded the capital's residents of the enduring harms that colonialism had wrought in Mozambique's social fabric, as if the seven years of independence, cleanup campaigns such as Operação Limpeza, and the reeducation program had failed to effect any change. "Lourenço Marques was the city of prostitutes[,] . . . the capital of murder, of theft, of moral degradation," Machel declared, as he listed several obstacles to social change. "The degradation of customs, alcoholism, drugs, prostitution, concubinage, the instability of the family, bribe, material and moral corruption," he concluded, "tear apart the moral and social fabric; they disintegrate the society and open the way to alien and bourgeois mentality. These are forms of cultural, social, and ideological subversion."[31]

To dismantle the enduring roadblocks that impeded socialist modernization, Machel laid out the following measures, which depended on enthusiastic participation from the masses. First, urban residents were to sharpen their vigilance in working places and residential areas, where the enemies were thought to have encamped as "lice and locusts." Residents were to scrutinize the lifestyle of their neighbors, detect misfits, and denounce them to local authorities. Second, party brigades were to carry out a general survey of urban areas. They would go from house to house to register residents and determine who deserved urban citizenship and its benefits, especially food rationing and housing. Third, the government would stop the influx of rural migrants to the cities. The government would send the excess parasitic urban population that was "in queues, producing nothing" back to the countryside so that the few resources available could be provided to the working people. "Only those who work have the right to eat in the new society that we are building," Machel told his listeners. "We cannot allow the parasites to go on sucking our blood."[32] To accomplish such a task, Frelimo would not use conventional police investigations. Rather, Machel called for neighborly surveillance, predicated on ideological perceptions of enemy behavior and visual signs that defined Xiconhoca, Frelimo's iconography of moral decay. As we shall see in the next chapter, the Mozambican people's vigilantism would provide the forensic intelligence that allowed authorities to identify the enemies and flush them out of the city. That Machel made no secret of the social groups to be targeted only reinforced the populist dimension to this kind of state surveillance. Unsurprisingly, the purge targeted the same demographics that interior minister Armando Guebuza had listed in the bill proposing legislation on reeducation camps. But there was a new twist. People already detained in reeducation camps and formal penitentiaries were to be sent to labor camps for five to six years under military guard, until they produced enough to "compensate the people for what they stole."[33]

If on the one hand the Ofensiva campaign reduced the number of reeducation camps and shrunk the detainee population, on the other, it expanded the power of state institutions at the local level to identify and punish deviants. Public vigilantism, which was voluntary and haphazard during the transition period, came to underpin state surveillance. In the long run, the Ofensiva empowered low-level state officeholders and ordinary citizens, who became increasingly militarized, to persecute and punish deviants, real and imagined.

SURVEILLANCE, THE CRIMINALIZATION OF UNEMPLOYMENT, AND THE THEATRICS OF PUNISHMENT

The conflation of real and imagined obstacles on Mozambique's road to socialism was a hallmark of Machel's rule. So, too, was the vehemence with which he harnessed his charismatic authority to correct structural impediments to development, which was far beyond his—or even the entirety of his administration's—capabilities. As a populist, exhortatory campaign, the Ofensiva classically illustrates the tensions inherent in socialist experiments—that is, the dissonance between high-minded ideals of modernity and objective social reality.[34] In Mozambique, the reality that Machel and his government confronted was an economy in decline, which could not meet the impoverished, largely illiterate, and agrarian population's most basic needs. Although the economic slide resulted in part from the global recession triggered by the 1973 oil crisis, the most important factors were the colonial settlers' acts of sabotage and their sudden withdrawal, along with the enormous challenge of pivoting an economy designed for a small minority (less than two hundred thousand settlers) to serve twelve million people.

The departure of colonial settlers deprived Mozambique of trained and experienced clerks in all sectors, from public services to private enterprises.[35] Although the economic and social chaos reverberated across the country, it manifested most visibly in urban areas, particularly in the capital. The settler exodus sparked a profound crisis of unemployment, created food shortages, and destroyed the chain of urban services. For instance, in 1974, hotels, restaurants, and domestic service employed about three hundred thousand Africans. Most of these jobs disappeared when settlers left the country.[36] In the countryside, the agrarian economy, which depended on *cantineiros* (European and Asian retail traders), suffered profound disruptions. With no market in which to trade their crops, peasants had little incentive to produce. The end of colonial rule also meant that peasants gained the freedom to seek better job prospects in towns.[37] The influx of rural migrants to towns had risen sharply since the early 1960s, but it accelerated during the transition and early years of independence. The number of residents in Maputo rose from about 400,000 in 1973 to 755,300 in 1978.[38] Unlike in the developed world, where industrialization accompanied—and, in most cases, fueled—urbanization, Mozambique saw its urban areas expand rapidly without concomitant growth in the industrialized economy.[39] Maputo's small industrial complex shrank drastically between 1973 and 1978, from 481 industries and factories to 211—a 56 percent reduction.[40]

Mozambique's challenges were only exacerbated by its economic dependence on its two most hostile neighbors, apartheid South Africa and Rhodesia—perhaps the Portuguese rentier colonial economy's most enduring legacy. As Frelimo endorsed the struggles for South African and Zimbabwean liberation, the two White regimes retaliated with measures to undermine the Frelimo government, from economic sabotage to military aid given to Frelimo's contras.[41] Apart from the disruption caused by the civil war (which began a few months after the declaration of independence), the biggest blow to Mozambique's economy came from the two largest employer sectors: transportation and migrant labor. A considerable proportion of southern Mozambique's population depended on income from performing migrant work. Between 80,000 and 110,000 mine workers were recruited annually to South Africa since the early days of the twentieth century. In a deliberate act of destabilization and in keeping with shifts to labor recruitment in South Africa's mining industry since the late 1960s, the apartheid regime reduced the number of Mozambican miners by 70 percent. By 1977, only 37,000 miners were recruited. South Africa also reduced the volume of transit goods from Mozambican ports by 60 percent, thus leaving thousands of dock workers unemployed.[42] Frelimo enforced UN sanctions against Rhodesia by barring the minority regime from using Mozambique's ports; the move cost Mozambique a crucial source of revenue and thousands of jobs (particularly in the second largest city, Beira). The combined effect of these factors compounded the economic crisis and the vast array of social challenges, from shortages in consumer goods and high rates of unemployment to urban overcrowding.

Frelimo leadership reacted to these economic challenges in emotive and typically moralistic terms. While recognizing the structural legacies of colonialism, party officials viewed the economic crisis as an ethical problem, evincing the lack of moral resolve from the people and their unwillingness to work and follow the party line.[43] Waning popular tolerance for enduring the sacrifices that the revolution demanded (particularly shortages in consumer goods and the breakdown of urban services) heightened President Machel's disgruntled assessment of the challenge at hand. He believed that people were unemployed not because they lacked work but because they were lazy and lived in towns as parasites.[44] He saw rural immigrants who moved to cities to seek a better life as idle people fleeing the hard work of tilling the soil and who were instead pursuing the easy life and the worldly

FIGURE 3.2. Partial view of Maputo's cimento, ca. 1980. The building on the far left is city hall. Beyond, the caniço stretches into the horizon. By 1980, the city had close to one million residents. Photo courtesy of Arquivo do Jornal Notícias (AJN).

pleasures that the city had to offer. The president and his party comrades concluded that the labyrinthine caniço areas where these so-called parasites agglomerated were breeding grounds for crime, immorality, and social disorder.

The imprint of Frelimo's long years of exile in Tanzania, where this kind of moralistic discourse dominated the public sphere in the 1960s, is unmistakable.[45] But Frelimo's discourse on idleness also had echoes of a century-old assumption that Africans were idle and keen on leading a parasitic lifestyle, an image Portuguese colonial authorities and European missionaries alike had advanced since the late nineteenth century.[46] The imperative to exert absolute control and to exploit the African workforce in the cheapest way motivated the colonial regime's discourse on African idleness; the implication that Africans did not belong in urban areas followed from this discourse.[47] As I discussed in chapter one, African urban elites—keen to maximize their chances of civil recognition under Portuguese rule—appropriated this discourse as they sought to elevate their community to respectable standing in the colonial society. Their newspapers exhorted Africans to be industrious and to earn their place in the city by conducting themselves properly as wage earners. Frelimo leaders shared this reformist vision. Their campaigns against vagrancy were informed by long-standing colonial anxieties about civility and urban disorder. In form and substance, they reproduced the very methods of social control and colonial violence that dominated much of the first half of the twentieth century in Mozambique. When their campaigns against urban anti-socials began in 1974, memories of when "everyone walked in fear" in Lourenço Marques and other cities were still fresh.[48]

Despite misguided perceptions of African idleness and parasitism, social scientists who surveyed the African urban population in colonial and early independent Mozambique documented the creative ways that people devised to navigate the narrow opportunities in places such as Lourenço Marques, where they made a living while contributing to the country's economic development. In 1957, sociologist Hillary Mitchell conducted a survey of Lourenço Marques's African residents. She observed the array of trades that people were engaged in and noted the indispensable role that such trades played in the social reproduction of Mozambique's African townspeople. Mitchell found that a considerable proportion of Lourenço Marques's active working force was self-employed. Most of the domestic utensils and amenities that furnished African homes in the caniço were produced by local artisans and tradespeople. Skilled masons built the houses, which were made of reed and corrugated iron (and occasionally of concrete). Two-wheel-cart pushers (*txovas*) were the town's lifeblood. They transported goods (particularly building materials and consumer products) from and to various corners of the city.[49] In 1968, anthropologist Rita-Ferreira confirmed Mitchell's findings. He argued that it was erroneous and unjust to "affirm that Africans (professionally qualified or not) were strictly dependent on activities created by Europeans and Asians, and that [without these activities] they would be incapable to elevate themselves from the level of subsistence of their ancestors." He regarded the adaptation and creativity that Africans developed in urban areas as "undeniable" and "worthy of attention."[50] After independence, studies of social life in Maputo confirmed Mitchell and Rita-Ferreira's observations. Subsequent studies revealed that, despite the high rates of official unemployment, most urban residents took part in several informal activities, which comprised a regimen of self-employment that contributed to the economy of the city.[51]

Frelimo leaders did not regard informal occupations as proper work. Stone masons, reed-house builders, txovas, petty traders, tradespeople, and artisans of all sorts found themselves labeled as parasitic vagrants, as "moral deserters" who fled work. The party criminalized their activities as well as their very presence in the city. Like prostitutes and drunkards, they were unworthy of urban citizenship and had to be *swept* and *flushed out* to the countryside. President Machel's Ofensiva rally of March 1980 provided guidelines for government officials on how to detect and eliminate these threats:

> We must know how many people live in each neighborhood, how many houses it has, how many shops and what their capacity is, how many people live in each house, and how many people in each household are employed. Only this way we can plan the right distribution of products to each area. First in Maputo, Beira and Nampula, we shall launch a major campaign to survey the situation, and this will later be extended to other towns. We shall form people's brigades in each neighborhood to go from house to house finding out who lives there and register them. Each neighborhood must have a complete register of its residents. The campaign will also allow us to discover and neutralize criminals, vagrants, prostitutes and social misfits.[52]

The president's speech and his instructions ran in every Mozambican newsreel and circulated in party bulletins. The masses were encouraged to closely study the speech so they could participate in the Ofensiva. Party cadres were urged to transform the president's words into actionable policies. And that is precisely what the twenty members of the Council of Ministers did in April 1980. In less than a month, the Council drafted a lengthy document with ten resolutions and fifty tasks to rid Maputo and other cities of those who allegedly skirted work.[53] The tasks were to be carried out by rank-and-file officers (*directores nacionais*). The details of the plan were confidential, and those charged with implementing it only learned of those sections of the document that governed how they were to implement their particular task.[54] While the overall plan was publicly announced, the particulars of its implementation were closely guarded. As we shall see, the party's aura of secrecy created enormous problems in the plan's implementation, not only because those charged with carrying out the program failed to understand the larger project but also because colleagues did not share information with each other; their instructions came with a warning that prescribed confidentiality.

Resolution number five of the Council's action plan is of particular interest, as it defined the tasks required to reorganize the capital city. Task number 29 called for the capital to be elevated to the administrative category of province, given its "special characteristics." Task 31 called for neighborhoods to be transformed into communal neighborhoods (*bairros comunais*). The limit of families in each bairro was fixed at 2,500 (about 12,500 people). The most populous neighborhoods were subdivided. For example, the 60,000-resident Bairro Central in the city's concrete core was subdivided into three bairros, Central A, B, and C. Bairro Maxaquene, at

56,000 residents the most populous in the caniço, was split in three, Maxaquene A, B, and C. In this new organization, each bairro's residential block (*quarteirão*) was limited to 50 families (about 250 people). A block's chief (*chefe de quarteirão*) was charged with running the block. The chief counted on the assistance of a ten-household supervisor (*chefe de 10 casas*) and a number of locally recruited militias. Above them was the neighborhood secretary (*secretário do bairro*). The secretary also chaired the neighborhood's party cell, or Grupo Dinamizador (GD), which included members of OMM (Organization of Mozambican Women), OJM (Organization of Mozambican Youth), and locally elected juries.[55] This spatial and bureaucratic rearrangement was meant to amplify people's vigilance and make it easy for local authorities to detect social misfits and the unemployed.

Although they occupied the bottom rung of the party-state's pyramidal hierarchy, local authorities at the neighborhood level wielded enormous power. Their own interpretation of party guidelines often defined the shape and course that the cleanup campaigns took. They knew the residents of their bairros and paid close attention to which families participated in the neighborhood's collective life and which did not. They knew which households upheld stringent moral standards and which did not. Weekend community activities and meetings afforded the perfect forums to assess where people stood in relation to party commandments. As one former chefe de quarteirão told me, families that failed to attend weekly meetings or join in the early morning sweeping of sandy streets were often blacklisted or looked upon with suspicion. People avoided walking in front of the house that belonged to the chefe de quarteirão or the bairro's headquarters, lest they attracted the scrutinizing gaze of local authorities.[56] After all, like Xiconhoca, the signs of moral decadence were ubiquitous. They were present in people's ways of dressing, of walking, of talking; they manifested through their material possessions; and so on. Most detainees in reeducation camps and the thousands rounded up in urban areas during Operação Produção were arrested, convicted, and expelled by local bairro authorities.

In addition to rearranging the city's residential areas, the Council's action plan included the creation of a cabinet team to carry out a more refined survey of Maputo. Aside from the "occupation of houses and rationing," the survey aimed at "the detection of the unemployed, vagrants, bandits, etc., in order to send them to green belts."[57] This was not a survey to help the government better understand the problems of Maputo but was rather an instrument to identify the targets of the forthcoming cleanup campaign. The survey sheet asked for the name of the bairro; the number of the block and the house (flat and street name for cimento residents); and place of work and identity papers (ID, work card, and the house's contract if rented) of the head of household. The survey also collected information regarding the number of people in each household; the size of the house in relation to its number of occupants; the age, degree of kinship, and professional occupation of the dependents of the head of household; and the location and number of the *loja do povo* (people's store) from which the household purchased its monthly groceries. It also inquired into the hygienic appearance and conservation of the house and the status of rent payment, if applicable.[58] This was a detailed inquiry to identify who should stay in the city and who should be banished. This was a state at work to make its population visible and easily susceptible to surveillance and social engineering.

The presidential Ofensiva kept the Council of Ministers occupied for two years. Urban reorganization and residential surveys notwithstanding, the Council was also working to stem the influx of rural migrants into the capital city. Again, colonial mechanisms of social control provided the model for action.[59] The party introduced a work card for civil servants in 1977; the following year, it was extended to all workers. According to Law 2/78, issued on March 30, 1978, in addition to regulating tax payment, the card allowed the government to "eliminate unemployment which is caused by the attraction that big cities exert over the youth." The card was also intended to help the government reward those who "produce wealth or render useful services to society" by restricting access to rationed consumer goods only to those who possessed a work card. The Ministry of Labor was the only entity that could issue a work card. Workers had to submit a form stamped by their employers to the ministry in Maputo or to its delegations in the provinces. The card had to be renewed every two years and be marked every three months. Anyone with a recognized form of waged labor was entitled to a work card. Self-employed workers had to obtain their stamped forms from the GDs in their residential areas.[60] Because the government did not outline which activities constituted self-employment, the law gave GDs immense discretionary power. It was up to the GD to decide if a particular kind of occupation constituted work. Self-employed workers found that their livelihoods—and lives—rested in the hands of GDs.

The Council sought to expand and expedite the documentation that delineated the urban working population in Maputo and all other urban centers. Until 1981, however, the production of work cards lagged. The Ministry of Labor faced many logistical problems. Due to chronic shortages, the necessary equipment was scarce. Paper, ink, and photographs were difficult to find. The centralization of the process in Maputo, where all cards were produced, complicated the logistics of distribution. To fix the problem, the Ministry of Labor decided to give districts the authority to issue their own work cards. As a result, by December 1981, a total of 150,585 cards had been issued. There was still a long way to go in documenting every worker, but the government was determined to "know exactly the number of the country's active working force."[61] The following year, the Ministry of Labor announced that, from 1982 onward, all working people would be required to possess a work card. From then on, only those with a work card could purchase consumer goods in the people's stores and benefit from all other urban services, which included housing, public transport, and healthcare. In June 1982, the Council and the party's Central Committee announced another move to control rural migrants: they added a residential card to the list of documents issued for every urban resident with recognized, waged work. Citizens visiting the cities were to be issued a temporary document, without which they could be arrested and expelled back to the countryside. From then on, to move around in the cities, urban residents had to carry a triad of documents: an ID, a work card, and a residential card.[62]

As the party introduced its new documentation requirements, security forces were already rounding up undocumented residents. On June 14, the same day the Council announced the residential card, police apprehended a thousand people in Maputo "for questioning." According to journalist Joseph Hanlon, "50 were wanted by the police and another 200 were charged as vagrants."[63] A month before, the police had claimed that the roundups were already reducing crime by 30 percent in Maputo.[64] The fabrication of impressive numbers reflected socialist Mozambique's privileged mode of governance. Numbers justified policy and showcased progress.

The repressive way in which the government documented urban residents and enforced compliance led to ever-growing demand for cards, as citizens sought to escape the wrath of security forces. As newspapers reported, the "avalanche" of people seeking IDs and work and residential cards overwhelmed registration agencies. Identification departments could not accommodate the people who congregated in long *bichas* (queues) inside and outside their buildings.[65] The Ministry of Labor and the registration agencies under the Ministry of Justice faced extraordinary demand throughout the country. By August 1982, in Maputo, only 110,000 residents had been granted resident cards. The situation was so out of control that the director of registration services went to the press to clarify who was entitled to a resident card.[66] Yet his clarification did little to soothe desperation among citizens or to deter the police from carrying out roundups. In fact, the police deliberately conducted some raids in front of registration agencies. Caught between the charismatic authority of the revolution's leader, who demanded results in the "battle against the enemy within," and a small bureaucratic machine (dys)functioning under extreme austerity, the Council hesitated but did not halt the process. New deadlines were arranged for each neighborhood to register residents and issue cards. GDs were given three weeks to complete the job.[67]

The party's sense of urgency in mapping Mozambique's urban working population through spatial reorganization, surveys, and documentation grew more acute as the party-state confronted the rapidly declining economy and struggled against its most significant internal foe, Renamo. The economic crisis was leading people to devise means of survival outside the legal bounds and restrictions of Frelimo's command economy. Smuggling and black markets for consumer goods spiraled out of control.[68] Backed strongly by South Africa, by 1982, Renamo was wreaking havoc in central Mozambique and advancing quickly toward the capital in the south. Frelimo did not recognize Renamo as a political entity but rather viewed the group as a gang of armed bandits at the service of external powers seeking to undermine the new republic and its stance against the region's minority regimes. The economic crisis and the war represented two sides of the same coin; the party-state knew this much.[69] The moral fervor with which it assessed its predicament, however, pushed the government toward more draconian measures of social control, which in turn deepened the crisis. In his final Ofensiva rally in Maputo on June 22, 1982, President Machel announced new rules for circulation in towns. In addition to mandating ID, work, and residential cards, he imposed a curfew in Maputo and distributed weapons to ordinary people to help security forces protect the city against armed bandits. But the guns were to be used against more than armed bandits: prostitutes, adulterers, the undisciplined, and moral deserters of work all fell within the party's proverbial and literal crosshairs.[70] In violation of Article 3 of the Constitution, which guaranteed citizens' individual rights and the "inviolability of domicile and secrecy of correspondence," security forces received instructions to extend their raids to residential areas and to carry out house-to-house searches for undocumented residents.[71]

A new phase of theatrical justice and spectacular punishment accompanied the craze for neighborly surveillance. From the colonial playbook, the party resurrected forms of punishment and instruments of inflicting physical and emotional pain previously deemed archaic. Mass trials, public ridicule, flogging, and executions by firing squad all returned in this period. In 1979, the party-state passed the Law for Crimes against the Security of the People and the People's State, a severe penal code that instituted the death penalty. Like the reeducation system, this new law did not replace the colonial penal code, and it contained all the contradictions that had doomed the bill legislating reeducation.[72] Frelimo leaders were as passionate in attacking colonialism and in vowing to *escangalhar* (dismantle) the colonial state as they were in praising colonial rule for its exercise of disciplinary power. In defending the reintroduction of chamboco, Machel told a mass rally that "violence is necessary in the exercise of power" and that "the Portuguese knew how to use power." He asserted that, like the Portuguese, "we have to use our power to punish with severity."[73] The parliament discussed and unanimously approved the reintroduction of flogging, except for one dissenting vote cast by Teodato Hunguana, who had been moved from the labor ministry to the justice ministry.[74] From what we know of his political commitments, his dissent does not come as a surprise. And the parliament, as Hunguana well knew, was the appropriate forum in which to voice a discordant opinion. Although it was lauded as the people's house, the parliament was in fact the party's private house, where members of the brotherhood of the elect could disagree. The rules of pensamento único were only broken if a member raised discord outside the house, to the larger public. Minister Hunguana knew where the line had been drawn and never spoke publicly against flogging.

Although the parliament justified flogging to punish smuggling and black marketeering, the punishment applied to all kinds of offenses, from the most severe to the more mundane (such as public displays of affection). The police conducted several roundups to detain people who subverted state market laws and sold goods above official prices. The new law, Law 5/83, contained instructions on how to flog offenders. Courts could condemn offenders for up to ninety *chicotadas* (strikes). No more than thirty lashes, however, could be administered at once. At least eight days had to pass until a new round of lashes could be inflicted.[75] Flogging was to be administered in public. It was not merely a form of physical punishment; it also sought to teach the public by shaming the offender. The first victim of the *lei da chicotada* was a man named Raul Cumbe, who was condemned for selling fifteen small cakes at the price of seventy-five meticais each, fifteen above the official price.[76]

Under the Ofensiva dictates, offenders could only be condemned by a jury within the new system of people's justice that entered into force in 1978. Given the sheer number of people detained as *candongueiros* (black marketeers) between 1981 and 1983, the trials took place in the marketplace, often in the open under the scorching sun. Some offenders were brought to trial dressed in gowns made of sacks and in clown hats, with plaques with defamatory inscriptions hanging from their necks: "I am a *candongueiro*, Xiconhoca!"[77] Pronounced guilty, the offenders were laid on the ground and flogged, after which they were either set free or sent to reeducation camps or to the euphemistically named green belts.[78] Mozambique's punitive state intertwined legal justice and public ridicule as twin instruments of its power.

The mass trials were invariably rushed. Judges faced pressure to deliver the "people's justice" in a short period of time. But the number of wrongdoers whose behavior they had to adjudicate was so high that due process became an impossibility. The Ministry of Justice admitted as much. In 1983, as part of the ministry's contribution in hastening the Ofensiva and the party's Fourth Congress resolutions, magistrates decided to accelerate trials to relieve the "congested" prisons, especially Maputo's Central Prison. The People's Tribunal of Maputo Province decided to hold trials on Saturdays, with the *meta* (goal) of holding ten trials during each session. The aim was to "allow a rapid sending of the defendants to Reeducation Centers and production units in order to relieve the prisons of congestion."[79]

Socialist Mozambique was a state of transparent, spectacular, and, in some cases, theatrical violence. Punishment was both modern and archaic, insidiously private and spectacularly public. The party called on the Revolutionary Military Tribunal (TMR)— established in 1979 to exclusively hear political crimes (particularly those related to armed banditry)—to step in and process civilian cases in 1982. As the war on smuggling and black marketeering took a more aggressive turn, the party-state gave TMR full power to try "economic sabotage." The Law for Crimes against the Security of the People and the People's State was amended to include death penalty by firing squad for smuggling. Until the archives of the former TMR are made available for consultation, we will not know how many people the military tried and executed. But from the available public record, 1982 and 1983 appear to have been the tribunal's busiest years. The TMR announced its sentences in public communiqués and newspapers, often with detailed information about the biography of each offender, accompanied by their photograph.[80] The biographical narration of guilt was a key method in Mozambique's jurisprudence. Public exhibitions similarly underpinned the enterprise. Firing squads carried out some executions before assembled crowds. One such public execution took place near the renowned dunghill of Bairro Hulene in Maputo in April 1983. Five of the six people executed were Renamo rebels. But one man, Gulam Nabi, was executed for "smuggling prawns and appliances." He had been condemned by a court of law in 1982 and was already serving his prison sentence. But, for his case, the party-state applied the amended law retroactively and sought to make an example of him.[81]

As mouthpieces of party-state commandments, newspaper editors hailed the public executions as "people's justice."[82] Indeed, public floggings

FIGURE 3.3. An offender is publicly flogged, 1982. In socialist Mozambique, punishment was both modern and archaic, at once insidiously private and spectacularly public. Scenes like this one were common in reeducation camps. Photo from *Público magazine.*

and executions were popular policies, cheerfully welcomed by the urban public. Hundreds of enthusiastic participants joined marches in support of the flogging legislation in Maputo.[83] As Joseph Hanlon commented in 1984, "The new measures met general approval. The extended death penalty is popular, just as the reintroduction of hanging in Britain would be."[84] Public support of the party's reformist and punitive policies shaped the course of the campaigns in the bairros as neighbors and relatives turned against one another in acts of self-policing and denunciation. As for party-state leadership, the stage was set to strike the final blow against the enemy within and to once and for all rid the cities of alleged moral deserters of work. With residential areas rearranged, urban populations surveyed, and worthy urban citizens documented, it was time to launch Operação Produção.

A PERMANENT STATE OF SIEGE: THE TWO STAGES OF OPERAÇÃO PRODUÇÃO

At the end of Frelimo's long-overdue Fourth Congress on May 21, 1983, President Machel inaugurated Operação Produção as part of the Congress's resolutions to expedite socialist development and eliminate hunger in Mozambique. Although Operação Produção had been in the making since Machel announced the initiative in March 1980, the government did not develop a concrete plan on how to carry it out. The Council's efforts to reorganize the cities' residential areas and to survey and document the urban population sought to identify so-called moral deserters of work, not necessarily to prepare for the campaign itself. In fact, when party leadership finally decided to implement the campaign, only the thirteen members of the party's politburo knew the details of what was to come. The two politburo members who also served as provincial governors, Marcelino dos Santos (Sofala) and Mário Machungo (Zambézia), delayed the campaign's start in their respective provinces for at least two months in order to give their rank-and-file officers enough time to prepare.[85] Those provincial administrators who did not have the same privilege were taken by surprise when thousands of banished urbanites arrived, and they largely failed to integrate the displaced into their provinces. The campaign was both anticipated and unexpected. It was expected because it was announced; it was unexpected because the campaign did not happen the year that Machel intended (1980) but rather three years later. The general public might well have forgotten the particulars of the president's vows to transform the cities into liberated areas by *sweeping* and *flushing out* their bourgeois decadence. Or the public might have taken the intermittent police roundups as the promised campaign. Government officials of all ranks hardly knew more. Although many had been working hard to map out the urban population following the Council's action plan, they had no understanding of the ultimate goal of their work. The broader picture remained secret. The Council had demanded secrecy in the lengthy action plan that it sent to a few high-ranking government officials, including the governor of Maputo Province. "The Council of Ministers draws attention to the fact that this Document as a whole is CONFIDENTIAL," the memorandum said; "National Directors and other staff should only be aware of the parts they need to implement the tasks."[86] It is probable that, outside the closed circle of Frelimo's politburo, the governor of Maputo and the city mayor were the only officials to be briefed about the incoming massive cleanup campaign.

When he announced the campaign, President Machel did not assign it a code name (his speech was no different from the various orations he delivered during his Ofensiva spree). The appellation *Operação Produção* was the creative work of interior minister Armando Guebuza and his staff. As soon as the president announced the campaign, the government sprang into action. Citizens and most bureaucrats had little time to prepare. The party gave bureaucrats three weeks to ready themselves. The government prepared the directive that would guide the operation on June 15. The document was released to the press on June 20. Ironically, the directive indicated June 20 as the campaign's beginning, which meant that the public learned of the operation on the same day that it commenced. In practical terms, the directive suspended the constitution and all other laws and deposited the country's sovereignty in its sole commandment. It imposed a state of exception that suspended the most basic of civil liberties: the right to mobility, the right to choose one's place of residency, the right to privacy, and, above all, the right to citizenship in one's own country. The directive contained ten articles detailing who would carry out the campaign as well as when and how it would be carried out. The number of government institutions involved indicates the priority that Frelimo placed on the campaign. Eleven ministries and four state departments were designated to constitute the Comando Operativo Central, or Central Operative Command (COC). This special commission would coordinate the campaign, and Guebuza assumed its helm. The constitutive members of the COC included the Ministries of the Interior, Defense, Security, Justice, Finance, Ports and Railways, Agriculture, Commerce, Industry and Energy, and Information; the National Commission of Planning; the State Departments for Labor, for Civil Aviation, and for Road Transportation; and the National Council of Production.[87]

Each province established its own Comando Operativo Provincial, or Provincial Operative Command (COP), headed by the provincial governor and involving local representatives of the same government institutions that constituted the COC. City mayors also belonged to COPs. Following the party-state's hierarchical structure, below COP came the District Operative Command (COD), headed by the respective district administrator. The COPs and CODs worked directly with Grupos Dinamizadores and chefes de quarteirão in residential and working places. On no other occasion before or after 1983 did Frelimo assemble such a robust bureaucratic machine to drive a cleanup campaign.

Residents had to produce three mandatory documents to prove their right to live in the city—namely, a residency card, a work card, and an ID or passport. The directive ordered people who failed to produce any of the three to be "detained immediately" and taken to *centros de verificação,* or verification centers (VCs), where teams of verifiers would assess their case and determine their fate. The verification teams were to consist of at least one public attorney, a locally elected judge, members of the local GDs, and a police officer. After verification, detainees were to be sent to *centros de evacuação,* or deportation centers, where transport would be waiting to take them out of the city. New admissions and urban hiring in the public sector and factories were temporarily suspended, though employers could request authorization from operative command offices for exceptional hiring. Anyone entering an urban area was required to carry a *guia de marcha* (marching order). This document stated the objectives and duration of their visit as well as the exact location of temporary residency. Frelimo mandated that visitors present their guia to local authorities directly connected with the Ministry of the Interior within forty-eight hours of their arrival so that they could receive authorization to enter the city. As the directive set forth, "Unauthorized presence leads to immediate detention and evacuation to a destination of the convenience of the authorities."[88]

Following the directive, the campaign unfolded in two stages: a fifteen-day voluntary phase, during which the "unproductive" were to submit voluntarily and choose where they wished to be relocated, and a coercive phase for the "recalcitrant." The voluntary phase began on June 20, and volunteers were to register with their local GDs and receive a guia de marcha for their chosen destination. The time between the two phases was astonishingly short. The fact that the government gave residents only two weeks to register to depart the cities indicates the campaign's true intentions. At no moment did Frelimo authorities consider the campaign to be a pacific process. Operação Produção was conceived as a compulsive campaign, and it was expected to be painful, like the "jigger" in one's foot that "hurts and draws blood."[89] In a secret directive distributed to COPs, the COC instructed authorities to include health personnel in the verification centers "for first aid."[90] The fact that the published directive listing COC members excluded the health ministry is revealing: the party-state attempted to disguise the campaign's violent nature.

Few people chose to leave the city during the voluntary phase; the majority flocked to the registration offices in a desperate attempt to obtain the required documents. Most people did not petition the registration office to request new documents but rather to collect identification they had been requesting for several months and sometimes for years. Since registration offices across the country always lacked the logistical capacity to satisfy high demand for documentation, many people, including those with formal waged employment, were undocumented when the coercive phase began on July 5. The directive did not indicate an end date for the coercive phase. Operação Produção was set to last "permanently" until all the "unproductive" were removed from the cities.[91]

In the early hours of June 5, the COC deployed the first sweeping brigades to the capital. Teams of local GDs, police officers, soldiers, and militias combed the streets and neighborhoods of Maputo, demanding that residents show the three required documents. The COC instructed the brigades

FIGURE 3.4. A police officer knocks on a residential home in a caniço bairro during Operação Produção in Maputo, July 1983. Most roundups took place late at night, when residents would be off their guard. Photo courtesy of Arquivo da Revista Tempo (ART).

to target specific locations with high concentrations of people, particularly in front of grocery stores, bakeries, and registration departments known for their long queues.[92] In just a few days, thousands of people were arrested and detained in verification centers. The COC installed thirty-eight verification centers around the capital city.[93] Unsurprisingly, the process did not develop as expected. In the first weeks and months, the authorities took most people directly to deportation centers, without passing through verification. For their part, the verification teams only assessed the cases of those who demanded much closer scrutiny of their papers. The process resembled the expedited trials that the party arranged during the previous intermittent roundups. But the number of cases was excessive, and the time required to determine people's fates was short. The time that the party afforded to process cases often followed from the availability of transportation for deported individuals. With party cadres working around the clock, due process took too long. As soon as trucks or buses arrived at the deportation center, deportees were loaded and driven away. Although the Ministry of Justice dispatched special mobile teams of attorneys to visit centers and attend to the most sensitive cases, irregularities, which spanned from the moment of arrest to deportation, riddled the operation.

The party-state's lack of logistical preparation soon became apparent. After Maputo's reorganization, a total of ninety-six neighborhoods comprised the city. Given that the COC only opened thirty-eight verification centers, residents of many neighborhoods could not request, much less obtain, the documentation that authorities demanded. The GDs in the bairros lacked a means of transportation. These limitations, however, did not prevent the government from carrying out detentions and deportations. They proceeded without verifying whether the deportees were unemployed or resided in the city rightfully. For example, in Bairro Luís Cabral, "there was no triage of cases of unemployment and prostitution," said Albino Massangai, a member of the verification brigade, in a roundtable that the Ministry of Justice convened in 1984 to evaluate progress.[94] Yet, even in those neighborhoods with verification centers nearby, brigades found it easier to take detainees to deportation centers. Alberto Zandamela recalled: "In Matola-Gare where I worked as chief justice, there were many cases where the police expelled peasants as unproductive without bringing them to the tribunal. When we received the complaints and concluded that they were innocent, the people were already in Niassa or other centers of production in the country." As Zandamela admitted, Matola-Gare was a rural area that happened to be near the capital city, and most residents were peasants. "That area had one particularity that maybe we did not pay attention to at the beginning of the operation," he said; "people work in the country in their family *machambas,* they collect firewood and make charcoal. These people never had work cards because they did not work in a company and had no employer." He concluded in perplexity, "So, is the peasant an unproductive?" Indeed, only a policy driven by moral dogma and prior judgment could have blinded authorities to such an obvious fact. Although the COC issued a second directive that clarified who should be expelled, at the beginning of the campaign, the brigades followed President Machel's call to cleanse the cities of everyone who lacked a work card. As Zandamela noted, "The police considered unemployed anyone without a work card and sent them to Niassa."[95] Charismatic and bureaucratic claims to authority collided throughout the campaign.

Although most victims were deported without their identities confirmed, verification centers afforded no safe haven. First, the centers were not equipped to accommodate or house the massive numbers of people awaiting verification of their papers. Detainees streamed in by the thousands, and the verification teams could not process all of these cases. Consequently, people stayed for weeks in the centers without food, water, and hygienic facilities. The COC had not factored such a crisis into its calculus. As Joseph Hanlon observed, "Evacuation and verification centers were set up with no assessment of needs and the Maputo city council was called in to dig latrines only when the shit began to pile up."[96] Reports from various

FIGURE 3.5. A verification team at work, Maputo, July 1983. Verification centers were short staffed and ill-equipped for the task. Here, the team is processing eleven cases at once. Note the detainees' submissive poses as they await their verdicts. Photo courtesy of Arquivo da Revista Tempo (ART).

CODs in Maputo indicated the COC's lack of support. COD operatives complained about the shortage of food and blankets for detainees before deportation, the absence of a means of transportation to expedite deportations, and the centers' unsanitary conditions.[97]

The government's lack of preparation for the campaign did not only affect detainees. Members of verification teams labored under taxing conditions. Some worked straight "for 48 hours without food and a deficient logistical support." One judge named Salomão Langa recalled, "In the first days we worked with many difficulties, without food and without rest because the roundups were constant and we had to expedite the cases."[98] Despite the Ministry of Justice's claim that its role in the campaign was a "great success" and that "legality and justice were duly served," it is hard to believe that hungry and sleep-deprived judges conducted fair hearings, especially when they processed hundreds of cases every day.[99] In fact, as Isabel Tiago conceded, "The quantity of people brought by the police to the verification centers was excessive." Tiago, an attorney stationed in a verification center, recalled that "for those cases in which the situation of unemployment of the accused was confirmed by the *responsáveis* of the *bairro,* the triage team sent them directly to deportation centers from where they were sent to production units."[100] *Responsáveis* (neighborhood authorities) amassed tremendous power during the campaign. Although attorneys dominated the legal procedures, it was often the members of local GDs who called the shots. Under the state of exception imposed by the campaign's directive, secretários de bairro and chefes de quarteirão were granted new powers as they led proceedings in the People's Tribunals. The Law of Judicial Organization, which instituted the people's justice and *tribunais de base* (local tribunals) granted neighborhood and village judges no power to pronounce sentences that deprived defendants of liberty. In other words, they could not sentence people to serve time in prison or reeducation camps. Only district and provincial tribunals retained this prerogative. During Operação Produção, however, the COC's directive vested local tribunals with the authority to sentence people for up to three years in production centers.[101] Local authorities used this power to pursue agendas of their own, settling scores and targeting rivals.

Verification teams struggled to determine who should be deported. District reports to Maputo's COP indicated that "there is lack of clarity in the definition of concepts of prostitute, vagrant, vagabond, unemployed, and domestic servant."[102] The challenges were so acute that the COC deployed brigades to right the wrongs that local commands had made when assigning victims to labor camps. The Provincial People's Tribunal in Maputo established an Operation Room, where officials analyzed information about the campaign, especially the most sensitive cases. The workings of Frelimo's bureaucracy, however, further complicated the process. Most district verification brigades were not aware of the operation's directive—not because the document did not reach their CODs but rather because team leaders kept the instructions to themselves and the mistakes continued. The reason for this breakdown is quite simple. The central government marked most directives with SECRET in red ink. The new directive bore the same designation, and team leaders assumed the document was for their own private consumption and did not share it with their subordinates. A mobile supervisory brigade discovered this problem across Maputo Province three months into the campaign.[103] Governor José Moiane organized a seminar on September 8–9, 1983, to address the issue and to evaluate the campaign's course in Maputo. Each COD presented a summary report and detailed their principal challenges to the governor. They all pointed to *falta de clareza* (lack of clarity) with respect to their targets and cited the COP's and COC's lack of support.[104] The seminar drew some recommendations for the COC, including the suggestion that the concepts of prostitution, vagrancy, and unemployment, including *empregado doméstico e artesanato* (domestic service and workmanship), had to be clarified. Brigades had deported many

FIGURE 3.6. "Voluntary" deportees about to board a plane to Niassa during the voluntary phase of Operação Produção, Maputo, July 6, 1983. Those who left during this stage could take their belongings with them. Photo courtesy of Arquivo da Revista Tempo (ART).

charcoal makers, housemaids, and housewives as unproductives.[105] As aircrafts loaded with unproductive deportees left Maputo every day, the finding came too late for tens of thousands of people. Many had already arrived in Niassa and Cabo Delgado in the country's far north.

Nevertheless, the COC deployed mobile teams of attorneys to oversee sensitive cases in verification and deportation centers across the city. The COC also composed a document that more clearly defined the key conceptual categories operative in the campaign: *prostitute, vagrant, vagabond,* and *unemployed.*[106] As Gita Honwana wrote in her report to the Ministry of Justice, cases involving the accusation of prostitution were the most difficult to resolve. Attorneys in the Operation Room spent hours debating how to define *prostitute.* They found no satisfying definition that they could agree on. Apparently, the COC's directive, though aiming to offer clarity, provided none. Its language proved more confusing than instructive. As Honwana noted, most of the accusations of prostitution were related to "subjective individual sentiments by *chefes do quarteirão* or the women in the OMM." Accusations of prostitution, she continued, "sometimes masked acts of retaliation for old scores in the *bairro.*" In verification centers, judges adopted different interpretations, "conflating single mothers, housewives, and minor and grown daughters living with their parents with prostitutes."[107] The government's legalist yet ambiguous conception of prostitution could not account for the myriad ways in which people at the local level understood the practice. Varied and conflicting local understandings of the categories that were to be purged, and not the government's commands alone, shaped the campaign.

Despite the intensity of state surveillance during the campaign, urban residents did not passively wait to be deported. People devised ways to subvert the operation and escape deportation. The verification centers recorded several cases of false documents and forged signatures.[108] According to Melchior Manuel, a COC member whose testimony Gita Honwana included in her report, "There was a substantial increase in crimes of falsification of documents."[109] Friends helped each other, lending or borrowing documents.[110] Even members of the GDs tried to rescue close friends and relatives by issuing false documents.[111] Bribery was frequent, especially in cases that involved illegal occupation of apartments or unpaid rent.[112] Some people sought soldiers' protection in exchange for services, much to local GDs' dissatisfaction. Albino Massangai recalled with bitterness the number of *comandantes* (soldiers) in his bairro who consorted with women he and his colleagues deemed prostitutes. "They 'nationalized' all single women during Operação Produção," he told Gita Honwana. He claimed that because his bairro (Luís Cabral) was near the train terminal where a large contingent of military forces were stationed to protect the cargo, most women in his neighborhood were soldiers' *amantes* (lovers). When he led his GD to round up the women and send them away, the soldiers demanded their lovers back. "I was threatened by one of these elements with a pistol," he said. "I was threatened for doing justice, for obeying the laws."[113] Conflicts between the party-state's branches flared often during the campaign. Opportunism, illegal transactions, and schemes of all sorts pervaded Operação Produção. This was an ironic outcome for a state program that sought to eradicate all forms of illegalities and to purify society in the name of socialist development and modernization. Yet, the campaign's most remarkable irony was the opportunity it provided local authorities and ordinary citizens to pursue their own agendas, often subverting the party-state's moralizing dicta. Most people expelled from cities during the campaign were not just apprehended in house-to-house searches or public roundups; they were framed and denounced by their neighbors, coworkers, and even close relatives. It is to these intimate politics of self-policing and denunciation that we turn in the next chapter.

4 ~ Vigilante Citizenship and the Politics of Denunciation, 1974–1984

> Power may control the public address system, but crowds also have a voice, generally a murmur, at times a roar.
>
> —John Lonsdale, "Moral and Political Argument in Kenya"

GIVEN THE acute shortage in human, material, and technological resources that the Mozambican government faced, how did they manage to identify, round up, and intern nearly 1 percent of Mozambique's population? With such a small military and police apparatus and no sophisticated system of surveillance, how did the regime identify its purge targets? The reorganization of urban neighborhoods and the documentation of urban residents as part of the Ofensiva campaign described in the previous chapter did not, on their own, give the government the capacity to expel so many people from the cities. In the few scholarly representations of Frelimo's urban cleanup campaigns, the party-state appears as the commanding force in a solo act of modernizing society and making the nation. Margaret Hall and Tom Young argued, for example, that "the effectiveness of the [Mozambican] state relied increasingly on a top-down coercion which placed a high premium on the state's capacity to reach out and mold society."[1] But this top-down perspective of Frelimo's governance neglected the forces from below without which the heavy hand of the state could not have reached the society it sought to mold. As Anne Pitcher aptly observed, the socialist experiment in Mozambique was not a dance of one but of multiple players. Constant negotiation, resistance, and cooperation between the state and social groups marked the experiment.[2]

In this chapter, I demonstrate how Frelimo's coercive capacity rested on the cooperation and willingness of ordinary people to banish those who did not fit into their ethical norms of urban citizenship. Citizens were not bystanders and passive recipients of state commandments. They participated enthusiastically in Frelimo's efforts to transform the moral outlook of urban society. I am less interested in how citizens resisted Frelimo's campaigns, in part because acts of resistance did not deter the regime from rounding up unwanted people and because the major form of opposition to Frelimo was the armed rebellion led by the Mozambique National Resistance from 1977 to 1992 (by far the most discussed subject on postcolonial Mozambique). My focus here is on the roaring voices of ordinary citizens whose sense of moral indignation aided Frelimo's project in direct and indirect ways. While attuned to the party's discursive archetypes and exhortatory harangues about proper civil comportment, urban citizens' participation in the cleanup campaigns was not always animated by political ideology. More often than not, they followed mundane dicta that emanated from the nitty-gritty complexities of everyday life in independent Mozambique. One site where these dicta are visible is in the heated debate over civic order and moral decorum that took place in the press. A vibrant public sphere animated by moral indignation took hold of the country as citizens debated which moral aesthetics should regulate individual and collective conduct in independent Mozambique. These debates were not new, and in both style and substance, they resembled older longings for civic order dating back to the early years of the twentieth century.[3] However, they were more vitriolic in condemning the supposed wayward lifestyle of city dwellers and in urging authorities to punish deviants and to drive them out of urban areas. While Frelimo's socialist rhetoric permeated public discourse and provided a new vocabulary and rhetorical ammunition against urban social decay, the fervor with which ordinary people articulated their views in the press often contrasted with the party line. The words of the public had material consequences that the party could not regulate.

The second site of public participation in the cleanup campaigns concerns the practices of self-policing and denunciation among urban residents. Publicly, people accused each other in residential and occupational meetings organized by Grupos Dinamizadores. Following instructions from party-state authorities, residents joined vigilante groups and sharpened their gaze on neighbors and colleagues, looking for signs of enemy behavior, which they reported to authorities either through speech or writing. Denunciation thus shifted into the private sphere. People often knew each other and employed vigilantism as a tool with which to settle personal conflicts and get rid of rivals or competitors for material and social resources—or sometimes even of embarrassing family members.[4]

That moral indignation seized a growing urban citizenry in a context of extreme austerity and material want is not surprising. Sociologists have long established that such tendencies are common among lower-middle-class citizens in their struggles for material well-being and upward mobility, especially when resources are scarce and the channels for such mobility are narrow.[5] Although I do not develop a sociological reading of the urban class structures of independent Mozambique, in part because of their incipient visibility in the period under analysis here, indignant voices often came from the middle ranks of the wage-working population.[6] They manifested their entitlement to urban citizenship through demands to exclude potential competitors in accessing the privileges of urbanity. It is therefore not surprising that their moral indignation—genuine, instrumentalist, and often self-serving—turned into a powerful weapon that aided Frelimo's reformist project in its most punitive fashion by denouncing as enemies to be expelled those undeserving of urban citizenship. Intimate enmity, self-policing, and denunciations are intrinsic elements of autocratic regimes obsessed with social engineering. These regimes have long relied on the willing help of ordinary people and the pervasive practices of vigilantism that were not always motivated by political or ideological conviction but by the most mundane forces of everyday life and by individuals seeking to pursue agendas of their own.[7] The combination of public moral indignation and competition for resources pushed Frelimo's reformist and punitive program beyond the party's control.

MORAL INDIGNATION AND THE MOZAMBICAN PUBLIC SPHERE

In 1977, a young university student named Samuel Nguja found himself living in the quarters of the newly established Centro 8 de Março in Maputo, a boarding house for students Frelimo had selected for training in specific fields to rapidly tackle the shortage in government clerks. Nguja was a native of Nampula in northern Mozambique. To him, the capital city seemed like a totally different world, with its high-rise buildings and busy streets. Walking around the acacia-lined streets of the city, Nguja observed the habits of his fellow young compatriots and found them offensively inappropriate. With a burning sense of duty, he wrote a letter to the editor of *Tempo*, the most widely read news magazine in Mozambique at the time. The editor published the letter with a poignant title: "Problemas da juventude: Namoro 1" (Problems of the youth: Dating 1). What prompted Nguja's intervention was the ways people dated and displayed affection in the city's sparse public gardens and parks. To him, public displays of affection conflicted with the revolutionary ethics of socialist Mozambique that Frelimo stood for.

Reproducing the ready-made socialist rhetoric of the ruling party, Nguja claimed that the youth had to contribute to the construction of socialism by ridding themselves of the old and "decadent vices," chief among them hugging and kissing in public. He postulated that the rise of the New Man depended on this purification process. "For me," he wrote, "hugging in the streets is scandalous and shameful. It's not right. It's wrong because it's a Western culture that we need to eliminate." He went on to say that dating in public "harms our revolution."[8]

Samuel Nguja used the pen to exercise his rights and duties as a citizen of independent Mozambique to address issues of public concern in the freshly introduced discursive archetypes of the ruling party. In so doing, he joined thousands of citizens all over the country whose sense of revolutionary duty was aroused by Frelimo's reformist exhortations. After several decades of censorship and marginalization under colonial rule, the independence of Mozambique opened wide the spectrum of active citizenship. The recent end of censorship and marginalization of citizens' voices further exacerbated the revolutionary fervor. The readers' pages of *Tempo* magazine proved to be the perfect forum for their newly awakened public engagement and interest in civic action. *Tempo* was founded in the dying days of colonial rule in Lourenço Marques as an independent and progressive paper, one that would render the marginalized and silenced African subjects visible in the White-dominated colonial press.[9] Like the other two papers that survived the transition to independence, *Notícias de Maputo* and *Notícias da Beira,* in addition to the national radio station, *Radio Moçambique, Tempo* became an enthusiastic vehicle for the party-state commandments and a privileged forum for public engagement with Frelimo's nationalist agenda. Writing letters to the editor was one way for citizens like Nguja to exercise their newfound freedom of expression after colonialism's censorship and marginalization, to participate in the revolution, and to keep up with fellow compatriots.

Nguja's article sparked a long debate in the magazine about social mores and the culture of dating in Mozambique.[10] A month after the publication of his letter, a clerk named Alfredo Simango sent a more passionate letter to the same editor, which he framed as a follow-up to Nguja's. The title of his article went straight to the point: "Um Africano verdadeiro não beija nem abraça na rua" (A true African neither kisses nor hugs in the street). Like Nguja, Simango was incensed by public displays of affection, which he denounced as foreign and un-African. "Going around arm in arm," he wrote, "is not correct. For a true African, kissing in the street is something shameful. To walk arm in arm or to embrace in the street is not love in our society;

it's an imported love." He went on to claim that for a father or mother to see their child kissing or hugging in the street "is shocking." He suggested that in the same way that violent movies were prohibited for people below eighteen years of age, romantic movies should also be forbidden for the young. "Dating among our youth," he asserted, "should be linked to the interests of the masses of workers and peasants."[11]

Vigilante citizens like Nguja and Simango articulated a puritan view of African authenticity that Frelimo leaders espoused: an austere and abstemious character whose sole drive was to serve the collective good and the revolution. Theirs was a revolutionary romanticism that sought to replace forms of intimacy viewed as foreign with quasi-mechanical interactions understood as advancing the goals of the ruling party. Their passionate postulations about appropriate African conduct exemplified the ways in which a significant section of the Mozambican public engaged with Frelimo's project. Although newspapers were not the only space where public opinions about urban decadence were articulated and debated in independent Mozambique, they offer us the best possibility to "penetrate the thinking of those who were implicated in the events of the past" in their own words and at the time of the events.[12] Yet, as public spaces that privilege the literate and largely urban minority over the illiterate and rural majority, newspapers are not representative of the national public. At the time of independence, Mozambique had an inordinately high level of illiteracy, estimated at above 90 percent. Therefore, the public that convened in such forums as *Tempo* magazine or *Notícias* accounts for a fraction of the Mozambican public that engaged with and embraced Frelimo's moralizing project. For instance, *Tempo* received more than three thousand letters to the editor in 1978 alone, of which they only published six hundred.[13] Clearly, my assessment of the public engagement with Frelimo's reformist project is conditioned by the selective bias of newspaper editors. The overwhelming majority of published writers of letters to the editor shared the puritanical passion of the party leadership in condemning urban decadence. Discordant voices tended to be few and far between. This was the work of editors who were often more inclined to publish those letters which reinforced the party line, thus silencing opposing views.

Scholars of the media in socialist Mozambique have revealed the ambiguity of Frelimo's censorship of the press. Whereas the party sought to control the country's address system by nationalizing all media outlets and directing them to mobilize the masses for the tasks of the revolution, the regime lacked manpower and the capacity to enforce institutional censorship. There was no cabinet where news was screened before publication.

This task was left to the discretion of devoted editors, most of whom had a long history of anticolonial activism and were initially aligned with Frelimo's revolutionary principles. It was up to them and their teams to report and publish news and commentaries according to their own interpretation of the party line.[14] Threading the line between ideological loyalism and independent thinking required a degree of self-censorship that carried risks. Although Frelimo did not purge newspapers, editions deemed inappropriate or out of step with the socialist revolution were occasionally removed from circulation. Some editors who stepped out of line suffered penalties. Fernando Lima, for example, was expelled from *Notícias* for his criticism of the anti-prostitution campaigns, which he denounced for focusing on women's styles of dress while ignoring the structural roots of the problem. In several of his editorials, he questioned the effectiveness of reeducation as a way to achieve social reform.[15] But independent-minded journalists like Lima were rare. Most navigated the opaque principles of the ruling party by infusing newspapers with the voices of the people. With more space than other dailies, *Tempo* magazine was the most successful at making its pages available to the masses to speak to each other and with governing bodies. The readers' pages occupied one-third of the magazine and was its most popular section.[16]

While editors were confined to their role as mouthpieces of the ruling party, readers had more space for independent writing and were not passive recipients of news. They were enthusiastic participants in news making, often pushing editors in certain directions and urging them to focus on particular themes at the expense of others. They saw newspapers as an extension of the public sphere, where aspects of daily life could be argued, contested, and mitigated. Moreover, their debates were not confined to one newsreel or a particular location. As Derek Peterson and Emma Hunter put it, "Texts had afterlives."[17] The debates that newspaper texts elicited traveled across different newspapers and across time and space. A piece from one newspaper, say *Notícias da Beira*, could be debated in *Tempo* or *Notícias* of Lourenço Marques/Maputo. Debaters were not simply animated by a blind allegiance to the ruling party and its reformist ideology, even if they employed the party's discursive poetics and relied on editors' bias to get their pieces published. While blind followers existed, we see evidence of self-motivated coparticipants in a public sphere engendered by a shared conviction that moral decrepitude and foreign cultural practices harmed Mozambique's reputation as an independent nation.

Newspapers were more than just news outlets; they were forums of civic argument that allowed citizens to intervene in national matters as dutiful agents of the revolution. People like Nguja and Simango built archives of newspaper articles from which they drew insights and points to argue for or against in their own letters to editors. Their writings had afterlives. They prompted action and determined who should be targeted in the urban cleanup campaigns against people deemed to be anti-social. The case of a young man named Cumbane illustrates this point. Three months after the publication of Alfredo Simango's article, Cumbane wrote an angry letter to *Tempo*'s editor to report on his February 1978 detention.[18] The police agents who detained him and his girlfriend found them holding hands in front of a coffee shop in Matola, an industrial township located a few miles from Maputo. Ignoring the couple's cries of innocence, the police agents on patrol asked the couple if they did not "know that here in the People's Republic of Mozambique it is forbidden to walk arm in arm?" The agents took them to a police station where "many other people were detained for not carrying IDs and for hugging on the street." The hugging offenders were ordered to form a line and handed a text published on January 1, 1978, in the letters-to-the-editor section of *Tempo.* It was none other than Simango's piece condemning hugging and kissing in public. Although no law prohibiting public displays of affection existed in Mozambique's legal code, printed texts like Simango's carried the weight of law. In the hands of law enforcement agents with basic or often no instruction at all, printed texts from newspapers were just as legitimate as those from a courthouse. After reading the article, the police inquired about the couple's marital status. "If you were single," wrote Cumbane, "they wanted to know if the man was known by his girlfriend's family." After the inquiry, the commander of the police station addressed the detainees. "He told us that indeed it's prohibited to walk arm in arm on the street because it's a shameful act, . . . a colonial vestige." The detainees were finally released near midnight, after several hours of lectures on proper moral comportment and exhortations to let go of decadent foreign habits that were contrary to the revolutionary ethics of socialist Mozambique.

Cumbane and his girlfriend were lucky to have been set free after spending hours in police custody. Several other couples were not as fortunate and ended up in reeducation camps for committing the same offense. As the editor of *Tempo* commented in reply to Cumbane's letter, such incidents were becoming increasingly common in all major cities across the country. Indeed, cases of detainees arrested for public displays of affection permeate the archival record of Niassa's reeducation camps. This crime was often listed as "liberalism" and "moral corruption." In some cases where couples were found kissing or in moments of intimacy, local authorities exhibited them to the public in shaming ceremonies that resembled the Nachingwea trial.[19]

Incendiary letters such as the ones written by Nguja and Simango reflected the widespread anxieties of ordinary citizens about appropriate moral behavior and conflicting notions of modernity in early independent Mozambique. These letters populated Mozambique's newspapers and inspired action. They demonstrate the extent to which ordinary people were invested in sanctioning the behavior of their fellow compatriots in line with the ruling party's punitive reformism. During cleanup campaigns, these moral sanctions enabled people to get rid of those they perceived to be unworthy of urban citizenship. This was the case in the first wave of public condemnations of short dresses or miniskirts in the capital city, which was inspired by Operação Limpeza's efforts against prostitution in September 1974. Unlike Tanzania or Uganda, where such campaigns were carried out by volunteers or young party pioneers, in Mozambique, conducting cleanup campaigns against those labeled anti-socials was an exclusive prerogative of security forces and party agents.[20] But the party's pronouncements against the indecency of women inspired action beyond their control. While security forces scanned the red-light district in search of women of ill repute, gangs of young men went into the streets of Lourenço Marques and harassed women in miniskirts, forcing them to wear the "respectful" and "traditional *capulana*."[21] On one occasion, the mob nearly killed a young Black girl for wearing a miniskirt, after molesting her at midday in front of the downtown market Vasco da Gama (today, Mercado Central). According to the reporter who reported on the case, no one in the crowded market came to the aid of the victim. Instead, some female vendors joined the aggressors while a crowd of about a hundred bystanders formed a circle to watch the spectacle. A courageous truck driver saved the girl from certain death. An environment of fear began to grip the city, especially in the bairros where the gangs were most active. "In the last three days," the reporter summed up, "no woman—elderly or young—has been able to walk the suburban streets in a dress or wearing a skirt, even below the knees, without covering her body from the waist down with a *capulana*. They cannot go out in public wearing pants either."[22]

Conflating a modern style of dress with prostitution was a far too common phenomenon in Africa and elsewhere.[23] Like their contemporary counterparts, especially in East Africa, where the miniskirt aroused passionate debates and mobilized action, the mobsters of Lourenço Marques/Maputo were taking the matter of urban indecency and the "shameful" conduct of urban women into their own hands. Although the party condemned such acts of voluntarist violence—averse as they were to what Ortega y Gasset called *mobocracy*—the writing was on the wall.[24] In the eyes of urban moral critics, the miniskirt was a trademark of licentiousness and a device that women used to deceive men. The revealing length of the miniskirt embodied the nation's postcolonial shame. No one made this point more bluntly than the famous poet laureate and journalist José Craveirinha. In a commentary published in *Notícias da Beira* five days after the first mob attack on short-skirted women in the capital city, Craveirinha supported the "ban on minis." He commended the "revolutionary" attitude of the capital's youth and asserted that the ban on miniskirts and their "replacement with the traditional *capulana*" was a welcome and necessary policy. He maintained that in the city of cement "the mini is an irreverent fashion," while in the caniço it "corresponds to a degraded condition of women." For him, any woman wearing a miniskirt in the caniço was not making a saucy fashion choice but was a prostitute. The mini was humiliating for men in the suburbs because it reminded them of the frustration of seeing their daughters and sisters selling their bodies to White men. Prostitution and the "inviting" short dresses that women wore were thus reminders of the humiliations of colonialism. The ban on the mini was, in the poet's words, the beginning of the "total decolonization of the Mozambican family."[25]

Vitriolic attacks on independent women and their fashion choices sometimes backfired. As the platform of debate widened and revolutionary vigilance sharpened, contributors had to be cautious in the way they framed their stories. The acute level of public scrutiny was such that one line or a small detail from a contributor's letter was enough to cause one to be seen as an enemy rather than a dutiful member of the revolutionary comradery. In 1977, Abílio Hauaniaca wrote to denounce women who "seduced" men in front of a cinema in Lichinga, Niassa Province, based on his "personal experience." He asked the authorities of Niassa to relaunch operation Pente Fino (fine comb), which, to his disappointment, had resulted in the detention of "only ten prostitutes" in the city—a low yield considering "the number of prostitutes that continue to lure men" in Lichinga. He mentioned a particular brothel where prostitutes worked and urged the police to go there to round up the "whores."[26] Three readers from his hometown, José Walemo, Manuel Luís, and José da Silva, wrote back to accuse him of being one of the promoters of prostitution. They found in Abílio's letter the evidence that *he* was an "agent of sexual corruption" himself.[27] How was it possible, they asked in their separate letters, that Abílio knew where the brothel was located and did not inform the local Grupo Dinamizador? By failing to inform the GD about the location of the brothel, Abílio was defaulting on his revolutionary duties. His claim that only ten prostitutes were detained during Pente Fino instead of the "hundreds that were actually sent to reeducation camps" was further proof that Abílio was not attentive to the revolutionary process underway and had to be reeducated.[28]

Judging from the volume of letters to editors in *Tempo* and *Notícias* with self-incriminating material, the scrutiny of the reading public could not suppress the people's urge to express their indignation at the moral lapses of their fellow citizens. Sometimes the indignation was such that readers joined forces to craft letters condemning urban indecency. Engagement with the revolution called for collective action. A group of three friends, Francisco Nhaduco, Paulo Chachine, and Diamantino Paulino, coauthored a letter to call for the ban of "immoral magazines" that "influence the youth in acquiring bad habits."[29] One of those bad habits was dancing. In several speeches during his mass rallies, President Machel denounced dances as bourgeois and exhorted the youth to abandon the practice and engage in revolutionary tasks to decolonize their minds instead.[30] Contributors to newspapers found in the president's call an opportunity to sharpen their gaze over neighbors in search of persistent signs of decadence and disobedience of party orders. Once infringers were found, contributors addressed them by full name, adding their home addresses and urging authorities to put an end to the violation and, if need be, take the infringers away. Carlos Agostinho do Rosário sent a letter to *Tempo* to report a dance organized by one Senhor Jenito, a fellow resident at Bairro do Aeroporto in Maputo. Addressing Senhor Jenito directly, do Rosário reminded him of President Machel's words in Cabo Delgado, where the supreme leader declared that "we do not want balls here in Mozambique." In very aggressive tone, he urged Senhor Janito to discontinue his "western practices," which "hinder our revolution."[31] Another anonymous group of friends identified themselves as "old and young *continuadores* (pioneers)." The title of their coauthored letter carried their message in unequivocal terms: "We don't want balls and freak parties in our country." They called upon the government to issue a decree forbidding "these legacies of colonialism" which "dishonor our daughters" and "harm the revolution."[32]

These passionate expressions of indignation were not confined to written texts in newspapers. They inspired action, providing essential information for authorities to locate unwanted subgroups. More often than not, security authorities relied on denunciations in letters to editors to carry out the cleanup campaigns. Incriminating denunciations did not need to be accurate. As was true of xiconhocas, the features of those who harmed the revolution were detectable in their fashion choices, in their cultural tastes, in their manners, and in the ways they displayed affection. When coupled with the effects of economic decline and the shortage of consumer goods in urban areas pressured by the influx of rural migrants in the late 1970s and early 1980s, these acts of vigilantism and denunciation took a more intimate character. The enemy within became both figurative and literal.

As the phase of transition gave way to the period of socialist consolidation in the early 1980s, the signs of economic decline were apparent and so was the inability of the state to provide urban services (housing, transportation, health, education, and, more importantly, food rationing).[33] This momentous change was reflected in the language and tone of those who expressed their opinions in the press. People were no longer content with simply denouncing what they viewed as social pathologies harmful to the revolution. They were now calling on the government to round up and remove from urban areas those who hindered access to urban resources by leading parasitic lives. As bichas and shortages of consumer goods became the order of the day, residents who felt entitled to claim urban citizenship, either because they were born in the city or because they had formal wage employment, embraced prejudiced ideas and vigorously endorsed the government's purges to stop rural-to-urban migration.

While letters to editors and public commentaries condemning civic disorder and calling on authorities to take action illustrate the extent to which Frelimo's reformist project found a fertile and receptive terrain, it was through the everyday practices of vigilantism, self-policing, and libel that ordinary people participated actively in urban cleanup campaigns. The network of informants that security services established throughout the country, the physical composition of Mozambique's most crowded residential areas (where most victims of roundups resided), and the citizens' willingness to turn in their neighbors, friends, colleagues, and relatives to authorities all contributed to shaping the geography of the cleanup campaigns and the demography of reeducation and labor camps.

In addition to letters to editors, the most prevalent form of denunciation was speaking ill about others in private to secretaries of GDs or in public during GD meetings in residential communities and workplaces. Citizens also provided libelous information about others to local agents of the Grupo de Vigilância Popular, or People's Vigilance Group (GVP). The GVP was a network of intelligence gatherers and community policing created in April 1978 by the secret services, Serviço Nacional de Segurança Popular, or National People's Security Service (SNASP). Since its founding in 1975, the agency was under the command of Jacinto Veloso, a veteran of the liberation struggle with the cabinet rank of minister of security.[34] In his memoir, Veloso noted that SNASP was modeled after the East German Stasi and the Soviet KGB, and its agents were trained by East German, Cuban, and Soviet experts.[35] The agency responded directly to the president and had full authority to "order and undertake inquiries, conduct searches and arrests it judged convenient." It could also "proceed to necessary requisitions, instruct processes and detain persons, determining their fate, namely to send them to competent police authorities, to tribunals, or to reeducation camps."[36] SNASP operated above the law, and its decisions "were not subject to appeal." Its powers to detain and condemn subjects were made retroactive to the period before September 1974, which means that it could persecute individuals for crimes or subversive acts committed before independence.[37] According to Veloso, the agency was a "very heavy machine with its own military personnel, jails, investigative agents, and many people in logistics and support, who often entered into clashes with the police and the army."[38] The number of full-time SNASP officers was estimated at 1,500 as of 1984.[39] Despite this significant number, the agency's real strength lay in the network of unpaid voluntary informants and onlookers in the GVPs.

The GVPs' main task was to watch over "saboteurs" and "lazy individuals," in what SNASP designated a "struggle against economic sabotage" in state enterprises.[40] They were active in every corner of society, including workplaces, residential areas, schools, and places of leisure or of worship.[41] Membership was voluntary. In July 1978, SNASP estimated that in Maputo Province alone there were 456 GVPs with around 17,000 members.[42] In August 1979, during the Second Seminar on Popular Vigilance held in Maputo, SNASP proudly announced that in many factories more than 23 percent of workers had joined GVPs, and in some factories more than 50 percent had volunteered.[43] One year later, the security agency claimed that 300,000 citizens were actively involved in GVPs across the country.[44] Although these statistics need to be treated with caution, given the general tendency by government officials to inflate numbers for propaganda purposes or to impress the party leadership, even exaggerated, these figures indicate the level of participation of ordinary people in efforts to police each other and provide information to SNASP about enemy actions.[45]

Volunteers to GVPs were often the lowest ranking workers. In residential areas, only people with "free time to spend" joined the groups, as membership often entailed frequent weekly meetings, night shifts, attending calls for help in cases of emergency, chasing petty criminals, and settling disputes between neighbors or relatives.[46] Like GDs, however, the GVPs were attractive to those seeking respectability, power, and influence. As members of the lowest party-state apparatus, the GVPs, like their colleagues in the GDs and militias, had advantages in getting ration cards. As widely reported in newspapers and fictionalized in Mozambique's literature, sometimes these local party-state agents took leading positions as organizers of lines for shops,

FIGURE 4.1. March of vigilantes in Maputo on the fifth anniversary of the GVPs, October 10, 1982. Some wear the GVP badge on their left arm. The second banner from the front reads: "Vigilance is the task of all the people." Photo courtesy of Arquivo da Revista Tempo (ART).

bakeries, or water fountains in the bairros, which allowed them to be the first in line or to put their acquaintances in front.[47] In the context of chronic shortages of basic consumer goods, these seemingly insignificant acts of trickery often determined which families got access to food and water and which did not. At the same time, it was from these voluntary vigilantes that the state gathered its intelligence and kept a permanent eye on the enemies of the revolutionary morality.

Although experts from the German Democratic Republic and the Soviet Union helped in setting up the GVPs, denunciatory and libelous practices were not new in Mozambique. The Portuguese secret police, the Polícia Internacional e de Defesa do Estado (PIDE), also relied on a network of informants to detect anticolonial activities during the liberation struggle.[48] However, unlike the Portuguese regime or the German Democratic Republic, Frelimo's government made no major secrets about the workings of its intelligence services and its network of informants.[49] Volunteers to the GVPs were handed forms to fill out in front of their colleagues and neighbors. Some received a badge to wear.[50] Vigilantism was not a private activity; it was a very public undertaking. Instructions on how to collect intelligence and denounce suspects were handed over in the open, published in newspapers, read in radio news hours, and discussed at public meetings.[51] Vigilantism was thus a very public and often intimate practice. In January 1978, *Tempo* published a SNASP appeal to all citizens to double their vigilance against the infiltration of enemies. The agency instructed citizens to be more

FIGURE 4.2. Maputo governor José Moiane and SNASP officers instruct the masses on vigilance in front of GVP headquarters in Maputo, April 1980. Vigilantism was not a secret activity but a very public undertaking. Photo courtesy of Arquivo da Revista Tempo (ART).

attentive in places of mass gathering, such as markets, bus stops, cinemas, restaurants, and concert halls. In residential areas, citizens were instructed to look out for "strange behavior" and report it to authorities. Special attention was to be paid to "people who cause agitation, make exaggerated noise and other acts of insolence in public."[52] Armed with a pamphlet produced by the Council of Ministers in 1977 on the mechanisms of enemy action against the revolution, SNASP officials held meetings with workers and residents to instruct them on how to detect the enemy.[53] They reminded workers and residents that the enemy lived in their midst. "Vigilance must begin in your households and in places where you spend time," said one SNASP official in a meeting with residents of Bairro Chamanculo in Maputo in 1979. The enemies, he continued, "live among the people, eat with the people, and play with the people."[54] He instructed residents to reinforce their vigilance and pay close attention to the conduct of their neighbors and relatives and to inform authorities about any suspicious behavior.[55]

This was not a sophisticated system of surveillance. Its main pillar was the enthusiasm of ordinary citizens who welcomed their role as vigilantes. This enthusiasm can be gleaned from the number of people who volunteered to join the GVPs as well as from the number of people detained during police round ups. In a political culture of transparency in which most operations were done in the open and the results widely showcased in the press, we do not need declassified documents to see the work of the GVPs and the role of ordinary citizens in providing information for the cleanup campaigns. When the police launched the operation against black marketeers and vagrants in June 1982 to tackle the shortage of consumer goods, the editor of *Notícias* dispatched reporters to hear public sentiments on the campaign and inquire into how citizens were helping the authorities. "Vigilance must begin in our own homes," said one forty-nine-year-old vendor in Xipamanine market named Alberto Napore. In tune with the party line, he added that "the unemployed must be forced to work" in state farms because "if they continue to live in the city they can easily be won by the enemy." Another interviewee, thirty-year-old Romeu Valente, declared: "We must begin vigilance in our neighbor's house because we know that these criminals are infiltrated in our midst."[56] He might have heard the SNASP agent and internalized his instructions. Bernardino Xavier, aged forty-three, also suggested that residents had to sharpen their gazes over their neighbors' houses and search for vagrants in their own families. "We must be vigilant," he said. "We must analyze the life of our neighbors and our relatives as well." For him, Maputo residents were to blame for the increase in vagrancy and unemployment in the city because "we send for our country relatives without any occupation, only to come and increase the rate of unemployment." It is as if he had memorized President Machel's speech at Ponto Final word for word. Twenty-three-year-old Francisco Nhantumbo, a bartender living in Bairro Laulane, was more cutting: "We don't need these elements in our city. In the [GD] meetings we must analyze the life of each resident in the bairro. It's during these gatherings that we have to denounce everybody that we suspect."[57]

It may well be that these random citizens were reproducing verbatim discourses they heard on the radio, read in the papers, or discussed in public meetings, but theirs were not simple opinions without consequences. The demography of reeducation camps indicates that citizens like Alberto Napore, Bernardino Xavier, and Francisco Nhantumbo meant business. In June 1982, during the same police operation mentioned above, residents of Bairro Inhagóia and Bairro Luís Cabral in Maputo called on the police to "go clean the vagrants" who "lived in the clover, spending the day drinking or sleeping" in their bairros.[58] A police brigade arrived at dawn and knocked on designated houses. According to the reporter who covered the event, the police knew exactly which houses to target. The night roundup yielded forty arrests. When the reporter asked the unnamed authority about the reasons for these detentions, he replied: "It is obvious these people are going to rob other people's houses at night." The accusers knew that, regardless of guilt or innocence, their unwanted neighbors would certainly be condemned and taken away. As the reporter observed, of the forty detainees sent to the police station, only five were identified as criminals. He also noted that, in that selective campaign, the police detained hundreds of individuals who were not criminals but rather "individuals accused of vagrancy." Most detainees, the reporter wrote, "were undesirable individuals denounced by the people." As the police officer in charge of the operation told the reporter: "During the early hours of the morning, the [police] vehicle brigade runs through the various streets of the city's neighborhoods looking for the residencies of undesirable individuals indicated by the population."[59]

As in other campaigns since the launch of the Ofensiva in 1980, the detainees of Bairros Inhagóia and Luís Cabral were sent to Maputo People's Tribunal, where Judge João Carlos Trindade pronounced their sentence. They were all condemned to serve up to two years in reeducation camps in northern Mozambique, after which they were to be sent to state farms. The judge told the reporter that, "although those vagrants were not accused of any crimes, they are on the margins of society, and their danger is accentuated because they do not have a means of subsistence."[60] After the Ofensiva was launched, this form of juridical proceeding resulted in thousands of people being condemned to reeducation. Under the terms of the Ofensiva, sentences for reeducation had to be pronounced by a judge after a proper trial. Unfortunately, these trials were often hasty proceedings. Compelled to deliver justice in a timely manner, judges could not keep pace with the number of detainees brought to the courts by the police. Sometimes the trials took place in the open, with judges delivering sentences for hundreds of detainees in just one day in the marketplace. Although the Ofensiva was meant to put an end to extralegal detentions, it did not resolve the contradictions of a justice system based on a moralistic understanding of wrongdoing. In his deliberations, Judge Trindade was not employing any penal code formally developed by the state. He was following the same unwritten moral codes that animated the extrajudicial phase of the roundups before the Ofensiva. Vagrants were not criminals, he agreed, but they lived "on the margins of society" and were therefore a threat to social order. In this and all other juridical proceedings involving the urban undesirables, it was the potential of urban disorder that stood trial, not the actual crime.

Because most people accused of vagrancy were informal and self-employed workers with no papers, they could not prove their worth as urban citizens of equal merit to documented urbanites who held formal employment. With a justice system in which offenders had no defense attorneys or benefactors, going to court was almost halfway to a reeducation camp. In many cases, beginning in 1980, arrested vagrants were tried in so-called

FIGURE 4.3. Residents celebrating after a meeting on people's vigilance in Maputo, 1980. The women, likely members of the local OMM branch, received capulanas to honor their zealous vigilantism. The words on the wall remind residents that "people's vigilance is the duty of every one of us." Photo courtesy of Arquivo da Revista Tempo (ART).

tribunais populares in their neighborhoods. Members of the local GDs, including selected chefes de quarteirão, leaders of GVPs, and representatives of local branches of the Organization of Mozambican Women (OMM) and Organization of Mozambican Youth (OJM), constituted the grand juries of these tribunals. Selected by the party as among the most respected members of their community, these juries had limited experience with legal procedures and edicts. They were largely "instructed to apply good sense in deciding disputes and dealing with minor infractions."[61] Legal scholars working in Mozambique at the time of the socialist experiment hailed the "truly popular nature" of these courts and the revolutionary justice delivered by "barefoot judges in the shade of a cashew tree."[62] But the premise of these courts—the use of "good sense" and the predominance of unwritten moral rules—often led to unjust decisions because the watching and testifying crowds often influenced the cases. Although these courts might have been effective in dealing with cases involving divorce or polygamy, they were largely deficient in delivering justice with respect to alleged vagrancy, prostitution, or any case during cleanup campaigns. On these occasions, extralegal proceedings and the mood of local residents dictated the fate of defendants. In October 1982, twelve young men accused of vagrancy stood trial in the people's court of Bairro Chamanculo. The police officer who directed the process declared that the defendants "had the habit of staying home during the day and of going out at night." This was often the supposed evidence provided to police authorities by local vigilantes and the cause of detention. In this particular case, the chefes de quarteirão who called on the police to arrest the twelve alleged vagrants did not attend the trial, and local residents testified in favor of ten defendants who were set free. The other two, who did not find any sympathetic soul among the attending crowd, were pronounced guilty and sentenced to "six months to three years of reeducation to be served in a camp indicated by the Ministry of the Interior."[63] The regime of public scrutiny and vigilantism empowered city dwellers to denounce others in ways that pushed the limits of government oversight. More often than not, acts of denunciation were self-serving.

THE LIBEL OF JOSSIANE GUAMBE

Frelimo's definitions of crime and enmity indiscriminately politicized and outlawed social behavior. The ambiguity of party-state instructions on how citizens and members of vigilante groups ought to observe and denounce suspicious behavior left ample room for independent and conflicting interpretations of what constituted suspicious behavior. Members of the GVPs, including professional agents of SNASP and government clerks at various levels, took advantage of this ambiguity to serve their own interests. Although the process of selecting volunteers involved a certain level of scrutiny, the GVPs, like the militias or GDs, were often infiltrated by opportunists and, in many cases, petty criminals who used the agency's badge to pursue agendas of their own.[64] The infiltration of dishonest people into the GVPs was so widespread that in 1980, during the Ofensiva, President Machel urged them to "purify their ranks."[65] As SNASP chief Jacinto Veloso reported in 1982, the Cabinet for Discipline and Control of his security ministry received "many letters, including phone calls" from citizens denouncing agents of SNASP for "improper conduct" and "abuse of power." Veloso asserted that, after investigations, his cabinet discovered that most of the information about the corruption of his agents was true. SNASP agents' various crimes included using their badges to dupe citizens for personal gain and, in furtherance of personal vendettas, to arrest and send innocent people to reeducation camps.[66]

The libel of Jossiane Guambe by Domingos Bila is a good example of how people manipulated the party-state discourse to persecute personal enemies. In June 1978, Domingos Bila wrote a letter to "his excellency" the governor of Maputo Province to "denounce Mr. Jossiane Guambe," allegedly a former PIDE agent. Like most letters addressed to political authorities, Bila's letter followed the bureaucratic and highly formulaic norms of addressing the state in accordance with standards introduced by the Portuguese colonial regime. He completed the official twenty-five-line application sheet (*folha de requerimento de 25 linhas*), with appropriate seals glued to the paper, and signed. Given the scarcity of these materials, producing the letter might have cost him a good sum of money. Bila was not denouncing somebody he vaguely knew. The laundry list of incriminating behavior that Bila compiled in his damaging letter indicates the level of intimacy of his denunciation. His letter included the exact number of Guambe's identification document, his original place of birth (Jangamo, in Inhambane Province), the exact addresses of his past and current residences (Bairros Inhagóia and Benfica), and his past and current professional occupation. Guambe was an itinerant seller of *mulala* (*Euclea natalensis*—a black root used as a toothbrush) and *soruma* (cannabis, which Bila described as "dangerous drugs for the people"). It was as if Bila had the complete curriculum vitae of the denounced on his table when he composed the letter.[67]

A true revolutionary citizen speaks in the language of revolutionaries. As Aminda Smith puts it, in socialist regimes, subjects learned to speak "to the state in its own language."[68] Bila made sure that his letter was populated with the appropriate vocabulary in vogue under Frelimo. To be credible, his words had to indicate his familiarity with the revolutionary discourse and convey the zeal with which he carried out his duties as a vigilante citizen. He called his victim a "great speculator" to suggest that Guambe's trade in mulala was fraudulent and contrary to the tenets of Frelimo's command economy. He also called Guambe an "opportunist" and a "traitor of the interests of the people." Bila's most serious accusation was that Guambe was a colleague of Chico Feio. And here is where he caught the attention of the authorities. Chico Feio was the infamous torturer of detainees who were under PIDE custody and was renowned for his sadism. He symbolized the most heinous features of the enemy. The name of the cartoon figure Xiconhoca was coined after him. Bila's reference to Chico Feio led authorities to assume that Guambe could have been Chico's colleague—that is, not in the sense that both worked for PIDE but rather that they were close friends (Chico Feio also lived in Bairro Inhagóia, where he suffered a brutal death at the hands of a mob as soon as the colonial regime fell).[69] Given the severity of Bila's allegations, Governor José Moiane dispatched two SNASP officers to investigate the case.

After interrogating Guambe, the two officers reported to the governor. The inquiry had not revealed "anything significant," they wrote, but the "subject is hiding something." Investigations had to continue until evidence was found that Guambe was a "dangerous *comprometido* whose place was a reeducation camp."[70] The fact that Bila was himself a trader in mulala—which he indicated in his denunciatory letter—did not raise any suspicion about the real motivation behind his accusation. It may well be that Guambe had been a PIDE agent and Bila was acting from a sense of duty in denouncing him. But other than the very detailed information about his victim's biography, Bila's two-page letter—handwritten in broken Portuguese—contained nothing objective about Guambe's activities as a PIDE agent. Instead, it had more on Guambe's speculative trade in mulala, which was also Bila's trade. That the two men knew each other well is evident. They might have been friends and rubbed shoulders in the busy markets or the labyrinthine streets of the bairros where they conducted their trade and competed for clients and who knows what else.

I did not have access to the archives of SNASP or the Ministry of the Interior—which were the main destinations of written denunciations—but it is not hard to imagine how letters like the one filled by Bila kept SNASP officers busy. I also do not know the circumstances under which the interrogation of Guambe took place or the outcome of the case. But the report to the governor by the two investigators clearly indicates that Bila's words were taken at face value. After all, his was the voice of the people, the source of revolutionary truth. Party leadership constantly recommended that security officers listen to the people.[71] It is safe to conclude that Bila took advantage of the regime of vigilantism to persecute his personal enemy, not the enemy of the revolution. He was one among many civilians who found a useful crack in the larger politics of reformism and used it to get rid of personal enemies. Intimate acts of denunciation like these reached higher heights during Operação Produção. In the largest of all of Frelimo's campaigns, the murmurs and roars of popular vigilantes grew even louder.

INTIMACY AND DENUNCIATION DURING OPERAÇÃO PRODUÇÃO

Unlike previous campaigns, which consisted of unannounced police roundups in designated locations, Operação Produção was largely a street-to-street and door-to-door sweeping campaign. While prior campaigns were short, lasting no more than a week or two, Operação Produção ran uninterrupted for about a year from June 1983 to May 1984 and then intermittently until May 1988. The few scholarly works on Operação Produção often draw a picture in which the party-state appears as the masterful agent, marshaling victims out of the cities in what is portrayed as an unpopular program.[72] However, the campaign was greeted with cheerful popular support. The government could not have rounded up the nearly one hundred thousand victims on its own; it needed the active and enthusiastic participation of ordinary citizens and of local authorities. They all played a central role in the campaign, leading the brigades in the house-to-house searches and indicating the places to be targeted and the people to be arrested.

While many people were arrested in public locations, an equal proportion of "unproductive" urbanites were detained at home. Security authorities often carried out their house-to-house searches in the late hours of the night or even at dawn so that they could catch people at their least guarded. For most victims targeted at home, the members of the campaign brigades who accompanied the police and took them to verification and deportation centers were not strange or unfamiliar. As Alfredo Langa told me in the Niassa village of Matama where I interviewed him, the person who got him deported knew him well. "It was 23:45 when they took me from my house," he said. "It was July, and the secretary of my neighborhood knew me personally. He knew that I was a handyman."[73] Operação Produção was an intimate campaign carried out by people who knew their victims. Their motives often betrayed the principles of the campaign that Frelimo upheld.

The layout of the bairros in the suburban areas exacerbated the intimacy of denunciation during Operação Produção by making it easy for vigilante citizens to incriminate their victims. For anyone who is familiar with the layout of Mozambique's urban neighborhoods, it is not hard to imagine the ease with which chefes de quarteirão, secretários de bairro, members of local GVPs, and vigilante residents identified their victims. In all major cities, most residents lived in the crowded and labyrinthine bairros. One common feature of these bairros—at least until the early 1990s—was the lack of privacy. Hailing from rural areas where homesteads were spacious and dispersed, most residents in the *subúrbios* built fences to demarcate the perimeter of their households and to protect their livestock. Built from discarded materials—corrugated sheet metal, reed, or wooden poles—fences were often used to conceal a family's poverty from the gaze of passersby. But this was often futile because, despite the fencing, residents lived in the open and could "hear the conversations of their neighbors and they [knew] a great deal about what happen[ed] in their homes."[74] This suburban configuration made it difficult to conceal secrets. Like ordinary Russians who resorted to whispering and keeping to themselves in order to escape the ever-listening ears of neighbors, many families in Mozambique learned to avoid talking politics.[75] But unlike the Russians, who could conceal their secrets behind the thick walls of their apartments, most Mozambican families in the bairros were exposed to onlookers and eavesdroppers. Most of their household activities took place in the front yard outside the house—from cooking, eating, doing laundry, and bathing to receiving guests. In these circumstances, it was not a difficult task for vigilantes to find their victims. A simple round in the bairro was enough to provide vigilantes with evidence to send the police to fetch a suspect resident. Walking in the crooked streets of a neighborhood like Inhagóia or Luís Cabral, vigilantes could easily hear a radio playing; they could see the smoke from cooking fires and smell the food; they could distinguish the nourished faces of children of one household from the hungry ones in the next, or see residents taking a nap under the shade of a mango tree or having drinks during work days. In many cases, such mundane scenes provided enough evidence to incriminate individuals. After all, vigilantes were not instructed to investigate and report objective facts but instead to denounce people based on suspicion. The sound of the radio could serve as proof that the resident was engaged in illegal activities that were harming the national economy, such as smuggling batteries or buying them from candongueiros or, even worse, getting them from South Africans in exchange for critical information about Mozambique.[76]

Carlos Sevene Matsinhe, who was denounced by neighbors in Maputo during Operação Produção, told me that he was a very industrious man. "My family never suffered from hunger because I always provided for them," he told me in front of his small hut in Unango, Niassa Province.[77] From their homes, Matsinhe's neighbors could see that in his house food was never wanting. Matsinhe was a fisherman and could exchange the yields of his fishing for foodstuffs. From the perspective of his less fortunate neighbors, Matsinhe could only be employing illegal methods to be able to provide for his family in a time of tremendous food shortages. Jealous of his fortune, Matsinhe's neighbors accused him of selling secrets to South Africans, who rewarded his traitorous acts with comestibles. This was all too familiar a story during Operação Produção.

In 2015, I interviewed a community of peasants in the rural village of Matama near Lichinga in Niassa. Unlike their counterparts in Unango, who were a mix of victims from the reeducation camps and those of Operação Produção, the villagers of Matama were all victims of the 1983 campaign. They all named the person who led the security brigades to their homes or who was behind their deportation. Alexandre Jorge told me that he had an altercation with the secretary of his bairro in Magoanine in Maputo. The goats of the *camarada secretário,* who lived across the street from Jorge, got into Jorge's machamba and ate his beans. Jorge went to the neighbor to demand reparations, and the conversation turned into a bitter fight. But the camarada secretário had the upper hand. When the campaign began, he

FIGURE 4.4. A resident presents his papers to a search brigade during Operação Produção. A member of the bairro's GD (far right, scratching his nose) accompanies the police officer, who inspects the resident's papers while carrying an AK-47 slung over his shoulder. The GD agent was likely a familiar face to the resident. Photo from *Tempo* (Maputo), July 1983.

found an opportunity to punish Jorge for his audacity in demanding reparations for the damage caused by the goats. "I had documents, but the secretary contributed to my deportation," Jorge said, "When the campaign began, he did not think twice to have me sent here."[78] Alberto Malate told a similar story. He was a txova pusher in Maputo, and like most cart pushers, he had no work card. But his little business was enough to get him and his family by. He was pushing his loaded cart when his neighbor pointed a finger at him, signaling the militias to detain him. "We were neighbors," he said. "The *chefe de quarteirão* was my neighbor, but because I had this little business, which was going well, he did not like me."[79] It is possible that the chefe de quarteirão was simply doing his duty and had no particular grievance with Malate. But this is unlikely, given that who got sent away and who stayed often turned on what kind of relationship residents had with their local authorities. We have no way of knowing whether all the cart pushers of Malate's neighborhood were sent away, but cart pushers did not disappear from Maputo's neighborhoods during or after the campaign. One may be tempted to dismiss Malate's claim that his neighbor was jealous of his success, but as Adam Smith once argued, the world of human action is moved by moral sentiments, jealousy or envy being the strongest among them.[80] Most of my interviewees claimed that envious neighbors played decisive roles in their deportation from Maputo to Niassa during Operação Produção.[81]

People on good terms with local authorities often found ways to evade deportation. For example, Manuel Cossa was saved twice by the secretary of his bairro in Matola. "He knew that I was a good man and twice he sent me back home." A self-employed painter, Manuel Cossa had no documents. But on his third arrest, the secretary could not rescue him again.[82] In some cases, local authorities protected people even if they led a wayward lifestyle. In small towns where local authorities seemed to have enjoyed considerable power, the outcome of the campaign was different. Ananias Tivane was the district political commissar in the agricultural township of Chokwé in Gaza Province during the campaign. He was in charge of the campaign and solicited his subordinates to produce lists of people to be deported from the town. They produced only one list with five people. As he told me, all five people were "foreign" women accused of prostitution. By *foreign* he meant outsiders who immigrated from neighboring districts. Although he knew several unemployed people, including youngsters who in his opinion "should have been sent to reeducation," no native of Chokwé was included on the list. As he put it, "They were using the campaign to get rid of those women for whatever reason. I could not do anything because I was afraid, there is a lot of witchcraft in Chokwé, and I didn't want to upset people." Powerless, Tivane drove the five women away.[83] Clearly, the local GDs took advantage of the campaign to target people they considered undesirable, using a criterion that would have shocked Frelimo authorities who justified sending people to the north as a way of breaking the tribal identities so inimical to nation building. Here, Chokwé GDs were subverting the mantra that "for the nation to be born, the tribe must die" by precisely targeting people they deemed to belong to different subethnic groups. Despite Frelimo's staunch anti-tribal stance, the campaign served tribalist agendas because vigilantes were more inclined to denounce people of different ethnic origins.

The campaign was subverted beyond the control of party authorities and their reformist agenda from the very beginning. In fact, as many reporters observed, to escape deportation, many people of "doubtful conduct" joined the militias and were involved in the cleanup of undesirables identified under their own criteria, not the party's. Reports from various operative brigades in charge of the campaign in Maputo acknowledged that their teams had been infiltrated by people who had no understanding of the directive guiding Operação Produção. As one report from the district of Boane to Maputo's Provincial Operative Command (COP) observed, many officials in charge of carrying out the operation "don't know about the existence of the directive defining vagrancy, prostitution, and this state of things can misconstrue the objectives of 'Operação Produção.'"[84] The campaign was launched without a master plan, and the very government departments that were instructed to carry it out were not informed of its particulars until a week before its commencement. With no time to prepare, COPs and CODs (District Operative Commands) welcomed anyone with enough enthusiasm to get the work done.

News reporters went from verification center to verification center and chose particular cases to highlight the irregularities of the campaign. The case of Mamã Lídia caught the attention of *Tempo* journalist Calisto Muianga, who recognized her as one of his neighbors among the mass of people awaiting trial in a verification center in Maputo. She had been dragged there by her chefe de quarteirão and his assistant, a militiaman named Sonda. Her case was brought to the attention of a mobile team of attorneys sent by the COC (Central Operative Command) to correct mistakes. One attorney asked the chefe de quarteirão why the lady was to be deported. The man pivoted and pointed to his assistant as the party responsible for her detention. Sonda was brought to the verification center to justify Lídia's deportation. His reply was intriguing: "Well . . . I mean . . . it is because this lady has no marriage certificate," he stammered, "and because the man she lives with is not the father of her children. Also, because in our neighborhood she does not greet us, she despises us."[85]

Verification centers across the country were full of cases like Lídia's. Although these kinds of "irregularities" were not necessarily gendered, as both men and women were victimized by authorities seeking to settle personal animosities, women were far more vulnerable.[86] As Kathleen Sheldon observed in her seminal study of women and politics in Mozambique, "Women were less likely to have a waged job that would provide the necessary papers, they were more likely to be illiterate and unable to follow the complicated directions to obtain the proper identification forms, and they generally were more apt to be outside of the bureaucratic structures of the government."[87] Lídia was a widow, a mother of three children, and living with a second husband. She was a housewife with no working papers, and as the reporter noted, she had no idea why she was to be deported. The reporter did not say anything about the exact motivations that led the chefe de quarteirão and militiaman to arrest her. But these two men might have seen her matrimonial situation as an affront, especially because the man she lived with moved into her house instead of taking her to his own. In patriarchal southern Mozambique, marital arrangements like these often aroused public condemnation in local communities. For citizens like Sonda and his colleague, Operação Produção was launched to put an end to similar "dishonorable" situations, not simply to tackle vagrancy and unemployment as party-state authorities proclaimed. Yet, there was also something else in Sonda's nervous justification of Lídia's arrest that suggests a tense relationship between them—perhaps a rejected proposal for an affair. The campaign may well have presented an opportunity for one of the two men who arrested her to either get his revenge or fix a "shameful" problem in his residential block.

The team of attorneys set Lídia free. But they could not oversee all the cases brought to deportation centers by vigilantes who viewed the campaign as a means to punish their own enemies or to settle domestic disputes. In the city of Beira, for example, the father of fifteen-year-old Heroísa Isabel took her to the deportation post himself. According to the reporter who covered the case, the angry father did not want to see his daughter going out with a certain individual, and so he "handed her to the authorities as a prostitute to be sent away." For this strict father, the campaign was a perfect occasion to teach a lesson to an "embarrassing" and "unruly" daughter. As the reporter observed, deportation centers across Beira received several identical cases.[88] A woman deported to Chipembe, Cabo Delgado, said to a press reporter: "I did not marry officially, so in my identity card it is still written 'single.' But I married a long time ago, I have children and everything. I explained this, but they did not listen to me."[89]

As in all previous cleanup campaigns, the government failed to prevent Operação Produção from descending into a juridical shamble, and the real power to deport individuals rested in the hands of urban residents and local authorities who were animated by personal agendas rather than by party ideology. The government's attempts to regain control were often sporadic. For example, in August 1983 the COC issued a new directive determining that the OMM had to take responsibility in dealing with cases related to women, particularly accusations of prostitution, that girls less than sixteen years of age were not required to carry work cards, and those between seventeen and twenty-three, as long as they lived with their parents, should not be deported.[90] In one of his visits to a verification center in Maputo, Armando Guebuza, the chief head of the COC, was shocked to see several pregnant women awaiting deportation to Niassa.[91] Although, on this occasion, the minister ordered the women's release, neither he nor any of the several mobile teams of attorneys could be present in all deportation posts established in the cities. Up until May 1984, when the campaign finally slowed down, local vigilantes continued to arrest and deport people out of personal vendettas and based on independent interpretations of the aims of the campaign. More than police roundups, it was these acts of vigilante citizenship and denunciation that provided the reeducation pipeline its punitive subjects.

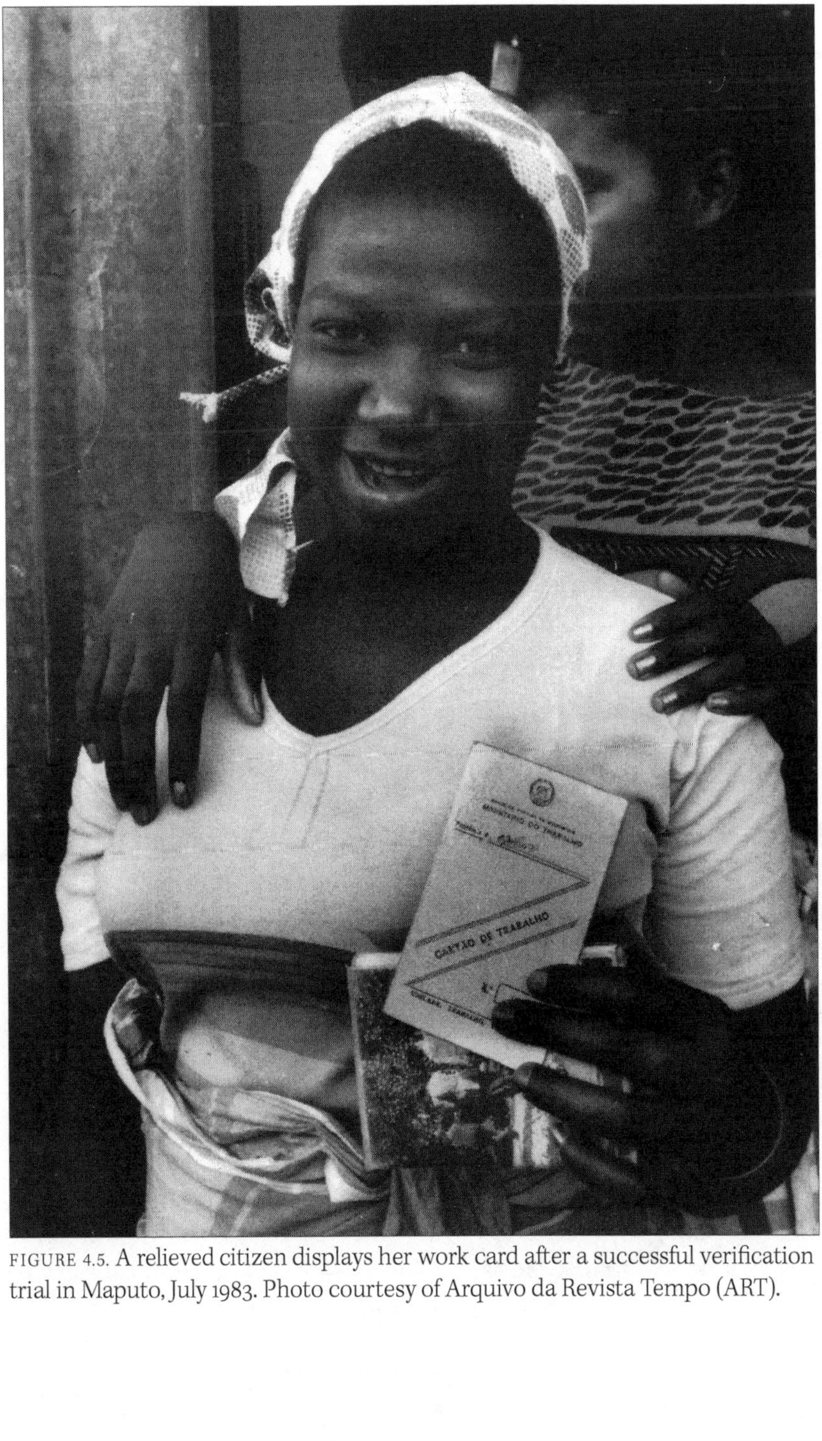

FIGURE 4.5. A relieved citizen displays her work card after a successful verification trial in Maputo, July 1983. Photo courtesy of Arquivo da Revista Tempo (ART).

5 ~ Reeducation Camps, Austerity, and the Carceral Regime

A Portrait from Niassa

IN AUGUST 1976, a reporter from the state-run newspaper *Notícias* visited the women's internment camp of M'sawize in the northern province of Niassa.[1] At the time of the visit, the camp housed 501 detainees. The reporter sought to document the progress that women detained for prostitution had made and to soothe those who doubted the righteousness of Mozambique's reeducation program. As concerns about Frelimo's human rights abuses circulated domestically and internationally, the reporter's lengthy article was meant to counter rumors that the party inflicted macabre punishment within the camps.[2] The reporter began by describing the place, juxtaposing the camp's physical features against the thick expanse of forest that surrounded the site. "A bamboo stick and thatch mark the entrance," he wrote. "Not far away, the first houses of reasonable dimensions plastered with clay and thatched roof; then a large open field." He sketched out the camp's spatial arrangement, which consisted of two parts. One area was reserved for overseers, with housing for warders, a secretariat, a station for radio transmissions, and a refectory. The other contained the detainees' quarters, a "series of sheds arranged length-wise, forming in the background a semicircle." He conceded that the camp's facilities were "very rudimentary pole huts, very exposed to cold." The newsman noted that the huts were "built by *reeducandas* (reeducatees) themselves and by local peasants." Betraying a sense of pride, the reporter observed that the detainees enjoyed a semifree regimen, a privilege that could only be possible in Mozambique, guided as

FIGURE 5.1. Detainees at M'sawize wait for a meal in the camp's refectory, August 1976. Each has her place in line marked by a tin cup and plate on the ground. The *Notícias* reporter stands on the far right. Photo courtesy of Arquivo do Jornal Notícias (AJN).

it was by Frelimo, the magnanimous revolutionary party. "For those who have certain doubts regarding the reeducation camps," the journalist assured, "we can say that there is no fence or enclosure that makes it look like a special camp. In fact, several kilometers away [from the camp], we could see women in reeducation, who moved about without authorization to the people's shop in the village of Msauise [*sic*] or to the Central Military Base to receive visits."[3]

In fact, Mozambique's reeducation camps did not include the features commonly associated with modern internment camps. They lacked erected barriers; they had neither fences nor central watchtowers. In all camps, the number of security personnel remained remarkably low in relation to the inmate population, rendering the surveillance regimen loose indeed. Despite authorities' attempts to control movement, detainees exercised considerable leeway inside and outside the camps. The freedom that the reeducation program apparently afforded detainees struck many observers who visited the camps in the 1970s and early 1980s. They were often left with the impression of having visited a typical rural settlement (*aldeia communal*).[4] Yet, unlike the ujamaa-inspired villages, the camps were inhabited by two groups with distinct visual markers. The group of detainees wore black uniforms and had shaved heads. Warders wore military fatigues and carried AK-47s. Aside from these two ominous features, little in the camps resembled a penal institution.

Given the physical resemblance between communal villages and reeducation camps, it is easy to buy into the false belief that the camps were not special and that they had the same panoptic function as the rural villages. Some scholars have assumed that Mozambique's communal villages served as biopolitical mechanisms of state surveillance, which aimed at rendering peasants "more legible and, thus, more amenable to state intervention."[5] If free villagers were subjected to a panopticon, what can be made, then, of the reporter's observation that the detainees of M'sawize were semifree and inhabited a benevolent place that seemed a detention camp in name only? Were reeducation camps internment camps at all?

The conditions that the reporter encountered in M'sawize, I argue, amounted to neither a panoptical institution nor a humane carceral regime. The freedoms he observed revealed austerity—scarce human and financial resources—which shaped the reeducation program from its inception to its demise. Frelimo authorities *intended* the camps to be strict disciplinary institutions. But they were never able to realize their panoptical ambitions of social and spatial legibility, discipline, order, and ethical transformation because they could not afford to do so. The same was true for communal villages. The sketch of the reeducation camp complex that I draw in this chapter illustrates the gulf that yawned between Frelimo's ambitions and the material conditions in which the reeducation program unfolded. If we are to accept the claims that the communal villages were panoptical, then what the reporter described admirably in M'sawize was a panopticon without sight.

Building on the archival record of Niassa's Department of Reeducation Services (DPSRN, Direcção Provincial dos Serviços de Reeducação do Niassa) and interviews with former detainees, this chapter illuminates a carceral regime whose architects faced human and material constraints. Conditions of austerity, argues Laura Bear, create new relationships and engagements between the state, its agents, and society, which are based on ever-evolving expectations of performance. Austerity yields the expectation that those who occupy the bottom of sociopolitical and economic hierarchies must do more with fewer resources.[6] Without material and human resources to run the reeducation program, state officials compelled detainees to build their own detention facilities, grow their own food, carry out political education on their own, and, in many ways, watch over their own carceral regimen. The detainees' self-surveillance did not arise from an ever-present monitoring eye endowed with modern, biopolitical technology. Rather, this state of affairs reflected the camps' remoteness and the state's inability to support the reeducation program it devised. Consequently, the reeducation program in Mozambique can be understood to have been a do-it-yourself enterprise that produced a penal regime not only distinct from internment camps elsewhere but also contrary to Frelimo's technocratic moralism and panoptical ambitions.

THE REEDUCATION CAMP COMPLEX

On paper, Frelimo established the camps to mentally decolonize and reform so-called wayward members of urban society and putative enemies of the socialist revolution. The party leadership envisioned the camps as pedagogical institutions where reeducatees would be transformed into New Men and New Women through corrective labor, political education, moral rehabilitation, and cultural enlightenment.[7] A month before the reporter's visit to M'sawize, President Machel instructed his top cabinet officers within the Council of Ministers "to give further attention" to the reeducation program. He stated that the camps should be designated to correct certain crimes and that reeducatees should be classified and interned according to their offenses. Pursuant to Machel's command, the Council envisioned camps specifically for drug addicts, prostitutes, drunkards, vagrants, the undisciplined, thieves, and so on. "Our general concern," the president said, "is to transform the Old Man into the New Man, to transform society. Now, all we need is to find the adequate means to achieve this goal."[8] To succeed in transforming "old men" into "new men," camp overseers were to be diligent gatherers of knowledge, observing the behavior of each detainee and recording improvement.[9] What Machel called for was a disciplinary institution akin to a modern, well-functioning pedagogical penitentiary.

Initially, the Ministry of the Interior (MINT) attempted to follow presidential instructions and intern detainees according to criminal categories. For example, in Niassa, the camps of M'sawize and Ilumba were reserved for prostitutes. Naisseco, also in Niassa, held "individuals considered drug addicts."[10] Chiputo and M'telela (in Niassa) and Chaimite (in Cabo Delgado) were established for Frelimo dissidents. This organizational scheme did not persist, however, and the reeducation camp complex rapidly descended into disorder. The camp of Sacudzo in Sofala Province held more than a thousand detainees, among them street children, nonconvicted thieves, undocumented civilians who failed to produce ID cards during police roundups, and sacked civil servants (including teachers, "undisciplined" soldiers, and police officers).[11] In Ruarua, common criminal offenders shared barracks with Frelimo guerrillas who had deserted during the liberation war. The Chicomo camp in Gaza Province contained 750 detainees, incarcerated on a wide range of charges.[12] Even M'telela, a camp designed for prominent political prisoners and meant to hold no more than 130 inmates, received those found guilty of common-law offenses. In general, each camp's inmate population comprised people from all over the country who had been detained by the state for all kinds of alleged wrongdoing.

With few personnel to run the reeducation program, the party-state vested the power to detain and distribute detainees throughout the camp complex in low-ranking officers who worked at the ground level. The party's rank and file often dispatched suspects to camps without trial or consultation with more senior authorities. MINT's lack of a centralized, bureaucratic body muddled the camp complex until the end of Mozambique's socialist experiment. The creation in 1976 of the Direcção Nacional dos Serviços de Reeducação (National Directorate of Reeducation Services, DNSR)—almost two years after the first camps opened—did little to remedy the challenges. The DNSR and its provincial subdivisions, the DPSRs (Provincial Departments of Reeducation Services), were understaffed and largely on the sidelines in deciding where detainees should go.[13] Given that anybody—from the highest-ranking officer to the lowest agent—could condemn others to reeducation without reporting to MINT and without needing to produce documentation, the government could never coordinate the process. In the end, the local DPSR decided where to send detainees. Since most people had not been formally sentenced and therefore lacked written records of their offenses (at least until 1980, that is, before the Ofensiva), they were arbitrarily distributed across the camps. Neither security nor DPSR officers had the time or the qualifications to conduct formal interrogations. In 1980, MINT attempted to organize the reeducation program by appointing a more capable officer, José Castiano Zumbire, to head the DNSR. Despite Zumbire's efforts, the camps continued to lack order with respect to how authorities distributed and classified detainees.[14]

Transportation to the camps further betrayed the system's lack of organization. Although MINT held jurisdiction over the reeducation program, its functions often coincided with those of the Ministry of Defense and SNASP (Serviço Nacional de Segurança Popular). It is unclear how these three organs made decisions to bring detainees to the camps, but each operated an eclectic network of military planes, trucks, and buses, which carried detainees to the country's far reaches without coordination. The government occasionally repurposed private and public buses to ferry incoming detainees. Army air bases built for the Portuguese counterinsurgency in the 1960s served as the main sites of operations. Flights in Russian-built cargo planes, known as Antanov, seem to have been employed to transport detainees from Maputo and Beira to the far north. But the camps' remoteness invariably meant a long journey. Equipped with inadequate means, security operatives had no choice but to be inventive. They often transported detainees under cover of night. Although most detainees knew that they were being sent to a reeducation camp, no one knew which one. From the moment of arrest to deportation, authorities gave detainees no information about their fate. By denying detainees a sense of their geographical position, reeducation authorities reduced the likelihood of escape during the trip and at the destination. Carlos Fumo, whom SNASP sent to Ruarua in Cabo Delgado, narrated the transportation tactics in our interview:

> After two weeks at Maputo's central prison, we were taken to the airport at dawn. We were all frightened, for we didn't know where we were going. They kept us at the army airbase. We saw army soldiers walking up and down, and nobody talked to us, so we had no idea what was going on. Suddenly, an Antanov arrived around 5 a.m. and we boarded. We arrived in Cabo Delgado at about 2 p.m. When we landed, they hid us in the bush inside the airport. We only knew that we were in Cabo Delgado thanks to a plate with the name of the province behind the bushes. Yet we still didn't know where we were going. At about 7 or 8 p.m. a military truck arrived and the armed soldiers shoved us inside the tailgate. We drove for hours and arrived at the site at 1 a.m. The camp commander came, looked at us in the eye, and went back to his office. We had not eaten or drunken anything since we left Maputo. Although the camp didn't have that many people, there were no rooms for us to sleep. There were no lodgings for newcomers. We spent the night in the open. Before sunrise they woke us up to march as soldiers, and later we went into the forest to cut down the bamboos to build our huts.[15]

Reeducation authorities often hid detainees in bushes because army airbases were located inside civilian airports and lacked space to await transportation to the camps. Preventing anxious and exhausted detainees from discovering their whereabouts posed a challenge to security operatives. And so, too, did taking them from the aircraft to the camps. In Niassa, an automobile trip from the provincial city of Lichinga to M'sawize (which takes three to four hours on a paved road) could take one to two days.[16] With no paved roads and with frequent interruptions to either repair the vehicles, which broke down amid rough, unpaved tracks, or to apprehend desperate detainees who attempted escape, the journey taxed captors as well as captives.[17] To help the guards pass time and ease tension, the travelers sang Frelimo anthems that celebrated the liberation saga and its heroes and mocked traitors and counterrevolutionaries. Silva Santana, a SNASP officer tasked with transporting detainees to Niassa and Cabo Delgado, recalled in our interview: "Before the civil war we traveled by bus, singing all the way. We initiated the songs and they had to sing along." For women, the journey to reeducation camps was more perilous. In the deserted sand tracks that led to M'sawize and Ilumba, far away from the public gaze, army guards often targeted female detainees for sexual assault. As Silva Santana told me, soldiers "took advantage of the girls along the way by forcing them into sex."[18] The torment of the journey—hunger, exhaustion, exposure to nature's elements, and cruel exploitation—presaged the reeducation program itself.

With very few exceptions, detainees built the camp infrastructure themselves. They collected logs from nearby forests to erect their huts. In Niassa and Cabo Delgado, they then plastered the open sides with mud, as local villagers would have done. But this labor-intensive task took longer to complete. In the two women's camps, the walls seem never to have been finished through the early 1980s, when camps were shuttered. In southern and central Mozambique, detainee huts were simply built with reeds. Such hasty and basic accommodations did little to protect detainees from weather conditions and natural threats—cold in the winter nights, snake bites on hot days, and other mortal hazards.[19] Although conditions across camps varied to some extent, the camps universally lacked comfort. Detainees slept on bare, sandy ground. Those who knew carpentry built wooden bed frames. Although the frames were rougher than the floor, they at least separated detainees from snakes and biting insects. In Niassa, the great nightmare was the cold. Even in men's camps, where walls were plastered, the mud often dissolved in rain or dried and peeled off. Few detainees had the strength to undertake the painstaking work of replastering the huts. The permanent struggle to find food in the hunger-stricken camps precluded such work. Consequently, most lodgings were left unprotected on the sides (see figure 6.2). Malarial mosquitoes and tsetse flies (responsible for trypanosomiasis, also known as sleeping sleekness) pervaded the barracks and found plenty of blood on which to feast. Camp overseers lived amid similarly inadequate conditions.

The layout of camp lodgings accorded with Frelimo's high-modernist ideal of how rural settlements should look in socialist Mozambique, with geometrically aligned, rectangular- or square-shaped houses. Communal villages were arranged in a similar fashion, with straight lines and a large central square reserved for the people's revolutionary activities.[20] The rectangular barracks within reeducation camps similarly opened to a square area known as *rassemblement*. A French term meaning "to assemble" or "to gather," *rassemblement* arrived in Frelimo's vernacular via the first group of guerrillas to train in Algeria in 1963. Like the village square, the rassemblement occupied the center of the camp's collective life. Meetings, roll calls, parades, cultural performances, and public punishment took place there.

To complement the camp's regular layout, detainees wore black uniforms. Each person received two pairs of khaki pants, two long- or short-sleeved shirts, a cap, and a pair of canvas boots. The black uniforms seem to have first been used by colonial security forces, most likely for recruits in training. It is possible that MINT found the supply in storage and repurposed the uniforms for reeducatees. No other color was better suited for the fallen urbanites sent to the countryside to be purified of their sins. Among other implications, the black uniform symbolized the state of suspended citizenship in which detainees lived (as a reeducatee, one lost all civil rights). At the same time, the uniform allowed party officers to exert control over inmates. The uniforms, then, represented perhaps the only palpable attempt to enforce within the camps a systematic order and to render the detainees legible. Peasant populations living near the camps were instructed to be vigilant and to inform authorities whenever they saw people dressed in black wandering about without armed guards. The uniform also gave camp life the military semblance that Frelimo authorities wanted to see.[21]

Camp authorities found it difficult, however, to keep all detainees in uniforms. The shortage in consumer goods that characterized the Mozambican economy made clothing a luxury, especially in rural areas. When the stock of uniforms ran out in the reeducation program's first two years, it was not replenished. By 1978, in most camps, detainees wore whatever they could find. Only on special occasions, such as a visit by a state official, did authorities demand that detainees wear their black uniforms. On such instances, camp overseers made sure that those detainees with better- or well-kept uniforms sat in the front and relegated those with more ragged uniforms to the back. Lack of soap and sewing materials made it nearly impossible to preserve the uniforms, much less to maintain good hygiene. The literal concept of uniformity became a matter of performance, enacted for those high in the state hierarchy to see. Austerity, instead of producing diligent reformers, compelled camp authorities to become managers who cultivated the appearance of uniformity. For the government, dressing detainees in the extremely impoverished countryside, where local populations still lived largely half-naked, also became fraught. Most of my interviewees recalled shocking encounters with nearly naked peasants in the villages close to their camps and the envy with which they were often met because of their "good looks" in black fatigues. In Niassa and Cabo Delgado, for example, detainees were known as *mkunya woripa,* or "white blacks." As former detainee Ché Mafuiane told me, "*Mkunya woripa* means that the person is black but at the same time he is white because he was dressed."[22] The label *white* does not refer to race here but rather to social status. For the Macua-speaking people in northern Mozambique's remote corners, the detainees represented relative privilege because they were dressed and "looked good" in their black garments. On the one hand, their perception was a clear indication of the scarcity and neglect in which local populations lived. On the other, it highlighted the cultural and social differences between the rural people of the northern provinces, where most camps were established, and the detainees, who had resided mostly in urban areas. That these urbanites—who appeared privileged to their rural counterparts—had to be fed and dressed by the state must have caused a great deal of confusion.

NIASSA AND THE AUSTERITY OF CAMP ADMINISTRATION

Niassa, the primary location for transforming Mozambique's anti-social elements and enemies of the revolution into New Men and New Women, was sui generis. Of the eight provinces that had reeducation camps, Niassa contained a record number of eight (see maps 0.1 and 5.1). When the party closed camps in all provinces targeted by the fast-spreading Renamo insurgency in 1981–82, Niassa became the sole nexus of reeducation. The need to populate this expansive and sparsely inhabited territory explains why the party established most camps there.[23] Niassa is both the largest and least inhabited of all Mozambique's provinces. Years of intensive slave trade, military raids by Ngoni armies from Mfecane-troubled Zululand, and the European wars of conquest in the late nineteenth century and early twentieth century contributed to the low population density of present-day Niassa.[24] The thirty-five years of plunder under the chartered Niassa Company (1891–1926) not only worsened local inhabitants' plight but also entrenched Niassa's status as the least developed corner of Mozambique (a ranking that the province holds to this day). Many people fled the violence by migrating west into Malawi and north into Tanzania. It is estimated that between 1920 and 1930, more than three hundred thousand people abandoned the area.[25] At the time of independence, only four hundred thousand people inhabited the extensive territory of 129,000 square kilometers (50,000 square miles).[26] At the same time, Niassa, together with the province of Cabo Delgado, enjoyed the status of sanctuary for the ruling party. It was in both provinces that Frelimo consolidated its liberated areas during the armed struggle. Niassa and Cabo Delgado were therefore perfect locations to anoint the urban *xiconhocas* in the liberation's holy land. Yet, the Portuguese colonial regime had often banished undesirables to Niassa because of its remoteness. The reeducation program only reinforced a long-held perception that Niassa was a place of punishment.[27]

However, Niassa proved a great challenge for DPSRN bureaucrats tasked with running the camps. The Direcção Provincial dos Serviços de Reeducação do Niassa (Provincial Directorate of Reeducation Services of Niassa) was established in early 1976 as part of MINT's first attempt to organize the reeducation program. The department reported directly to MINT and to the local governor, making the program doubly subordinated. Except for the governor and the local security units (the police and the army), the department kept the camps' locations and administrative matters secret even from members of Niassa's executive body and provincial assembly.[28] According to MINT directives, the department had to submit monthly reports to the ministry and to the governor, documenting conditions on the ground. While camp commanders supplied the department with information for the reports, DPSRN directors made frequent journeys into the province's far reaches to assess the camps for themselves. It is their efforts that offer a glimpse of life inside the camps and the challenges that camp authorities faced in realizing Frelimo's salvationist ideals. Although the camps did not all function in the same manner, as most of the rules depended on both geographic location and individual camp overseers, the picture that emerges of Niassa's camps is generally representative of the entire reeducation complex.

Initially, the DPSRN was responsible for overseeing five reeducation camps: Naisseco (Revia), Chiputo, M'sawize, Ilumba, and M'telela. Although M'telela's high-profile detainees formally fell under SNASP's exclusive responsibility, the DPSRN functionally assumed charge. In 1976, the five camps held over two thousand inmates in total. But in the same way as the number of inmates fluctuated, the number of camps also varied over time. In November 1978, MINT opened a second camp for male detainees in M'sawize, very close to the women's camp already there.[29] The Naisseco detainees were initially held in Revia, from where they were moved due to the former camp's unhealthy location. They were again moved in early 1979 to Unango, the site of an old military garrison and penitentiary, thirty kilometers from Lichinga. After the presidential Ofensiva of 1979 and 1981 and the resulting wave of amnesties, Chiputo, Unango, and M'sawize closed, and the inmates—most of whom were forbidden from returning to their original homes—were compelled to stay and transform their former camps into Cities of the Future. Yet, as the government shuttered some camps, it broke ground on others. Muoco, for example, was likely established in 1981 for expelled police officers, though it never featured in DPSRN reports.

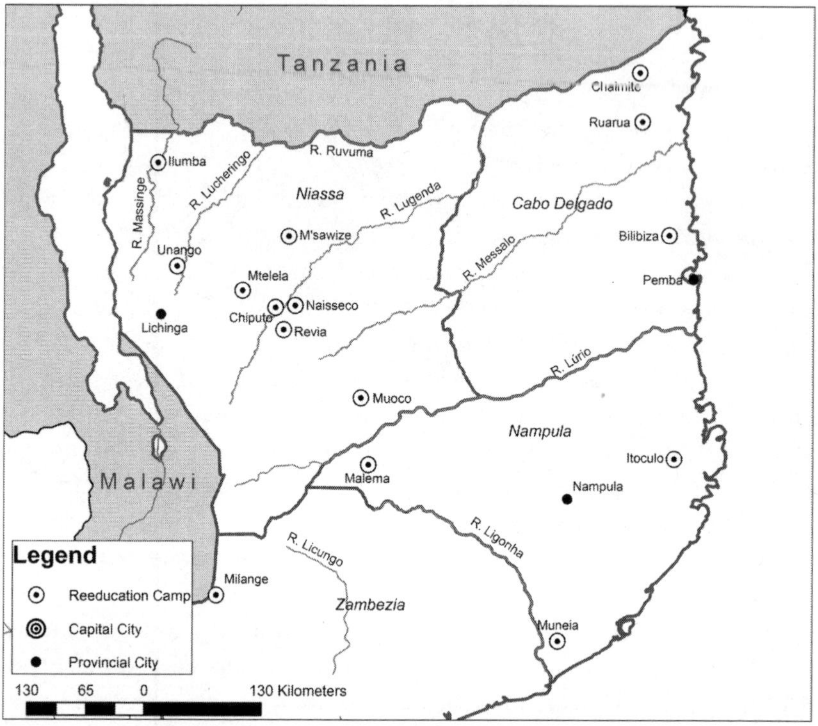

MAP 5.1. The reeducation camp complex of northern Mozambique. Niassa Province housed the greatest number of camps (eight). Courtesy of Clark Library, University of Michigan

The DPSRN occupied a small office in Lichinga's single government building. Two of its most diligent and prolific directors, Francisco Taibo and André Trabuco, recorded much of its bureaucratic work. Their reports include many complaints about the difficulties of administering the camps. It is from them that we know that the DPSRN lacked basic equipment and was chronically short of personnel. In May 1976, the department had only seven staff members and no typewriter. To produce its reports and attend to the camps' vast needs, the DPSRN had to borrow a typewriter, which only became available when other departments did not need the precious machine. The department possessed a total of seven vehicles, of which five trucks were to carry rations and detainees. But only two trucks were operational, and the rest were reported to be damaged "due to the rough roads" of Niassa.[30] Most DPSRN vehicles were abandoned along the tracks leading to the camps while the department waited for spare parts. In his report of May 1976, Taibo requested repairs for broken vehicles and reminded MINT in Maputo that his request was urgent, so that "the camps do not feel abandoned."[31] Until his tenure ended later that year, MINT had not replied to his correspondence, and most of DPSRN's vehicles remained out of commission. His substitute, Trabuco, was also met with silence as he pressed the capital for urgent assistance.[32]

Unable to provide the DPSRN with equipment to run the reeducation camps, MINT chose not to respond. It is possible that MINT clerks were wrestling with other state departments responsible for distributing equipment and goods to other state entities beyond the reeducation complex. But there was very little to distribute in a young country with so many acute demands. As the reeducation camp complex came into being and the camp population grew, Frelimo also confronted the twin challenges of stabilizing the country amid transition and governing with few qualified cadres. The threat of military invasion by Rhodesia and South Africa loomed. Abandoned schools, hospitals, and factories required immediate attention. As the government allocated insufficient resources, reeducation camps slipped to the bottom. And among the ten provinces, none was lower in priority than Niassa. Most supplies—from staple items such as clothing, soap, cooking oil, and sugar to administrative necessities such as paper, pencils, typewriter ink, and so on—had to be shipped from the capital at the country's southern tip. Niassa residents suffered from chronic shortages. Rural areas were the worst off, in Niassa and elsewhere across Mozambique. Located in the most remote areas, reeducation camps were thus at the lowest extreme of Frelimo's thin chain of resource allocation. MINT ignored the reports of DPSRN directors and similarly gave little regard to the provincial governor. The two DPSRN directors received the full support of Governor Manave, who often signed the reports they wired to Maputo. Sometimes the governor added a note of his own, reiterating the DPSRN complaints and highlighting the urgency of the directors' request for basic tools needed by the department.[33] The Niassa reeducation department's archive testifies to the exhaustion of understaffed and ill-equipped bureaucrats, who labored within the material constraints of a nation in crisis. As the years passed, DPSRN directors did not bother to elaborate on the difficulties they faced. They reproduced old reports and stamped them with a new date. After 1977, they ceased to meet their monthly deadlines. One report soon accounted for three months, sometimes more. Lacking paper and ink for the typewriter, by 1979 they stopped writing altogether. Overburdened MINT authorities in the capital seemed to have neither noticed nor cared.[34]

By necessity, DPSRN operatives and camp administrators assumed multiple roles and employed detainees in the day-to-day task of running the camps. According to MINT directives, each camp was to include five responsáveis, each with a deputy who managed specific aspects of camp life. The five responsáveis included a chief of the camp (the highest position within the camp), a military camp commander, a political commissar responsible for political education and ideological indoctrination, a responsável for agricultural production, and a responsável for cultural activities. The camps were also meant to have a secretariat, which would include at least one or two typists to produce the required monthly reports.[35] Generally, the chief of the camp and his deputy were police officers on the MINT payroll, as were the typists. The rest of the responsáveis and warders were former Frelimo guerrillas and veterans of the liberation struggle who had little academic instruction and who were on the Ministry of Defense's payroll. The number of warders to staff in each camp was never specified. But the general consensus—even among the central government's top members—was that the camps were alarmingly short of guards and qualified overseers. For example, in July 1976, the Council of Ministers proposed training at least a hundred camp overseers. The Council presented this number as an initial, urgent necessity but stressed that, in the long run, the camps would need more cadres.[36] During the First National Seminar on Reeducation held in Maputo in November 1976, MINT proposed a two- to three-month training program for camp overseers. The training package was to include political education, sociology, psychology, administration and bookkeeping, mathematics, geography, and constitutional law.[37] Talks by high-ranking party officers and guided visits to productive units were to supplement the program. Camp overseers would become well versed in farming practices (including husbandry of small animals), production planning, storage and food-conservation techniques, hygiene and first aid, and sports and cultural activities.[38]

If MINT was aware of the resources and technical training necessary to run the reeducation program, the ministry failed to deliver on its ambitious plans. As Rhodesia's aggression toward Mozambique escalated into a civil war, the conflict consumed almost all newly recruited security cadres.[39] With its priorities elsewhere, the government recruited no new professional camp supervisors for the reeducation program. The training program remained a desk initiative. In M'sawize, the chief commander Silência David and her deputy, Judite Florêncio, commanded a platoon of seventeen female guards. The few warders guarded and sought to reeducate 501 inmates. Such disproportionate ratios were present in almost all reeducation camps, where a handful of soldiers guarded hundreds of detainees.[40] In the Chicomo camp in Gaza Province, commander Jaime Rebich had fifteen soldiers to guard 750 inmates.[41] Yet, it was not only guards who were in short supply. The camps also lacked responsáveis. In Niassa, only one camp, Chiputo, could fill the five designated positions. In the rest,

FIGURE 5.2. Detainees and a warder pose for a photograph in Unango, unknown date. This photo was taken during the construction of one of the camp's barracks. The detainees wore fodder sacks while working to avoid damaging their uniforms—the only clothes they had. That only one armed warder is pictured suggests that there were very few in the camp. Photo courtesy of Arquivo da Revista Tempo (ART).

overseers took on two or more positions, often serving as commanders, political commissars, and responsáveis for production.[42] Whereas the capital's political leadership dreamed of specialized and professional reeducators, austerity forced camp authorities to improvise. Their impromptu decisions not only combined and collapsed various responsibilities but also corroded the camp's hierarchy.

To alleviate the shortage of guards, overseers appointed detainees to serve as auxiliaries to patrol units. Fellow reeducatees pejoratively called these detainee-guards Gatos Vermelhos (Red Cats).[43] Other fortunate detainees were appointed to positions as administrative assistants, teachers, and heads of working platoons. These positions elevated detainees to a level of respectability among their warders. They were also exempted from some of the most taxing and menial activities, such as farming and felling trees, and they enjoyed more freedom to move in and out of the camp.[44] The environment that the *Notícias* newsman found so reassuring in M'sawize—with detainees coming and leaving at will—revealed the shortages that organically shaped and conditioned Mozambique's reeducation camps, not the ruling party's magnanimous ethos.

The porous nature of the carceral regimen, however, should not be taken to mean that detainees had total freedom. Camp overseers instituted other forms of authority to keep the internees within camp vicinities and to prevent escape. The semifree women that the *Notícias* reporter saw along the road that linked M'sawize with the nearby village could only travel in that open stretch of Mavago District. The camps' remote location, coupled with the fact that transportation occurred in the dark, kept detainees confined. Like most camps in Niassa, Cabo Delgado, Nampula, and Sofala Provinces, M'sawize was established in an unmarked forest—in this case, within the country's largest hunting reserve (Reserva de Caça do Niassa). The reserve is well known for its lions and other dangerous fauna.[45] The camp was some three hours' walking distance from the nearest village. To reach the provincial city of Lichinga by foot took two to three days. The area had been one of Frelimo's *zonas libertadas* during the armed struggle, and the party maintained a small military base (Base Central) hundreds of miles away from the camp. Local communities were often instructed to report to authorities if detainees came to their villages.

Many detainees attempted to flee, and some successfully navigated the forests and attained the freedom they longed for. Generally, those escapees who prevailed were locals familiar with the area. With their fluency in local vernaculars, they could convince villagers to let them go or even alleviate their thirst and hunger along the perilous journey.[46] But these were exceptional cases. Most detainees did not dare brave the wilderness because they knew neither the local geography nor the languages. The dangers of the forest and fear of predators served to keep detainees in line. In June 1976, the administrator of Niassa's Majune District informed the DPSRN that eight detainees had fled from Naisseco. One of them, João Manhiça, was "eaten by a lion and we do not know about the other seven."[47] Manuela Nascimento, who worked for Niassa's Caritas (an international humanitarian organization of the Catholic Church) and visited most reeducation camps, told me that her traveling team often had to stop to bury human remains. "Sometimes it was only half the body," she recalled, "or just the bones."[48] Camp overseers publicized these chilling cases to discourage escape attempts. Sometimes, to inspire fear of the bush, overseers forced detainees to bury the partial and disfigured remains of their devoured companions.[49]

In describing the elements that underpin a panoptic institution, Michel Foucault remarked: "Full lighting and the eye of a supervisor capture better than darkness, which ultimately protected. Visibility is a trap."[50] Mozambique's reeducation camps inverted the features of such an institution. Frelimo's complex was a blind panopticon that relied on the camps' remote location, wild surroundings, and the terrors of nighttime in the bush to keep its subjects in line. Few urbanites dared to confront the roaring of lions, the growling of hyenas, and the shrill of owls.[51] The camps' locations were, for the most part, enough of an obstacle to curb escapes. Therefore, control within the camps hinged neither on the "monitoring eye" of state agents and armed guards nor on the square-shaped huts and rassemblement that formed their architectural apparatus. Rather, it rested in the camps' remoteness and the detainees remaining ignorant of their location. This logic explains why it was crucial that detainees not learn where they were to be transported. Likewise, it accounts for the absence of maps within the camps. In most cases, maps were forbidden even among wardens. As one former detainee in Sacudzo recalled, even lectures on Mozambique's geography were delivered without a map.[52] Here, the interplay between austerity and a fragile carceral regime came into focus. Mortal threats in the natural world, menaces that lurked in the night—these were the techniques of surveillance that shaped Mozambique's reeducation camps. In the context of extreme austerity, the dangers of the wilderness did the work of surveillance.

THE SOCIAL COMPOSITION OF THE INMATE POPULATION

For camp authorities forced to do so much with so few resources, the inmate population's social composition exacerbated the challenge of keeping detainees in line and in conformity with the reeducation program. As DPSRN director André Trabuco impressed upon his superiors in the capital, the party predicated the reeducation program on detainees acknowledging their wrongdoing. Repentance and self-transformation were only possible if detainees accepted their guilt and appreciated why they received such harsh treatment in the reeducation camps. Of course, the entire enterprise made a fruitless mockery of the humane principles that ostensibly underpinned Frelimo's revolutionary project.[53] From the reeducation program's inception, camp overseers in Niassa and elsewhere realized that the people they were to transform into New Men and New Women should never have been arrested.

When the *Notícias* reporter visited M'sawize in 1976, he did not speak to any of the 501 detainees who watched him walk around the premises with a mix of amusement and fear. The newsman was only allowed to speak to the camp's chief commander. Although he did not mention her name in his lengthy article, DPSRN reports reveal that she was Silência David.[54] Upon his arrival, the reporter was greeted with revolutionary chants and folk dances: "At the center for meetings," he noted, "a few hundred women wearing mostly black uniforms sang songs and danced."[55] The

FIGURE 5.3. Female reeducatees welcome the *Notícias* reporter in M'sawize, August 1976. Their hair was cut short in an attempt to clear away the signs of urban degradation and alienation (wigs and straightened hair). While some wear a black uniform, others are dressed in their usual clothes. Photo courtesy of Arquivo do Jornal Notícias (AJN).

three photographs that accompanied his news article were small in size and afforded only a partial glimpse of the inmates. But the original photographs, which I found in the *Notícias* archive in Maputo, give a better view of the women. One of them shows some reeducatees seated in an unwalled hut that served as a refectory, and a line of metal dishes on top of small tins used as drinking cups (figure 5.1). The reporter, who was cut off in the photograph that the newspaper published, is standing nearby. In the news article, a caption indicates that each dish marked an inmate's place in the line for the eagerly awaited meal. Some reeducatees wore black uniform shirts—or what remained of them. Others—who most probably arrived after the uniforms had run out—had capulanas tied in place of trousers or wore ordinary clothes. Another photograph, which was not published with the news article, shows inmates clapping and singing (figure 5.3). Their faces are close to the camera. Most are young. Their eyes and facial expressions transmit something that I cannot quite read. No one smiles. They were surely singing and clapping against their will. All had their hair shorn—it had been cut off as soon as they arrived in the camp in an attempt to eliminate the signs of degeneration and alienation (wigs and straightened hair) supposedly bred by the corrupting urban environment from where they hailed.

Mozambican and international journalists produced several similar portraits. Although instructive, they present only a mass of nameless people living in desperation. The portraits say nothing about their individual stories. We know, for example, that at least four camps—namely, M'telela and Chiputo in Niassa, and Chaimite and Ruarua in Cabo Delgado—held political prisoners and Frelimo deserters. Yet these camps also received the urban anti-socials who constituted most detainees. Who, then, were these reeducatees, and under which charges were they being held captive? What do we know about their age, marital status, professional occupation, and place of origin? Seeking answers to these questions not only illuminates the argument of this chapter but also serves to recover the reeducation complex's nameless victims.

In 1978, the DPSRN compiled several lists that included details about 827 detainees from the Naisseco and M'sawize camps. The authors' goal was to alert Governor Manave and MINT authorities in Maputo of the arbitrary ways in which most detainees were arrested in their places of origin and the offenses for which they were being held indefinitely in the camps.[56] Although they proposed the release of all 827 detainees, they made clear that their list showed that there was a much larger problem in Niassa's reeducation camp complex. While speaking of selected detainees, these exceptional records illustrate the social composition of Niassa's inmate population, which can be used to extrapolate broader characteristics that defined the whole reeducation camp complex in Mozambique.

In their illustrative sample of 827 detainees, DPSRN officials counted 580 men and 247 women. They came from every province in Mozambique, although Maputo and the neighboring town of Xai-Xai in Gaza Province predominated. The place of origin for sixty-three detainees was not indicated. Although most inmates were single, the number of married people of either gender was considerable. At least 203 male detainees were listed as married and 267 as single. There were 147 single women and 90 recorded as married. The inmate population skewed young, with an average age of about twenty-five years. Excluding infants living with their detained mothers, detainees' ages ranged from ten to seventy-seven. Given the high levels of illiteracy that carried through the first years of independence, many detainees did not know their exact age when asked. Table 5.2 illustrates that the illiteracy rate was higher among female detainees than their male counterparts. The youngest male detainee in Naisseco was ten-year-old Carlos Vasco Machel from Chibuto (Gaza), who was "falsely suspected of theft."[57] The oldest male reeducatee was Zacarias Cossa, aged seventy-seven, who was condemned for manslaughter in Maputo—the gravest crime to appear on all lists.[58] Among the female detainees, the youngest were two girls, Elisa Fernando and Georgina Macone, both aged fifteen. One was detained for an unknown transgression; the other for prostitution. The oldest *reeducanda* was Elina Tembe, aged fifty-three. She was detained in Maputo for "selling alcoholic drinks."[59]

TABLE 5.1. MARITAL STATUS OF 827 DETAINEES FROM M'SAWIZE AND NAISSECO

Marital Status	Men	Women
Single	304	147
Married/Amancebadas	203	90
Divorced/Separated	1	1
Widowed	5	7
Undeclared	52	17

TABLE 5.2. AGE OF 827 DETAINEES FROM M'SAWIZE AND NAISSECO

Age (Years)	Men	Women
10–17	52	15
18–25	198	52
26–35	103	31
36–45	61	13
46–55	64	7
56–65	27	0
66–75	9	0
Over 76	1	0
Unknown	65	129
Total	580	247

The offenses for which the 827 detainees on the lists were held captive encompassed a miscellaneous body of petty trivialities, from minor theft, adultery, and fights with relatives and neighbors to drinking alcohol and smoking hemp. But the majority were undocumented urbanites who failed to produce identification papers during roundups in places of leisure. Among the female detainees, the most common causes for detention were prostitution, marital disputes, and adultery. Yet the overwhelming majority of female detainees (135 in total) were held without any known offense. Their offense record reads as *motivo desconhecido* (unknown) or *sem motivo* (without offense).

TABLE 5.3. OFFENSES OF 827 DETAINEES FROM M'SAWIZE AND NAISSECO

Offense	Men	Women
Undocumented during roundups	170	28
Unknown	55	135
Alcohol and cannabis (production, consumption, and sale)	84	0
Prostitution	0	58
Minor theft	46	0
Suspected theft	43	0
Vagrancy, gambling, unemployment	31	5
Theft of cattle	24	0
Fights with neighbors, friends, relatives	22	29
Corruption (sexual and moral), adultery, marital disputes	22	18
Discord with Grupo Dinamizador or local authorities	15	7
Fencing (dealing in stolen goods) or black marketeering	8	0
Work-related	6	0
Possession of foreign currency (SA rand) or illegal border crossing	5	0
Traditional healing and sorcery	4	0
Political dissent or speaking ill of the party/leaders	4	0
Comprometido (PIDE agent)	1	0
Religious fanaticism or Jehovah's Witness	1	0
Serious theft	1	0
Murder or rape	0	0
Other	5	0
Total of recorded offenses	547	280

Most of the offenses for which people had been arrested were so trivial to that DPSRN officers did not conceal their outrage and disappointment about such detentions. Francisco António Manuel, a fisherman from the coastal town of Quelimane in Zambézia Province, was arrested because "he pushed somebody in the line for bread" (*empurrou uma pessoa na bixa do pão*). Manuel, forty-two years old and married, arrived in Naisseco on January 25, 1975. When DPSRN documented his case, he had been in detention for three years. Marcelo Francisco, a twenty-one-year-old resident of Beira, was serving an indefinite sentence in Naisseco "for entering the premises of the custom services without permission." Similarly, António Chavane, sixteen, was found wandering in the vicinity of Maputo's airport, for which he was sent to Niassa. Security operatives had found Sebastião Gabito Mazive, a self-employed locksmith, in the rubbish hill of Hulene, Maputo, while he was scavenging for scrap metal to use in his workshop. Unable to produce an ID and a work card, he was taken as a vagrant to Niassa.[60] The camps generally held undocumented victims of the cleanup campaigns against vagrancy and alcoholism, irrespective of their age, for several years. Carlos Bassequete, sixty-three years old, was detained for "vagrancy and for having no profession." Fernando Rafael, fifty-one, from Chipungabera in Sofala, "was found sleeping in the market." Fifty-two-year-old Cristina Magaia, like Elina Tembe, was detained for "producing alcoholic drinks" in Maputo. And fifty-year-old Luís Chibaquela Chissicu was "found drunk on the street" in Maputo. His intemperance earned him an indefinite sentence in Naisseco. In 1977, he had been detained for two years.[61]

Many people were serving sentences under unproven allegations of minor theft. Since no indictments were produced and no judicial hearings were held before 1980, suspicion amounted to conviction. Filipe Mucotonheni, who could not give his exact age when questioned by DPSRN officers, "was accused of stealing sugar." João Timbana, from the village of Marracuene in Maputo Province, "was accused of stealing potatoes." Twenty-year-old Rodrigues Ndzeco, also from Maputo, was "accused of stealing a radio." Valente Joaquim, thirty-one, from Niassa, "was accused of losing a pig" under his care. And twelve-year-old José Macavana from Bairro Infulene in Maputo was arrested for suspicion of "stealing 200 Escudos," or roughly six dollars.[62] They all spent three years in reeducation.

Even for those detainees who confessed to their felonies, the penalty far exceeded the alleged crime. For example, fifteen-year-old Samuel Afani "stole two chickens" when he was thirteen. When interrogated in 1978, two years had passed since he arrived in Naisseco.[63] Most of the confessed crimes consisted of stealing cattle in the rural areas near Maputo (Ressano Garcia and Moamba) or of buying illegal goods (particularly clothing and appliances). The party considered carrying foreign currency, particularly rand from neighboring apartheid South Africa, a grave crime. A fifty-eight-year-old miner named Rafael Mucave paid heavily for being "found with lots of money on his return from South Africa."[64] Although the government's attempts to eliminate foreign currency stemmed from illegal monetary exports that depleted Mozambique's national reserve bank during the transition period (1974–76), Mucave was the victim of excessive zeal and opportunism.[65] With 30 percent of southern Mozambique's population dependent on migrant labor in South Africa, it was not uncommon for returning residents to carry cash in rands. It is plausible that people keen on keeping Mucave's earnings sent him to Niassa. The reeducation program provided ample opportunity for such unscrupulous acts motivated by material gain. Similarly, in the civil sector, the reeducation program allowed rank-and-file government authorities to rid themselves of unwanted subordinates for all kinds of petty faults. A driver named Jacinto Chongo took the car from his work and drove home in Maputo's Bairro Hulene "without authorization." For this unsolicited escapade, his boss sent him to Niassa.[66] Domingos Francisco Trindade, aged fifty-two, was also serving an indefinite sentence in Niassa because "he broke the fin of a car."[67]

Discord among local authorities—the Grupos Dinamizadores, militias, or army soldiers and police officers—often ended with arrest and deportation. Failure to participate in local party meetings and collective public works (such as cleaning the streets or building the bairros' headquarters) could be used to blackmail and then incriminate residents. But most disputes were motivated by jealousy, vengeance, or retribution for personal offenses, as well as refusal to consent to local authorities' demands. Francisco Quebe, sixty-four, was in detention because "he refused to give his daughter to a member of the *Grupo Dinamizador*" of his bairro in Maputo. Francisco Zumpuza, also sixty-four, shared the same fate for "refusing to offer his daughter to an agent of the FPLM (the army)."[68] Protective fathers were not the only ones to pay heavily for refusing to give the hand of their beloved daughters. Women who refused local authorities' sexual advances—irrespective of their marital status—were sent to reeducation camps. Anastácia Cabona, a resident of Tete, "refused to wed a police officer named José Sabora," for which she spent three years in M'sawize.[69] Sometimes it only took a simple disagreement with a chefe de quarteirão or a secretário do Grupo Dinamizador (GD) to be deported to Niassa. Such was the case for Augusto Matias, who had been in Naisseco since May 1975 for "arguing with the secretary of the GD."[70] The reeducation program not only allowed government officers and local authorities to pursue their own agendas and vendettas but also entitled almost anyone in a position of relative power to act against an opponent. In such a fraught environment, trifling acts of indiscipline or recklessness could earn someone several years of detention. This was the case of a sixteen-year-old boy named Eduardo Mabuie, who "argued with the driver of a public bus" in Maputo. The unruly boy might have been fourteen when the offended driver took him to the police station from where he was then sent to Niassa.[71]

Yet others were condemned to reeducation by their own relatives, friends, and neighbors after skirmishes of various kinds. Marital disputes ranked high in this category. João Rafael, a forty-two-year-old resident of Quelimane, was arrested because "he had an argument with his wife." Similarly, twenty-five-year-old Rosa Ajudante from Vilanculos in Inhambane "had a disagreement with her husband." Domestic violence also constituted grounds for detention. Ganani João, aged fifty-seven, was sent for reeducation for "beating his wife." Similarly, fifty-year-old Viola Chirondo from Chimoio "beat his wife for committing adultery."[72] Ordinary people rid themselves of offending relatives and friends by calling local authorities or filing a case with the police. The transgressions were overwhelmingly minor. Twenty-two-year-old Chico Charles "had an argument with his father" (*brigou com o pai*) in Homoine, Inhambane, which resulted in his indefinite internment in Naisseco. Sixteen-year-old Ernesto Ofiço from Bairro Mafalala in Maputo was deported for "fighting with his brother." The list of such cases stretches very long. Zacarias Pandire, aged thirty, from Chibabava in Sofala Province, was said to have "beaten his mother." Inácio Francisco, a twenty-three-year-old resident of Manhiça, "spent his cousin's money" without consent. Eusébio Francisco, a young boy of seventeen from Quelimane, "fled from school."[73] Sixty-four-year-old Matendenja Sebuie from Guijá in Gaza Province was in Niassa for "fighting with a friend." And Manuel Naife, aged thirty-eight, a worker in the cashew factory of Cumbane in Inhambane "pushed off his friend for cuddling his wife in front of him." This offended but aggressive husband arrived in Naisseco in December 1975 and was still there in August 1977 when DPSRN recorded his case.[74]

Many of the offenses that can be classified as political crimes were derisory. Fifty-year-old Ardinho Soprimo was in detention because "he said that Frelimo is not good." His ungracious comment cost him two years in Naisseco.[75] Another detainee named Decamata Bambo from Beira was arrested because somebody accused him of "tearing off a photograph of the President."[76] His outrageous act yielded three years of detention.

Further details about the reeducation camps' inmate population can be gleaned from the DPSRN lists. The professional occupations recorded from detainees in Naisseco and M'sawize, for example, indicate that most of the inmates were not the parasites and idle vagrants that the authorities claimed they were. As table 5.4 illustrates, the people sent to reeducation camps were engaged in a motley of urban trades. It is not surprising that most people held the sorts of positions most upended by the flight of White settlers—namely, housekeepers (listed as *mainatos* and *empregados domésticos*), bartenders, restaurant cooks, and servants. Many worked in industries that became volatile and unstable during the transition and were also heavily impacted by the settler exodus: carpenters, electricians, plumbers, masons, bricklayers, painters, clerks, and stockkeepers. Miners also featured prominently, as did farmers who lost work because of the transitional crisis. These lists do not indicate, however, whether detainees were employed at the time of arrest. Given that only four people (one man and three women) were listed as unemployed, it is likely that most people were actively engaged in occupations of their trade when they were arrested.

TABLE 5.4. PROFESSIONAL OCCUPATIONS OF 827 DETAINEES FROM M'SAWIZE AND NAISSECO

Trade	Men	Women
Housekeeper, cook, servant, bartender	79	17
Carpenter, electrician, plumber, blacksmith	41	0
Clerk, stockkeeper, typist	37	3
Driver, driver's assistant	37	0
Farmer (camponês/agricultor), charcoal maker	35	40
Mechanic	32	0
Mason, bricklayer, painter	29	0
Vendor, shopkeeper	29	9
Student	28	7
Miner, migrant worker	24	0
Factory worker	22	11
Fisher, sailor	16	0
Housewife	0	40
Baker	10	0
Tailor, shoemaker / shoe repairer	8	11
Guard	7	0
Civil servant	5	0
Nurse, health worker, hospital servant	4	1
Stevedore	4	0
Watchmaker / watch repairer, repairer of appliances	4	0
Fireman	2	0
Army soldier, police officer	1	1
Declared unemployed	1	3
Other	14	2
Unrecorded trades	109	104
Total of recorded trades	578	249

The portrait that comes into focus from the DPSRN detainee lists reveals broader trends among the inmate population across Mozambique's reeducation complex. Detainees served indefinite sentences in remote camps for the most trivial of transgressions or unproven suspicion of wrongdoing. The accusations that ensnared them largely came from people who knew the detainees and sought revenge or to gain advantage by sending them away. Camp authorities found it difficult to convince unjustly detained prisoners that they had to undergo reeducation. If the camps were intended for social misfits and vagrants, few detainees could be said to belong to those categories. Most detainees held jobs, even if informal ones; they supported families and dependents. Based on their offenses, few qualified as enemies of the socialist revolution, at least as far as camp authorities were concerned.

That the DPSRN should produce such lists three years into the reeducation program illustrates a significant feature of Mozambique's internment camps. The DPSRN, like reeducation departments in other provinces, was meant to produce monthly reports detailing reeducatee behavior and improvement. Officers were to open biographical files for each detainee from the day of entry and record their evolution from fallen to saved. This work was never carried out. The DPSRN was ill-equipped to run the reeducation program as planned. Frelimo's perpetual shortage of qualified cadres meant that only the least prepared were employed in reeducation camps. They not only lacked technical abilities to carry out their duties, but they also faced permanent shortages in bureaucratic materials (paper, ink, and pens). Therefore, detainees were never permanently registered, nor was their behavior meticulously observed. The very methods that define modern penal institutions were absent from Frelimo's camps. The so-called monitoring eye was dormant if not blind. Simply put, the camps were a dumping ground; they were sites of abandonment where people were sent and forgotten. That it took three years for DPSRN overseers to carry out what was meant to be a monthly routine reveals a panopticon gone awry. No permanent seeing machine monitored the detainees, and no individualized classification was made. The austerity in which the camps operated made it impossible for such work to be realized. Instead of a disciplinary system, it took two dedicated rank-and-file bureaucrats, who were personally motivated and at risk of losing their positions, to create the lists of disproportionately penalized offenders.

Outraged by the sheer injustices they observed in Niassa's camps, Francisco Taibo and André Trabuco produced the lists to call the provincial governor and MINT back to reason, not for panoptical considerations. I do not know what verdict Governor Manave issued after he read the extensive lists sent to him and the pleas to release the detainees. Since the bill meant to legislate on the reeducation program never became law, who had the authority to release detainees remained legally undefined. The general understanding was that the minister of the interior had the last word on this matter, second only to the revolution's supreme leader, President Machel. Yet, on several occasions, Governor Manave consented to DPSRN's suggestions to release a detainee when he was presented with evidence of their innocence or the undisputed fact of the impracticality of their reeducation in the province. For example, in April 1978, when the DPSRN submitted yet another list of thirty-seven arbitrarily arrested detainees and suggested that they be repatriated, the governor authorized their release. One of the female detainees, forty-year-old Maria Lindri from Quelimane, had been "detained for being single." In this case, the governor wrote the following on the top corner of the file: "Concordo com a sua devolução" (I agree with their repatriation).[77] But the release of 827 detainees was certainly something that the governor could not decide without consulting his superiors in Maputo. The archival record is silent here.

ETHICAL CRISIS AND THE BUREAUCRATIC PAINS OF REEDUCATION

Studies of socialist Mozambique have documented that fabricated or inaccurate reports by rank-and-file bureaucrats eager to curry favor or afraid to reveal the true state of affairs was one reason why Frelimo often set ambitious goals—be they for public administration or state-run enterprises—the ultimate outcome of which was the socialist experiment's collapse.[78] This interpretation implies that Frelimo leaders were not aware of conditions and capabilities at the local level, where centrally planned policies entered into force. While they were certainly ignorant of most economic and social sectors, it is hardly the case in relation to reeducation camps. From the outset, the party-state leadership knew of the reeducation program's shortcomings. DPSRN officers informed Frelimo leaders of reeducation's ineffective nature. In his final report of May 1977, André Trabuco called for his superiors to pay more attention to the camps' challenges and needs as well as the flaws that spanned the entire reeducation initiative. He told them that, with shortages in appropriate equipment and qualified personnel, the high-minded reeducation program was a facade. Considering the politically charged environment in which he worked and the strictly pyramidal and authoritarian regime that restrained party-state officials (even at the highest level) from making comments that could jeopardize their political careers, the extent to which Trabuco challenged decisions from the top is remarkable.[79] "With the present report," he wrote, "besides observing the monthly routine duty, we want to try to sensitize those to whom it may concern, about certain aspects that embarrass the Reeducation Services of this province, and we want to take our points of view and suggestions to your highest consideration."[80] After briefly repeating the usual complaints about lack of equipment and support—some of which were copied and pasted from previous reports—Trabuco dedicated two pages (out of four) to a section with the header *pontos de vista* (points of view). In it, he lectured his superiors about the program's irregularities and the delicate position of camp overseers, especially when it came to explaining to reeducandos why they were being reeducated and what reeducation meant in such wretched conditions. He claimed that the situation was made worse by the fact that many detainees were in fact innocent and, at most, only suspected of felony. It is worth citing him in full here:

> We have received in this Province many *reeducandos* whose causes of detention, as stated in their respective *guias de marcha* and biographical files, create in us a sense of wonder. It is stated as a motive of detention *suspected of theft, suspected of use of drugs, suspected of prostitution or simply corruption,* and there are even files without any kind of annotation. Now, this creates a certain embarrassment for us, because we are left not knowing the truth when we hear *reeducandos* complain about the ways in which they were arrested. We do not know if, in fact, a simple suspicion constitutes enough cause for one to be detained. We are presented with elderly people with ages between 50 and 60 years old, who are implicated in issues that can easily be resolved with a constructive criticism in their communities. We think that this method of work does not contribute in any way to combat crime. Quite the opposite; it foments terror and discontentment among the people. And for those politically less enlightened, it discredits the revolution, thus misconstruing the Party and the Government's objectives in creating Reeducation Centers.[81]

André Trabuco chose his words carefully. He knew he was treading on thin ice. Many people paid a heavy price for making far less critical comments about the ruling party and its policies. Trabuco evidently knew of Ardinho Soprimo, who was detained for years for uttering that "Frelimo was not good." But he rose above fear of his superiors and addressed the state in its own language. He never questioned the reeducation program's righteousness. He was pained by its implementation. He closed his impressive report by suggesting that the party-state structures responsible for detentions should carry out their work meticulously and that they should investigate the denunciations and libels with forensic care to avoid sending innocent people to reeducation camps. He insisted that only those people proven guilty of having committed serious crimes should be subjected to reeducation and that the elderly (who were already frail) should not be sent to the camps. And the young, most of whom had their schooltime interrupted and were idly roaming in the camps—thus compromising "their tomorrow and the future of our Land and People"—should be sent to schools in the province. "If we are allowed," he added, "we would like to assert that the success of a reeducation camp depends particularly on the acceptance of the process by the *reeducandos*, yet that acceptance is only possible if they recognize the reason for their detention."[82]

As chief of the DPSRN, André Trabuco was building on the work of his predecessor, Francisco Taibo. Their words and actions suggest that not all rank-and-file officers in charge of reeducation camps were insensitive to detainees' fates or silent about the program's flaws. They took their work seriously, even if doing so could cost them their privileged positions in the government. Several of their reports contained lists of citizens who had been arbitrarily detained and included requests for authorization to release them.[83] Despite the silence of authorities in the capital—who often insisted that people had to be self-reliant and inventive to find solutions for local challenges—these two officers persisted in reminding the capital of the inhumane conditions that inmates and wardens faced in the camps and how many aspects of the reeducation program were an embarrassing stain on the country's justice system. Their carefully chosen words echoed those of Teodato Hunguana in his juridical comment about Minister Guebuza's failed bill. Like Hunguana, DPSRN officers were also ignored, and the contradictions of the reeducation program continued. As the next chapter illustrates, the camps were sites of social abandonment. Their wretched conditions victimized captives and captors alike.

6 ~ Abandonment and Everyday Life in Reeducation Camps, 1974–1982

SIMEÃO MAZUZE, also known as Salimo Muhamed, is a noted musician in Mozambique. Among his many hits is the song "Bilibiza." After I learned that Bilibiza was the name of a reeducation camp in Cabo Delgado Province and that the musician had been interned there in the late 1970s, I arranged an interview with him. "This song has a special meaning that I will never forget," he told me. Although our many conversations about reeducation camps were cheerful, sometimes satirical, our first encounter was emotional. "This song is dedicated to all reeducation camps, which I consider concentration camps because they concentrated many Mozambicans," he said in a trembling voice as he wiped the tears from his face. The thought of Bilibiza took him to the darkest moments of his life. He spent three years in several reeducation camps in central and northern Mozambique, namely Sacudzo, Bilibiza, and Chaimite. After a small grievance with his boss at Maputo's air force base, where he was responsible for overseeing army aircrafts, on April 10, 1977, Mazuze was sent for reeducation without trial. In his midtwenties, he was freshly married and awaiting the birth of his first child. Sacudzo in Sofala Province was his first detention camp. It was there that he composed the first version of the song in Changana, his mother tongue. In 1978, he was moved to Bilibiza after attacks by Renamo made it impossible for the government to maintain reeducation camps in central Mozambique. As a member of the small group of detainees whose artistic talents exempted them from the most tasking labor in the camps, he continued to perform the song and conveniently changed the lyrics from "Ya 'bamba le Sacudzo" to "Ya 'bamba le Bilibiza."[1]

Ya 'bamba le Bilibiza, a hi fambeni hi ya kuvona
(Life is hard in Bilibiza, let's go see it)
Bilibiza kuni tinenha, a hi fambeni hi ya kuvona
(There are brave men in Bilibiza, let's go see it)
Bilibiza ka rimiwa, a hi fambeni hi ya kuvona
(There's farming in Bilibiza, let's go see it)
Bilibiza ka fundiwa, a hi fambeni hi ya kuvona
(There's education in Bilibiza, let's go see it)
Bilibiza kuni makwayela, a hi fambeni hi ya kuvona
(There's kwayela dance in Bilibiza, let's go see it)

These simple lyrics sum up some typical aspects of everyday life in Mozambique's reeducation camps: hardship, farming, political education, and cultural activities. But the picture of the camp that Mazuze's song painted is a sanitized one. Taken literally, the message of the song is more in tune with Frelimo's sloganeering about the goals of the reeducation program. The line "Ya 'bamba le Bilibiza" is vague. It can mean "Life is hard," as I have translated it. But it can also mean something different. The word *'bamba* does not appear in any dictionary of Changana or its sibling language Ronga. Although I asked him several times during our conversations, Mazuze did not give a clear definition of what he meant by it. He also never mentioned censorship of his lyrics. But, since he performed this and other songs he wrote to entertain camp overseers and important visitors during camp festive days, it is unsurprising that no outward dissent appears in the song and that no line is present that puts the camp in a negative light.

At first glance, Bilibiza emerges in the song as a place of industrious men, of social and cultural renewal, and as therefore worthy of public attention ("A hi fambeni hi ya kuvona"). This is the image that Frelimo authorities envisioned in setting up the camps: bands of idle urbanites being transformed into industrious and upstanding citizens through hard labor, political indoctrination, and cultural awakening. But "Ya 'bamba le Bilibiza" could also mean that the chamboco was ringing hard on people's bodies in the camp, an allusion to the most pervasive form of punishment in the camps.[2] According to musician and music scholar Rufus Maculuve, the use of ambiguous language in musical compositions to convey coded messages was a common practice in socialist Mozambique. Salimo Muhamed was a master of this technique.[3] The lyrics of "Bilibiza" may give the impression that it celebrates the reeducation program, but melodically the song sounds more like a denunciation. And what it denounces is the brutality of the camp regimen and the sense of abandonment that reeducatees experienced.

This chapter expands the argument introduced in chapter five about the role of austerity in shaping the penal system of reeducation. While the previous chapter focused on the organic workings of the camp complex and the bureaucratic challenges that camp authorities in the Niassa Province faced in carrying out their duties, in what follows, I explore social life inside the camp complex. I illustrate the ways in which shortages and decrepit infrastructures organized and delimited daily life in the camps. Functioning in extreme conditions of austerity, camps were spaces of social abandonment.[4] The wretchedness of camp life—hunger, cold, and disease—did not victimize only detainees; it affected camp overseers as well. Captives and captors suffered the same privations. If detainees yearned for freedom, camp warders and their commanders also longed to be released from their duties and moved to better worksites. When conditions became unbearable, both inmates and warders braved the dangerous forests to find freedom or died trying. All camp dwellers—detainees and overseers both—experienced in relatively equal measure the agony of abandonment. At the same time, there emerged in the camps forms of sociability among detainees and overseers that undermined Frelimo's high-minded, austere ideals of reeducation. Drinking, indulgence, and all sorts of illicit transactions characterized social life in the camps.

WORK AND THE DAILY CAMP ROUTINE

One of the main features of Mozambique's reeducation camps was the lack of a system of regimentation of detainees' daily routine. Despite several attempts to produce a centrally coordinated program for the camps, the Ministry of the Interior (MINT) was never able to pass any regulations with detailed rules governing day-to-day camp operations. The ministry was short of capable people to develop such rules, and its administrative capacity was overstretched, given the ministry's many responsibilities. Consequently, camp supervisors had to come up with their own plans on how to keep detainees busy. Although a tentative program was introduced later in 1980 when José Zumbire was nominated director of the National Directorate of Reeducation Services (DNSR), the program still left much of the daily camp routine up to supervisors to decide.[5] The consensus was that detainees had to work in the fields (*machambas*) from which their food was to come. But unlike penal labor camps elsewhere, where productivity and output were often prioritized over other activities, in Mozambique the camps had no economic relevance. There were no production quotas and no defined number of hectares for the fields. The produce from machambas was entirely for the inmates—and still the camps often fell short. Not only did the camps lack appropriate implements for agriculture (hoes and axes were the only tools available), but they also had no qualified agricultural experts. Therefore, camps were not self-sufficient. They depended almost entirely on rations from Provincial Departments of Reeducation Services (DPSRs)—but these rations often failed to arrive. Every weekday, armed camp warders marched brigades of detainees to the fields, where they grew a few rain-dependent crops that provided the camps' staple foods: corn, manioc, and beans. Small vegetable gardens, which could only be worked on the banks of nearby rivers, were often left to individual initiative. Although in some camps detainees collected timber and produced charcoal, subsistence agriculture was the most serious work in which they were engaged.

Despite the hardship of farming, detainees were subjected to very little regimentation in reeducation camps. The daily routine in most camps began very early in the morning. "Dawn at 4:30 in the morning. Cleaning and breakfast. Then farm. Lunch. Farm again." This is how Silência David summarized the daily program of M'sawize as she guided the *Notícias* reporter who visited her camp in August 1976. "In the evening, they eat again," she continued. "However, we do not always have enough food, so sometimes nobody eats at night."[6] As in Frelimo's former training camps, the day often started with a whistle, which signaled detainees to form a line in the rassemblement. The chief commander took the roll and gave the instructions of the day. Organized as brigades of twenty-five to forty people, some groups would work the machamba, others would cut and collect wood, and still others would fetch drinking and cooking water from nearby rivers. Others would build the huts and, in the case of M'sawize, continue work on the road that would link the camp with the nearby village (to allow trucks to deliver rations and bring more detainees).

After roll call, detainees had a cup of sweet tea (if there was sugar) and a piece of manioc or some cornmeal porridge for breakfast. They then joined their working platoons and marched to the fields (see figure 6.1). Other work consisted of felling trees for use in local construction, as firewood, and for the production of charcoal. In some camps, such as M'telela and Chiputo, there were groups of artisans who were excused from the hard labor of tilling the land. These artisans produced woodwork (such as benches, doors, and bed frames) and carried out minor carpentry and masonry maintenance work inside the camp. Other artisans produced utensils such as baskets and

FIGURE 6.1. Detainees at work on the banks of a river in Inhassune, Inhambane Province, 1976. Photo courtesy of Arquivo do Jornal Notícias (AJN).

mats that, like charcoal, they sold in nearby villages. Yet, market-oriented artisanal production often depended on the enthusiasm and organizational skill of the responsável for the camp industry (who could be a detainee) as well as on the support of camp overseers who sold the produce and used the money to buy food.[7]

After work, detainees returned to the camp for lunch. A team of selected detainees prepared the food. These teams seem to have been rotated daily or weekly. Detainees known for being good cooks often held their positions permanently. Cooking was the most sought-after job in the camp because it allowed detainees to be closer to the source of food—a guarantee of more generous portions than the meager ones that the majority received.[8] The staple food was beans served with corn meal, or *chima* (in other places in East and Southern Africa it is known as *ugali, sadza,* or *uswa*). Generally, the food was poorly cooked and unseasoned. For urbanites used to a more refined diet, the roughness of the camps' rations was challenging. As Carlos Fumo recalled of Ruarua, "We practically lived like savages, we had no food."[9] Occasionally, on good days, the camps served game meat. But this only happened in certain camps near hunting reserves, such as M'sawize and Sacudzo.[10] Some detainees were able to supplement their meager meals with a piece of fresh fish from nearby rivers. However, given the lack of fishing hooks and nets, catching fish in the camps took great skill and patience. For those who worked in vegetable gardens, the unpalatable taste of chima and beans could be improved with some green leaves.

FIGURE 6.2. Detainees share a meal inside their hut in Unango, 1984. Note that one detainee (front right) uses a spoon while the others eat with their hands. In some camps, cutlery was a symbol of status. The lodging has wooden bed frames, but the mud on the unskillfully plastered wall has dried up and fallen off, leaving detainees exposed to the elements. Photo by Naíta Ussene. Courtesy of Arquivo da Revista Tempo (ART).

Mealtime betrayed the makeshift character of the carceral regimen. As soon as their rusty iron dishes were filled, the reeducatees sat wherever they wanted in the vast open camp and in the company of close inmates or friends (see figure 6.2). In his Kafkaesque novel *Campo de trânsito*, Mozambican fiction writer and historian João Paulo Borges Coelho captured mealtime in the re-education camp with satirical yet informative detail.[11] Most detainees were modern urbanites who had adopted the Portuguese colonial notion that cutlery was a symbol of civilization. For most urban southerners, eating with at least a fork or a spoon was the norm, whereas eating by hand was tantamount to backwardness. In the camps, detainees had to learn how to eat by hand because cutlery was a luxury that only a few—often senior detainees—could afford. Like other metal tools (such as knives), forks and spoons were markers of hierarchy inside the camp. Those who obstinately maintained their "civilized" ways of eating used bark or hardened leaves in place of spoons.[12] Camp overseers ate the same unpalatable food, but theirs was often prepared in separate pots by somewhat better cooks. As hard as some camp overseers tried to keep a kind of hierarchical and statutory distance from detainees, camp life offered few options. Differentiation was through uniforms, warders' firearms, and the undisputed reality that some were captors and others were captives. The camps were so resource poor that overseers had to make a real effort to distinguish themselves from the captives. At times, they ate in the open, like their captives. At others, they concealed themselves in a less visible spot that detainees were not allowed to approach.[13]

In most camps, where farming was only done in the morning, lunch marked the end of daily work for most detainees. They spent the remainder of the day very much on their own. Most detainees spent the afternoons chatting or, on hot summer days, daydreaming under the cool shade of a tree or, in the chilly dry season, warming up in the sun in the open rassemblement. Some detainees spent their free time patching up their ragged uniforms or sewing their worn shoes. Others, the most industrious, tended to their small vegetable gardens or else they tried to improve their lodgings, which, given their rudimentary nature, were in a permanent state of disrepair. Except for the women's camps of Ilumba and M'sawize, where political education seemed to have been mandatory from the outset, in most camps it was optional (at least until the late 1970s). Therefore, those thirsty for knowledge spent the two hours after lunch attending the political commissar's lectures. Those allowed to hunt braved the forest with a couple of guards on their heels. The less sober found a shady spot to smoke hemp or to drink *cajulima,* a locally distilled and highly intoxicating brandy. In many cases, affluent detainees sneaked to the nearby villages for alcohol or to alleviate their urge for a smoke, even though they risked being caught and punished. However, punishment for smoking hemp or drinking only happened in case a cruel guard decided to enforce a camp rule that was often overlooked. (Camp warders were themselves frequent visitors of the village for the same reason.)[14] The most creative detainees joined the folklore groups known as Grupo Cultural Polivalente (Multipurpose Cultural Group). Membership in these highly selective groups earned detainees a free pass from the heaviest labor. The groups were responsible for cultural production and entertainment of all sorts, including plays, choirs, dancing, and poetry. They spent most of the day rehearsing the numbers to be presented on Saturday and Sunday afternoons or on the many scheduled revolutionary holidays. Occasionally, they performed for important visitors.[15]

There was no set time to return to camp in the afternoon. Hunger led everyone to the kitchen line for supper as the falling sun cast its last reddish rays from above the trees surrounding the camp. If available, the meal was invariably the same as the one eaten at lunch. Sunset marked the end of the day. With no electricity and no lights, at night the dense darkness of the camp was often dotted with the sparks of fires around which detainees gathered for a last chat, trying to warm up before bedtime during the colder months. Small lights might shine inside the lodgings of camp overseers, the only camp residents lucky enough to have a candle or a paraffin lamp—a few of the little luxuries that differentiated captors from detainees. If there was a permanent monitoring eye in the camp, surely it went totally blind at night.

THE FACADE OF EDUCATION

Frelimo authorities regarded education, in conjunction with hard labor, as the main instrument for the rehabilitation of detainees. On paper, each camp was to have a pedagogical program and at least one political commissar responsible for the political and ideological (Marxist-Leninist) education of detainees. In reality, the camps lacked basic educational materials, classrooms, and cadres able to carry out the program. Few camps had a political commissar qualified to teach, which compelled camp commanders to entrust the task to educated detainees, who had to improvise, given the lack of clear orientations and didactic materials. André Trabuco, one of the chief officers of Niassa's reeducation department, characterized the education program of the camps as a facade or at most a meaningless activity.[16]

MINT made the poor state of political education the main subject of its First National Seminar on Reeducation held in Maputo in November 1976. The seminar concluded that, while manual labor was undoubtedly a crucial component of reeducation, a meaningful political program had to be created, one informed by scientific socialism. "For example," the agency stated, "production has to be studied" and detainees had to learn that it was "through production that humanity evolved"; they had to learn about the "role of the surplus and the emergence of class division in society," the "current revolutionary process in Mozambique," and the pursuit of a "classless society."[17] Learning the history of Mozambique's colonial domination, the rise of Frelimo, and the struggle for liberation was key to transforming detainees into awakened, conscious New Women and New Men. The seminar determined that the "implementation of a meaningful political program implied the organization of reeducatees according to a military structure." In short, camps needed to have a monthly plan that dictated all activities. Each Saturday afternoon, camp overseers were to meet and carefully study the execution of the plan and establish new programs. The daily program mandated two hours for political study.

The meticulous pedagogical ideas about how detainees were to be reeducated betrayed the contradictions between plan and possibility so characteristic of socialist experiments. Political education had to include lectures, the production of a camp journal, and the collective study of newspapers. There were detailed instructions on how the two hours of political education had to be spent. One hour was to be dedicated to lectures; half an hour to debate and clarification of doubts; and the other half hour to commentaries on daily news and such issues as "the definition of the enemy, the behavior and erroneous ideas among reeducatees, exposition of new initiatives," and so on. For the program to be successful, a designated group of detainees had to listen to the 12:30 p.m. news broadcast on a battery-powered radio set and then explain it to all detainees during the general assembly. Even so, austerity meant that only one radio set could be allocated to each camp for this purpose. The small size of the radio set and the absence of loudspeakers meant that the few who could listen to the program served as amplifiers and broadcasters. In addition, camps were to introduce gymnastics, sports, and cultural activities. Professional training was to be implemented in crafts such as carpentry, mechanics, and art. In their capacity as chief political instructors, political commissars had to select a group of exemplary detainees to serve as aides, who were to prepare—under their supervision—the materials for the lectures. Each class was limited to twenty to forty students. Political commissars were to inform detainees that participation in these activities was a "decisive step towards their freedom."[18]

Despite these high hopes, a lack of resources limited the party's ability to realize its reformist ambitions. These detailed instructions were part of a wider culture that characterized Frelimo's socialist regime—namely, a culture of wishful governmentality divorced from reality.[19] In the end, little if anything changed in the educational program inside the camps. DPSRN (Provincial Directorate of Reeducation Services of Niassa) officers continued to be greatly concerned about the level of education of many camp overseers in Niassa. In April 1977, six months after the Seminar on Reeducation recommended special training for camp supervisors, André Trabuco noted that the "political and technical capabilities" of Niassa's camp officers "are minute."[20] He sadly informed his superiors that in Ilumba, for example, "the various programs are being implemented with much difficulty due to lack of personnel in quantity and quality to materialize the instructions." The main difficulties were in literacy and political education. "The camp lacks personnel capable of understanding the instructions through political documents, *Tempo* magazine and newspapers, and interpreting them," he wrote.[21]

Because schoolbooks were in short supply in the country and none could be sent to reeducation camps, newspapers and magazines were the only didactic materials available to camp instructors. Even though these materials arrived in the camps several months after they had been published, instructors based their lectures on editorials, news articles, and, more importantly, government communiqués and speeches by Frelimo leaders. President Machel's speeches were the primary—and often the only—guiding tools for political and ideological education. Taught by people with "minute" instruction, it is not difficult to imagine the theatrical nature of the lectures that reeducatees attended every day after returning from the fields. Seated under the shade of a tree, as was often the case because there were no huts to serve as classrooms, detainees listened as their political instructors read aloud a section of a speech by the president or a piece of news. A discussion of the content of a months-old news article would follow. If the commissar happened to be versed in Frelimo's socialist maxims or knew a few facts about the history of the armed struggle, that lecturer would throw in some ready-made slogans about the virtues of collective labor, the class struggle, the heroic saga of the liberation war, or global imperialism and the actions of internal enemies seeking to undermine the revolution. Instructors kept no records of who attended the lectures and made no assessment of inmates' pedagogical progress. Thus, with no training for instructors and no didactic materials, political education amounted to nothing more than propaganda, mobilization, and moral exhortation. Silência David, the chief of the women's camp in M'sawize, explained her political work among putative prostitutes in the following terms: "Political education is part of our working methods. At first, if we said 'Viva Frelimo,' nobody responded. Nobody understood why they were brought here, why they had to suffer this much and endure these life conditions. To explain what the lives of these women represented in the colonial society, to explain the kind of society we want to build in Mozambique, to explain why they are in this isolated place, a political explanation was necessary."[22]

Like her colleagues in other camps, Silência David measured the success of her political work by looking to the military discipline that detainees showed in parades and during roll calls or to the hundreds of raised fists in the air as detainees shouted "Viva Frelimo!" in unison. For most camp authorities, the point of reeducation was to help detainees understand why they had to endure isolation and suffering in such remote places (a difficult task given that most detainees were innocent). Obedience to camp commandments and military orderliness in parades were often the only measures of detainees' submission to the reeducation program. Ana Maria, who was detained in a dance club in Maputo at the age of eighteen and spent two years in M'sawize, told me sarcastically: "I learned to be a soldier. I did not need any reeducation, but I was reeducated. I did not dance anymore, for example."[23] Another former detainee, who was seventeen when he was sent to Sacudzo, said to me in anger: "I don't think I was reeducated. Quite the opposite, I cultivated hatred and resentment."[24]

Four years after the First National Seminar on Reeducation, the government realized that little had been done to implement an effective educational program in the camps. During the Second Seminar, which was held in Maputo in January 1980, the new interior minister, Mariano Matsinhe, urged participants to improve the situation, but he merely listed the same tasks outlined in 1976. Nevertheless, he lauded the "successes achieved," and claimed that they "attest to the righteousness of Frelimo's political line and the measures taken by the government for the reeducation of thousands of vagrants and delinquents who swarmed the urban areas of the country."[25] The minister's statement not only reveals the inability of the government to accept its shortcomings but also a blind belief in the idea of reeducation. Party leadership attributed the limitations or failures of the program to bad implementation and enemy sabotage; for them, the principle behind the program was necessarily righteous and holy. For officers like André Trabuco and his colleagues entrusted to carry out the program, the contradictions between high-minded ideals and reality were hard to ignore—especially because camp conditions eroded the fragile difference between detainees undergoing reeducation and camp warders responsible for reeducating them, thus undermining any sense of hierarchy.

HUNGER AND COLD

The remote location of the camps and the government's inability to provide for them, combined with the rickety lodgings in which detainees and warders lived, exacerbated the sense of purposelessness with which some camp authorities and inmates regarded the reeducation program. In the rainy summer months between October and April, roads became muddy and treacherous, making it difficult for the government to supply camps with food on a regular basis. The dry and cold season between May and August came with another set of challenges because camps lacked winter clothes and camp accommodations offered little protection against the elements. The privations that governed the camps nearly flattened the difference between captives and captors, but without this separation, the carceral regime could not function as designed. The harsh conditions of the camps made detainees and warders both captives in punitive institutions functioning under extreme scarcity.

Although the *Notícias* reporter who visited the women's camp of M'sawize in August 1976 lauded the loose ambience of reeducation, his report painted a grim picture of life in the camp. His editorial strategy made sure that his main point was not lost on readers. He printed in bold letters the words of his only interlocutor, chief commander Silência David. Her statements were cries of abandonment. "Difficulties here are plentiful," she told him, "beginning with the lack of food."[26] The reporter ensured that his readers would not miss the weight of desperation in her words and the sense of urgency with which they were uttered. The reporter was the first person from Maputo to visit the camp since its foundation in late 1975, and Silência David knew that it would be several months until another important figure came around again. She seized the moment, hoping that the reporter would carry her cry for help to authorities in the capital and to the wider public. "We go very hungry here," she said. "Rations hardly reach us. Trucks break down in the rough roads and the food rots and never reaches us here. Many people have anemia. Even now, we only have rations for just one meal in the barn. In addition, the food quality is very poor. Usually, we only have beans and maize flour."

The unpaved, rough paths that led to the camps in the vast and mountainous territory of Niassa presented huge difficulties for the distribution of rations and other provisions. Vehicles could not reach the camps because the camps were located on the other side of rivers that lacked bridges and because the unpaved roads, opened when the camps were first established, had been rapidly reclaimed by vegetation. In M'sawize, detainees had to carry loads of rations on their heads from the village to the camp, "a path that is very time consuming and difficult for it is a very long walk."[27] To bring rations to Ilumba from Base Central Ngungunhana, the reeducandas had to cross the Lindi and Messinge Rivers. "The River Messinge is very large, and crossing is done by a pneumatic canoe," noted Francisco Taibo in one his reports. The road from Base Central, he added, "does not guarantee a normal course, that is why vehicles take many days to reach the camp." Providing rations for the Naisseco camp took great effort. "Since the beginning of the rainy season up to April," insisted the tireless DPSRN chief, "our vehicles unload the ration in the village near the river, 22 km away from the country-town of Majune. From here the ration is carried by *reeducandos* to the camp, in a journey that takes two days. This is the reason why the camp was forced to go without food for several days."[28] An SOS radio message from Ilumba to Lichinga on April 20, 1976, informed the provincial governor that, after going six days without food, everyone in the camp was confined to bed. Two days later, the same radio operator delivered a desperate message in which the camp commander asked why authorities were not replying to their cry for help and that people were already "losing consciousness" because of hunger.[29]

In their diligent and often desperate reports, DPSRN directors Francisco Taibo and André Trabuco informed MINT and Governor Manave that the geographic location of Niassa's camps and the state of its infrastructure posed life-threatening challenges not only for inmates but for camp overseers as well. The M'sawize camp, Taibo wrote in May 1976, only "possesses wooden provisional lodgings, with walls and ceiling covered with grass. The camp environment is bad and unhealthy because the rain and the cold come easily in the barracks, thus causing many diseases due to humidity." In M'telela, where some masonry existed given that it was a former colonial military base, lodgings were not enough for all detainees. As Taibo noted in his report, "Some detainees live in huts that do not offer conditions for a camp destined for reactionaries who, for their qualification, deserve a special vigilance." M'telela detainees were mostly political dissidents who camp authorities regarded with a certain degree of reverence. Although the leadership in the capital was often silent about the desperate pleas for help from the camps, they ultimately conceded to closing Revia in February 1976 because the camp "did not offer any sanitary conditions, and there was high mortality among detainees."[30] All inmates were moved to a new camp in Naisseco.

Another dangerous reality was the lack of proper infrastructure for the climates in which the camps were located. By Mozambican standards, Niassa is very cold during the dry season, which stretches from May to September. With most of its territory more than 1,000 meters (3,280 feet) above sea level, the median temperature is 16°C (60°F). During the peak of the dry season, temperatures usually drop to 8°C (46°F) or lower.[31] The rudimentary nature of camp lodgings left inmates exposed to the chilling temperatures. The fact that inmates and wardens slept on the bare floor due to a lack of bed frames and mattresses only exacerbated the situation. "In all camps, there are no beds for *responsáveis* nor *reeducandos*," Francisco Taibo reported to his superiors. In a tone that betrayed his exasperation, he told the governor that "it is assumed that the abundance of diseases, apart from exposure, is the result of sleeping on the bare floor, for humidity is a great enemy of men."[32] The lack of blankets made an already alarming situation unbearable. Most detainees were arrested in light summer clothes in the warm streets of Maputo, Beira, and Nampula. The government did not consider that they would subsequently need winter clothes. As Silência David lamented to the *Notícias* journalist, "We do not have clothes to wrap up. The cold is unbearable, and the houses have no protection on the sides. We have no blankets. We only give out blankets to those who had nothing to cover up."[33] Her use of the second person is significant. Everybody in the camp, detainees and camp overseers alike, faced the same hardships. They all went hungry, they were all cold, they all fell sick, and they all felt abandoned.

HEALTH

Starvation and the inhospitable conditions of reeducation camps correlated with outbreaks of diseases that affected detainees and camp overseers. Each camp was equipped with a rudimentary health post and a first-aid attendant. However, with very limited medical expertise and a shortage of medicines, there was little that camp medics could do to alleviate the torment of the sick. Easily curable diseases often led to death. Hunger, exposure to cold, and the poor sanitary conditions of the camps were the most common causes of severe health problems. Starvation caused swelling of the body (especially legs) and gastrointestinal complications, including acute diarrhea. Dizziness was a constant malaise, especially for those in advanced stages of malnutrition. Camp obituaries pointed to cases of tuberculosis, asthma, trypanosomiasis, malaria, bilharziasis, elephantiasis, amebiasis, and scabies. In the women's camps of M'sawize and Ilumba, there were several cases of syphilis.[34]

The most widespread disease directly related to poor sanitation and hygiene was tungiasis, locally known as *matequenha*. This sinister condition is caused by a small sand flea that penetrates the epidermis (normally toes and fingers and, in severe cases, any part of the body), causing intense itching and inflammation of the skin. Victims in advanced stages of infection have painful ulcers and deformation of the affected area (often nails or entire toes), leading to difficulty in walking. Several unpublished photographs in the archives of *Notícias* and *Tempo* show emaciated reeducatees with matequenha, walking on their heels with the aid of a walking stick (figure 6.3). "Many people died of *matequenha* here," a former nurse who worked in Unango told me in Niassa.[35] In addition to sand fleas, snakes and snakebites

FIGURE 6.3. A reeducatee suffering from matequenha walks with the help of a stick in Unango, Niassa, June 1984. Most detainees lacked shoes and thus lived barefoot, which exposed them to the sand fleas that cause tungiasis. Photo by Naíta Ussene. Courtesy of Arquivo da Revista Tempo (ART).

were common, particularly in the working fields.[36] Several detainees suffered from festering, untreated wounds for months on end without medical assistance. In May 1976, Francisco Taibo reminded his superiors that "all reeducation camps need health care." He went on to suggest that "in the absence of comrades with training in nursing, at least health workers of the Rural Assistance Health Service, who have skills to replace a nurse, should attend the camps." He closed his report by saying that "it is also convenient that the camps receive medical visits once in a month."[37]

Reeducation camps stretched the already limited capacity of Niassa's government to provide free health care for all. Although this was an enormous challenge throughout the country, the situation in Niassa was far more extreme. The flight of Portuguese settlers left Mozambique with only thirty medical doctors and a few hundred nurses for a population of twelve million. Concentrated in major cities, the health services inherited from the colonial regime only covered 7 percent of the population.[38] To reverse the scenario, Frelimo resorted to its medical expertise developed in liberated areas in the 1960s. During the armed struggle, Frelimo had initiated a free primary health service that became the cornerstone of Mozambique's health policy. Hospitals and clinics were nationalized, and a network of rural health posts was established in areas that had never benefited from such services before. Compared to the colonial period, the nationalization and rapid expansion of health care was indeed a significant improvement and a major gain of independence.[39] However, the expansion of health facilities came at the cost of the quality of services provided. As the Council of Ministers recognized in 1980, "We have been preoccupied with quantity rather than quality."[40] In rural areas, peasant populations relied on paramedics of the Rural Assistance Health Service. These paramedics were volunteers who worked part-time and had only six months of first-aid training. As the Provincial Health Directorate of Niassa reported in 1980, "In a total of 75 health units [in rural Niassa], 44 were governed by non-qualified personnel (*serventes* and military aiders)."[41] It was from these good-willed medics that camp overseers often sought relief when detainees and their own comrades fell sick. Yet, getting assistance from paramedics was uncertain. Not only were they poorly prepared and unequipped, but because of their status as volunteers and part-time workers, they often left their posts unattended to tend to personal affairs. In June 1976, Francisco Taibo, who had gone on a work visit to the camp of Naisseco, reported: "Many people are sick, and there are no medicines. The health post in the near village of Revia has no nurse and the camp's aid station is empty. On our way back we had to bring with us those who are seriously sick."[42]

Reeducatees and camp overseers who were critically ill often had to be taken to district hospitals, which were far from the camps. Since camps had no vehicles on duty, camp overseers had to request transportation from the DPSRN office in Lichinga. Such requests often took several days to be met. During the peak of the rainy season, when the unpaved roads become muddy and impervious to vehicles, only helicopters could rescue the sick. Several SOS radio messages from various camps, particularly Chiputo, Naisseco, and Ilumba, reached the desk of the DPSRN director and of Niassa's governor, asking for urgent transport for sick detainees and warders. One message from Naisseco, dated April 21, 1978, asked for a helicopter to take a seriously ill camp commissar in Chiputo to the hospital. When the DPSRN denied the request, claiming that Niassa did not have a helicopter available, the exasperated camp commander sent another radio message, this time to the governor, to complain about the DPSRN's shortcomings.[43]

These enormous logistical demands far exceeded the powers of the unequipped, understaffed, and underfunded DPSRN. Although on other occasions a helicopter was arranged to rescue the sick, such effort required the cooperation of the army department in the neighboring province of Nampula.[44] To make matters worse, epidemic crises put the ineffective health service in Niassa's reeducation camps under greater pressure. In September 1980, an outbreak of measles affected all the districts with camps, especially Majune and Mavago. The epidemic immediately resulted in 145 deaths.[45] Most victims were children. The village of M'sawize, including the two reeducation camps in the area, were the most affected.[46] The realty was that hygiene- and sanitation-related epidemics spread rapidly inside the camps. Scabies, for example, was a common malaise that quickly passed from one detainee to another, especially during the dry season. The chilly temperature of Niassa's winter discouraged detainees from going down to the river to bathe. The scarcity of food also made personal hygiene come second, as detainees often sold or exchanged their provisions of soap. "We distribute soap here," said Silência David in her conversation with the *Notícias* newsman in M'sawize, "but they often exchange it for food. The same happens with clothing."[47] Consequently, many detainees suffered from scabies.

The situation was even more dreadful in the women's camps. Given the total inexistence of sanitary pads, female detainees had to be inventive to attend to their hygienic needs. When I asked former M'sawize reeducatee Ana Maria about this subject, she said bluntly: "We invented." They made makeshift pads from old clothes. In extreme situations, she told me, "we used corn leaves for pads."[48]

Given the DPSRN's incapacity to provide health care and given the shortage of staff to fill the vacant positions as camp medics, most camps selected detainees and entrusted them to serve as nurses. They administered vaccines (when vaccines were available) and prescribed drugs (often aspirin, the most common medicine in the infirmary, for all kinds of ailments without any formal diagnosis).[49] The medical skills of these spontaneous health technicians were questionable and sometimes shocking. One of my interviewees gave me a remarkable account of how he became the chief nurse of the men's camp in M'sawize. José Júlio Pereira, also known as Zequinho, was eighteen when he arrived at M'sawize in 1982 to serve an indefinite sentence. His tender age saved him from the same fate as his older companions, who were tried by the Revolutionary Military Tribunal (TMR) for their Renamo-related activities and sentenced to death by firing squad.[50] In 1980, Zequinho had escaped from Chia, a reeducation camp for "undisciplined" pupils in Matutuíne (Maputo Province). He had been confined there for nearly a year for smoking cigars in the schoolyard and for peering at his teacher's panties in class. A camp escapee, he sought better prospects in South Africa. Undocumented and inexperienced, he was soon arrested and deported back to Mozambique. At the border post, while waiting to cross back to Maputo, Zequinho fell into the hands of recruiters for Renamo. Zequinho was trained in firearms and espionage in Johannesburg and sent back to Maputo to distribute anti-Frelimo propaganda and recruit malcontents to the rebel movement. It was during this activity that a friend of his—a dutiful vigilante—denounced him to SNASP (National People's Security Service), and the entire clandestine network of Renamo activists connected to him was arrested and tried by the TMR in 1982. From a group of thirteen, Zequinho was one of three defendants not condemned to death by firing squad.[51] In M'sawize, the Makonde camp commander and his wife, who gave Zequinho the pet name Americano (due to his "whiteness"), granted him a second chance because of his frailness, good looks, and mixed-race background. "I used to sit and chat with the commander while his wife prepared something for us to eat," he told me. "When I fell sick his wife took care of me." After recovering from a malarial fever that nearly killed him, Zequinho began working in the infirmary where the commander's wife had nursed him back to health. "I treated people, dressed the wounds, and administered vaccines. Even the commander's wife got several vaccine injections from me when she had malaria. I had a good notion of injections," he said, with a hint of pride in his sad eyes. When I asked him how and where he learned these skills, he at first evaded the question with a "here and there," but at my doubtful look, he came to the truth. "To be honest," he said, "I learned from the drugs. I used to inject myself with cocaine, after having experimented with all kinds of drugs. From that experience, I learned to look for veins and apply injections."[52]

Zequinho's was an extraordinary case. However, sick detainees and camp overseers had little choice but to trust their lives to those whose medical expertise was acquired in similarly unconventional circumstances. To escape the dreadful conditions of labor fields, many detainees sought employment in camp infirmaries. And camp commissars were quick to accept convincing claims of medical expertise from reeducatees, especially those with experience in the health sector, regardless of their occupation.[53] It is unsurprising, then, that most of the sick who reached the Lichinga hospital from reeducation camps were gravely, if not terminally, ill. In most cases, the hospital suggested that such patients—after recovering (and if they survived)—should not be sent back to the camp. In September 1981, Rogério Cunha, a general practitioner and chief medic at the Lichinga hospital, recommended that Benedito Chivambo, a reeducatee from M'sawize with "diabetes mellitus and an incurable diabetic ulcer in the leg," be sent home because the camp's infirmary "has no conditions for his treatment."[54] It is unclear from the archival record whether camp authorities acceded to his recommendation.

SOCIAL LIFE

Apart from the harsh labor conditions, poor diet, unhealthy living environment, and scant health care, life in Mozambique's reeducation camps was also governed by unwritten rules about temperance and abstinence. Detainees were expected to cultivate austere moral habits, to stay away from alcohol and drugs, and to remain chaste. The architects of the reeducation program envisioned life in the camps as close to monastic. However, much of the social life inside the camps subverted these idealistic goals. Living under conditions of extreme want, detainees and warders created new forms of sociability inside and outside the camps that undermined Frelimo's technocratic moralism. Such subversions included drugs, alcohol, sex, and all kinds of illicit trades. As Ana Maria told me, "If you did not smoke you had to learn to smoke. If you did not drink, there you had to drink. Otherwise, you would go crazy and die alone." And she added: "Many people began smoking hemp in the camps."[55] The dormant panopticon of Mozambique's penal colonies could not tame these realities of human nature.

Throughout Mozambique, rural populations had always planted hemp in their gardens. The distillation of *cajulima* from sugarcane and the production of fruit-based moonshines was also a centuries-old tradition.[56] The presence of detainees near rural villages provided a market—incipient as it was—for the intoxicating and inebriating supply that was never wanting in most rural homesteads. Generally, detainees exchanged with villagers the few but very precious goods that they received as part of their rations (mainly soap and clothing) for alcohol and hemp. As Felizardo Chaguala recalled, in Sacudzo, a small group of detainees often went to the nearby village during or immediately after work, endowed with goods collected from several detainees, such as bars of soap, pieces of cloth, and occasionally money. The drinks were consumed in the village because bottles were harder to conceal. But the group would bring the hemp to the camp and share it with fellow detainees.[57] Although smoking and drinking were forbidden and one could be flogged if caught, camp warders often ignored this unwritten rule. Some warders and camp commanders also had a taste for cajulima and hemp. Sometimes detainees and warders ventured together to purchase hemp and cajulima in nearby villages. It was common for warders to send detainees to procure the goods for them or for detainees to bribe warders with hemp to avoid punishment.[58] As Ana Maria and Ché Mafuiane pointed out in our conversation about M'sawize and Chaimite, these arrangements between detainees and warders put all camp dwellers on the same level. "We did not sit at the same table with the camp commander," Ana Maria told me, "but I can say that we smoked with them."[59] In fact, some camp overseers were not only smokers but were also engaged in the hemp trade inside and outside the camps. As former SNASP operative Silva Santana told me, many soldiers bought hemp from rural villagers and transported it to urban areas using Soviet-made airplanes, which were rarely inspected at airports. Austerity could also provide camp authorities and security officers connected to the reeducation program with an opportunity to accumulate wealth. Silva Santana was himself a prosperous hemp trader in the 1970s and 1980s. As he boasted to me, "I built a very nice house with the sale of hemp."[60]

This was one of the many contradictions of the reeducation program. For people detained for smoking, drinking, or so-called sexual corruption, the reality of life inside the camps was a bitter irony. For those who never smoked and did not drink, the camps seem to have initiated them in these habits. Although not all detainees led unrestrained lives, few—captives and captors alike—lived up to the monastic aspirations that political authorities envisioned from the high seat of power in the capital. President Machel was incensed when he first visited the camps of Niassa in 1979 and Cabo Delgado in 1981. In Naisseco (Niassa) and Ruarua (Cabo Delgado), the president discovered that, among many other things, drunkenness and recklessness were the order of the day. Reeducatees and reeducators all lived in "disgusting" conditions and "unruliness."

Although Machel attributed the chaos in those two camps to an internal enemy deliberately seeking to undermine the revolutionary program, he acknowledged that reeducation was rife with contradictions that reproduced the very social ills that the program was meant to eliminate.[61]

The president's findings could not be truer than in the two women's camps of Ilumba and M'sawize. Here there was little that the female camp supervisors could do to prevent the frequent visits of soldiers and paramedics stationed in the military garrisons several miles away from the camps. In 1976, the DPSRN compiled a list of pregnant detainees in the two camps to illustrate how out of control the situation had gotten. While some women were already pregnant when they got to the camps, many fell pregnant after arriving.[62] The archival record is largely silent about the circumstances that led to pregnancies in the camps. But one case was recorded in August 1977 because of the shocking penalty that the offenders faced. The case involved an employee of Niassa's reeducation services contracted to build a brick house in M'sawize. The unnamed man was caught having sex with an unnamed reeducatee. According to the report, it was the fourth time that the couple were caught, and this time they were punished. The camp commander forced the offending couple to repeat the act in the rassemblement in front of everyone. When the couple refused, they were forced to push a barrel of oil around the rassemblement completely naked as all the detainees sang a revolutionary anthem and clapped.[63]

Although this was a case of a civilian who could be subjected to such a humiliating penalty, most visitors to the camps were soldiers with considerable leverage over camp overseers and who compelled detainees and female warders to have sex with them. The subordinate status of female warders is well captured in Licínio Azevedo's film *Virgem Margarida*. Detainees were aware of this weakness in the carceral regimen and sought to use it to their advantage. A relationship with a military officer could offer rewards to a hungry and cold detainee or a solitary warder. Soldiers could provide food, blankets, soaps, and occasionally some time out of the camp in more comfortable lodgings. These recompenses often stirred frictions in women's camps as jealousy and competition for lovers and protectors spread among detainees and warders. Because warders had the upper hand, they used their power to punish competitors for the attention of their loved ones. In M'sawize, Ana Maria recalled, "Sometimes female guards inflicted senseless punishment on girls that flirted with their men." While female detainees remained in the camp if they became pregnant, often delivering their babies and rearing them there, pregnant female warders were immediately removed from the camp and replaced.[64]

But this was not simply a story of men forcing women into unwanted affairs. As one paramedic put it in an application letter to Niassa's Governor Aurélio Manave, "Love happened."[65] In November 1978, MINT moved discharged police officers and comprometidos from a reeducation camp in Nampula Province and resettled them in a new camp on the opposite bank of the Lugenda River, near M'sawize.[66] It is unclear why MINT decided to place a men's camp near a women's one. With the two camps separated only by the river—which is often shallow during dry season—the grassy banks along the running water became a perfect spot for lovers' encounters. In our conversation, Ana Maria interpreted the establishment of a men's camp near her camp as a knavish act on the part of camp overseers who, in her understanding, wanted to satisfy political prisoners with whom military authorities in Niassa had some kind of close relationship. Only further research could confirm this claim. Nevertheless, and according to Ana Maria, "honest romantic affairs" took place when the male detainees arrived. These affairs often began as payment for small favors: fixing somebody's falling hut or sharing a piece of fresh fish or game meat. Given men's ability to fish and hunt, their camp was constantly visited by female reeducatees desperate to "kill their hunger" (*matar a fome*) or to get a better meal for their infants. No disciplinary measure could tame detainees' desire to seek lovers, and indeed, after some time, detainees no longer needed to hide their river crossings. As Ana Maria recalled, "Our 'jumping the fence' to the other side was something visible, especially because on the other side of the river there were better conditions. People wanted to eat, and they had to eat."[67] The word *fence* does not stand for any erected physical barrier here. It is a reference to the illicit act of leaving one's home to meet a lover. The consequence, in Ana Maria's words, was a "shower of pregnancies" that soon befell the camp.[68]

Falling in love and exchanging wedding vows was also part of camp social life. In September 1976, a twenty-four-year-old nurse named António Muianga wrote to Governor Manave to ask for his permission to marry Filomena Matangue, a reeducatee at Ilumba. The couple met in Base Central Ngungunhana, the small military garrison where António was temporarily stationed. In Niassa and Cabo Delgado, military garrisons were often used as distribution points for rations destined for other camps. Given the poor state of the roads leading to the camps, the vehicles from the provincial reeducation services often unloaded rations at a military garrison, and detainees then carried the supplies on their heads back to their respective camps. A walking trip from Ilumba to Base Central could take two or more days.[69] It was most likely on one of these trips that António met and fell in love with Filomena, who was in detention for smoking hemp. In his petition, António promised the authorities that if she continued with her vice after their marriage, he would send her back to the camp himself.[70] The archival record is silent on the verdict of António's heartfelt request. Other requests to wed female detainees were less poignant.[71] But they all reveal the complex world inside Mozambique's reeducation camps, where the elusive power of a modern seeing machine and of technicians of behavior was almost nonexistent.

MOTHERHOOD

The gendered dimensions of internment also indicate the makeshift character of the reeducation program and the government's inability to anticipate its social consequences. Although a few female detainees were interned alongside men (for example, in camps like M'telela and Chiputo, which were designed for political dissidents), most women were detained in the exclusively female camps of Ilumba and M'sawize. Most were accused of prostitution, some were "religious fanatics" (Jehovah's Witnesses), and others were accused of sorcery, adultery, brewing and selling alcohol, and other moral offenses.

The *Notícias* reporter who visited M'sawize in 1976 was shocked by the age range among detainees in the camp. "There were children of tender age and elderly women," he wrote.[72] Either because he was not allowed to see them all or because he chose to omit the fact, the reporter did not mention any pregnant women or their newborn babies. However, a report from Niassa's DPSRN to Governor Manave dated June 1976 noted that forty-six children were born in M'sawize in May 1976, and thirty-one children were born in Ilumba in the same month. In the most guarded camp of M'telela, there were four births.[73] By October 1976, there were fifty-two babies in M'sawize and thirty-nine in Ilumba.[74] This means that eighty-one women—at least in those three camps—were already pregnant when they were arrested in November 1975, and fourteen either got pregnant in the camps or became pregnant in the subsequent arrests that took place after the first massive cleanup operations of 1975. Another report indicated that seventy-six women in both M'sawize and Ilumba were interned with their children, who ranged from ages zero to thirteen. The list includes the name of each child, their age, and the name of their mother. Flora Moisés Machel—the younger sister of President Machel—was among the mothers detained with a one-year-old.[75]

Unlike female warders, who could be released from their duties when pregnant, for female detainees the consequences of sexual encounters (forced or consensual) were often disastrous. As one of the leading inmates in her group, Ana Maria recalled being selected to go to Lichinga to help identify dead babies and their respective mothers in the provincial hospital.

"In the center where I was," she told me, "250 newborn children died. It was the first time that I entered a morgue."[76] Although I could not confirm these numbers in the archival record, several reports to Niassa's governor from reeducation camps as well as from Lichinga's hospital indicate that many reeducatees delivered stillborn infants or that their newborn babies did not survive the first days.[77] Some detainees delivered in the camp or at the health unit in the nearby village, but most had to be evacuated to the hospital in Lichinga because of the delicate condition of their pregnancies. Although the high rate of child mortality was a national problem—and more so in the extremely underdeveloped Niassa—a pregnancy in a reeducation camp was more likely to be an ill-fated case. The lack of appropriate medical assistance, the prevalence of untreated diseases, the harsh living conditions (especially malnutrition and intensive manual labor), and the inexperience of inmates who were in most cases first-time mothers: all these circumstances combined to produce disastrous calamities.[78] As Ana Maria told me, "Everything was missing for someone who was pregnant."[79] The 1980 annual report from Niassa's Provincial Health Directorate observed with alarm the inappropriate conditions in which women gave birth in the province. Even when women gave birth in health units, the report lamented that "most of the deliveries are assisted by unqualified health workers."[80]

For those lucky mothers whose babies survived the often complicated deliveries, nursing and raising a child in a reeducation camp was extremely difficult. In establishing reeducation camps for women, MINT did not contemplate the needs of mothers. Malnourished mothers produced little milk, and when their breasts ran dry, they were forced to feed their children whatever they could find. To wrap their babies, they often tore their capulanas or their own tattered clothes. Sometimes, not even a needle was available to sew the clothes, leading women to resort to rudimentary but very creative solutions to dress their children. As André Trabuco reported in April 1977, in M'sawize, "women use bamboo needles to sew children's clothes due to lack of appropriate needles."[81] Given that children in local villages had more or less the same ragged appearance, in the eyes of camp overseers—including authorities from the provincial government—the situation was considered normal.

CULTURE

If romantic affairs and their often tragic outcomes betrayed the camps' lack of social hygiene, cultural activities, a key component of the reeducation program, offered reeducatees and warders an important outlet from the pains and boredom of detention. Each camp had a Grupo Cultural

Polivante (Multipurpose Cultural Group, GCP) that performed every Saturday or Sunday afternoon. From the early days of the liberation struggle, Frelimo considered culture to be a central vehicle for nation building and for the making of the Homem Novo.[82] Often encompassing folkloric song and dance, and sometimes poetry and visual arts, culture was defined in pragmatic and instrumental ways. It was a visible and performative act that could be displayed in classrooms and playgrounds and could be heard in chants and folk dances from all corners of the country. Its role was to teach people about the rich mosaic that colonialism attempted to destroy and to foster a new national identity.[83] Like nature and society, culture was a malleable corpus that could be transformed at humanity's will. It could be assembled, sorted out, and synthesized to produce a multicolor yet unitary expressive form. For instance, to form a valuable culture for the new society, the sculptures and the exhilarating *mapiko* mask dances of the Makonde people in Cabo Delgado could not stand on their own, isolated and without reference to other cultural expressions. They had to be associated with *makwaela* dances from Manhiça or *timbila* xylophones from Zavala in the south. Cultural expressions were not to be bound to geographical locales or possessed by specific ethnic communities; they were to be shared by all, learned by all, and performed by all people, "from Rovuma to Maputo." This utilitarian understanding of culture was inscribed in a resolution from the 1970 conference on education and culture: "Let dance, sculpture, song, which are traditionally cultivated, be combined with painting, written literature, theater, artistic craftwork. Let's make the creation of some become of all, men and women, young and old, from North and South, so that a new revolutionary and Mozambican culture may be born from all of us."[84]

However, in the same way that individuals could only become new social beings by cleansing themselves of the impure effects of colonialism and feudalism, culture had to be purified and rearranged to serve the goals of the revolution. Expressions seen as representing aspects of the old society were excised from dances and songs and replaced with revolutionary themes. *Poesia de combate* (combat poetry)—a literary genre that was especially encouraged—had to contain meaningful and easily decipherable messages extolling the liberation saga and vilifying the enemies. As the introduction to the first anthology of Frelimo's poesia de combate provided, "Poetry does not speak of myths, of abstract things, but rather of our life as struggle, of our hopes and certainties, of our determination, of our love for our friends, of nature, of our country."[85] Scholars have rightly called Frelimo's cultural aesthetics "socialist realism."[86] Mapiko dancers were prohibited from performing numbers that exalted lineage or ethnic rivalries. Songs and plays that

FIGURE 6.4. Detainees assembled at the rassemblement for cultural activities during President Machel's visit to the Chaimite camp in Cabo Delgado, October 1981. Photo courtesy of Arquivo do Jornal Notícias (AJN).

glorified polygamous chiefs, initiation rites, and other rituals shrouded in secrecy were utterly banned.[87] Cultural producers working across all genres were armed with an array of ready-made revolutionary vocabularies (*palavras de ordem*) to include in their art.[88] Hymn composers, most of whom had trained in Christian churches' choral groups, inserted new lyrics into old religious melodies.[89] Nachingwea—the mythic headquarters of Frelimo during the struggle—was the powerhouse of the party's cultural production. On Saturday afternoons, people gathered at the rassemblement for *actividades culturais*. The party encouraged them to assimilate and perform the various cultural expressions of Mozambique, whether from the urbanized south or the less developed north. In 1972, Samora Machel, a vibrant chorister himself, was convinced that "today a new culture is being developed based on traditional forms with a new content dictated by our new reality."[90]

The new cultural aesthetics tested and developed in Nachingwea and other guerrilla bases became the mainstay of reeducation camps' cultural activities. In the Council of Ministers of July 1976, President Machel urged the authorities in charge of reeducation camps to "promote culture." He instructed them on the kinds of cultural activities detainees ought to perform. "For example," he said, "prostitutes must do theater about the life that they led [before detention], about what it is to be a prostitute." He insisted that "theater, music and dance should be a constant part of life in reeducation

FIGURE 6.5. A GCP choir performs during a presidential visit to Ruarua, Cabo Delgado Province, October 1981. Photo courtesy of Arquivo do Jornal Notícias (AJN).

camps." For him, culture was "a form of liberation."[91] Therefore, every Saturday or Sunday afternoon, detainees gathered at the rassemblement to see their GCP perform. The GCPs could present multiple cultural numbers in just one session. These included choirs singing Frelimo's anthems; groups performing makwaela, mapiko, or *ngalanga* dances; individual or collective recitation of poems written by detainees; and performance of plays. In accordance with the presidential directive, camp overseers held these sessions to cultivate the sense of national pride that detainees were believed to lack. Attending actividades culturais was mandatory in all camps—failure to be present was punished severely. These punishments, however, appear to have been unnecessary because many attended the cultural sessions with enthusiasm.

Aside from photographs and a few poems, no surviving records of the cultural activities performed by the GCPs surfaced from the archives. Simeão Mazuze, who was a professional musician and painter before detention, told me that he directed a play about Ngungunhane, the last emperor of Gaza (the precolonial kingdom that ruled much of southern Mozambique in the nineteenth century).[92] In Frelimo's official history, Ngungunhane was a national hero who resisted Portuguese colonial occupation and was defeated in 1895 because, among other reasons, he was betrayed. Although Mazuze did not remember the details of the play, it is not difficult to imagine its plot and the moral lesson it was meant to impart on the audience: the heroism of resistance, the necessity of unity against the enemy, and the ubiquitous presence of traitorous enemies within.

Although there was no strict censorship in the camps, cultural production followed a defined script that comported with the official history. Like cultural producers outside the camps, GCP artists had to employ the ready-made vocabulary of revolution in their art. Following Samora Machel's prescription of what revolutionary literary works (particularly poetry) had to look like, detainees composed poems celebrating the deeds of the liberation struggle. Two of the only three poems that I found in the archives have unsurprising titles: "Poesia 25 de Setembro de 1977" (Poem 25 September 1977) and "A luta armada" (The liberation struggle). The third was simply entitled "O meu poema" (My poem). They were written by anonymous detainees in M'telela to celebrate the thirteenth anniversary of the liberation struggle—a national holiday. The first three stanzas of the poem "A luta armada" are illustrative of the kind of unpalatable poetry that Frelimo socialist realism encouraged not only in the camps but nationally:

THE LIBERATION STRUGGLE

I
Nobody can stop the people's decision
No, no one can destroy the strength of a united people
A determined people is like a storm
No one can stop nor destroy it
II
Once colonialism
Wanted to test the people's strength and resolution
Since 25 of September of 1964 the enemy was smashed and trampled
He, well-armed and prepared by his generals
III
But with the determination of the people from Rovuma to Maputo
They left without farewell
Completely defeated and unmasked[93]

This kind of revolutionary adulation dominated much of the cultural production in the first years of the revolution. Poems like these permeated newspapers in the free world. The camps were no different. In the camps, too, cultural creativity was restricted to Frelimo's revolutionary dicta. There was little space for spontaneous, elaborate, and abstract expression. Culture had to be readable and easily accessible. Its message had to be clear. Songs, plays, dances, poetry: they all followed the same script in exalting the liberation struggle and its heroes, in praising the vanguard party, and in condemning the enemies.[94] The last stanza of "O meu poema" is unequivocal in its exaltation of the heroes and denigration of the enemies:

> My poem!
> My poem on the 13th anniversary of our struggle for national liberation makes me like!
> My poem!
> I shall never let ants nor flies in my house, that is, the reactionaries and their lackeys.
> My poem!
> It makes me analyze, the Mozambican heroes.
> Down with the ambitious!
> Viva Frelimo, the vanguard Party of the socialist revolution![95]

Despite the straitjacketing restrictions of the official cultural script and the improvised nature of most productions, detainees and warders appreciated the GCP performances. They mostly occurred on public holidays or during official visits by party-state authorities. For such special occasions, the camp's responsável for culture or the political commissar took charge by supervising rehearsals and preparations to make sure that the scripts, lyrics, and poems had no improper formulations or subversive messages. Official visits were perhaps the only times when camp supervisors were nervous because the visits were as much to check on detainees' discipline as on the supervisors' ability to carry out their duties properly. On these occasions, detainees were made to look the best they could. Those with less ragged uniforms were put in the front row, whether seated on the floor or standing, while the GCP performers took center stage in front of the wooden balcony where the illustrious visitors sat.

GCPs allowed detainees with artistic inclinations before detention to improve their artistry and develop new skills. For example, Simeão Mazuze composed some of his most popular songs in the three camps where he served his sentence. He enjoyed a very successful artistic career after detention, including an acclaimed role in the 1985 film *O tempo dos leopardos* (The times of leopards), Mozambique's first feature film after independence.[96] His success in the film was due to his experience acting in plays he cowrote and directed in reeducation camps. His friend Ché Mafuiane, who was an athlete before detention, went on to pursue a modest career in the prestigious theater company Mutumbela Gogo and an equally modest musical career in Mazuze's band, Xigutsa Vuma.[97] For some detainees who joined the GCPs, culture helped forge social bonds that endured well beyond reeducation.

However, one should be cautious not to overstate the significance of the GCPs in Mozambique's cultural life. Mazuze, Mafuiane, and a few others were exceptional cases. Like everything else in the camps, the GCPs were shaped by the shortages endemic to the reeducation program. Cultural producers had to work in very tight circumstances; not only did political commissars control the themes and moral lessons of their creations, but detainees also lacked the most basic tools for artistic production. There were no musical instruments (except for improvised drums in certain camps); paper for compositions and poetry was scarce, so the majority of artistic creations had to be memorized.[98] Most importantly, not all camps had talented artists like Mazuze. In M'sawize and Ilumba, for example, actividades culturais were boring, and detainees were uninterested, which led camp authorities to complain that Niassa's Organization of Mozambican Women (OMM) needed to be more involved in the camps' cultural and social life.[99] Burdened by motherhood and the struggle to feed themselves and their children, female reeducatees had little energy for singing and dancing. With much higher levels of illiteracy than men, there were few who could write plays or poetry. Unlike her friend Ché Mafuiane, who had good memories of camp cultural activities, Ana Maria was resentful: "If the problem was to learn to sing, farm, and march like soldiers, there was no need to take us so far away from home and abandon us in those camps."[100]

DISCIPLINE AND PUNISHMENT

In public pronouncements, party-state authorities often denied that physical punishment was part of reeducation. "Punishment is not the objective of reeducation," said President Machel in 1981; he instead described the objective as "the reintegration into society of the man who went astray."[101] However, for former detainees, including for my informants, the part of everyday camp life that they remember most vividly is the gruesome physical violence they faced. The archival record hints at what detainees suffered under certain camp commanders, but it is generally silent about the kinds of disciplinary methods employed to remonstrate wrongdoers inside the camps: felling trees (*destronca*), digging holes, floggings, and weeks of solitary confinement in wet and muddy underground cells. My informants had vivid recollections of these types of punishment.

The ways in which camp supervisors attempted to enforce the unwritten rules of internment also demonstrate the peculiar features of the reeducation camps. MINT never issued directives about how to handle disciplinary cases. There were no written rules about what detainees were allowed and what they were forbidden inside or outside the camp. Despite this absence, there was a general understanding that detainees should not drink alcohol, smoke marijuana or do any kinds of drugs, or engage in sexual activities among themselves or with local villagers. Fleeing from camp was out of the question. Everyone was compelled to work. In some camps, attending political lectures was mandatory. Hunting and going to the nearby villages without authorization were forbidden. The enforcement of these regulations was often left to the discretion of camp commanders and their deputies. Given the loose security in all the camps, detainees frequently broke the rules. When it came to enforcing discipline, each camp developed its own distinctive character—character that depended largely on the commander in charge and that was thus constantly evolving, given how frequently supervisors were rotated through camps.

Except for solitary confinement and for the felling of trees (which often took place in the bush), all other forms of punishment were invariably a public spectacle, performed or meted out in the rassemblement in the presence of all inmates. There were no individualities in this eyeless panopticon. Punishment had little to do with the private soul or with individual reformation. Punishment was about degradation and theatrical pedagogy. While wardens chastened offending detainees, the other inmates formed a circle in the rassemblement and sang from Frelimo's repertoire of revolutionary anthems. Ché Mafuiane and André Macovo recalled one of the songs from Chaimite: "A wile mucolonyi, a wile, a wile mucolonyi, a wile" (The colonialist has fallen, he has fallen).[102] All the techniques of physical punishment came from the playbook of Frelimo's guerrillas and were all refined during the struggle for liberation when disciplining deviant soldiers and civilian populations under guerrilla authority.[103]

Destronca was one of the most prevalent forms of punishment and was employed in almost all camps. The daunting task did not only consist of cutting a tree down but also of uprooting it with a simple ax. The task could take days, and the punishment did not end until the tree was completely uprooted. "You could take a week, that was up to you," recalled André Macovo. "They waited for you with a rifle while you were at it, tired, hungry, or sick, they forced you to do it until it was done."[104] Any offense could be punished with destronca, depending on the mood of the camp supervisor. Sometimes, the task was used sadistically to "welcome" detainees arrested for serious crimes, such as collaboration with Renamo. Zequinho, the paramedic who arrived at M'sawize in 1982 at the age of seventeen, was greeted with destronca. He recalled his experience:

> As soon as I jumped out of the helicopter, they gave me an ax to uproot a big tree. You could see sparks coming out from the impact of the ax on the wood. But you had to bring the tree down with all its roots. I had never held an ax before. I lived in the city. My hands were torn and bled. But I could not stop. Whenever I stopped, they hit me with the butts of their guns. I worked until it was dawn, and I ended up fainting because of exhaustion and hunger. They poured water on me and told me to continue the work. I could not go on. My ax was bloody. I fell sick. I had fevers for a month.[105]

Callusing the palms of recently arrived urbanites was one goal of this form of punishment, thus beginning the mental and physical transformation that was the object of reeducation, turning lazy city people into hard-working peasants. Camp commanders may well have been replicating on detainees what Samora Machel did to them in Nachingwea when he demanded to see their hands callused.

Some camps were renowned for their cruel forms of punishment. Chaimite and Ruarua in Cabo Delgado and M'sawize in Niassa had underground solitary cells known as Xiconhoca (an allusion to the caricature figure that represented Frelimo's archenemy). These cells were holes dug in the camp and then covered with wood. In Chaimite—a former Portuguese military base—the cell was established in a pit that the Portuguese army once used to stock weaponry. These pits were always kept wet and muddy, and detainees were sent there naked.[106] Simeão Mazuze, who was sent to such a cell in Chaimite, recalled: "Although each reeducation camp had its rules, punishment was almost the same. There was a place called Xiconhoca where a person wearing only a sack was confined, excluded from all other *reeducandos.* They tucked you inside the site and then they poured water. After a while earthworms began to rise out. I do not know if they were really worms, but they pierced you, and you could not sleep. After spending several days there they sent you to fell black wood trees."[107]

The crimes for which detainees were sent to these ghastly places varied. Some were very serious. José Júlio Pereira was sent to the cell for two months for attempting to escape from M'sawize in 1985. "It rained and the pit was filled with water and mud," he told me. "I ate and did everything else there. I got very sick. That's when they took me out."[108] An escape attempt was one of the gravest offenses. André Macovo recalled that he ventured out of the camp at Chaimite one day in 1977 to spend a night with a woman in a nearby village. Upon his return, he was sent to the Xiconhoca.[109]

Other motives were mundane and arbitrary. Chaimite authorities punished Simeão Mazuze in this gruesome way for calling one of the warders *senhor* instead of *camarada*. Mazuze told me that, upon hearing the word *senhor*, the warder rang his whistle and summoned all detainees to the rassemblement. "Some people were three or four miles away working in the fields, but they had to come running." The offended guard informed the detainees that their colleague was a reactionary and had to be disciplined. Asked if Mazuze's fault warranted punishment or not, all detainees raised their hands in agreement. Naturally, they were afraid to oppose an authority figure and end up sharing Mazuze's inevitable fate. The offender tried to argue that the warder was indeed a senhor because he oversaw all detainees, and that the detainees were camaradas because they were all in the same subordinate category. His argument only made his case worse. He was flogged in front of the crowd to the soundtrack of a revolutionary anthem performed by his own companions. After the beating, he was stripped naked, dressed in a sack, and thrown into the underground solitary cell. "I was kept there for twenty-two days," he recalled. "It rained, I was wet, and this time I was alone. I only came out once to bathe in the river. When they finally took me out, I ran around the camp like a madman."[110]

Chamboco was the most common form of chastisement. It was invariably inflicted in highly choreographed public spectacles, a revolutionary anthem sounding in the background. Other forms of punishment included undressing and burying detainees up to the neck or forcing them to lie down in the middle of the open rassemblement and face the sun with eyes wide open. This malicious castigation—well captured in Licínio Azevedo's *Virgem Margarida*—was often inflicted on hot summer days when the sun was at its peak. Sometimes detainees were castigated like cadets, with intensive physical drills like crawling or running for hours around the rassemblement carrying or rolling heavy objects (wooden poles or drums).

Some of the most sadistic forms of punishment were inflicted on Jehovah's Witnesses, whom Frelimo authorities pejoratively called religious fanatics. Although most were interned at Carioco in Milange, Zambézia Province, they were also scattered throughout other camps. Devoted to their creed of only bowing before God, Jehovah's Witnesses obstinately refused to pay homage to the national flag and anthem and refused to shout the *vivas* to the ruling party. One camp commander in Naisseco was notorious for employing gruesome forms of torture against "recalcitrant" Jehovah's Witnesses. He "frequently ordered [detainees] to be tied with ropes soaked with saltwater."[111] This form of torture left many detainees crippled. In 1978, when Governor Manave was informed about the abuses at Naisseco, he ordered the commander to be detained and sent to another reeducation camp as a prisoner. During the Ofensiva campaign and his second visit to Cabo Delgado and Niassa in 1981, President Machel was also shocked by reports about torture in Ruarua and ordered the arrest of the camp commander.[112]

Of all camps in the reeducation complex, M'telela stood out for its special category as a camp reserved for the most notorious political prisoners. Aside from the high security penitentiary in Maputo, M'telela seems to have been the only place where political prisoners were interned. The camp was established in a former Portuguese army garrison in the district of Majune to house some of the "traitors" showcased in Nachingwea. Frelimo former vice president Uria Simango, his wife Celina, politician Joana Simeão, dissidents Lázaro Nkavandame, Paulo Gumane, Father Mateus Gwengere, and several other prominent figures who defected from Frelimo during the liberation struggle and attempted to create alternative parties were sent to M'telela in November 1975. The number of inmates never surpassed 140. The regimen was rigorous, and no outside visitors could enter without written authorization from Niassa's governor and from President Machel.[113] It was the most feared camp, and the one detainees were the most afraid of being transferred to. In an article published in 1996, Dalmazia Colombo, an Italian nun working in the Diocese of the Catholic Church in Lichinga at the time, described M'telela as an extermination camp on par with Auschwitz and the Siberian Gulag.[114] Father Inácio told me that, to this day, the invocation of M'telela still raises discomfort in Niassa. "People do not want to talk about that place here; it is a great shame that our province bears," he said.[115]

These bitter references to M'telela stem from the fact that the prominent figures listed above did not leave the camp alive. They were all executed in a covert operation (possibly in 1979), under circumstances that have never been fully explained.[116] Among the executed was a young Catholic priest from Cuamba (Niassa) named Estevão Mirassi, who was detained by Governor Manave in 1977 for speaking up against Frelimo's authoritarianism.[117]

It is likely that many less prominent detainees were also executed in M'telela pursuant to the governor's orders. A former commander in the famed camp of Nachingwea during the liberation war, Governor Manave was known for being very autocratic and for condemning to reeducation or even execution individuals who seemed to challenge his authority. Those who knew and worked with him in Niassa had a set of terms to describe him: *implacável* (implacable) and *carrasco* (hangman) were some of them.[118] Terms like *Tanzania individual* or *lenha* (firewood) were code words for execution in Niassa, possibly coined by the governor.[119] João Trindade—who served as Niassa's chief justice between 1979 and 1981—told me that Governor Manave was "the maximum authority in the province, he was above everything, including justice. The last word on everything was his. It was up to him to decide who died and who lived."[120] There is a famous story in Lichinga—told in whispers—that he once sent a young man to a reeducation camp for dating his daughter without his consent.[121] He was both implacable and jealous. His notoriety in Niassa equals that of M'telela.

However, the archival record paints a different picture of M'telela. Although the camp was very harsh, living conditions there seem to have been relatively decent compared to other camps. The status of some detainees like Simango commanded some reverence from camp overseers and a much higher concern for their well-being.[122] With the few resources they had, camp overseers tried to alleviate the pains of internment for the prisoners. Some detainees lived in stone houses and were thus protected from the elements. They could write letters to relatives, although they could not mention the name and the actual location of the camp. The treatment they received from warders was generally courteous, with few cases of physical punishment (except in the case of escape attempts). The sadistic forms of punishment that were prevalent in other camps seem to have been rare in M'telela. Prominent political prisoners were executed by soldiers who did not work in the camp complex, and the act did not take place in the camp in front of all inmates. Detainees who had been sentenced to death were taken out in military convoys—often under the pretense that they were being set free or transferred to other camps.[123] At least in M'telela, punishment was not a public spectacle. The fact that the camp included both male and female detainees also made its social life slightly less austere than that in other camps.

DEATH

Mozambique's reeducation camps were not designed to kill detainees. Except the high-profile cases of covert executions of political dissidents in M'telela and possibly in Ruarua, detainees perished due to the harsh conditions of the camps, namely starvation, disease, mental breakdown, and physical punishment. Many were killed by lions and similar predators while trying to escape. Warders faced these threats as well. Yet, no postmortem investigations were ever carried out, even when the victims died in a hospital, and no one was held responsible for the deaths. The defining condition of the *homo sacer*, argues Agamben, is that he or she can be killed without the commission of a crime; nobody is held responsible for his or her death.[124] This is not to say that detainees in Mozambique were entirely consumed by the specter of death. There was more to camp life than suffering. Yet, death was a permanent reality inside the camps, hence the number of pages that DPSRN officers and camp overseers dedicated to recording deaths, and the vivid memories of some of my interviewees who had to bury their fellow detainees.

One detail that surfaces from the archival record is that once the unfortunate detainees breathed their last, no hint of dignity was given to their bodies. Dead reeducatees were unceremoniously buried in the bush, sometimes in unmarked common graves. Camp authorities rarely notified the deceased's relatives.[125] Quantifying the number of detainees in Mozambique's camps is an impossibility, given the paucity of information; the death toll is only slightly easier to estimate. Although camp overseers informed the DPSRN about deaths in their camps, they did not provide mortality statistics. It is likely that many deaths went unrecorded either due to negligence or fear of reprimand (particularly in deaths that resulted from punishment). From the spotty archival record between 1976 and 1977, the DPSRN was informed about the death of close to one hundred reeducatees.[126] Given the inconsistency of reporting and the incomplete state of Niassa's archives, this figure is likely underinclusive and accounts for just one year. Although no records were kept for the critical years of the civil war (1983–88), in which deaths were counted as part of the casualties of the conflict, it is fair to estimate that the number of detainees who perished was well over a thousand.[127]

There were many ways to die in the camps. As DPSRN officers frequently and desperately reported, camps were under the constant threat of hunger and starvation. In their weakened states, detainees easily succumbed to diseases, most of which were caused by the inhospitable conditions of their lodgings. Although some reports included the cause of death, most were plain statements from camp commissars. When reports of death reached the desk of the DPSRN, the deceased had already been buried. An August 24, 1976, radio message from Base Central informed Lichinga that Naisseco reeducando Nuno Maumede died of pneumonia and was buried on August 21. The same message indicated that reeducanda Marta de Lurdes died in M'sawize on August 24 and was buried shortly after. The cause of her death was not mentioned.[128] Most of the death communiqués evince complete insensitivity, as in the following one, dated June 30, 1976, which reported the death of a reeducatee in Ilumba: "We hereby inform the passing in this camp of a *reeducanda* named Rosa Agostinho. The said marginal was the daughter of Agostinho Armando and Beatriz Manuel, from Buzi district, Sofala province. Revolutionary greetings. Unity, Work, Vigilance."[129]

Apart from starvation and disease, the remote location of reeducation camps was a factor in the camps' death toll. Reaching the camps during the rainy season was a deadly endeavor, particularly those camps, like Ilumba,

M'sawize, and Naisseco, that were located beyond riverbanks from Lichinga. During the rainy season, the Lugenda becomes a very powerful river, carrying vast quantities of water downstream. Food carriers trying to cross the river on boats or while using bridges improvised from tree trunks were often swept away by strong currents and never seen again. A situation report from Naisseco to DPSRN, dated August 1977, disclosed that reeducatee Wiliamo Nguenha was taken by the current while trying to cross the river. His body was found the following day.[130] Camp overseers did not escape the dangers of Niassa's wilderness. On May 23, 1976, the river current washed away Naisseco typist Bonifácio Lesta Tomás. He had been tasked with supervising the opening of a road that linked Naisseco to a new sawmill where detainees produced timber. He and the camp commander had used a bark to cross the Lugenda River. "The bark turned in midstream," reported Francisco Taibo, "and the typist disappeared. His body was never found."[131]

People also found death in their desperate search for freedom. Although escape attempts were daunting adventures, given the wild surroundings of the camps and the long and treacherous journey to the city, some detainees took advantage of the camps' loose security and braved the forests. Camp guards also took to the forests and crossed the border to neighboring countries to escape the harsh conditions of reeducation camps.[132] It is difficult to know from the archival record how many escapees succeeded. The reports about runaways in the DPSRN files indicate that some detainees were either recaptured or devoured by predators. Remains of runaways were occasionally found along the roads of rural Niassa, with clear signs of attack by lions or other animals.[133]

Although few reports talk about suicide, some detainees attempted to take their own lives in the camps. One report referred to a failed suicide attempt by Joana Simeão in M'telela, on June 9, 1976. Simeão was one of the prominent political prisoners in M'telela, along with Uria Simango. According to the camp's report, Simeão asked the guards if she could be moved to a different room, calling on them several times during the night. Her request was not granted. She was found unconscious in the morning with a ribbon around her neck.[134] The camp commander, with no medics to turn to and unsure of what to do, asked Francisco Taibo to "come to the camp urgently."[135] When he was informed about the case, Governor Manave dispatched the province's chief medic, who was on duty in Mecula District, to go to see Simeão.[136] Joana Simeão's high-profile status and the staff's urgency in finding her care shows that, at least until 1976, political prisoners were still held in high regard. There is nothing in the archival record that helps elucidate how the situation changed so much that Simeão and her companions were executed in 1978 or 1979. Nevertheless, as Tzvetan Todorov once observed, suicide in internment camps was "an opportunity to exercise free will"; it was an act of "defiance, not desperation."[137]

Dead detainees were buried in unmarked ditches in the bush. Unlike in the Soviet Gulag, where at least a numbered plate marked the location of each grave, in Mozambique's camps, not even a wooden pole was placed to mark the last resting place of detainees.[138] In cases of mass deaths (some of which occurred in the inhospitable camp of Revia in early 1976), bodies were thrown in unmarked mass graves. While few cases of mass death were reported, the use of unmarked graves was widespread throughout the reeducation camp complex. Additionally, little effort was made to notify the relatives of the deceased. Upon receiving death reports, the DPSRN often sent them to the governor's cabinet, who in turn informed the government of the province of origin of the deceased. But such information rarely reached the families. Detainees arrested in 1974 and 1975 arrived in Niassa before the reorganization of peri-urban neighborhoods into bairros comunais or the resettlement of rural communities in communal villages. By 1977, much of the composition of peri-urban and rural settlements had changed. Because writing letters was a privilege granted only to a few people, detainees were unable to communicate with their relatives and often lost track of their whereabouts. Neither MINT nor camp overseers had complete files with detailed information about detainees' origins. The spotty records kept by the DPSRN were based on the testimonies of detainees themselves. Information in the files was organized in columns, included for the detainee's name, generic place of origin (often the district or province, with no indication of home address), age, and the cause of detention.[139] Consequently, relatives were not and could not be informed when detained family members passed away.

MINT was aware of the situation and attempted to address it. In April 1978, MINT distributed a circular to DPSRs in all provinces with camps, urging them to inform authorities about deaths no more than forty-eight hours after their occurrence. The ministry complained that despite orders already given to provincial DPSRs, there were still many problems with how camps reported deaths—they either reported deaths irregularly or much too late. "This causes, as it is obvious, embarrassing situations for the *estruturas* that have to inform the concerned relatives," the circular remarked.[140] In addition to informing authorities about deaths with urgency, camps were instructed to include information about the origins of the deceased to facilitate the location of their relatives. Camps were also instructed, "as much as possible, to report on the causes of death" as well as "the exact date of death."[141] However, the circular said nothing about returning the corpses to relatives to allow them to properly bury the deceased. The bodies were not returned because of the distance, the cost of transportation, and the lack of a refrigerated morgue for storage until transport was available.[142] But, more significantly, bodies were not returned in order to conceal from the public the suffering that plagued the camps. The speedy burial of the remains of detainees originally from Niassa who could easily be returned to relatives proves this point. Abiti Maunde Issufo, a reeducatee at M'sawize, died in the hospital in Lichinga from an undisclosed disease on February 2, 1977. She was originally from Chitambe in Massangulo, a few miles away from the city. Even so, she was buried immediately, after which authorities sent an "urgent" message to the district of Mandimba, entreating the district administration to locate and inform her relations.[143]

Not returning the corpses was a deliberate act that was intended to keep society ignorant of the human cost of the reeducation program. To this day, no dignity has been restored to those who paid a very high price for the socialist experiment. Many families are still in the dark as to the whereabouts of their relatives who were abducted from the cities and sent to camps to be transformed into New Men and New Women. This historical wound, as Dipesh Chakrabarty would call it, is a vivid reminder of the cost of high-minded schemes of social engineering that Mozambique has yet to address.[144]

7 ~ Wretchedness and Survival during Operação Produção and the Civil War, 1983–1989

On a hot summer night in late 1983, António Jorge was sleeping in his hut in the M'sawize camp in Niassa when a commotion outside his hut woke him up. To his shock, the camp commander rushed in, wearing only his underwear and carrying two AK-47s. He handed one to António Jorge and told him to get ready to fight because the camp was being attacked by Renamo rebels. An academic who had been detained without trial, António Jorge told the commander that he never handled a rifle. Besides, he asked, what was he to fight for? To defend his own detention? The commander thought for a short while, shook his head in visible confusion, and rushed out.[1] In the following days, months, and years, like all the other camps and villages in Niassa, Cabo Delgado, and Nampula Provinces, M'sawize was plunged into the horror of the civil war. The camp—once a space of social abandonment and privation, where a revolutionary morality was being forced on allegedly decadent urbanites—became a war zone. The blurry line that had separated detainee from warder and camp from village suddenly disappeared.

When António Jorge arrived in M'sawize, the camp had few detainees. By that time, which followed Machel's Ofensiva campaign between 1979 and 1982, the number of reeducatees had significantly decreased throughout the country. The Ofensiva resulted in amnesty for many detainees and the closure of numerous camps. The growing number of Renamo rebels had initially prompted the government to close the camps south of the Zambezi River, setting some detainees free and arbitrarily moving others to the north of the country. But the expectation that Zimbabwe's independence would bring lasting peace and a decade of rapid economic development animated Machel's decision to pardon most reeducatees in Niassa, Cabo Delgado, and Nampula Provinces. Free detainees were not allowed to return to their original homes. They had to stay in the north and participate in the local implementation of PPI (Plano Prospectivo Indicativo) by either transforming their camps into socialist villages or joining new state farms along the Lugenda and Messalo river valleys. For those detainees like António Jorge who remained in the few reeducation camps that were still operational, for a short period, living conditions improved slightly due to the reduced camp population. But in May 1983, the government launched Operação Produção in a last effort to purge the cities of moral decadence and provide rural areas with the necessary manpower to produce food and push the country toward self-sufficiency. Niassa alone received more than twenty thousand deportees, most of whom were sent to the few remaining reeducation camps, like M'sawize, and to nearby villages and state farms in Unango, Matama, and similar places.

This new flood of people pushed the logistical capacities of Niassa to its limits. Even if the campaign did not attract Renamo directly, it coincided with the arrival of the rebels in the region. The combined effect of the campaign and the civil war was catastrophic. Pardoned detainees starting to rebuild their lives, current reeducatees, and Operação Produção deportees found themselves in the middle of the conflict and left to fend for themselves. Their trials and struggles for survival were not different from those that villagers throughout the country faced. But, unlike villagers who had never been forced from their homes, these urbanites had been removed from the safety of the cities and dumped in an unfamiliar countryside where war actively raged. António Jorge was lucky to return to Maputo before the collapse of M'sawize without ever having had to fight to defend his own detention. Many of his fellow detainees and Operação Produção deportees did not share his luck.

AMNESTY, DEVELOPMENT, AND THE CITIES OF THE FUTURE

When President Machel visited Niassa in October 1979 in preparation for the Ofensiva campaign, he had two goals in mind. One was to assess the reeducation program and verify for himself the damning report produced by the task force that he had instructed to investigate allegations of illegalities in the camps. He accomplished this goal by visiting the camps and holding meetings with detainees and camp supervisors. His second goal was to identify suitable areas for his cherished Niassa Development Program. Part of the PPI section designed for Niassa, the project called for four hundred thousand hectares of arable land and the establishment of at least three state farms in Matama, Unango, and M'sawize; it also included several other smaller agrarian initiatives.[2] In several speeches during his visit, Machel reiterated the idea of populating Niassa as one way of speeding the development of the province. Yet, the thousands of hectares were not to be farmed by Niassa peasants, nor were Niassa peasants the ones who would receive the technical and financial assistance established by the project. Instead, unwanted urbanites were to be the main agents of development. Their task was to transform Niassa's wilderness into socialist villages and, in the process, transform themselves into New Men and New Women. Niassa would be "the great school of the marginal" elements of Mozambican society: vagrants, prostitutes, and criminals.[3] At the end of his visit, the president gave amnesty to detainees in selected camps. All detainees in Chiputo were set free. The inmates from the insalubrious camp of Naisseco were moved to a better location in Unango and then set free a year later. The women's camps of Ilumba and M'sawize were shut down in the following months.[4]

The pardoning of reeducatees was intertwined with Machel's developmental vision for Niassa. Although Machel granted amnesty and closed some camps, detainees were not free to return home. Instead, they were to participate in the development program by transforming their former detention camps into lucrative and respectable agrarian towns where their families would join them.[5] In other words, this was not the end of the reeducation program but an attempt to integrate the camps into the developmentalist agenda. The obsession with reforming the mores of the ex-detainees was not abandoned in this attempt. The family unit—the bedrock of a morally upstanding society—was to be the basis of the agrarian, socialist towns, which were aptly called Cidades do Futuro (Cities of the Future). President Machel commanded camp authorities to locate the wives and children of male ex-detainees and send for them. For those with no families, authorities would "procure" wives for them from local communities. Speaking to a crowd of attentive listeners in Lichinga as he laid out his plan of marrying bachelor ex-detainees to local women, Machel sneered: "We are here, aren't we? Among Mozambicans, what is the problem?" If the bachelors were not happy with local women, Machel remarked, prostitutes from urban areas

FIGURE 7.1. President Machel gives amnesty to detainees at Ruarua and commands them to transform the camp into a City of the Future, October 1981. Amnestied detainees were not allowed to return home. They were to stay in northern Mozambique and work in development projects designed in the PPI. Photo courtesy of Arquivo da Revista Tempo (ART).

would soon join them and they could pick and choose. "Women who persist with prostitution, drugs, will come here too. They will marry drug addicted men. This is a serious decision that the government will take," he said.[6] The scheme overlooked female ex-detainees. Given that reeducandas were considered prostitutes, no effort was taken to locate their relatives or attempt to bring their families to Niassa. It remains unclear what happened to most amnestied women, whether they were free to return to their places of origin or settled permanently in Niassa.

Between 1980 and 1982, ex-detainees worked with some enthusiasm to transform their former detention camps into proper agrarian villages. The local government selected M'sawize and Unango to be the pilot Cities of the Future. It gave municipal authority to a small team of party cadres who had been tasked with coordinating the scheme.[7] Francisco Cuinica, a dynamic party cadre who rose from Frelimo's Central Committee for mass organizations in Maputo to temporary director of the nationalized Sena Sugar Estate in Luabo, took charge of Unango as mayor. Although he was never officially sworn in and his position remained ad hoc until the collapse of the scheme, he embraced his new functions with eagerness and established himself as a prominent leader in Niassa. He quickly organized a task force to locate and mobilize the families of ex-detainees to move to Niassa.[8] According to Cuinica, on paper, the relocation of ex-detainees' families was not compulsory. But party officials employed coercive measures to force women and children to pack up and move to the north.[9]

The scheme proved more difficult than expected. After causing many years of separation and cutting off communication, the reeducation program had broken many families apart. Despite its coercive power, Cuinica's task force could not convince most families to relocate to Niassa. The task force's persuasive abilities often depended on the level of education, occupation, seniority, marital status, and property ownership of the families involved. For poor families deeply disrupted by the disappearance of their members, especially a breadwinning father and husband, fear of party-state authorities was very high; such families were thus more likely to give in and move to Niassa. But for families that had successfully withstood the absence of a father or husband, especially if the mother or wife was educated, materially independent, or, as was often the case, remarried, resettling in Niassa was out of the question. But the biggest challenge was finding the families of ex-detainees in the first place. In the reshuffled cityscapes from which most ex-detainees hailed, addresses and the toponyms of residential neighborhoods were not the same after the Ofensiva, and the bairros in cities like Maputo and Beira had changed significantly in the eight years since independence.

FIGURE 7.2. A detainee is reunited with his wife and child in Unango, October 1981. The family unit was the bedrock of Frelimo's moral society. In Niassa and Cabo Delgado, ex-detainees and their families were to be the foundation of agrarian socialist towns (Cities of the Future), which would develop from the ruins of former reeducation camps. Photo courtesy of Arquivo da Revista Tempo (ART).

By mid-1982, only three hundred families were reunited in Unango.[10] There, a state farming company under the able directorship of Paulo Zucula provided paying employment for all ex-detainees. The farm produced mainly corn and beans, and it enjoyed a modest harvest in its first season in 1981–82.[11] In 1981, two years after his first visit, Machel returned to Niassa and Cabo Delgado to assess the progress of his development program. In Cabo Delgado, Machel extended amnesty to 684 detainees in the Chaimite camp. He instructed camp authorities to send the sick and the elderly back home. The young and fit, like André Mavoco and Ché Mafuiane, were sent to state farms, primarily to the sisal plantation in N'guri.[12] The president promised government support, including the provision of electricity, schools, hospitals, and farming implements. New socialist cities would rise from these country outposts, and the ex-detainees would be hailed as heroes of labor, the epitome of the socialist New Men.[13]

After years of suffering and destitution, most ex-detainees and their families were caught up in the optimism of rural development; they thus enthusiastically committed to the project of rebuilding their lives.[14] In Unango, they built their homes on the slopes of the mountain for which the area is named and cultivated the vast plains watered by the Lucheringo River. A few agrarian technicians from the German Democratic Republic and China offered expertise and advanced equipment to the farm. As employees of the state farm, ex-detainees received a modest salary, permitting them to purchase the basic goods that had been a luxury in the reeducation camps, such as bars of soap and secondhand clothes. Although most Unango residents had their own family farms (especially those who were not employed by the state farm), they were expected to participate in the city's cooperative. The municipal council installed a rudimentary health post and built an elementary school and a secondary school to service the city's population, which was two thousand and growing.[15] For a short period of time, life seemed possible in Niassa.

However, things unraveled quickly, and the sense of optimism gave way to desperation. The Niassa Development Program suffered from the same maladies that afflicted all other development projects under Frelimo's command economy. In Frelimo's grand scheme, agriculture was to provide the means for industrialization. The government gave priority to mechanized or semi-mechanized large-scale state farms. In the words of Merle Bowen, the "strategy antagonized the peasantry" not only because it ignored the needs and capabilities of smallholders but also because it channeled no resources to them. Frelimo operated on a dualist framework that distinguished the formal, market-driven economy from the informal, subsistence-oriented peasantry. The party saw the large-scale state farms as the only sector capable of dynamizing the economy, whereas smallholders had to be brought into the economy by first being organized into cooperatives and then gradually integrated into the formal sector as wage laborers. In other words, while the formal sector needed investment, the informal sector only needed mobilization. This ill-conceived policy ignored the fact that family farming accounted for more than three-quarters of the country's crop output. The PPI budget called for 75 percent of agricultural investment to be allocated to state farms, 25 percent to cooperatives, and nothing to family farming. Despite the party's heavy-handed mobilization, cooperatives did not take off because peasants continued to opt for family farming. Consequently, the government neglected the peasantry and focused on state-run enterprises. Thus, "of agricultural investment between 1977 and 1983, about 90 percent went to the state sector, 2 percent to cooperatives, and virtually nothing to small-scale family farming."[16]

Despite the investment in imported heavy machinery, hybrid seeds, fertilizers, and financial backing, state farms like Unango and Matama performed poorly and failed to accelerate the much-expected development in

Niassa. There were many loose links in the value chain, including deficient marketing structures, insufficient transport networks, lack of managerial and technical expertise, and inadequate supply of operational items like gas and spare parts.[17] Although Paulo Zucula had some agrarian expertise and counted on the assistance of some East European experts in Unango, his colleague in Matama, Caetano Massaka, knew nothing about farming. As Massaka put it in his resignation letter addressed to the minister of agriculture in 1984, he had "no training in agriculture," and none of the hundreds of ex-detainees under his command knew how to drive a tractor, how to operate a combine harvester or how to maintain and repair machines.[18] When machines broke down, mostly because of inadequate use and lack of appropriate maintenance, they were simply left to rust. In Matama, twenty out of forty tractors were not operational and only seventeen out of forty-six tillage plows were in use due to lack of spare parts. There was no coordination between the company and the provincial department of agriculture responsible for supplying the farm with seeds and equipment. When 120 tons of seed potatoes arrived in 1983, the farm had no land prepared for planting, no water pump to irrigate the new crop, and not enough workers to do the job.[19] Although in theory, the farms required little permanent manpower, the process of mechanization was incomplete, which left them dependent on peasant labor, especially during planting and harvesting. Yet, during these periods of intensive labor needs, the farms competed with family farming and could not meet their quotas. While large areas of land could be cleared by machines, few hectares were cultivated, and considerable quantities of crops (especially grain) were left unharvested. Additionally, the Niassa market was too small to absorb the farms' produce, and transportation to the larger market in Nampula Province was not efficient.[20] Like all other state farms across the country, Unango and Matama thus did not yield any profits, and the living standards of their employees did not improve.

However, life in the Cities of the Future was much better than in the reeducation camps. For the first time since 1974, the DPSRN (Provincial Directorate of Reeducation Services of Niassa) had few camps and few detainees to oversee. Although reeducatees continued to arrive, particularly in M'sawize, their numbers were manageable. As a result of Machel's Ofensiva in the judicial branch of the government, from 1980 onward, people could only be sent for reeducation after a formal trial.[21] The Ofensiva seemed to have solved the problem of indiscriminate detentions; the PPI seemed to have infused the populace with a sense of developmental optimism; and the revolution seemed to be moving away from the initial voluntarist phase, with its intermittent cleanup campaigns and spectacles of violence, toward a more directed path of state-led progress and the rule of law. However, the years between 1979 and 1982 were the calm before the storm. The launch of Operação Produção in June 1983 rolled back the few gains the Ofensiva had achieved in the administration of justice. Niassa became one large reeducation camp, a massive penal colony where tens of thousands of expelled urbanites were abandoned and left to fend for themselves.

OPERAÇÃO PRODUÇÃO IN NIASSA

Operação Produção had been in development since 1979 and was meant to be implemented in 1980. However, the party-state never announced a plan for how to carry it out. Although President Machel declared that the campaign would be launched as early as March 1980, the particulars of the operation remained a secret only known in the high echelons of power. When the campaign was finally announced in May 1983, officials in the provincial and district administrations, including the security forces, knew as much as the general population about its details. The central government never notified the rest of the branches of government about the details of the operation. Everybody was unprepared for the campaign, particularly in the provinces and districts where the so-called unproductive were to be relocated.

Niassa received the largest contingent of expelled urbanites. According to the province's police department, between June 1983 and May 1984, Niassa "welcomed" fifteen thousand "unproductive" deportees, mainly from Maputo and Beira.[22] This figure is not to be trusted because the police did not keep records of those who arrived in Niassa; it was instead an estimate that the police department produced for the sake of reporting when the government brought the campaign to an end in 1988. The figure also does not include the number of families who arrived to join their relatives in 1984. Journalist Rui Zunguza, who assessed the campaign in Niassa one year after its launch, estimated that for each deportee, at least three family members joined.[23] We may never know exactly how many people ended up in Niassa, but the number was certainly far more than the fifteen thousand reported by the province's police department.

The effects of the campaign in Niassa were felt immediately. In September 1983, only two months after the beginning of the compulsive phase of the campaign, the new governor, Colonel Sérgio Vieira, sent a wire to Minister Guebuza—the head of the Central Operative Command (COC)—requesting more tools because the province had received more than ten thousand *improdutivos* and it had only three thousand hoes. He warned that if the situation was not addressed immediately, the "unproductive will continue to be unproductive due to lack of instruments of labor."[24] This wire tells us two things. First, it confirms that more people were sent to Niassa than the figure presented by the local police department would suggest because the intensive phase of the campaign continued until May 1984. More people arrived from Sofala and Zambézia Provinces, where the campaign began two months later.[25] Second, the wire confirms that no advance preparations were made for receiving the expelled urbanites. The three thousand hoes that the province had in its possession were not enough for the people arriving by the thousands every week. Those hoes may have been intended not for the newcomers but instead for local peasants. This means that the few resources that the local government possessed—which could barely meet the demands of the local population—now had to be shared with people arriving from outside of the province. The cries of abandonment and the frequent desperate wires to the capital for support returned. But this time they did not come from the isolated—and largely ignored—camp overseers and DPSRN officers; they came from the governor himself. He, too, felt abandoned (and, in a way, betrayed) during Operação Produção.

After serving in various branches of the government in Maputo (chief of staff, president of the National Bank, and minister of agriculture, among others), Sérgio Vieira expected Operação Produção to be like the previous campaigns he witnessed from the capital—that is, brief and theatrical. He believed only a few hundred urbanites would be sent to Niassa to set an example and warn away those who had thoughts of migrating to the cities. Because party leadership framed the campaign as a battle against hunger and unemployment, Governor Vieira expected deportees to arrive with tools, at least some knowledge of farming techniques, tents for temporary shelter, and appropriate clothing. He was shocked and revolted by what he saw. A minimum of four planes arrived to the airport in Lichinga every day, unloading nearly nine hundred people. Most people came with only the clothes they had been wearing at the time of detention. It was July, and the cold in Niassa was unforgiving. The local Provincial Operative Command (COP) had not prepared sufficiently for the scope of the task at hand. It became clear to the governor that Niassa was unprepared to receive the number of people sent from Maputo and other cities.

If running the reeducation camps and the Cities of the Future was challenging, Operação Produção only made things worse. The tremendous daily administrative demand of processing, accommodating, and distributing nine hundred people to the various labor camps consumed all the energy of the provincial government. For two months, everything else stopped. The COP had been allocated only six small trucks for the task. Together, the six vehicles could only transport two hundred people per day. Faced with nine hundred daily arrivals, the administration had to mobilize more vehicles from elsewhere in the province. This meant that other important activities could not continue. The period between June and August is harvest season in northern Mozambique. With vehicles being deployed to transport people from the airport to the city and from the city to the various labor camps, crops were left unattended and rotting. In addition, the number of vehicles mobilized to transport the newcomers was consuming the limited fuel supply, which was also used to run the generators that provided light for Lichinga and many of Niassa's towns. Without electricity, there was no water. Governor Vieira was desperate and enraged. His telegram to Minister Guebuza on July 16, 1983, did not conceal his feelings, and warned of the impending crisis if the capital city continued to send nine hundred people every day. "We fear that the accumulation in Lichinga of these elements without being able to evacuate them," he wrote, "could seriously disturb the conditions of hygiene, health, and order in the city."[26]

The conditions in which most deportees were kept before their relocation to labor camps were inhumane. As soon as they landed at the airport, the Niassa COP drove them to Lichinga's trade fair, Feira de Exposição do Niassa (FEN).[27] They were housed there in the few exhibition rooms until they could be distributed to various labor camps and to state farms. Because the COP had few cars available for transport, the process was slow, and FEN became a ghetto. Many people stayed there for months until transport became available. As Francisco Cuinica recalled, "People were lodged like animals." Rooms with capacity for only five people housed hundreds. The sanitary conditions were repulsive, and little food was provided.[28] Celina Nhantumbo, who spent one month at FEN while waiting for transport to a labor camp, remembered the place as "deplorable."[29]

Hunger, cold, and disease reduced the number of deportees before relocation, as some people died at FEN. Children and the sick were the first victims of the unbearable conditions there. Manuela Nascimento, a local resident in Lichinga, remembered seeing dead bodies on the street near the fair. "Many people came here already sick, many died on the streets," she told me. "It was common to see cadavers there."[30] Governor Vieira's telegram to Minister Guebuza was a desperate attempt to stop the influx of more people. His political discipline and respect for hierarchy prevented him from being more aggressive in his message. But he was profoundly irritated. Francisco Cuinica recalled that the governor exploded once at the airport during another flood of arrivals, when several planes brought hundreds of people from Maputo: "This is worse than Nazism," he heard the governor say.[31] To make matters worse, the line of communication with Maputo was interrupted for four days in early July 1983. Unable to speak with the capital, the governor could not coordinate or request support from the central government, or even intervene to prevent more people from coming to the province.[32] On September 3, 1983, he sent another telegram, asking the head of the COC to at least improve the organization of deportations to give Niassa the time and means to prepare. This time, his tone was less sentimental.

> Concerning Operation Production, we would like [to] suggest [to] Your Excellency some points that would help improve [the] efficiency [of the operation]. First, we must know at least 4 days [in] advance [the] movement [of] airplanes with two objectives [:] to send cargo [in their] return and to have here arranged the means [of] immediate evacuation of the [unproductive]. Second, notify us with 4 days [in] advance of the list of those being sent and their cases so [that] we can draw up a plan for [their] distribution and immediate evacuation as indicated in point one. Third, given that in wintertime, and our winter is relatively cold, [the] deportees should bring with them [at] least clothes and blankets, as well as tents for immediate shelter. Fourth, the province faces permanent difficulties [such as] lack of soap and medicines. Agglomerations [of] people can create serious problems for us. So, in our suggestion: a) Make prior medical inspection of deportees to prevent cases of cholera, hepatitis, tuberculosis, and other contagious diseases. b) Send [at] least soap with [the] deportees to ensure [the] indispensable hygiene that prevents unfortunate situations.[33]

What the governor was asking for in this telegram was an idealized, coordinated process that Guebuza simply could not deliver. The campaign had been out of control from day one. Verification and deportation centers in Maputo, Beira, Nampula, and other cities faced the same logistical constrains. They were understaffed and working nonstop to verify the cases of thousands of arrested citizens per day. There was little time to produce lists of people before sending them away. Deportation centers in the cities had also become ghettos due to transportation shortages. In these centers, authorities were only concerned with getting as many people out as quickly as possible. They could not inform the provinces of destination four days in advance because airplanes were not adhering to a predictable, coordinated schedule. The COC in Maputo had lost control of the campaign from its inception and was unable to direct where it went.

Aside from its social cost, Operação Produção had material and financial consequences for Niassa. The entire campaign cost Niassa 63,856,756 meticais ($1,596,418.90 at the rate of 40 meticais per dollar).[34] This money was mostly used to cover the cost of fuel, to distribute the unproductive to the various labor camps across the province, to feed them, to provide them with seeds and hoes, and for minor logistical expenses. This amount was many times more than the entire budget for reeducation camps between 1975 and 1983.[35] Yet, it was not enough to meet the needs of tens of thousands of people.

Despite the logistical difficulties, lengthy wait, and pain that deportees experienced at FEN, the COP managed to send them to ten of the fifteen districts of Niassa—namely, Cuamba, Lago, Lichinga, Majune, Mandimba, Marrupa, Maúa, Mavago, Muembe, and Sanga.[36] The distribution was random. Some people went to state farms and others to the Cities of the Future in Unango and M'sawize. Some went to reeducation camps, particularly to M'sawize. But the majority went to uninhabited rural areas, in a process that reproduced the initial phase of the establishment of reeducation camps. With only a hoe or an ax—or, in most cases, with no tools at all—the unproductive were given some seeds for beans and corn and told to clear the land for their *machamba* and to build the huts for the night and for the years to come. This was their new home.

UNANGO, MATAMA, AND M'SAWIZE: WHAT KIND OF HOME?

In July 1984, Rui Zunguza and Naíta Ussene, two seasoned *Tempo* magazine reporters, went to Niassa to document the integration of the unproductive one year after their deportation from Maputo and other cities. The pair produced a moving and detailed report about living conditions in Unango and Matama in the wake of Operação Produção. While Ussene took photographs, Zunguza, a perceptive journalist, collected testimonies from several deportees and local authorities directly involved in the campaign. They were all cries of abandonment and despair.[37]

The distribution of the unproductive was left to the discretion of local COPs. Fortunate deportees went to villages and state farms, which were only minimally equipped to accommodate them. The communities to which they were sent were rarely informed about the process beforehand. Most were surprised when trucks arrived with loads of visibly confused urbanites.[38] The manner in which deportees were brought into villages resembled a slave market. But here, there was no buying, and accepting slave labor was a requirement rather than a choice. As soon as the truck discharged the deportees in each village, the local villagers were summoned and instructed to take one person into their family. "Adopt a child" was the phrase authorities used for the procedure. Each head of household was given time to evaluate the newcomers, who were made to stand in a line in the center of the village, and to choose a sympathetic face. There was no time for introductions. This was an encounter of strangers who spoke different languages and who were being forced to live together. Most villagers did not speak Portuguese. The newcomers had no idea what language was spoken in Niassa. The idea was that each village household would adopt one deportee who would help the family in the fields for at least a year; during this time, the deportee would acclimatize, learn to farm, and eventually establish his or her own household. As José Ngovene recalled, "In my group we were 500 people, more than the villagers. When all villagers had chosen their 'children,' the less respected among them were forced to take one more because we were too many. The villagers were forced to take us in, because everything was coercive at that time."[39] This was the solution that Niassa's COP found for handling people who had arrived with no means of surviving on their own. Villagers had no say in the proceedings, and so the burden of the campaign fell on their shoulders.

In state farms, the situation was somewhat better but not without problems. Unango and Matama had extensive agricultural fields that were managed in the same way as all state farms in Mozambique. They were highly mechanized enterprises and did not need to employ many workers. In fact, the hundreds of ex-detainees were more than enough to run the two farms. They spent most of their time without work. Labor was only necessary during harvest. Many studies of Frelimo's agrarian policy indicated that this was one of the factors behind the massive migration of people to the cities. Frelimo's emphasis of highly mechanized agriculture exacerbated the problem of rural and urban unemployment.[40] The driving premise of Operação Produção was the belief that peasants were fleeing the hoe, creating a surplus of labor in the cities while depriving the countryside of its workforce. Nothing could be further from reality. When the campaign began, Paulo Zucula, the director of Unango, requested a hundred people to help with the harvest. The COP sent him 250. In July 1984, when he was interviewed about the process, Zucula said that "*Operação Produção* transferred its problems to us, and its problems exacerbated ours."[41] The company did not have enough housing to accommodate the newcomers. The campaign began during the busiest time of year for the company because all workers were engaged in the harvest. They had no time to build huts for the deportees. The consequences were devastating. Many people were sick, hungry, and without shelter. The company did not have fuel to transport the sick to the hospital in Lichinga.

Similarly, the COP sent six hundred people to the state farm of Matama. But this was many times more people than the company could manage because, despite the farm's considerable size, there was not enough work to go around. In the end, the company sent two hundred people to a construction company "as a loan." Like Unango, Matama did not have enough lodgings or food for the newcomers. A desperate testimony by a deportee named Eduardo Nhamusua in July 1984 summed up the dire situation: "Many [people] here are sick. Since I was born, I did not know that a sack serves as a blanket. Here each person struggles to get five to six sacks. We rip them and we use them as a blanket. The result of this is that the dust that the person absorbs every night accumulates in the lungs and causes mortal diseases. The authorities here have never met with us to know about our concerns and to help us solve them."[42]

Hunger, cold, disease, and unsanitary housing claimed many lives. Pedro Vanombe told Zunguza about a colleague who died as soon as he arrived in Matama. Gabriel Julião was more bruising in his testimony: "We sleep like bags, we eat like pigs, and when [we fall] sick we are considered a piece of a machine," he cried. "Not long ago our colleague died. He fell ill and was not taken to the hospital. He stayed with us in those barracks. They only removed the body the following afternoon."[43]

Life was difficult in Niassa during Operação Produção. People longed to go back home. "I had a better life in Maputo, here we have no plate, no pan, no blanket, nothing," said Argentina Macuacua, who went to Unango with her six children to join her deported husband. She left four other children behind but could not think of having them join her. Now she knew that the party's promises of a better future in Niassa were all empty. Her six children were starving and cold. When the COP sent secondhand clothes for the company to sell to the deportees, there was nothing for children. "When the clothes arrived, they did not count with our children," she said. Another deportee, Eduardo Nhamusua, lamented nostalgically: "In Maputo at least we had something, chicken, a plate, wife. We came here thinking that we would contribute to the development of our country according to the instructions of the Fourth Congress. But the life we lead here discourages us from working with our maximum strength and will." From his testimony, Nhamusua had clearly believed the party's propaganda and gone to Niassa during the voluntary phase in the hope of improving his life and contributing to the revolution. His colleague, Pedro Vembene, spoke while holding a pan of rotten maize flour to show the reporter how desolate the situation was (figure 7.3). He pointed to a group of old and young people who had nothing to do in Matama and asked: "That old man there, he can't even walk, isn't he unproductive here in Niassa? What about these sixteen and seventeen-year-old boys, what future do they have here?"[44] The reporters had no answers to give.

FIGURE 7.3. Rui Zunguza interviews a group of deportees in Matama, June 1984. Pedro Vembane shows the rotten maize flour that the company distributed to workers. Photo by Naíta Ussene. Courtesy of Arquivo da Revista Tempo (ART).

For women and children who went to Niassa to join husbands and fathers who had been deported, the situation was more complicated. With the campaign so poorly organized, the family members that arrived later needed luck to find and be reunited with their relatives. There were several cases of family members that went to one district while their relatives were in another or even an entirely different province. In other cases, whole families arrived at the same time but were separated. Delfina Chaúke went to Niassa with her five children. The COP sent her to Matama, but her husband had fled, and nobody knew his whereabouts. "I don't know what to do," she told the reporter. "I am alone with the children. I have no relatives here. The company refuses to sell me food to feed my children. They say I'm not an employee. But what am I to do with the children?" The year 1984 was the peak of the economic crisis in Mozambique, and hunger loomed large everywhere. With crops left to rot while trucks were busy distributing people, Niassa had little food that year. Companies received more workers than they really needed, and they were forced to restrict rations of food. Without a contract and having to fend for her children alone, Delfina Chaúke was left vulnerable and an easy target for local militias seeking to take advantage of her. "Every night the militias come to my house, they accuse me of being *candongueira* and other things, but what will I do with my children? If I were alone there was no problem, but the children?"[45]

FIGURE 7.4. Ailing deportees and ex-detainees wait for medical care in Lichinga, June 1984. With no lodgings, they lived in the open, in the vicinity of the hospital and the local police station. Photo by Naíta Ussene. Courtesy of Arquivo da Revista Tempo (ART).

Rui Zugunza and Naíta Ussene saw and photographed hundreds of people who were lost in Lichinga and unable to locate their relatives. Most found shelter at FEN, at the police station, and at the hospital, where they were left to their own devices (figure 7.4). Local authorities told them to return to Maputo, but they would have to find the money for airfare on their own. To purchase a ticket, most sold all the belongings that they had brought to Niassa in the hopes of beginning a new life. Even if they succeeded in purchasing a ticket (and many did), they still ran the risk of being arrested again in Maputo as vagrants.[46] Zunguza summed up the situation by claiming that the campaign against the urban unproductive produced the rural unproductive. "The deportees who have become unproductive in Niassa are made up of two groups of people," he wrote. These groups consisted of "women unable to locate their husbands and former workers and students unjustly deported. Today these people suffer from serious psychological problems."[47]

The two reporters did not travel to the uninhabited areas where most deportees were sent to build their own villages. Nor did they go to reeducation camps, where detainees and deportees lived together in what became an imprecise and peculiar form of internment. The overwhelming majority of deportees went to the district of Mavago and settled near and within the reeducation camp of M'sawize. According to Zequinho, in 1983, the camp had fifty reeducatees. Just a few months after the beginning of Operação Produção, the camp's population had climbed to three thousand. "People died every day," he told me. "They arrived very weak and were put to work immediately. I buried some of them myself."[48] Interviewees from Niassa described cases of people who spent days walking back to Lichinga from Mavago, trying to find relief from hunger. Although the COP stationed militias to prevent people from leaving their designated areas, most militia units did not stay for more than a month, returning to Lichinga due to food shortages and hunger.[49]

In addition to hunger and destitution, matequenha wreaked havoc in the unsanitary lodgings where deportees lived, claiming many lives.[50] Soap for personal hygiene was unavailable. Despite Governor Vieira's insistent requests, not even a single box of soap was sent to Niassa for deportees until after he was relieved of his post in late 1984. His substitute, Mariano Matsinhe, also failed. His requests for assistance from the capital fell on deaf ears. Abandoned and desperate, most people returned to Lichinga with the faint hope of finding their way back to Maputo or Beira. But danger lurked in the bush. To this day, stories of people who had been devoured by lions while traveling back to Lichinga during Operação Produção are ubiquitous in Niassa's collective memory. Much of Mavago is part of Niassa's game reserve, and the COP placed no one in that territory in order to prevent desperate people from venturing through the jungle back to the city. We may never know how many people perished in Niassa. In the vast expanse of abandonment that Niassa became, most who died are unaccounted for. Much like the reeducatees who had died in the camps and then been unceremoniously buried in unmarked graves like Agamben's *homo sacer,* the victims of Operação Produção in Niassa vanished without a trace.

Despite the dangers of the journey, by 1985, many people had abandoned the rural areas where they were dumped and sought refuge in Lichinga. Some gathered at the air force base at the airport, hoping to catch a flight back home. When he was informed of the large number of people camped out at the air force base, Governor Matsinhe instructed the provincial tribunal to "collect" them and "submit the people to trial." He further directed the tribunal to condemn them all to be reeducated and sent to Sanga District, one of the few districts in Niassa that still had reeducation camps in operation.[51] Under the terms of the directive that governed Operação Produção and instituted a state of exception, the desperate deportees at the air force base were unproductive and had committed the crime of desertion from work. As the campaign's directive had already determined, "unauthorized presence [in the cities] leads to immediate detention and deportation to a destination of the convenience of the authorities."[52] The destination Governor Matsinhe found convenient was the reeducation camp. He did not care that people were fleeing from hunger, matequenha, and the war that was, by 1985, already ravaging all the villages and labor camps.

WAR, DISPERSAL, DESPAIR

The civil war that harrowed Mozambique for sixteen years from 1977 to 1992 is the most covered topic in the country's postindependence history.[53] However, scholars have largely ignored the connection between the origins of the conflict and those of the reeducation program and the cleanup campaigns. The camps and the campaigns contributed to cementing anti-Frelimo sentiments, especially among the segment of Mozambican society that was already opposed to Frelimo's socialist ideology. The camps were also the first source of recruits for the rebel movement.

André Matsangaissa, the founding leader of the Mozambique National Resistance (MNR, later renamed Renamo) escaped from the Sacudzo camp in Sofala Province in October 1976. A former Frelimo soldier, he was arrested in September 1975 "for allegedly stealing army property"; he was condemned for reeducation. His was not the only anti-Frelimo organization. Several other dissatisfied groups operated independent of each other to resist Frelimo. The most notorious was the Malawi-based Partido Revolucionário de Moçambique (PRM), which led military incursions in Zambézia Province, and Voz da África Livre, a small Rhodesia-based group that waged a political campaign against Frelimo through radio broadcasts. The main actors in the Voz da África Livre were White settlers who left Mozambique after Frelimo took power in 1974.[54] Although these groups eventually came together to form Renamo, in early 1977, they all competed for prominence in the resistance movement against Frelimo. They also competed in drawing support for their ill-defined causes, especially from the Rhodesian regime.

In 1976, Frelimo decided to enforce UN sanctions against the pariah state of Rhodesia, which the Portuguese colonial government had ignored since the mid-1960s. The sanctions consisted mainly of barring the landlocked country from accessing the sea through Mozambique. From the time that Cecil Rhodes's British South Africa Company had established the colony of Southern Rhodesia in the late nineteenth century, most of the colony's trade was serviced at the port city of Beira. Although Rhodesia redirected trade to South African ports, the White minority regime perceived Mozambique's open confrontation as a serious offense. Enraged by Frelimo's closure of their main outlet to the world and by Mozambique's backing of

Zimbabwe's nationalist movements, the Rhodesian regime sought to retaliate. Their strategy was to undermine Frelimo through radio propaganda and the formation of a small military unit that would assist the Rhodesian army in fighting the Zimbabwean nationalists that operated from Mozambique. This unit would have no autonomy and no political agenda of its own. Rhodesia was not interested in regime change; it wanted instead to pressure the government to change its anti-Rhodesia stance.[55] Matsangaissa thought otherwise. He believed that armed rebellion by Mozambicans, rather than ideological propaganda, was the only effective way to challenge and undermine Frelimo. He took it upon himself to assemble an army to convince the Rhodesian military authorities of his strategy. The reeducation camp of Sacudzo would provide the manpower he needed.

Matsangaissa's first attempt to recruit men at Sacudzo in December 1976 led to his recapture. He spent two days walking alone from the Rhodesian border to the camp, armed with a pistol. When he reached the camp, he was arrested for "being absent from the camp without permission." By then, acts of armed rebellion had taken place in Manica Province near the border with Rhodesia. Frelimo did not want to recognize the seriousness of the threat to its power or acknowledge its own role in inciting opposition. The government gave little thought to the fact that its harsh policies were feeding resentment inside Mozambique. At Sacudzo, Matsangaissa was under no special surveillance. He escaped again in early 1977 and went back to Rhodesia. In May he returned to Sacudzo, this time leading a small band of armed men. Although some scholars have called his operation a raid, in reality, he faced no opposition because the camp had few armed guards.[56] Renamo veteran Hermínio Morais, who took part in the assault, told me that when they reached the camp the guards put their weapons down, and no shots were fired while they were there. Moreover, Matsangaissa did not have to use force to recruit people to his cause. They voluntarily joined after he delivered a speech about the need to resist communism and oppression.[57] Much later, Renamo would resort to coercive recruitment and kidnappings, but in those formative days, the rebel leader employed only his own persuasive powers; people were free to join or to remain in the camp.

While many detainees opted to stay rather than take up arms against the government, some joined the rebels. One of the fifty detainees that followed Matsangaissa was Juliano Cumbane. When he was twenty-one years old, he was removed from a commercial bank in Maputo where he had quickly risen to management after the sudden departure of the Portuguese. He was accused of leading a bourgeois lifestyle and sent for reeducation. As he told me, Matsangaissa's speech was uplifting and convincing.[58] Until camp security sounded the alarm and a squad to chase the rebels was assembled, Matsangaissa and his volunteers had made considerable progress toward the border with Rhodesia. The squad spotted them just as they were about to cross the border. Shots were exchanged. The group dispersed, but Matsangaissa managed to reach Mutare with twenty-eight of his new recruits. In Mutare, the Rhodesian Central Intelligence Office (CIO) had established a base in Odzi for the rebel group.[59] Some of Matsangaissa's recruits from the Sacudzo camp went on to become Renamo's main military leaders. According to Juliano Cumbane, fifteen of Renamo's top generals were recruited in reeducation camps in Sofala Province. With his managerial skills, Cumbane became Renamo's head of war materials and logistics, as well as a member of the rebel's general staff.[60]

Due to its proximity to Rhodesia, the Sacudzo camp played a key role in Renamo's early days. It was an easy target for the rebels, which boosted their confidence and convinced the CIO of their viability as a serious force against Frelimo.[61] Even after Matsangaissa's daring assault, the Sacudzo camp continued to supply the rebels with new and eager recruits. Camp security was never tightened, and the rebels took advantage of this laxity by establishing a covert network that helped willing detainees escape to join them. Edmundo Tanasse was one of the detainees who kept the pipeline going. Although he did not think of joining Renamo himself, when he was approached by a Renamo recruiting agent, he promptly volunteered to help disseminate the word among his fellow detainees and guide them through the pipeline. Tanasse had been arrested for embezzlement in Maputo (a crime he confessed to) and was one of the higher-status detainees who had the freedom to go in and out of the camp at will. As a former serviceman in the colonial army, he handled rifles better than the camp guards could. He was put in charge of hunting parties to supply the camp with game meat in times of extreme hunger. The confidence that the camp authorities bestowed on him allowed Tanasse to go frequently to the nearby village of Paiva de Andrade (today Vila da Gorongosa), where he met and developed a long relationship with a local single mother. His partner's son was a Renamo recruiting agent. They both worked together to smuggle willing detainees out of the camp to Odzi. As he told me, he recruited a total of twenty-six people for Renamo during the two years that he was in Sacudzo, between 1977 and 1979.[62]

Although camp authorities never discovered the underground pipeline, the government realized the danger of running camps at the epicenter of an insurgency. The government started by reducing the number of inmates in Sacudzo. Some inmates, like my interviewee Felizardo Chaguala (who was eighteen years old at the time), were set free.[63] Others, like Beto Tembe, were sent to the military training center at Dondo (Sofala Province), with the intention of integrating them in the newly formed militias that were being deployed to fight Renamo and the Rhodesians.[64] The majority, however, were moved to other reeducation camps further north in Nampula, Cabo Delgado, and Niassa. The camp was finally closed in 1979, together with all camps south of the Zambezi River, where the rebels were active. But it was too late. By then, Renamo had grown from a small, erratic band of bandits numbering 76 men in 1977 to a well-funded and well-trained army of 1,350 men, with its permanent headquarters inside central Mozambique.[65] The camps had done their job. As one Renamo veteran put it, "Reeducation is what fueled the resistance."[66]

Frelimo's failure to associate the camps with Renamo was partly due to its belief that the rebels were puppet agents of Rhodesia with no mind of their own. This major misconception led to perhaps the biggest mistake that Frelimo made, which occurred when Zimbabwe became independent and Renamo moved from Odzi to Phalaborwa in South Africa. Frelimo was convinced that the rebels would be easily crushed once their masters had lost power in Rhodesia. The Frelimo delegation that took part in the Lancaster House negotiations, which culminated in Zimbabwe's independence, did not raise the issue of the rebels in discussing the conditions for a peaceful transition. Mozambique's intelligence services underestimated both apartheid South Africa's willingness to fill the void left by Rhodesia and Renamo's ability to secure South Africa's support. As Juliano Cumbane told me, at the same time that Zimbabwean soldiers were landing in air bases near Mutare, arriving from Mozambique and other neighboring countries, he and his Renamo colleagues were flying out to Phalaborwa in plain sight.[67] Despite the South African takeover, Mozambican authorities attributed little agency to Renamo (hence their mistaken conclusion in 1984 that only dialogue with South Africa would bring peace). Until the ruling party was forced to seek a negotiated settlement directly with the rebels to end the war in the late 1980s, Frelimo continued to regard Renamo as armed bandits with no political agenda.

In addition to Frelimo's institutional and resource limitations, Frelimo's strategic oversight proved advantageous to the rebels. After wreaking havoc in nearly every village south of the Zambezi River by 1982, Renamo moved northward and began operating in Niassa in September 1983, three months after the beginning of Operação Produção.[68] The two events were not necessarily connected—that is, Renamo did not follow in the path of the mass deportations.[69] But the campaign undoubtedly fueled the civil war in Niassa and in northern Mozambique more broadly, in the same way that the reeducation camps had played an important role in starting the war. The thousands of destitute and justifiably angry urbanites in forced exile were an attractive source of potential recruits for the rebels. It is unclear how many people Renamo recruited from among the deportees. By then, the rebels had abandoned using persuasion to recruit members and instead resorted to kidnappings and forced enlistment, especially of children. My interviewee José Ngovene told me that he recognized some of his former fellow Operação Produção deportees among the rebels when they attacked Unango in early 1985.[70]

However, in Niassa, Renamo based its military strategy less on recruiting people than on controlling territory. Of the categories into which Robert Gersony divided Renamo's operational strategy—namely, taxation, control, and destruction—Niassa was a "control zone."[71] According to Hall and Young, it was in control areas that Renamo established its bases and where local people "experienced extreme degrees of forced labor, especially involving porterage duties and other abuses."[72] This is precisely what happened to most deportees who fell into the hands of Renamo in Niassa.

Beginning in late 1984, Renamo launched several attacks in villages where deportees were relocated. With the largest state farm in the province, Unango was one of Renamo's major targets. After ransacking their targets and destroying all they could, the rebels often kidnapped the residents and took them to their bases.[73] Renamo's main stronghold during the entire course of the war was in the district of Maúa. According to Hermínio Morais, who stayed there for two months to train rebels on railway sabotage, the area was chosen for its remote location between mountain peaks, which made deploying government troops there impossible. But it also had a substantial concentration of peasants and readily available sources of food.[74] Although many people died in the attacks, those who were kidnapped were taken to Maúa and subjected to the same regime of exile and forced labor they experienced in government camps.[75] Renamo was not interested in winning them over to their cause. The rebels' actions were instead geared toward disrupting any governmental program and populating their strongholds with laborers who could secure food for their soldiers.

For many deportees, particularly in Unango, the effects of the war were ironic to say the least. Most received military training and joined the militia corps.[76] Although the militias were trained for defensive combat, most were deployed in military operations in the battlefield. To protect his City of the Future, Francisco Cuinica formed a militia unit made up of ex-detainees and Operação Produção deportees. He armed them and had them literally defend their own imprisonment. Unlike the M'sawize commander who found it ridiculous that António Jorge should bear a weapon to defend his own detention, Cuinica was not bothered by conflicts of consciousness. He had a city to defend, and he worked with the few resources he had at his disposal. His colleagues in other places in the province used the same approach. As he put it in our interview, the war effort in Niassa was "sustained by *ex-reeducandos* and *improdutivos*."[77]

However, as the years went on, there was little to defend in Unango. Production was halted and disorder settled in. Danger was everywhere and no one was safe. The story of how the director of the farm, Paulo Zucula, escaped from certain death is part of Niassa's oral history today. Due to intense rebel activity in the area, the provincial army commander had warned him not to travel without military escort on the only road linking Lichinga and Unango, but Zucula still insisted on taking a team of eight European cooperantes to the farm, supposedly to test out new equipment and farming techniques. When the rebels ambushed his minibus, Zucula ran away, accompanied by the one passenger who had been sitting with him in the front cabin. The rest were seized by the rebels and killed on the spot.[78] After this incident, the government removed nearly all foreign cooperantes from Niassa and repatriated them.[79] A small monument still marks the place of the tragedy.

By 1986 and 1987, the war had disrupted all government initiatives and upended life in Niassa for everyone. Hunger was pervasive, including in the capital city of Lichinga.[80] The logistical challenges that camp authorities and the COC had wrestled with to carry out the government's reformist projects now plagued the army. Underresourced and ill-equipped, neither the army nor the militias could protect the reeducation and labor camps, state farms, villages, and Cities of the Future from the constant Renamo assaults. In Sanga District, where the M'sawize camp was located, thousands of destitute and hungry ex-detainees and Operação Produção deportees wandered from one village to another to escape the rebels and, increasingly, the abuse from disorderly government soldiers. As the district administrator reported, Operação Produção deportees were starving because "they did not produce due to the war" and no rations were available.[81] In Unango, militia men were out of control. To feed themselves, they took food from the local population by force.[82] Soldiers stationed in Muecanhe complained about the lack of munitions, food, and clothing, and they also reported having felt helpless when Renamo rebels kidnapped women in the area.[83] Desperate, the district administrator of Sanga asked that "sick and elderly individuals" who came as improdutivos be relieved of their misery and sent home.[84] By 1989, the situation was so critical that the same administrator asked to move the district headquarters to Unango, where Cuinica's militias seemed to have secured some kind of military stronghold despite Renamo's constant assaults.[85]

To compound an already alarming situation, the rebels destroyed power lines and telephone posts, thus cutting off lines of communication with the provincial capital. These acts of sabotage increased the isolation and the sense of abandonment that local authorities always felt in Niassa. If government authorities felt abandoned and helpless, one can only imagine how urbanites caught in the middle of the war felt. It is not germane here to narrate the details of individual and collective suffering that the war brought to a people that had already sustained too much pain. The victims of Operação Produção suffered as much as the over five million Mozambicans all across the country who were directly affected by the war.[86] The estimated death toll for the entire war is one million; this figure includes those relocated urbanites who perished.[87] But what made their suffering even heavier is the fact that the government was supposed to protect them but instead forced them into the middle of a conflict they had already escaped when they migrated to the capital city from countryside villages in southern Mozambique. It is one thing to face the ravages of war in one's own home. It is altogether another to face them in an unfamiliar land.

Nevertheless, neither the war nor the permanent state of abandonment destroyed the human spirit of most deportees. Even in the most hopeless places, acts of kindness and love still took place. Carlos Sevene and Adelaide Matsolo are an extraordinarily moving case. Both were kidnapped by Renamo and taken to Maúa in 1985. Carlos Sevene was an industrious fisherman in Maputo before Operação Produção. His wife, who had joined him in Unango from Maputo, abandoned him to live with a man in the army. Adelaide Matsolo was sent to Unango from Maputo to join her deported husband. During the attack, her husband disappeared (possibly taken to a different rebel base or killed). Alone and destitute, Adelaide wandered aimlessly in the village, which was under Renamo control. For months, she lived as an indigent, and everyone believed her to be severely mentally ill. Carlos Sevene found her naked and unconscious in the middle of the village and took her to his shack. He covered her body with fabric torn from his only pair of pants. Together, they navigated the torments of exile, war, forced labor, and kidnapping in government camps and Renamo bases until the war came to an end in 1992. Like many of their fellow deportees who survived the war but had no means to return to Maputo, they went to the only place they had known in Niassa, the Future City of Unango. Piece by piece, they built a home on the slopes of Unango Mountain and formed a small community of southerners in permanent exile. When I interviewed them in 2015, they were both in their midseventies, and their only concern was that their marital union had never been officiated through *lobolo* (bride price) in the presence of Adelaide's relatives who, they believed, still live in Maputo.[88]

The story of Carlos and Adelaide is one among many in Niassa. It is a story of human resilience and of how people in conditions of extreme want and destitution nevertheless preserved a sense of dignity and humanity. Similar examples of how people repaired their lives after the ravages of the civil war, all without the help of the government, could be found everywhere in rural Mozambique. What is remarkable about deportees like Carlos and Adelaide is that they had to make sense of the ruin that the socialist experiment brought to their lives and live with the fact that there would be no homecoming for them. Although they hoped for some recompense from the government—an apology at the very least—they also knew they could not expect much.

Epilogue

CONSUMED BY the war effort and politically exhausted, Frelimo leaders were victims of their own messianic socialism. In October 1986, they lost their charismatic leader in a plane crush. Scholars have debated whether it was an accident or a deliberate act by enemies of Mozambique.[1] But without Samora Machel, the party lost its political vitality and sense of purpose. Pensamento único, the party's most valued principle, lost its gravitas. One by one, all the party's discursive maxims faded away from the public sphere. There was no more talk of revolution, of Homem Novo and his nemesis Xiconhoca, or of the other ideals for which many had suffered and died. The tasks of moving the country away from socialism, restructuring the economy, and finding a way out of the civil war were left to Machel's successor, Joaquim Chissano.

In 1987, Chissano's government implemented the first structural adjustment program (SAP), thus taking the path that most African countries had taken in the face of dysfunctional and unproductive economies. To fulfill the conditions required to receive economic assistance from the International Monetary Fund and the World Bank, the government had to cut back its bloated bureaucracy, shrink the public sector, reduce the size of the labor force, and privatize parastatals or else balance their budgets. State farms like Unango and Matama in Niassa and Muaguide in Cabo Delgado laid off hundreds of workers, most of whom were ex-detainees and Operação Produção deportees. The government was too burdened by the war and the structural adjustment program to consider transporting people back to their places of origin. In the capital, there was no talk of reversing the disaster of the cleanup campaigns. Unemployed and destitute, most ex-detainees and Operação Produção deportees flocked to the cities of Lichinga, Nampula, and Pemba in the hopes of catching a flight back home. Their status was undefined. While the police continued to arrest them as vagrants and send them back to the countryside, the army compelled many to join the militias and fight Renamo.[2] Although reeducation as a penal institution was still in force, by then most camps had simply been abandoned. In Nampula, ex-detainees and Operação Produção deportees found refuge in the airport's air force base, hoping to board a military plane back to Maputo. As one reporter who paid them a visit put it, they were sent to reeducation camps to be transformed into New Men, but they came out as indigents, abandoned to their fate.[3]

On May 7, 1988, Joaquim Chissano visited Niassa. The new president could not ignore the pitiful sight of thousands of indigents roaming aimlessly in the streets of Lichinga. In a statement that did not make the headlines and was instead buried in the midst of news stories about the devastation of war and the prospect of a negotiated settlement with Renamo, Chissano declared that Operação Produção was officially over and that everyone was free to go home.[4] Although a salvationist himself—like the other New Men forged in the struggle—Chissano differentiated his presidency from Machel's. He surrounded himself with a younger cohort of technocrats who did not share the Nachingwea old guard's ideological commitment to socialism.[5] He trusted these technocrats to lead Mozambique's transition from socialism to a neoliberal laissez-faire system, a process that Anne Pitcher calls "transformative preservation."[6] As Pitcher notes, the new leadership quickly dropped the language of revolution without any attempt to explain why the socialist experiment had failed. Their focus was on satisfying the terms on which donors had conditioned economic stabilization. The most important of these terms was getting Renamo to the negotiation table to discuss an end to the war. In 1989, the party held its Fifth Congress, which had one main agenda: to strike the very word *socialism* from the country's constitution, thus paving the way to a multiparty system along the lines of neoliberal reformism. The post–Cold War era had begun.

Chissano did not distance himself from Machel, but his political philosophy was based on forgetting the past and on moving forward. The victims of the socialist utopia, just like the victims of the civil war, were to bury their sorrows, lick their wounds, and get on with their lives as if nothing had happened.[7] This was the message of his statement in Lichinga. Although international newspapers reported that the party "acknowledged the mistake" it had made in launching Operação Produção, Chissano made no apologies and said nothing about reparations or help for victims.[8] People were to find their own way home and deal with the psychological effects of their traumatic past on their own. Unlike other postconflict societies, Mozambique would not establish a commission on truth and reconciliation. In time, it became apparent that the settlement that the government had finally reached with Renamo bequeathed Mozambique with a negative peace.[9]

In the absence of state assistance, the Catholic Church stepped in and mobilized resources to help people return home. Domestically, the Catholic Church had been the most vocal critic of the reeducation program and cleanup campaigns. The Church underwent a radical transformation after Mozambique's independence and was no more the quiescent, largely pro-regime institution it had been in the colonial period. According to Éric Morier-Genoud, it became an independent-minded African institution and sought to rehabilitate its public image by speaking up on behalf of the poor and oppressed.[10] This new outlook displeased the party and led to open confrontation. However, the Church was determined to play a leading role in Mozambique's public life. By 1988, the Church was instrumental in peace talks. Through Caritas—a relief organization whose mission is to help the needy and vulnerable—the Church mobilized resources in Germany and in England to assist ex-detainees and Operação Produção deportees.[11] They started repatriating people in 1988 by air and by boat from the port city of Pemba. Because the war was far from over and many people were still dispersed across the vast expanse of rural northern Mozambique, few people benefited from these initial repatriation efforts. It was only after the peace treaty was signed in Rome in 1992 that Caritas was able to gather more people and ship them home. This work of repatriation continued well into the early 2000s.

The social fractures that the reformist project created among those directly affected had no easy fix. While returning home was a festive occasion for some, it brought sorrow for others. The cleanup campaigns had torn families apart. But they also created new families and new communities. Repatriation could not right the wrongs of the past without wronging the present. Many people had formed new families in northern Mozambique; some former detainees had in fact been compelled to find spouses among local communities. Now that Caritas was offering return transportation to Maputo, many people abandoned their spouses and children and went home.[12] But not everyone risked losing twice. Many, like my interviewees Celina Nhantumbo, Cacilda Sithole, and Alfredo Langa, bade farewell to their companions and stayed to take care of their new families in Niassa.[13] As the leading officer at Caritas in Niassa, Manuela Nascimento witnessed most of these tragic events unfold. With six children of her own already, she adopted four abandoned children whose parents had either died during Renamo attacks or simply disappeared in the seesaw of repatriation.[14]

Despite its humanitarian efforts, Caritas was unable to locate and repatriate everyone. While some people opted to stay, others returned to the north after failing to settle in their places of origin. After several years of exile, many people were unable to locate their relatives. This was especially the case for those who returned to their rural homes in Inhambane, Gaza, and Maputo Provinces. The war had destroyed many villages and dispersed many communities. After learning that no one from his family in Vilanculos (Inhambane) survived the war, Sebastião Manhique went to Maputo, where he struggled to make a living, and then decided to return to Lichinga.[15] During the austere times of structural adjustment in the early 1990s, life in Maputo was as tough as in Niassa. After longing for many years to return home to Maputo, José Ngovene finally did so in the mid-2000s. But he could not face the fact that his old friends now led comfortable, middle-class lives, and he was a destitute peasant. "I saw that they all lived in beautiful houses," he told me in Unango, "yet I was smarter than them. I would have had a heart attack if I stayed in Maputo and thought about the life that was stolen from me. I will rather stay here as a poor peasant."[16]

This was the price that many people paid for the morality of revolution. In Mozambique, like elsewhere, the seductive discourse of liberation and socialism came with new chains. It promised to liberate, yet it created new prisoners.

Notes

INTRODUCTION

Epigraph: Samora Machel, "FRELIMO's Tasks in the Struggle Ahead," in *Mozambique: Revolution or Reaction?* (Oakland, CA: LSM Information Center, 1975), 14.

1. FRELIMO changed its name to Frelimo in 1977, when it became a Marxist-Leninist vanguard party. Because my study deals mostly with the vanguard party, I use the name Frelimo for both the front and the party.
2. For details, see Norrie MacQueen, *The Decolonization of Portuguese Africa: Metropolitan Revolution and the Dissolution of Empire* (London: Longman, 1997).
3. See A. D. Harvey, "Counter-coup in Lourenço Marques: September 1974," *International Journal of African Historical Studies* 39, no. 3 (2006): 487–98; Benedito Machava, "Galo amanheceu em Lourenço Marques: O 7 de Setembro e o verso da descolonização em Moçambique," *Revista crítica de ciências sociais*, no. 106 (May 2015): 53–84.
4. See António Rita-Ferreira, "Moçambique post-25 de Abril: Causas do êxodo da população de origem Europeia e Asiática," *Moçambique: Cultura e história de um país* 8 (1988): 122–69; Fernando Couto, *Moçambique 1974: O fim do império e o nasciemento da nação* (Alfragide: Caminho, 2011); Ribeiro Cardoso, *O fim do império* (Alfragide: Caminho, 2011); Aurélio Le Bon, *Mafalala 1974: Memórias do 7 de Setembro, a grande operação* (Maputo: Movimento Editora, 2015).
5. MHN, Samora Machel, "Message from the President of FRELIMO on the Occasion of the Investiture of the Transitional Government of Mozambique," 20 September 1974; AGGPM, MINT, Circular 6/GMI/976, "Assunto: Objectivos dos centros de reeducação," 5 January 1976.
6. For similar examples, see Paul Boyer, *Urban Masses and Moral Order in America, 1820–1920* (Cambridge, MA: Harvard University Press, 1978); Andrew Lees, *Cities Perceived: Urban Life and Society in European and American Thought, 1820–1940* (New York: Columbia University Press, 1985); Andrew Lees, *Cities, Sin, and Social Reform in Imperial Germany* (Ann Arbor: University of Michigan Press, 2002); James Holston, ed., *Cities and Citizenship* (Durham, NC: Duke University Press, 1999); Sueann Caulfield, *In Defense

of Honor: Sexual Morality, Modernity, and Nation in Early Twentieth-Century Brazil (Durham, NC: Duke University Press, 2000).

7. David Martin, "The (Political) Facts of Life on Mozambique's Sin Street," *Chicago Sun-Times,* 6 October 6, 1974.
8. *Daily News,* 3 November 1975.
9. "FRELIMO cria campos de reeducação," *A capital,* 20 November 1974.
10. *Daily News,* 3 November 1975.
11. MHN, Jay Ross, "Mozambican Reeducation Camps Raise Rights Questions," *Washington Post,* 7 May 1980.
12. With scant statistical evidence to turn to, I draw my estimates from camp reports from various provincial departments of reeducation (DPSRs), as well as from Jean Tartter, "Government and Politics," in *Mozambique: A Country Study,* ed. Harold Nelson (Washington, DC: American University, 1984), 201; Herbert Howe, "National Security," in Nelson, *Mozambique,* 277; Omar Ribeiro Thomaz, "Escravos sem dono: A experiência social dos campos de trabalho em Moçambique no período socialista," *Revista de antropologia* 51, no 1 (2008): 191; Carlos Quembo, *Poder do poder: Operação Produção e a inveção dos "improdutivos" urbanos no Moçambique socialista, 1983–1988* (Maputo: Alcance, 2017).
13. Michel Foucault, *The Punitive Society: Lectures at the Collège de France, 1972–1973* (New York: Picador, 2018).
14. Christian Geffray, *La cause des armes au Mozambique: Anthropologie d'une guerre civile* (Paris: Karthala, 1990).
15. Michel Cahen, *Mozambique: La révolucion implosée; Etudes sur 12 ans d'indepéndance, 1975–1987* (Paris: Editions L'Harmattan, 1987).
16. João Paulo Borges Coelho, "Protected Villages and Communal Villages in the Mozambican Province of Tete (1968–1982): A History of State Resettlement Policies, Development and War" (PhD diss., University of Bradford, 1993); Harry West, *Kupilikula: Governance and the Invisible Realm in Mozambique* (Chicago: Chicago University Press, 2005).
17. Bertil Egerö, *Mozambique: A Dream Undone; The Political Economy of Democracy, 1975–84* (Uppsala: Nordiska Afrikainstitutet, 1987); Merle Bowen, *The State against the Peasantry: Rural Struggles in Colonial and Postcolonial Mozambique* (Charlottesville: University of Virginia Press, 2000); Kathleen Sheldon, *Pounders of Grain: A History of Women, Work, and Politics in Mozambique* (Portsmouth, NH: Heinemann, 2002); Anne M. Pitcher, *Transforming Mozambique: The Politics of Privatization, 1975–2000* (Cambridge: Cambridge University Press, 2002); Yussuf Adam, *Escapar aos dentes do crocodilo e cair na boca do leopardo: Trajectória de Moçambique pós-colonial* (Maputo: Promédia, 2006); Éric Morier-Genoud, *Catholicism and the Making of Politics in Central Mozambique* (Rochester, NY: University of Rochester Press, 2019).
18. Maria-Benedita Basto, *A guerra das escritas: Literatura, nação e teoria pós-colonial em Moçambique* (Lisbon: Vendaval, 2006); Paolo Israel, *In Step with*

the Times: Mapiko Masquerades of Mozambique (Athens: Ohio University Press, 2014); Drew Thompson, *Filtering Histories: The Photographic Bureaucracy in Mozambique, 1960 to Recent Times* (Ann Arbor: University of Michigan Press, 2021); Colin Darch and David Hedges, *Samora Machel: Retórica política e independencia em Moçambique* (Salvador: Edufba, 2018).

19. Lars Buur, "Xiconhoca: Mozambique's Ubiquitous Post-independence Traitor," in *Traitors: Suspicion, Intimacy, and the Ethics of State-Building*, ed. Sharika Thiranagama and Tobias Kelly (Philadelphia: University of Pennsylvania Press, 2009), 24–47; Maria Paula Meneses, "Xiconhoca, o Inimigo: Narrativas de violência sobre a construção da nação em Moçambique," *Revista crítica de ciências sociais*, no. 106 (May 2015): 9–52; João Cabrita, *Mozambique: The Tortuous Road to Democracy* (New York: Palgrave, 2000); Barnabé Ncomo, *Uria Simango: Um homem, uma causa* (Maputo: Edições Novafrica, 2004); Victor Igreja, "FRELIMO's Political Rule through Violence and Memory in Postcolonial Mozambique," *Journal of Southern African Studies* 36, 4 (December 2010): 781–99; Adelino Timóteo, *Os últimos dias de Uria Simango* (Maputo: Edição do Autor, 2017).
20. Thomaz, "Escravos sem dono"; Quembo, *Poder do poder.*
21. Sarah LeFanu, *S Is for Samora: A Lexical Biography of Samora Machel and the Mozambican Dream* (Scottsville, South Africa: University of KwaZulu-Natal Press, 2012); Allen F. Isaacman and Barbara S. Isaacman, *Mozambique's Samora Machel: A Life Cut Short* (Athens: Ohio University Press, 2020); Cristiano Matsinhe, "Biografias e heróis no imaginário nacionalista Moçambicano," in *Moçambique: Ensaios*, ed. Peter Fry (Rio de Janeiro: Editora UFRJ, 2001), 181–223.
22. Allen F. Isaacman, *A Luta Continua: Creating New Society in Mozambique* (New York: Foundation of State University of New York, 1978); Joseph Hanlon, *Mozambique: Revolution under Fire* (London: Zed Books, 1984); John Saul, ed., *A Difficult Road: The Transition to Socialism in Mozambique* (New York: Monthly Review Press, 1985); David Hoile, *Mozambique: A Nation in Crisis* (London: Claridge, 1989); Hans Abrahamsson and Anders Nilsson, *Moçambique em transição: Um estudo da história do desenvolvimento durante o período 1974–1992* (Gothenburg/Maputo: CEE-ISRI, 1994); Margaret Hall and Tom Young, *Confronting Leviathan: Mozambique since Independence* (London: Hurst, 1997); Alice Dinerman, *Revolution, Counter-revolution and Revisionism in Postcolonial Africa: The Case of Mozambique, 1975–1994* (London: Routledge, 2006).
23. Igreja, "FRELIMO's Political Rule," 781–99; Timóteo, *Os últimos dias.*
24. Machel, "FRELIMO's Tasks in the Struggle Ahead."
25. Buur, "Xiconhoca," 26–27.
26. James Aho, *This Thing of Darkness: A Sociology of the Enemy* (Seattle: University of Washington Press, 1994), 26; see also Barrington Moore, *Moral Purity and Persecution in History* (Princeton, NJ: Princeton University Press, 2000); Wendy Goldman, *Inventing the Enemy: Denunciation and Terror in Stalin's Russia* (Cambridge: Cambridge University Press, 2011).

27. AGGPN, DPSRN/MINT, "10 Seminário Nacional de Reeducação, documento de apoio no. 2: Projecto de programa para os centros de reeducação," November 1976, 1.
28. Giorgio Agamben, *Homo Sacer: Sovereign Power and Bare Life,* trans. Daniel Heller-Roazen (Stanford: Stanford University Press, 1998); João Biehl, *Vita: Life in the Zone of Social Abandonment* (Berkeley: University of California Press, 2005).
29. As Laura Bear argues, conditions of austerity create new forms of relationships and engagements between the state, its agents, and society, which are based on new expectations of performance. One of the central outcomes of austerity is the expectation that those at the bottom of sociopolitical and economic hierarchies must do more with less. *Navigating Austerity: Currents of Debt along a South Asian River* (Stanford: Stanford University Press, 2015).
30. On Frelimo's modernization of politics, see João Cravinho, "Modernizing Mozambique: Frelimo Ideology and the Frelimo State" (PhD diss., Oxford University, 1995).
31. Odd Arne Westad, *The Global Cold War: Third World Interventions and the Making of Our Times* (Cambridge: Cambridge University Press, 2005); Vladimir Shubin, *The Hot "Cold War": The USSR in Southern Africa* (London: Pluto Press, 2008).
32. Anne M. Pitcher and Kelly Askew, "African Socialisms and Postsocialisms," *Africa: Journal of the International African Institute* 76, no. 1 (2006): 1–14; Kelly Askew, "African Socialism," *Oxford Bibliographies Online,* last modified February 22, 2018, https://doi.org/10.1093/obo/9780199846733-0200.
33. See Donald Donham, *Marxist Modern: An Ethnographic History of the Ethiopian Revolution* (Oxford: James Currey, 1999); Mohamed Camara, *His Master's Voice: Mass Communication and Single Party Politics in Guinea under Sékou Touré* (Trenton, NJ: Africa World Press, 2005); Jay Straker, *Youth, Nationalism, and the Guinean Revolution* (Bloomington: Indiana University Press, 2009); Andrew Ivaska, *Cultured States: Youth, Gender, and Modern Style in 1960s Dar es Salaam* (Durham, NC: Duke University Press, 2011); Mike McGovern, *Unmasking the State: Making Guinea Modern* (Chicago: University of Chicago Press, 2013).
34. Andrew Burton and Hélène Charton-Bigot, eds., *Generations Past: Youth in East African History* (Athens: Ohio University Press, 2010); Emily Callaci, *Street Archives and City Life: Popular Intellectuals in Postcolonial Tanzania* (Durham, NC: Duke University Press, 2017). For one of the early discussions of these campaigns in East and Central Africa, especially with regard to women, see Audrey Wipper, "African Women, Fashion, and Scapegoating," *Canadian Journal of African Studies* 6, no. 2 (1972): 329–49.
35. Derek R. Peterson, *Ethnic Patriotism and the East African Revival: A History of Dissent, c. 1935–1972* (Cambridge: Cambridge University Press, 2012); Derek R. Peterson and Edgar Taylor, "Rethinking the State in Idi Amin's Uganda: The Politics of Exhortation," *Journal of Eastern African Studies* 7, no. 1 (2013):

58–82; see also N. Tutashinda, *As manifestações da 'autenticidade' Africana* (Lisbon: Cadernos Ulmero, 1978).

36. The recent controversy over dress codes in Kenya's parliament exemplifies the continued prevalence of postcolonial efforts at moral reform, whose roots can be traced to Victorian ethics and etiquette. See John Lonsdale, "Threads and Patches: Moral and Political Argument in Kenya," in *State, Power, and New Political Actors in Postcolonial Africa,* ed. Alessandro Triulzi and M. Cristina Ercolessi (Milan: Fondazione Giangiacomo Feltrinelli, 2004), 27–52; Peterson, *Ethnic Patriotism,* 286–89.
37. See Jean-François Bayart, "Africa in the World: A History of Extraversion," *African Affairs* 99, no. 395 (April 2000): 217–67; Jean-François Bayart, *The State in Africa: The Politics of the Belly,* 2nd ed. (Cambridge, UK: Polity Press, 2009); Achille Mbembe, *On the Postcolony* (Berkeley: University of California Press, 2001); Patrick Chabal, *Power in Africa: An Essay in Political Interpretation* (New York: St. Martin's Press, 1992); Patrick Chabal and Jean-Pascal Daloz, *Africa Works: Disorder as Political Instrument* (Oxford: James Currey, 1999). For a critique of this scholarship—generally characterized as Afropessimism—see, among many others, Ernest Harsch, "African States in Social and Historical Context," *Sociological Forum* 12, no. 4 (December 1997): 674; Michael Karlström, "On the Aesthetics and Dialogics of Power in the Postcolony," *Africa* 73, no. 1 (February 2003): 57.
38. Straker, *Youth, Nationalism,* 15; Peterson, *Ethnic Patriotism,* 35–36.
39. Priya Lal, *African Socialism in Postcolonial Tanzania: Between the Village and the World* (Cambridge: Cambridge University Press, 2015), 30; Emmanuel Akyeampong, "African Socialism: Or the Search for an Indigenous Model of Economic Development?," *Economic History of Developing Regions* 33, no. 1 (January 2018): 69–87. See also Jeremy Friedman, *Ripe for Revolution: Building Socialism in the Third World* (Cambridge, MA: Harvard University Press, 2021), 124–210.
40. William Friedland and Carl Rosberg, eds., *African Socialism* (Stanford: Stanford University Press, 1964); Carl Rosberg and Thomas Callaghy, eds., *Socialism in Sub-Saharan Africa: A New Assessment* (Berkeley: University of California Press, 1979); Crawford Young, *Ideology and Development in Africa* (New Haven: Yale University Press, 1982); Barry Munslow, ed., *Africa: Problems in the Transition to Socialism* (London: Zed Books, 1986); Marina Ottaway and David Ottaway, *Afrocommunism,* 2nd ed. (New York: Africana Press, 1986); John Markakis and Michael Waller, eds., *Military Marxist Regimes in Africa* (London: Frank Cass, 1986); Edmond Keller and Donald Rothchild, eds., *Afro-Marxist Regimes: Ideology and Public Policy* (Boulder, CO: Lynne Rienner, 1987).
41. This is not to dispute Jeffrey Byrne's contention that Algeria was a major source of inspiration and a destination of revolutionaries from what we now call the Global South. It is rather to emphasize the more central role that Tanzania played as the base of all liberation movements in southern

Africa and beyond. See Jeffrey Byrne, *Mecca of Revolution: Algeria, Decolonization and the Third World Order* (New York: Oxford University Press, 2016).

42. Julius Nyerere, *Freedom and Unity* (Dar es Salaam: Oxford University Press, 1967), 162; Julius Nyerere, *On Socialism* (Dar es Salaam: Oxford University Press, 1969), 19; Julius Nyerere, "African Socialism: Ujamaa in Practice," *Black Scholar* 2, no. 6 (February 1971), 3–4.
43. A. S. Bukenya, preface to *The Arusha Declaration and Christian Socialism* (Dar es Salaam: Tanzania Publishing House, 1969), viii.
44. John Lavoie, "The University Student and Nation-Building in Modern Africa," in *Arusha Declaration,* 27. See also Adrian Hastings, "Christian Faith and Social Commitment," in *Arusha Declaration;* David Westerlund, "Christianity and Socialism in Tanzania, 1967–1977," *Journal of Religion in Africa* 11, no. 1 (1980): 30–55. For a broader examination of socialism and religion, see, among others, Denys Turner, *Marxism and Christianity* (Oxford: Blackwell, 1983).
45. Ahmed Sékou Touré, *Afrika and Imperialism* (Newark, NJ: Jihad Publishing, 1973), 8, 29; Ahmed Sékou Touré, "Revolution and Religion," *African Democratic Revolution* 144 (March 1980): 9, 12.
46. Léopold Senghor, *On African Socialism* (New York: Frederick A. Praeger, 1964), 162–63.
47. Joe Slovo, "Shared Values: Socialism and Religion," *African Communist* (1994): 46–49.
48. Adom Getachew, *Worldmaking after Empire: The Rise and Fall of Self-Determination* (Princeton, NJ: Princeton University Press, 2020).
49. John Marcum, *Conceiving Mozambique* (New York: Palgrave Macmillan, 2018), 94.
50. See Abigail Meert, "From Students to Soldiers: Radical Politics and the Ugandan Exile Community in Dar es Salaam, 1967–1979" (lecture, African History and Anthropology Workshop, University of Michigan, Ann Arbor, MI, November, 28, 2023).
51. On Operation Vijana and other anti-indecency campaigns in Dar es Salaam, see Ivaska, *Cultured States;* Andrew Burton, "The Haven of Peace Purged: Tackling the Undesirable and Unproductive Poor in Dar es Salaam, ca. 1950–1980s," *International Journal of African Historical Studies* 40, no. 1 (2007): 119–51.
52. See James Brennan, "Blood Enemies: Exploitation and Urban Citizenship in the Nationalist Political Thought of Tanzania, 1958–1975," *Journal of African History* 47, no. 3 (2006): 389–413.
53. Jocelyn Alexander and Gary Kynoch, "Introduction: Histories and Legacies of Punishment in Southern Africa," *Journal of Southern African Studies* 37, no. 3 (September 2011): 410.
54. Malyn Newitt, *A Short History of Mozambique* (Oxford: Oxford University Press, 2017), 156–57.
55. Newitt, 157.

56. LeFanu, *S Is for Samora,* 85.
57. José Cabaço, *Moçambique: Identidades, colonialismo e libertação* (Maputo: Marimbique, 2010), 289.
58. For the roots of Frelimo's ideology, see, among others, Sonia Kruks, "From Nationalism to Marxism: The Ideological History of FRELIMO, 1962–1977," in *Studies in Power and Class in Africa,* ed. Irving Leonard Markowitz (Englewood Cliffs, NJ: Prentice-Hall, 1977), 237–56; Luís de Brito, "Le FRELIMO et la construction de l'etat national au Mozambique" (PhD diss., Université de Paris 8, 1991); Luís de Brito, *A Frelimo, o Marxismo e a construção do estado nacional, 1962–1983* (Maputo: IESE, 2019).
59. Michel Foucault, "Governmentality," in *The Anthropology of the State: A Reader,* ed. Aradhana Sharma and Akhil Gupta (Oxford: Blackwell, 2006), 131–43.
60. Samora Machel, *Discursos de Samora Moisés Machel, presidente da República de Mozambique,* 5 vols. (Maputo, 1980). See references to Machel's address in José Cabaço, "O Homem Novo: Breve itinerário de um projecto," in *Samora: Homem do povo,* ed. António Sopa (Maputo: Maguezo, 2001), 112; José Cabaço, *À sombra da utopia: Quando eu era nós* (Maputo: Fundação Fernando Leite Couto, 2021), 243.
61. See Stuart Schram, *The Thought of Mao Tse-Tung* (Cambridge: Cambridge University Press, 1989).
62. Frelimo employed the noun Homem Novo (which was often written with initial capital letters) as a gender-neutral category, meant to account for both men and women. My addition of Mulher Nova, which was not Frelimo's preferred formulation, is an attempt to capture the gendered dimensions of the party's discourse and praxis. For Frelimo's gendered politics, see, among many others, Stephanie Urdang, *And Still They Dance: Women, War, and the Struggle for Change in Mozambique* (London: Monthly Review Press, 1989); Sheldon, *Pounders of Grain.*
63. Ministério da Educação e Cultura, *O Homem Novo* (Maputo: MEC, 1977).
64. Samora Machel, *The Enemy Within* (Maputo: Department of Information and Propaganda, 1982).
65. Benedito Machava, "Reeducation Camps and the Messianic Ethos of Mozambique's Socialism," in *Socialismes en Afrique,* ed. François Blum et al. (Paris: Editions de la Maison des Sciences de L'homme, 2021), 319–56.
66. As Margaret Hall and Paul Young observed in their study of postcolonial Mozambique, Frelimo leaders had "an image of themselves as an embattled vanguard of 'fighters against darkness and superstition' surrounded by legions of enemies, shepherding the masses towards progress and enlightenment." *Confronting Leviathan,* 74.
67. Klaus-Georg Riegel, "Marxism-Leninism as a Political Religion," *Totalitarian Movements and Political Religions* 6, no. 1 (June 2005): 98.
68. This argument rests on the concept of political religion, which Emilio Gentile defines as "the sacralization of a political system founded on an

unchallengeable monopoly of power, ideological monism, and the obligatory and unconditional subordination of the individual and the collectivity to its code of commandments." The sacralization of politics in modern society, claims Gentile, occurs when "an entity such as a nation, state, race, class, Party, or movement is transformed into a sacred entity," and it "claims for itself the prerogative to determine the meaning and fundamental aim of human existence for individuals and the collectivity." Rising from the ebullient political environment of nineteenth-century Europe, political ideologies such as nationalism and philosophical doctrines such as socialism gave rise to political projects that took a secular religious dimension. Fascism and communism are the two extreme examples of sacralization of politics in the twentieth century. Emilio Gentile, *Politics as Religion* (Princeton, NJ: Princeton University Press, 2006), xv–xiv; see also Erich Voegelin, *Political Religions,* trans. T. J. DiNapoli and E. S. Easterly III (New York: Edwin Mellen Press, 1986), originally published as *Die politischen Religionen* (Vienna: Bermann-Fischer, 1938).

69. In a similar vein, Mozambican sociologist Elísio Macamo argues that Frelimo was driven by an "eschatological nationalism." See "Power, Conflict and Citizenship: Mozambique's Contemporary Struggles," *Citizenship Studies* 21, no. 2 (January 2017): 198. Under Kissinger's classification of leadership, Frelimo's approach falls within the prophetic category as opposed to the statesmen category. Henry Kissinger, *Leadership: Six Studies in World Strategy* (London: Penguin, 2022).
70. Igal Halfin, *From Darkness to Light: Class, Consciousness, and Salvation in Revolutionary Russia* (Pittsburgh: University of Pittsburgh Press, 2000), 1–2, 6.
71. João Paulo Borges Coelho, "Politics and Contemporary History of Mozambique: A Set of Epistemological Notes," *Kronos* 39, no. 1 (November 2013): 20; see also João Paulo Borges Coelho, "Um itinerário histórico da Moçambicanidade," in *Portugal na viragem do século: Língua Portuguesa, a herança comum,* ed. Fernando Rosas and Maria Rollo (Lisbon: Assitio & Alvim, 1998), 87–126. Terence Ranger used the term *patriotic history* to characterize the same eschatological reading of history in Zimbabwe. See "Nationalist Historiography, Patriotic History and the History of the Nation: The Struggle over the Past in Zimbabwe," *Journal of Southern African Studies* 30, no. 2 (June 2004): 215–34.
72. Hall and Young, *Confronting Leviathan,* 75. See MHN, "Desalojemos o inimigo interno do nosso aparelho de estado: Texto do discurso proferido pelo Presidente Samora Machel no comício popular de 18 de Março," *Notícias,* (Maputo), 18 March 1980.
73. "Fazer de todo o país uma zona libertada," *Tempo,* 4 September 1977, 361.
74. "Purifiquemos as nossas fileiras para avançar rumo ao socialismo," *Notícias,* 9 May 1978.
75. AGGPM, MINT, "Objectivos dos centros."

76. As Derek Peterson concluded from his study of patriotic thought in East Africa, "The prospect of national independence . . . made the work of moral reform more urgent. New freedoms entailed new prisoners." *Ethnic Patriotism,* 283.
77. Patricia O'Brien, "The Prison on the Continent: Europe, 1865–1965," in *The Oxford History of the Prison: The Practice of Punishment in Western Society,* ed. Norval Morris and David Rothman (Oxford: Oxford University Press, 1998), 178–201; Aryeh Neier, "Confining Dissent: The Political Prison," in Morris and Rothman, *Oxford History of the Prison,* 350–80.
78. Angela Davis, *Are Prisons Obsolete?* (New York: Seven Stories, 2003); Michelle Alexander, *The New Jim Crow: Mass Incarceration in the Age of Colorblindness* (New York: New Press, 2010); Elizabeth Hinton, *From the War on Poverty to the War on Crime: The Making of Mass Incarceration in America* (Cambridge, MA: Harvard University Press, 2016); Heather Schoenfeld, *Building the Prison State: Race and the Politics of Mass Incarceration* (Chicago: University of Chicago Press, 2018); Didier Fassin, *The Will to Punish* (New York: Oxford University Press, 2018).
79. Florence Bernault, ed., *A History of Prison and Confinement in Africa* (Portsmouth, NH: Heinemann, 2003); Caroline Elkins, *Britain's Gulag: The Brutal End of Empire in Kenya* (London: Pimlico, 2005); Dior Konate, *Prison Architecture and Punishment in Colonial Senegal* (Lanham: Lexington Books, 2018); Anna Mester, "Iberian Atlantic Imperial Carcerality: Vestiges of Colonial Disciplinary Violence in Cape Verde, Equatorial Guinea, and Mozambique" (PhD diss., University of Michigan, 2016).
80. Fran Buntman, *Robben Island and Prisoner Resistance to Apartheid* (Cambridge: Cambridge University Press, 2003); Derek R. Peterson, "The Intellectual Lives of Mau Mau Detainees," *Journal of African History* 49, no. 1 (2008): 73–91; Jocelyn Alexander, "Nationalism and Self-Government in Rhodesian Detention: Gonakudzingwa, 1964–1974," *Journal of Southern African Studies* 37, no. 3 (September 2011): 551–69; Munyaradzi Munochiveyi, *Prisoners of Rhodesia: Inmates and Detainees in the Struggle for Zimbabwean Liberation, 1960–1980* (New York: Palgrave Macmillan, 2014).
81. Daniel Branch, "Imprisonment and Colonialism in Kenya, c. 1930–1952: Escaping the Carceral Archipelago," *International Journal of African Historical Studies* 38, no. 2 (2005): 239–65; Florence Bernault, "The Shadow of Rule: Colonial Power and Modern Punishment in Africa," in *Cultures of Confinement: A History of the Prison in Africa, Asia, and Latin America,* ed. Frank Dikötter and Ian Brown (Ithaca, NY: Cornell University Press, 2007), 55–94.
82. Katherine Bruce-Lockhart, *Carceral Afterlives: Prisons, Detention, and Punishment in Postcolonial Uganda* (Athens: Ohio University Press, 2022).
83. Andrea Purdeková, *Making Ubumwe: Power, State and Camps in Rwanda's Unity-Building Project* (New York: Berghahn, 2015).
84. Enrique Ros, *La UMAP: El Gulag Castrista* (Miami, FL: Ediciones Universal, 2004); Joseph Tahbaz, "Demystifying las UMAP: The Politics of Sugar,

Gender, and Religion in 1960s Cuba," *Delaware Review of Latin American Studies* 14, no. 2 (December 2013); Van Toai Doan and David Chanoff, *The Vietnamese Gulag* (New York: Simon & Schuster, 1986); Tran Tri Vu, *Lost Years: My 1,632 Days in Vietnamese Reeducation Camps* (Berkeley: University of California Press, 1988).

85. Galina Ivanova, *Labor Camp Socialism: The Gulag in the Soviet Totalitarian System* (New York: M. E. Sharpe, 2000); Anne Applebaum, *Gulag: A History* (New York: Anchor Books, 2003); Klaus Muhlhahn, "The Concentration Camp in Global Historical Perspective," *History Compass* 8, no. 6 (June 2010): 543–61.
86. Agamben, *Homo Sacer,* 174.
87. Giorgio Agamben, *State of Exception,* trans. Kevin Attell (Chicago: University of Chicago Press, 2005), 23.
88. AGGPN, DPSRN/MINT, "7a Sessão Ordinária do Conselho de Ministros de 9 de Julho de 1976, síntese XI-parte: Centros de reeducação," Maputo, 9 July 1976, 4.
89. MHN, "Machel's Speech on Unjust Detentions in Re-education Camps," *Summary of World Broadcasts* (London), no. ME/6846, 6 October 1981, p. B/1.
90. Michel Foucault, *Discipline and Punish: The Birth of the Prison* (New York: Vintage, 1995), 200–204, 294.
91. West, *Kupilikula,* 176.
92. Writing about the aspirational nature of political institutions in independent Mozambique, David Morton has argued that "the Frelimo state was, in many aspects, an almost fictive entity needing people to fill it with content and meaning." *Age of Concrete: Housing and the Shape of Aspiration in the Capital of Mozambique* (Athens: Ohio University Press, 2019), 17.
93. Nicolas van de Walle, *African Economies and the Politics of Permanent Crisis* (Cambridge: Cambridge University Press, 2001); Frederick Cooper, *Africa since 1940: The Past of the Present,* 2nd ed. (Cambridge: Cambridge University Press, 2019).
94. AGGPN, DPSRN, SR/78, "Relatório referente ao mês de Fevereiro, Março, e Abril de 1977, Lichinga," 30 April 1977.
95. See Dalmazia Colombo, "Ntelela: Campo di sterminio," *Missione in directa,* March 1996; Cabrita, *Mozambique,* 96; Ncomo, *Uria Simango,* 22–23; Marlon Duncan, "Mozambique: Machel Re-education Camps Teach a Tough Lesson," *To the Point,* June 3, 1977; José Ramalho, "Alarm Spreads as Executions Continue," *To the Point,* June 1, 1979; José Pinto de Sá, "A história inédita dos 'centros de reeducação' em Moçambique: Os campos da vergonha," *Público magazine* 277 (June 1995).
96. Arthur Kleimann, Veena Daas, and Margaret Lock, eds., *Social Suffering* (Berkeley: University of California Press, 1997); Biehl, *Vita.*
97. See Jeanne M. Penvenne, *African Workers and Colonial Racism: Mozambican Strategies and Struggles in Lourenço Marques, 1877–1962* (Portsmouth, NH: Heinemann, 1995); Allen F. Isaacman, *Cotton Is the Mother of Poverty:*

Peasants, Work, and Rural Struggle in Colonial Mozambique, 1938–1961 (Portsmouth, NH: Heinemann, 1996); Valdemir Zamparoni, "Entre Narros e Mulungos: Colonialismo e paisagem social em Lourenço Marques c. 1890–1940" (PhD diss., Universidade de São Paulo, 1998); David Hedges, ed. *História de Moçambique*, vol. 2, *Moçambique no auge do colonialismo, 1930–1961* (Maputo: Imprensa Universitária, 1999); Eric Allina, *Slavery by Any Other Name: African Life under Company Rule in Mozambique* (Charlottesville: University of Virginia Press, 2012).

98. James Saymour and Richard Anderson, *New Ghosts, Old Ghosts: Prisons and Labor Reform Camps in China* (New York: M. E. Sharpe, 1998); Aminda Smith, *Thought Reform and China's Dangerous Classes: Reeducation, Resistance, and the People* (New York: Rowman & Littlefield, 2013).
99. José Moiane, "O direito e a justiça nas zonas libertadas," *Justiça popular* nos. 8/9 (January/June 1984): 11–14.
100. "A contribuição do nosso partido para o enriquecimento do Marxismo-Leninismo," *A voz da revolução*, no. 70, 1980, 21–24.
101. Licínio Azevedo, *Virgin Margarida* (Maputo: Ebano Multimédia, 2012); Licínio Azevedo, *A última prostituta* (Maputo: Ebano Multimédia, 1999).
102. See Victor Igreja, "Politics of Memory, Decentralisation and Recentralization in Mozambique," *Journal of Southern African Studies* 39, no. 2 (June 2013): 313–35.
103. Anne M. Pitcher, "Forgetting from Above and Memory from Below: Strategies of Legitimation and Struggle in Post-socialist Mozambique," *Africa: Journal of the International African Institute* 76, no. 1 (2006): 88–112.
104. João Paulo Borges Coelho, *Campo de trânsito* (Maputo: Ndjira, 2010).
105. I thank the late Professor Fernando Arenas for providing me with a copy of *Virgem Margarida.*
106. Ana Maria, interview with author in Matola-Kongoloti, 12 December 2014.
107. Lynne Viola, *The Unknown Gulag: The Lost World of Stalin's Special Settlements* (New York: Oxford University Press, 2007).
108. On the "accidental" nature of postcolonial African archives, see Jean Allman, "Phantoms of the Archive: Kwame Nkrumah, a Nazi Pilot Named Hanna, and the Contingencies of Postcolonial History-Writing," *American Historical Review* 118, no. 1 (February 2013): 104–29; Edgar Taylor, "Risk and Labour in the Archives: Archival Futures from Uganda," *Africa* 91, no. 4 (August 2021): 532–52.
109. Benedito Machava and Euclides Gonçalves, "The Dead Archive: Governance and Institutional Memory in Independent Mozambique," *Africa* 91, no. 4 (August 2021): 553–74.
110. AGGPN, DPSRN/SR, "Relação das crianças que se encontram nos campos com as suas mães," n.d.
111. AGGPN, DPSRN/SR, "Correspondência expedita, 1979–1981."
112. Ann Laura Stoler, "Matters of Intimacy as Matters of State: A Response," *Journal of American History* 88, no. 3 (December 2001): 893–97; Allman, "Phantoms of the Archive," 129.

113. Ann Laura Stoler, *Carnal Knowledge and Imperial Power: Race and the Intimate in Colonial Rule* (Berkeley: University of California Press, 2002), 18–19.
114. Frank Ankersmit, "Manifesto for an Analytical Political History," in *Manifestos for History*, ed. Keith Jenkins, Sue Morgan, and Alun Munslow (London: Routledge, 2007), 180.
115. Joseph Strayer, introduction to *The Historian's Craft*, by Marc Block (New York: Vintage Books, 1953), vii.
116. Marta Barroso, "Pena que não continuemos a ter campos de reeducação," *DW África*, September 29, 2012, https://www.dw.com/pt-002/pena-que-não-continuemos-a-ter-campos-de-reeducação-diz-joaquim-chissano/a-16258686.
117. "Campos de reeducação devem inspirar novo sistema prisional," *Media Fax*, October 8, 2010.
118. Michel-Rolph Trouillot, *Silencing the Past: Power and the Production of History* (Boston: Beacon Press, 1995).
119. Dipesh Chakrabarty, "History and the Politics of Recognition," in Jenkins, Morgan, and Munslow, *Manifestos for History*, 77–87; James Scott, *Seeing Like a State: How Certain Schemes to Improve the Human Condition Have Failed* (New Haven, CT: Yale University Press, 1998).
120. Alf Ludtke, "Introduction: What Is the History of Everyday Life and Who Are Its Practitioners?," in *The History of Everyday Life*, ed. Alf Ludtke (Princeton, NJ: Princeton University Press, 1995), 4.
121. As Derek Peterson argues, "Discourses—self-serving and partisan as they are—have real social and material lives. Texts, poetry, song, narratives and other discursive genres concretize changeable social relations, inspire action, invite emulation, and do work in the real world of human ambition and action." "Conversion and the Alignments of Colonial Culture," *Social Sciences and Missions* 24, no. 2–3 (January 2011): 215.
122. Arlette Farge, *The Allure of the Archives* (New Haven, CT: Yale University Press, 2013), 121.

CHAPTER 1: REVOLUTIONARY MORALITY AND THE STRUGGLE FOR MOZAMBIQUE, 1968–1974

1. CDSM, Pasta 2, Documentos da Frelimo, Frelimo, "II Conferência do Departamento de Educação e Cultura (DEC): Recomendações," September 1970.
2. CDSM, Frelimo, "DEC: Recomendações."
3. Jean Comaroff and John Comaroff, *Of Revelation and Revolution*, vol. 1, *Christianity, Colonialism, and Consciousness in South Africa* (Chicago: University of Chicago Press, 1991). In African studies, the term *elite* is controversial because it often fails to capture the social position of educated Africans in colonial contexts in a historically accurate way. Alternative terms such as *middle class, middle figures,* or *intermediaries* do not take us far either. See Robert Miller, "Elite Formation in Africa: Class, Culture and Coherence," *Journal of Modern African Studies* 12, no. 4 (December 1974): 521–42;

Benjamin Lawrence, Emily Osborn, and Richard Roberts, eds., *Intermediaries, Interpreters, and Clerks: African Employees in the Making of Colonial Africa* (Madison: University of Wisconsin Press, 2006), 3–34; Jason Sumich, "Elites and Modernity in Mozambique" (PhD diss., London School of Economics, 2005); Jason Sumich, *The Middle Class in Mozambique: The State and the Politics of Transformation* (Cambridge: Cambridge University Press, 2018).

4. CDSM, Frelimo, "DEC: Recomendações," 3.
5. Frantz Fanon, *The Wretched of the Earth* (New York: Grove Press, 2004).
6. Frantz Fanon, *A Dying Colonialism* (New York: Grove Press, 1965). The parallelism between Machel's and Fanon's reasoning does not mean that Machel or Frelimo at large were influenced by Fanon. In fact, Fanon had few if any admirers within Frelimo.
7. CDSM, Frelimo, "DEC: Recomendações," 4–5.
8. See Sonia Kruks, "From Nationalism to Marxism: The Ideological History of FRELIMO, 1962–1977," in *Studies in Power and Class in Africa,* ed. Irving Leonard Markowitz (Englewood Cliffs, NJ: Prentice-Hall, 1977), 237–56; Barry Munslow, *Mozambique: The Revolution and Its Origins* (London: Longman, 1983); Allen F. Isaacman and Barbara S. Isaacman, *Mozambique: From Colonialism to Revolution, 1900–1982* (Boulder, CO: Westview, 1983); Luís de Brito, "Une relecture nécessaire: La genèse du parti-état Frelimo," *Politique Africaine,* no. 29 (1988): 15–27; Luís de Brito, "Le FRELIMO et la construction de l'etat national au Mozambique" (PhD diss., Université de Paris 8, 1991); João Mosca, *A experência socialista em Moçambique* (Lisbon: Instituto Jean Piaget, 1999); Michael Panzer, "Building a Revolutionary Constituency: Mozambican Refugees and the Development of the FRELIMO Proto-state, 1964–1968," *Social Dynamics* 39, no. 1 (March 2013): 5–23.
9. For recent and fascinating work emerging in this field, see Paul Landau, *Spear: Mandela and the Revolutionaries* (Athens: Ohio University Press, 2022); Natasha Telepneva, *Cold War Liberation: The Soviet Union and the Collapse of the Portuguese Empire in Africa, 1961–1975* (Chapel Hill: University of North Carolina Press, 2022); Luise White and Miles Larmer, "Introduction: Mobile Soldiers and the Un-national Liberation of Southern Africa," *Journal of Southern African Studies* 40, no. 6 (December 2014): 1271–74; Luise White, "Students, ZAPU, and Special Branch in Francistown, 1964–1972," *Journal of Southern African Studies* 40, no. 6 (December 2014): 1289–303; Jocelyn Alexander, JoAnn McGregor, and Blessing-Miles Tendi, "The Transnational Histories of Southern African Liberation Movements: An Introduction," *Journal of Southern African Studies* 43, no. 1 (January 2017): 1–12; Jocelyn Alexander and JoAnn McGregor, "African Soldiers in the USSR: Oral Histories of ZAPU Intelligence Cadres' Soviet Training, 1964–1979," *Journal of Southern African Studies* 43, no 1 (January 2017): 49–66; Daniel Keiser, "'Makers of Bonds and Ties': Transnational Socialisation and National Liberation in Mozambique," *Journal of Southern African Studies* 43, no. 1 (January 2017): 29–48; Clinarete

Munguambe, "Nationalism and Exile in an Age of Solidarity: Frelimo-ZANU Relations in Mozambique (1975–1980)," *Journal of Southern African Studies* 43, no. 1 (January 2017): 161–78.

10. Eduardo Mondlane, *The Struggle for Mozambique* (London: Zed Press, 1983), 167–69; Michael Panzer, "A Nation in Name, a State in Exile: The FRELIMO Proto-state, Youth, Gender, and the Liberation of Mozambique, 1962–1975" (PhD diss., State University of New York, 2013).
11. Brito, "Une relecture nécessaire," 6–17.
12. This crisis has been in the limelight in the historiography of contemporary Mozambique, yielding perhaps one of the most heated debates on the history of Frelimo. It has been chronicled in several studies with varying perspectives. For earlier accounts of the crisis, see, among many others, Walter Opello, "Pluralism and Elite Conflict in an Independence Movement: Frelimo in the 1960s," *Journal of Southern African Studies* 2, no. 1 (October 1975): 66–82; Munslow, *Mozambique: The Revolution*, 102–13; Isaacman and Isaacman, *Mozambique: From Colonialism*, 96–97. For the most recent account, see Georgi Derluguian, "The Social Origins of Good and Bad Governance: Re-interpreting the 1968 Schism in FRELIMO," in *Sure Road? Nationalisms in Angola, Guinea-Bissau and Mozambique*, ed. Éric Morier-Genoud (Leiden: Brill, 2012), 79–101.
13. CDSM, Frelimo, "DEC: Recomendações."
14. Valdemir Zamparoni, "Frugalidade, moralidade, e respeito: A política do assimilacionismo em Moçambique, c. 1890–1930," X Congresso Internacional da Associação Latino-Americana de Estudos Afro-asiáticos, Rio de Janeiro, Brasil, 2000, https://aladaainternacional.com/wp-content/uploads/Frugalidade-moralidade-e-respeito.pdf.
15. See Jan van Butselaar, *Africanos, missionários e colonialistas: As origens da Igreja Presbiteriana de Moçambique (Missão Suiça), 1880–1896* (Lausanne: Département Missionnaire des Eglises Protestantes de la Suisse Romande, 1987); Patrick Harries, *Butterflies and Barbarians: Swiss Missionaries and Systems of Knowledge in South-East Africa* (Oxford: James Currey, 2007); Teresa Cruz e Silva, *Protestant Churches and the Formation of Political Consciousness in Southern Mozambique, 1930–1974* (Basel: P. Schlettwein, 2001).
16. See Aurélio Rocha, *Associativismo e nativismo em Moçambique: Contribuição para o estudo das origens do nacionalismo Moçambicano* (Maputo: Texto Editores, 2006); José Moreira, *Os assimilados, João Albasini e as eleições, 1900–1922* (Maputo: Arquivo Histórico de Moçambique, 1997).
17. For the history of these associations, see Jeanne M. Penvenne, "João dos Santos Albasini (1876–1922): The Contradictions of Politics and Identity in Colonial Mozambique," *Journal of African History* 37, no. 3 (1996): 419–64; David Hedges, ed., *História de Moçambique*, vol. 2, *Moçambique no auge do colonialism, 1930–1961* (Maputo: Imprensa Universitária, 1999); Raúl Bernardo Honwana, *Memórias* (Maputo: Marimbique, 2010), 101–2; Raúl Bernardo Honwana, *The Life History of Raúl Honwana: An Inside View of Mozambique from Colonialism to Independence, 1905–1975*, ed. Allen F. Isaacman (Boulder, CO: Lynne Rienner, 1988).

18. Alf Helgesson, "Church, State and People in Mozambique: An Historical Study with Special Emphasis on Methodist Developments in the Inhambane Region" (PhD diss., University of Uppsala, 1994), 253. On worldly asceticism, see Max Weber, *The Protestant Ethic and the Spirit of Capitalism* (New York: Charles Scribner's Sons, 1976), 4, 126.
19. David Hedges and Aurélio Rocha, "O reforço do colonialismo, 1930–1937," in Hedges, *História de Moçambique,* 2:67.
20. Jeanne M. Penvenne, *African Workers and Colonial Racism: Mozambican Strategies and Struggles in Lourenço Marques, 1877–1962* (Portsmouth, NH: Heinemann, 1995), 64.
21. Jeanne M. Penvenne, "We Are All Portuguese! Challenging the Political Economy of Assimilation: Lourenço Marques, 1870–1933," in *The Creation of Tribalism in Southern Africa,* ed. Leroy Vail (London: James Currey, 1989), 255–88; Valdemir Zamparoni, "Entre Narros e Mulungos: Colonialismo e paisagem social em Lourenço Marques c. 1890–1940" (PhD diss., Universidade de São Paulo, 1998); Allen F. Isaacman, "Colonial Mozambique, an Inside View: The Life History of Raúl Honwana," *Cahiers d'etudes africaines* 28, no. 109 (1988): 73.
22. John Lonsdale, "Writing Competitive Patriotisms in Eastern Africa," in *Recasting the Past: History Writing and Political Work in Modern Africa,* ed. Derek R. Peterson and Giacomo Macola (Athens: Ohio University Press, 2009), 256.
23. Penvenne, "We Are All Portuguese," 272.
24. CRL, "Ku ti kulisa" [To dignify ourselves], Secção Landina, *O brado africano,* 14 November 1924.
25. Hlonipha Mokoena, "'The Hardness of the Times and the Dearness of All the Necessaries of Life': Class and Consumption in Bilingual Nineteenth-Century Newspapers," *Social History* 45, no. 4 (October 2020): 456.
26. For a historical and literary examination of the newspaper *O brado africano,* see César Braga-Pinto and Fátima Mendonça, *João Albasini e as luzes de Nwandzengele: Jornalismo e política em Moçambique, 1908–1922* (Maputo: Alcance Editores, 2014).
27. CRL, Zeferino Franklin, "A ndondyo" [Education], Secção landina, *O brado africano,* 9 March 1922; "A byala" [Alcohol], Secção landina, *O brado africano,* 7 August 1926; "A ntiro wa psakunwa" [The work of drinking], Secção landina, *O brado africano,* 7 August 1926.
28. CRL, G. T., "O alcoolismo ni bubabyi bya lifuba" [Alcoholism and tuberculosis], Secção landina, *O brado africano,* 9 August 1924; Jimson Sungwini, "A ndyingo" [Temptation], Secção landina, *Clamor Africano,* 31 December 1932.
29. CRL, "Ku ti kulisa."
30. Joaquim Chissano's memoir offers insightful examples of his gradual transformation from a Tsonga nativist to a nationalist activist and revolutionary leader in the 1960s. The persistent conflation of civility and politics pervades his entire book. Joaquim Chissano, *Vidas, lugares e tempos* (Maputo: Texto Editores, 2010), 163–64, 229.

31. In Mozambique's Protestant churches, Juventude is the organizational collective of bachelor young adults who have finished their training in the Mintlawa (youth patrols) and are ready to enter adult life. See Elisabeth Morgenthaler, *Catecismo da Juventude: Tidyondzo ta Mintlawa* (Johannesburg: Central Mission Press, 1956); Igreja Presbiteriana de Moçambique, *Buku dra jaha: O livro do rapaz* (Maputo: Momento, 1991); Paulino Ricardo, "A Missão Suiça e a educação não formal nas comunidades Ronga, 1930–1960: O caso das Mintlawa" (licenciatura diss., Universidade Eduardo Mondlane, 2006).
32. For a biography of Eduardo Mondlane, see André Daniel Clerc, *Chitlangou: Son of a Chief* (Westport, CT: Negro University Press, 1971); Herbert Shore, "Resistance and Revolution in the Life of Eduardo Mondlane," in Mondlane, *Struggle for Mozambique;* Teresa Cruz e Silva, "Identity and Political Consciousness in Southern Mozambique, 1930–1974: Two Presbyterian Biographies Contextualized," *Journal of Southern African Studies* 24, no. 1 (March 1998): 223–36; Nadja Manghezi, *O meu coração está nas mãos de um negro: Uma história da vida de Janet Mondlane,* 2nd ed. (Maputo: Livraria Universitária, 2001); Robert Faris, *Liberating Mission in Mozambique: Faith and Revolution in the Life of Eduardo Mondlane* (Eugene, OR: Pickwick, 2014).
33. Faris, 17.
34. CDSM, Frelimo, "DEC: Recomendações." See also Ministério da Educação e Cultura, *O Homem Novo* (Maputo: Ministério da Educação e Cultura, 1977).
35. Examples include Marcelino dos Santos, Jorge Rebelo, Sérgio Vieira, and Óscar Monteiro. This group's initiation into Marxism took place during their college years in Portugal. Influenced by the Portuguese Communist Party, they professed a classical European Marxism, more aligned with the ideology of outlawed communist parties across the Western world. See Sérgio Vieira, *Participei, por isso testemunho* (Maputo: Ndjira, 2010).
36. Eduardo Mondlane, "The Evolution of Frelimo," in *The African Liberation Reader: Documents of the National Liberation Movements,* ed. Aquino de Bragança and Immanuel Wallerstein (London: Zed Press, 1982), 2:121–22.
37. Lopes T. Ndelana, *Da udenamo a Frelimo e a diplomacia Moçambicana* (Maputo: Marimbique, 2012), 63.
38. On China's role in African liberation struggles, see Alan Hutchison, *China's African Revolution* (Boulder, CO: Westview, 1976); Martin Bailey, "Tanzania and China," *African Affairs* 74, no. 294 (January 1975): 39–50.
39. Hélder Martins, "Samora na luta armada (1965–1968)," in *Samora: Homem do povo,* ed. António Sopa (Maputo: Meguezo, 2001), 111.
40. For details on the liberation struggle and Portugal's counterinsurgency measures, see Joel das Neves Tembe, ed., *História da luta armada de libertação,* vol. 1 (Maputo: Ministério dos Combatentes, 2014); John Cann, *Counterinsurgency in Africa: The Portuguese Way of War, 1961–1974* (Westport, CT: Greenwood Press, 1998).
41. I. I. Potekhin, *The Stalinist Theory of Colonial Revolution and the National Liberation Movement in Tropical and South Africa,* Scholarly Book Translation

Series (Annapolis: Research and Microfilms Publications, 1967), originally published in *Sovetskaya etnografiya*, no. 1 (April 1950): 24–40.

42. Ho Wei-yang, *Communist China's Policy in Africa*, Scholarly Book Translation Series (Annapolis: Research and Microfilms Publications, 1967), originally published in *Aussenpolitik (Foreign Policy)* 2, no. 3 (March 1961), 162–68.
43. Telepneva, *Cold War Liberation*, 15; Jeremy Friedman, "Soviet Policy in the Developing World and the Chinese Challenge in the 1960s," *Cold War History* 10, no. 2 (May 2010): 247–72.
44. Ana Bouene Mussanhane, *Protagonistas da luta de libertação nacional* (Maputo: Marimbique, 2012), 260–61; Steven Jackson, "China's Third World Foreign Policy: The Case of Angola and Mozambique, 1961–93," *China Quarterly*, no. 142 (June 1995): 401–22.
45. Martins, "Samora na luta armada," 99–115. See also the interview in José Moiane, "O direito e a justiça nas zonas libertadas," *Justiça popular* nos. 8/9 (January/June 1984): 11–14.
46. Cândido Mondlane recalled that the political commissariat of Frelimo's army, Forças Populares de Libertação de Moçambique (FPLM), was made up almost entirely of militants trained in China. Mussanhane, *Protagonistas*, 260.
47. Luís de Brito, João Paulo Borges Coelho, and José Negrão, "História da luta armada de libertação nacional" (unpublished manuscript, 1985), 48–55.
48. See the debate between Michel Cahen, "Check on Socialism: What Check? What Socialism?," *Review of African Political Economy*, no. 57 (July 1993): 46–59, and John Saul, "Eduardo Mondlane and the Rise and Fall of Mozambican Socialism," *Review of African Political Economy* 32, no. 104/105 (June–September 2005): 309–15.
49. Mussanhane, *Protagonistas*, 264–65.
50. E. Mondlane, "Evolution of Frelimo," 2:121.
51. E. Mondlane, 2:121.
52. Faris, *Liberating Mission*.
53. Nelson Mandela, *Long Walk to Freedom* (Boston: Little, Brown, 1994), 187.
54. Joe Slovo, "Shared Values: Socialism and Religion," *African Communist* (1994): 46–49.
55. Shore, "Resistance and Revolution," xxi.
56. Aquino de Bragança, "O Marxismo de Samora," *Três continentes* 3 (September 1980): 43–50; Ian Christie, *Samora Machel: Uma biografia* (Maputo: Ndjira, 1996), 245.
57. Munslow, *Mozambique: The Revolution*, 108.
58. AGGPN, Documentos da FRELIMO, Uria Simango, "Situação sombria na FRELIMO," 3 November 1969. In this pamphlet, which was also published as *Gloomy Situation in Frelimo*, Simango denounced what he saw as a forceful and illegal takeover of power by the southerners. While some of his claims were true—for example, the rampant use of corporal punishment in guerrilla bases and the execution of deviant soldiers—his long letter showed his lack of political tact.

59. "Comunicado do Comité Central," in *Datas e documentos da história da FRELIMO,* ed. João Reis and Armando P. Muiuane (Lourenço Marques: Imprensa Nacional, 1975), 79–80.
60. Colin Darch and David Hedges, "'Não temos a possibilidade de herdar nada de Portugal': As raízes do exclusivismo e vanguardismo político em Moçambique, 1969–1977," in *Territórios da língua Portuguesa: Culturas, sociedades, politicas; Anais do IV Congresso Luso-Africano-Brasileiro de Ciências Sociais, Rio de Janeiro, 1 a 5 de Setembro de 1996,* ed. G. V. Boas (Rio de Janeiro: Universidade Federal do Rio de Janeiro–Instituto de Filosofia e Ciências Socials, 1998), 135–49.
61. Frelimo, "Revolutionary Education," in de Bragança and Wallerstein, *African Liberation Reader,* 3:194–95.
62. CDSM, Pasta 2, Documentos da Frelimo, Samora Machel, "Nota de estudo para os instrutores compreender a nossa tarefa," 6 December 1970, 10.
63. As philosopher Byron Kaldis notes, "There are moments when [Karl Marx himself] writes in the tonalities of an Old Testament prophet." Byron Kaldis, ed., *Encyclopedia of Philosophy and the Social Sciences* (Thousand Oaks, CA: SAGE, 2013). For further discussion of Marxism and morality, see Steven Lukes, *Marxism and Morality* (Oxford: Clarendon, 1983); Kai Nielsen, *Marxism and the Moral Point of View: Morality, Ideology, and Historical Materialism* (London: Westview, 1989); Nicholas Churchich, *Marxism and Morality: A Critical Examination of Marxist Ethics* (Cambridge, UK: James Clarke, 1994).
64. Allen F. Isaacman and Barbara S. Isaacman, *Mozambique's Samora Machel: A Life Cut Short* (Athens: Ohio University Press, 2020).
65. See John Lewis, *Leadership in Communist China* (Ithaca, NY: Cornell University Press, 1963); Stuart Schram, *The Thought of Mao Tse-Tung* (Cambridge: Cambridge University Press, 1989), 123–28.
66. Machel's personal archive in Maputo includes all the books by Mao Zedong. From my analysis, most of his Marxist assertions come from volume 4 of Mao's *Selected Works.*
67. Schram, *Thought of Mao,* 123–28.
68. Frelimo, *Qualidades de um membro do Comité Central,* in Reis and Muiuane, *Datas e documentos,* 87–110.
69. Cann, *Counterinsurgency in Africa;* João Paulo Borges Coelho, "Protected Villages and Communal Villages in the Mozambican Province of Tete (1968–1982): A History of State Resettlement Policies, Development and War" (PhD diss., University of Bradford, 1993), 173.
70. Samora Machel, "Leadership Is Collective, Responsibility Is Collective," in *Mozambique: Sowing the Seeds of Revolution* (London: CFMAG, 1974), 16.
71. Machel, 16–20.
72. Slavoj Žižek, *For They Know Not What They Do: Enjoyment as a Political Factor* (London: Verso, 1991), 261.
73. See Barrington Moore, *Moral Purity and Persecution in History* (Princeton, NJ: Princeton University Press, 2000); Mary Douglas, *Purity and Danger: An*

Analysis of Concepts of Pollution and Taboo (London: Routledge Classics, 2002).

74. Yinghong Cheng, *Creating the "New Man": From Enlightenment Ideals to Socialist Realities* (Honolulu: University of Hawai'i Press, 2009), 1; Joshua Muravchik, *Heaven on Earth: The Rise and Fall of Socialism* (San Francisco: Encounter Books, 2002).
75. Cheng, *Creating the "New Man,"* 4.
76. Cheng, 1; Carlos Del Toro, *Cuba: Towards the New Man* (Chamber of Commerce of the Republic of Cuba, 1969).
77. Žižek, *For They Know Not What They Do,* 262.
78. Žižek, 262.
79. Frelimo, *Qualidades,* 87–110.
80. Carlos Siliya, ed., *Samora Machel na memória do povo e do mundo: Discursos,* vol. 1 (Maputo: CPHLLN, 2011). For Frelimo's official publications, see Colin Darch, "As publicações da FRELIMO: Um estudo preliminar," *Estudos Moçambicanos,* no. 2 (1981): 105–20.
81. CDSM, Pasta 2, Documentos da Frelimo, Josina Muthemba, "Relatório, 1968–1969: Palestra sobre militante da Frelimo," 26 January 1969.
82. See Mao Tse-Tung, "On the Reissue of the Three Main Rules of Discipline and the Eight Points for Attention: Instruction of the General Headquarters of the Chinese People's Liberation Army," in *Selected Works of Mao Tse-Tung* (Oxford: Pergamon Press, 1961), 4:155.
83. Frelimo, *Qualidades,* 87.
84. This point addressed one of the key issues in the internal schism that ended with the assassination of Eduardo Mondlane in February 1969 and the expulsion of Vice President Uria Simango in May 1970.
85. Frelimo, *Qualidades.*
86. Comaroff and Comaroff, *Of Revelation and Revolution,* 1:63.
87. Matias Mboa, *Memórias da luta clandestina* (Maputo: Marimbique, 2009), 56; Martins, "Samora na luta armada," 111. For signs of this austerity in Machel's formative years, see Gerhard Liesegang, "Samora Moisés Machel: Os anos de formação, 1933–1963," in Sopa, *Samora: Homem do povo,* 28–31.
88. CDSM, Machel, "Nota de estudo," 10.
89. AGGPN, Documentos da FRELIMO, Centro Político, "Acta da reunião do pelotão do curso político," 26 March 1974.
90. CDSM, Machel, "Nota de estudo"; CDSM, Pasta 2, Documentos da Frelimo, Samora Machel, "Sobre algumas questões referentes à natureza e funcionamento do campo de instrução," July 1970.
91. Isaacman and Isaacman, *Mozambique's Samora Machel,* 71–72.
92. Sarah LeFanu, *S Is For Samora: A Lexical Biography of Samora Machel and the Mozambican Dream* (Scottsville, South Africa: University of KwaZulu-Natal Press, 2012), 166.
93. AGGPN, Documentos da FRELIMO, "Curso de formação política," 1974.

94. José Cabaço, *Moçambique: Identidades, colonialismo e libertação* (Maputo: Marimbique, 2010), 278.
95. LeFanu, *S Is for Samora,* 166
96. Cabaço, *Moçambique: Identidades,* 279; Borges Coelho, "Politics and Contemporary History," 23.
97. LeFanu, *S Is For Samora,* 167.
98. Samora Machel, "The Liberation of Women Is a Fundamental Necessity for the Revolution," in Machel, *Sowing the Seeds of Revolution,* 32.
99. Mao Tse-Tung, "Sobre a grande vitória no nordeste e o movimento de educação ideológica de tipo novo no exército de libertação," in *Obras escolhidas de Mao Tse-Tung* (Beijing: Edições em Línguas Estrangeiras, 1971), 1:313.
100. For example, admission to the Mintlawa in the Swiss-Presbyterian mission in southern Mozambique entailed a similar ceremony in which candidates had to recount their background before a circle of experienced patrol members and instructors. See Elisabeth Morgenthaler and André D. Clerc, *Le mouvement des equipes ou patrouilles "Ntlawa" au Mozambique* (Lausanne: Mimeo, 1950); Clerc, *Chitlangou,* 171.
101. Fanon, *Wretched of the Earth,* 12.
102. Comaroff and Comaroff, *Of Revelation and Revolution,* 1:65.
103. Clerc, *Chitlangou,* 168.
104. Machel, "Internal Corruption," in de Bragança and Wallerstein, *African Liberation Reader,* 2:130.
105. Frelimo, "Self-Criticism," in de Bragança and Wallerstein, *African Liberation Reader,* 2:124. In his 1946 autobiography, Eduardo Mondlane offers a similar picture of how his Ntlawa team practiced criticism and self-criticism: "This is a society in which people speak openly. Every resolution made is put down on paper. The following week it is examined and discussed to see what has become of it. But the missionary does not preach at us. He sets us talking and allows contrary opinions. So the discussion never flags. It is a sharp battle of tongues and wits." Clerc, *Chitlangou,* 151.
106. CDSM, Pasta 2, Documentos da Frelimo, Josina Muthemba, "Relatório, 1968–1969: Reunião do D. D.," [Nachingwea], 19 August 1968.
107. CDSM, Muthemba, "Palestra."
108. CDSM, Muthemba, "Palestra."
109. Tobias Kelly and Sharika Thiranagama, "Introduction: Specters of Treason," in *Traitors: Suspicion, Intimacy, and the Ethics of State-Building,* ed. Sharika Thiranagama and Tobias Kelly (Philadelphia: University of Pennsylvania Press, 2009), 3.
110. James Aho, *This Thing of Darkness: A Sociology of the Enemy* (Seattle: University of Washington Press, 1994), 23.
111. Moore, *Moral Purity;* Douglas, *Purity and Danger.*
112. Hannah Arendt, *The Origins of Totalitarianism* (San Diego: Harvest Book, 1985), 423.
113. Žižek, *For They Know Not What They Do,* 262.

114. "Das contradições no nosso seio," *A voz da revolução,* January 1970, 7.
115. CDSM, Pasta 2, Documentos da Frelimo, "Definição do inimigo," 1970, 2.
116. "Tarefas das bases de apoio," *A voz da revolução,* no. 20, December 1973, 3–4.
117. CDSM, Machel, "Nota de estudo," 5.
118. CDSM, Machel, 5.
119. CDSM, Machel, 5.
120. CDSM, Machel, 5.
121. Anthony Giddens, *Émile Durkheim* (New York: Penguin, 1978), 81.
122. See *Tortura na colónia de Moçambique 1963–1974: Depoitmentos de presos políticos* (Porto: Afrontamento, 1977).
123. See James Saymour and Richard Anderson, *New Ghosts, Old Ghosts: Prisons and Labor Reform Camps in China* (New York: M. E. Sharpe, 1998); Aminda Smith, *Thought Reform and China's Dangerous Classes: Reeducation, Resistance, and the People* (New York: Rowman & Littlefield, 2013). Chinese punitive techniques of reeducation in Nachingwea are mentioned in José Moiane, "O direito e a justiça nas zonas libertadas," *Justiça popular* nos. 8/9 (January/June 1984): 11–14.
124. "Tarefas das bases," 4.
125. *Rassemblement* is a French term that means "to assemble" or "to gather." It was brought into Frelimo's vocabulary by the first group of guerrillas trained in Algeria in 1963.
126. Sebastião Mabote as reported in CDSM, Muthemba, "Reunião."
127. Chefe Ripua, a guerrilla officer, testified in the Nachingwea meeting of August 1968 that "from 1965 to 1966 there was no punishment in Cabo Delgado, but political re-education, and most soldiers were orderly. The undisciplined were very few." CDSM, Muthemba, Reunião.
128. Testimony by Chefe Ripua in CDSM, Muthemba, "Reunião."
129. Testimony by Chefe Ripua in CDSM, Muthemba, "Reunião."
130. CDSM, Muthemba, "Reunião."
131. Due to his close association with guerrilla commanders, Mondlane was more sensitive to their complaints that discipline was key to the success of the struggle. In contrast, his deputy, Uria Simango, remained averse to arbitrary punishments, and the commanders increasingly saw him as an obstacle. See testimony by Mariano Matsinhe in Mussanhane, *Protagonistas,* 567.
132. Machel, "Leadership Is Collective," 17. Students of European Puritanism will recognize in Mao's and Frelimo's codes of conduct Cromwell's New Model Army, "with its rigid camp discipline, its elaborate rules against every imaginable sin from looting and rapine to blasphemy and card-playing." Michael Walzer, *The Revolution of the Saints: A Study in the Origins of Radical Politics* (Cambridge, MA: Harvard University Press, 1965), 13.
133. Francisco Carmona and Emílio Beúla, "No contexto da revolução: Na Frelimo era norma fuzilar pessoas," *Savana,* 4 September 2009, 2–4.
134. Paolo Israel, "Utopia Live: Singing the Mozambican Struggle for National Liberation," *Kronos* 35, no. 1 (November 2009): 122.

135. See various editions of *A voz da revolução.*
136. The guerrilla intelligence kept detailed records about who committed what fault and where. Samora Machel took great interest in this effort. In 1979, when he visited the reeducation camp of Chiputo in Niassa (which exclusively hosted Frelimo deserters), Machel knew the names of most inmates and the details of how they had sealed their fate. More than once, he confronted inmates and corrected their statements, especially those he had trained directly. AGGPN, Serviços de Reeducação do Niassa, Documentos Dispersos, 1976–1984, "Inquéritos a desertores," 1979. See also "Chiputo: de traidores a heróis da reconstrução," *Tempo,* Número Especial Dedicado à Viagem Presidencial à Província do Niassa, 20 December 1979, 6–11.
137. "Frelimo militants expose traitors," *Daily News,* 20 March 1975.

CHAPTER 2: POLITICAL TRANSITION AND THE BIRTH OF THE REEDUCATION PIPELINE, 1974–1976

1. Samora Machel, "FRELIMO's Tasks in the Struggle Ahead," in *Mozambique: Revolution or Reaction?* (Oakland, CA: LSM Information Center, 1975), 14–17.
2. Michel Foucault, *The Punitive Society: Lectures at the Collège de France, 1972–1973* (New York: Picador, 2018), 45–106.
3. MHN, *Daily News,* 3 November 1975.
4. AHM, "Recuperação de marginais em Inhambane," *Notícias,* 30 October 1974; "Inhambane: Campos de recuperação começam a funcionar," *A tribuna,* 11 November 1974; "Em Inhambane: Recuperação de marginais," *Notícias,* 12 November 1974. Two episodes of violence in the capital city marked the transition to independence. The first episode was the settlers' rebellion on September 7, 1974, the day Frelimo and the new Portuguese government signed the peace agreement in Lusaka. Most settlers felt betrayed by the agreement, which recognized Frelimo as the only legitimate political force in Mozambique. The bloodier events of October 21, in which disoriented Portuguese soldiers clashed with Frelimo guerrillas, were in some way a continuation of the crisis of September 7. For details on these events, see James Mittleman, "State Power in Mozambique," *Issue: A Journal of Opinion* 8, no. 1 (Spring 1978): 4–11; A. D. Harvey, "Counter-coup in Lourenço Marques: September 1974," *International Journal of African Historical Studies* 39, no. 3 (2006): 487–98; Benedito Machava, "Galo amanheceu em Lourenço Marques: O 7 de Setembro e o verso da descolonização em Moçambique," *Revista crítica de ciências sociais,* no. 106 (May 2015): 53–84; Ribeiro Cardoso, *O fim do império* (Alfragide: Caminho, 2011).
5. "Operação policial para eliminar focos de banditismo: Comunicado," *A tribuna,* 28 October 1974; "Povo exige nome de agitadores," *A tribuna,* 28 October 1974. The few White settlers detained in this operation were later sent to Niassa and, after a few months, deported to Portugal.
6. Ana Bouene Mussanhane, *Protagonistas da luta de libertação nacional* (Maputo: Marimbique, 2012), 145.

7. In angry and vengeful acts similar to those of Algeria's departing *pied noirs,* some Portuguese settlers sabotaged and destroyed factory machinery and agricultural implements; some killed their cattle and ransacked their houses. There were also cases in which homeowners left the water taps open, flooding their houses before leaving. See Joseph Hanlon, *Mozambique: Revolution under Fire* (London: Zed Books, 1984), 48. For a literary depiction of these events, see the humorous novel by João Paulo Borges Coelho, *Crónica da rua 513.2* (Lisbon: Caminho, 2006). Ryszard Kapuscinski captured the madness of the end of empire in Luanda, Angola, in *Another Day of Life* (New York: Penguin, 1988). See also Pamela Gupta, *Portuguese Decolonization in the Indian Ocean World: History and Ethnography* (London: Bloomsbury, 2018).
8. See David Wield, "Mozambique: Late Colonialism and Early Problems of Transition," in *Revolutionary Socialist Development in the Third World,* ed. Gordon White (Lexington: University Press of Kentucky, 1983), 75–113.
9. The reeducation of society's wayward members was one of the key topics during the first meeting of the Council of Ministers, July 9–25, 1975, which the meeting minutes attest to: "The Council of Ministers deliberated to concede priority to the issue of reeducation of detainees, which will be carried out by the Ministries of the Interior and of Justice." AGGPN, "Programa geral de actividades do Conselho de Ministros: Tarefas e funções que competem a cada ministério; Decretos do Conselho de Ministros," 25 July 1975, 6.
10. AHM, "Recuperação de marginais."
11. "FRELIMO cria campos de reeducação," *A capital,* 20 November 1974.
12. Albino Magaia and Ricardo Rangel, "Prostituição: Tráfico sexual mata a fome," *Tempo,* no. 211, 13 October 1974.
13. The term *caniço* (reed) refers to the labyrinthine bairros in Mozambique's cities, whose houses were mostly built of reed and other precarious materials. This was in contrast to the cement housing of the urban core, or *cidade de cimento.* See David Morton, *Age of Concrete: Housing and the Shape of Aspiration in the Capital of Mozambique* (Athens: Ohio University Press, 2019).
14. Magaia and Rangel, "Prostituição."
15. Luise White, *The Comforts of Home: Prostitution in Colonial Nairobi* (Chicago: University of Chicago Press, 1990).
16. Krisno Nimpuno et al., *The Malhangalane Survey: A Study of an Unplanned Settlement in Maputo, 1976* (Gothenburg: Chalmers University of Technology, 1977).
17. Areosa Pena, "O bairro do caniço muda de face," *Tempo,* 2 May 1971, 33. Although mobility in the racially segregated urban areas was restricted for all Africans, women faced even harsher restrictions. While African men had been forced to carry transit passes since 1914 to circulate in urban areas, women who wanted to move from one location to another additionally needed the approval of their fathers, brothers, or any male tutor. These

colonial laws reinforced the notion of the city as a male space. Even after the Portuguese revoked the racial laws in 1961, Mozambique's gendered cityscapes remained the same, with the number of urban male residents far surpassing that of women. See António Rita-Ferreira, *Os Africanos de Lourenço Marques* (Lourenço Marques: Instituto de Investigação Científica de Moçambique, 1968), 156.

18. Rita-Ferreira, 279.
19. In 1976, there were 500,000 inhabitants in Lourenço Marques (excluding the satellites of Matola and Machava). By 1980, the city had reached 740,000 inhabitants (383,000 men and 356,000 women). See AGGPM, RPM-CCR/DNE, "10 recenceamento geral da população: Projecções demográficas," vol. 10, 1980.
20. For an examination of the foundations of male anxiety over independent women, see, for example, Carole Paterman, *The Disorder of Women: Feminism and Political Theory* (Stanford: Stanford University Press, 1989); Elizabeth Wilson, *The Sphinx in the City: Urban Life, the Control of Disorder, and Women* (Berkeley: University of California Press, 1991); Judith Walkowitz, *City of Dreadful Delight: Narratives of Sexual Danger in Late-Victorian London* (Chicago: The University of Chicago Press, 1992); Dorothy Hodgson and Sheryl McCurdy, eds., *"Wicked" Women and the Reconfiguration of Gender in Africa* (Portsmouth, NH: Heinemann, 2001); Signe Arnfred, *Sexuality and Gender Politics in Mozambique: Rethinking Gender in Africa* (Woodbridge, UK: James Curry, 2011).
21. Derek R. Peterson, *Ethnic Patriotism and the East African Revival: A History of Dissent, c. 1935–1972* (Cambridge: Cambridge University Press, 2012).
22. For an analysis of Frelimo's multiple discursive vocabularies, see Anne M. Pitcher, *Transforming Mozambique: The Politics of Privatization, 1975–2000* (Cambridge: Cambridge University Press, 2002), 78; Maria-Benedita Basto, *A guerra das escritas: Literatura, nação e teoria póscolonial em Moçambique* (Lisbon: Vendaval, 2006).
23. "Para onde foram as prostitutas?," *Tempo*, no. 237, 31 August 1975. See also Kathleen Sheldon, *Pounders of Grain: A History of Women, Work, and Politics in Mozambique* (Portsmouth, NH: Heinemann, 2002), 155; Omar Ribeiro Thomaz, "Escravos sem dono: A experiência social dos campos de trabalho em Moçambique no período socialista," *Revista de antropologia* 51, no. 1 (2008): 178.
24. AJN, "Desferido golpe eficaz na prostituição e intermediários: Encerrados os cabarés da Major Araújo, mulheres desejam mudar de vida," *Notícias*, 10 June 1975.
25. AJN, "Desferido golpe eficaz."
26. MHN, *Daily News*, 3 November 1975; "FRELIMO cria campos de reeducação," *A capital*, 20 November 1974.
27. MHN, International Commission of Jurists, "Mozambique's Re-education Camps," *Review of the International Commission of Jurists*, no. 27 (December 1981): 14–15.

28. Fernando Lima, "Como encarar à prostituição," *Notícias,* 13 August 1976.
29. Jeanne M. Penvenne, *Women, Migration and the Cashew Economy in Southern Mozambique, 1945–1975* (Rochester, NY: James Currey, 2015), 155–79; Sheldon, *Pounders of Grain.*
30. AGGPM, Secretariado Nacional da OMM, Departamento de Assuntos Sociais, "Documento de orientação para resolução de problemas sociais prioritários," Maputo, 1977, 4. For the history of the OMM and its role in the revolution, see Barbara S. Isaacman and June Stephen, *A mulher Moçambicana no processo de libertação* (Maputo: Instituto Nacional do Libro e do Disco, 1982); Stephanie Urdang, *And Still They Dance: Women, War, and the Struggle for Change in Mozambique* (London: Monthly Review Press, 1989).
31. See the description of Machel's vigorous condemnation of single mothers at OMM forums in Arnfred, *Sexuality and Gender Politics,* 8.
32. "República popular de Moçambique: A 1a ofensiva," *Tempo,* no. 252, 3 August 1975.
33. "Combate ao álcool: Governo toma medidas," *A tribuna,* 7 December 1974.
34. "Campanhas contra o álcool: Comité em acção," *A tribuna,* 22 November 1974; "Comité do bairro combate alcoolismo," *A tribuna,* 25 November 1974; "Mafalala: Luta contra alcoolismo," *A tribuna,* 26 December 1974.
35. CDSM, IPM, "Questões partidárias," 21 May 1975.
36. "Campanhas contra o álcool."
37. As a member of the editorial board of *Tempo* magazine, Albino Magaia had a full platform at his disposal to aid his comrades in the revolutionary task of cleaning up the cities. See Jacimara Sousa Santana, *Mulheres Africanas de Moçambique na revista "Tempo" (1975–1985)* (Itajaí: Casa Aberda, 2014), 66. These campaigns do not feature in Emídio Xavier Machiana, *A revista "Tempo" e a revolução Moçambicana* (Maputo: Promédia, 2002).
38. "Para onde foram as prostitutas?"; "O combate para acabar com a prostituição faz parte da luta contra o capitalismo: Part 1," *Notícias,* 18 November 1977.
39. AGGPM, "Síntese do relatório do primeiro semestre de 1978 do governador da província de Maputo à sua excelência o presidente da Frelimo e presidente da República Popular de Moçambique," Maputo, 31 July 1978.
40. José Capela, *O vinho para o preto: Notas e textos sobre a exportação do vinho para África* (Porto: Afrontamento, 1973; repr., Porto: Centro de Estudos Africanos, 2009); José Capela, *O álcool na colonização do Sul do Save, 1860–1920* (Maputo: Edição do Autor, 1995).
41. "Rusga em Quelimane: 144 detidos," *Notícias,* 24 December 1974.
42. Penvenne, *Women, Migration,* 55.
43. Penvenne, 61–62. For a literary account of these raids, see Calane da Silva, *Xicandarinha na lenha do mundo* (Maputo: AEMO, 1987).
44. See Matias Mboa, *Memórias da luta clandestina* (Maputo: Marimbique, 2009), 58; Dinis Muhai, "Da mecânica aos grupos de esclarecimento," in *Mafalala 1974: Memórias do 7 de Setembro, a grande operação,* by Aurélio Le Bon (Maputo: Movimento Editora, 2015), 148.

45. "Para onde foram as prostitutas?"
46. For a compelling study of leisure in colonial Lourenço Marques, see António Sopa, *A alegria é uma coisa rara: Subsídios para a história da música popular urbana em Lourenço Marques, 1920–1975* (Maputo: Marimbique, 2014).
47. MHN, Jay Ross, "Mozambican Reeducation Camps Raise Rights Questions," *Washington Post,* 7 May 1980.
48. H. G. Adler, "Ideas toward a Sociology of the Concentration Camp," *American Journal of Sociology* 63, no. 5 (March 1958): 521.
49. Tzvetan Todorov, "Communist Camps and Their Aftermath," *Representations* 49 (Winter 1995): 120–32.
50. AGGPN, DPSRN/SR, "Indevidamente detidas, M'sawize," n.d.; AGGPN, DPSRN/SR, "Casos duvidosos, M'sawize," n.d.; AGGPN, DPSRN, "Relação nominal de nacionais detidos arbitrariamente se propõe o seu regress à procedência," 24 March 1978.
51. Igal Halfin, *Intimate Enemies: Demonizing the Bolshevik Opposition, 1918–1928* (Pittsburgh: University of Pittsburgh Press, 2007), 2.
52. Barrington Moore, *Moral Purity and Persecution in History* (Princeton, NJ: Princeton University Press, 2000), 74.
53. Halfin, *Intimate Enemies,* 2, 14.
54. Robert Lifton, *Thought Reform and the Psychology of Totalism: A Study of "Brainwashing" in China* (New York: W. W. Norton, 1961), 24–25; Martin Whyte, *Small Groups and Political Rituals in China* (Berkeley: University of California Press, 1974), 74. See also Aminda Smith, *Thought Reform and China's Dangerous Classes: Reeducation, Resistance, and the People* (New York: Rowman & Littlefield, 2013).
55. "A confissão de Uria Simango," *A tribuna,* 14 May 1975. The final section of Simango's confession also appeared in *Datas e documentos da história da FRELIMO,* ed. João Reis and Armando P. Muiuane (Lourenço Marques: Imprensa Nacional, 1975), 323–25.
56. "Frelimo Militants Expose Traitors," *Daily News,* 20 March 1975; "Frelimo Exposes Traitorous Clique," *Daily News,* 23 April 1975.
57. "Frelimo Militants Expose Traitors."
58. For similar examples of revivalist public self-disclosure in East Africa, see Peterson, *Ethnic Patriotism,* 105–26.
59. "Frelimo Exposes Traitorous Clique."
60. Paolo Israel, "Utopia Live: Singing the Mozambican Struggle for National Liberation," *Kronos* 35, no. 1 (November 2009): 109.
61. *Ndungu* is a Swahili term for "comrade." "Frelimo Militants Expose Traitors."
62. "Frelimo Militants Expose Traitors."
63. "Frelimo Exposes Traitorous Clique." The militants were singing the famous yet sinister hymn "Frelimo aina mwisho" (Frelimo has no end). For a discussion of this and other songs, see Paolo Israel, *In Step with the Times: Mapiko Masquerades of Mozambique* (Athens: Ohio University Press, 2014), 228.

64. *Nachingwea* (Maputo: Instituto Nacional de Audiovisual e Cinema, n.d.).
65. "Frelimo Militants Expose Traitors."
66. "Confissão de Uria Simango," in *Uria Simango: Um homem, uma causa,* by Barnabé Ncomo (Maputo: Edições Novafrica, 2004), 417–37.
67. Ncomo, 337.
68. AGGPN, Documentos da FRELIMO, Uria Simango, "Situação sombria na FRELIMO," 3 November 1969.
69. Anthropologist Karin Barber defines *addressivity* as the "way the text [written or spoken] addresses a reader or listener." *The Anthropology of Texts, Persons and Publics: Oral and Written Culture in Africa and Beyond* (Cambridge: Cambridge University Press, 2007), 138.
70. See AGGPN, Documentos da FRELIMO, "Os graves acontecimentos de 1968 e as divergências ideológicas ao nível da direcção," 1970.
71. Ncomo, *Uria Simango,* 215.
72. João Cabrita, *Mozambique: The Tortuous Road to Democracy* (New York: Palgrave, 2000), 83; Ncomo, 337.
73. "A confissão."
74. MHN, Ross, "Mozambican Reeducation Camps."
75. See Maria Paula Meneses, "Xiconhoca, o Inimigo: Narrativas de violência sobre a construção da nação em Moçambique," *Revista crítica de ciências sociais* no. 106 (May 2015): 9–52; MHN, David Ottaway, "Chinese-Style Public Shaming: Subtle Mozambican Force Used on Ex-collaborators," *International Herald Tribune,* 9 March 1979.
76. "Frelimo Militants Expose Traitors." President Machel failed to fulfill this intention. Although in 1979 and 1981, Frelimo released most tried as traitors at Nachingwea, Simango, his wife Celina, Joana Simeão, and several other prominent political dissidents were executed in a covert operation after serving two years of detention in M'telela. Unlike other cases in which alleged traitors and enemies of the revolution were executed in public—and had their photographs and short biographies published—the case of Simango and his company is still cloaked in mystery. For details on the fate of Simango, see Cabrita, *Mozambique,* 100–103; Ncomo, *Uria Simango,* 331–47.
77. AGGPN, DPSRN/MINT, Serviços de Reeducação, Centros de Reeducação, "Comentários à proposta de lei," January 1976; AGGPM, MINT, Circular 6/GMI/976, "Assunto: Objectivos dos centros de reeducação," 5.
78. See "Centros de reeducação em Moçambique," *Tempo,* no. 264, 23 March 1976.
79. Igal Halfin, *From Darkness to Light: Class, Consciousness, and Salvation in Revolutionary Russia* (Pittsburgh: University of Pittsburgh Press, 2000), 1–2; 6.
80. AGGPM, MINT, "Objectivos dos centros."
81. AGGPM, MINT, "Objectivos dos centros."
82. AGGPM, MINT, "Objectivos dos centros."
83. AGGPN, DPSRN/MINT, "Proposta de Decreto Lei/77 sobre reeducação," 1976.
84. AGGPN, DPSRN/MINT, "Proposta de Decreto Lei/77."

85. AGGPN, DPSRN/MINT, "Proposta de Decreto Lei/77."
86. Jeanne M. Penvenne, *African Workers and Colonial Racism: Mozambican Strategies and Struggles in Lourenço Marques, 1877–1962* (Portsmouth, NH: Heinemann, 1995), 6; Malyn Newitt, *História de Moçambique* (Lisbon: Europa-America, 2012), 341.
87. See "As fontes do sanguessuga," *Tempo*, 1 January 1978, 20–25.
88. William J. T. Mitchel, *Iconology: Image, Text, Ideology* (Chicago: University of Chicago Press, 1986), 9.
89. Lars Buur, "Xiconhoca: Mozambique's Ubiquitous Post-independence Traitor," in *Traitors: Suspicion, Intimacy, and the Ethics of State-Building*, ed. Sharika Thiranagama and Tobias Kelly (Philadelphia: University of Pennsylvania Press, 2009), 26–28.
90. LeFanu, *S Is for Samora*, 85.
91. While the abstract and unachievable concept of the New Man has vanished from Mozambique's public memory and political rhetoric, Xiconhoca lives on in the postsocialist era. His offspring, *Nhoca Jr.—O Filho de Xico* (*Nhoca Jr.—Xico's Son*), appears regularly in the independent weekly newspaper *Savana*. The newspaper *A verdade* recently coined the term *xiconhoquice* to classify the xiconhocas of the week in the political scene of present-day Mozambique. See Penvenne, *Women, Migration*, 30.
92. James Aho, *This Thing of Darkness: A Sociology of the Enemy* (Seattle: University of Washington Press, 1994), 28.
93. AGGPN, DPSRN/MINT, "Proposta de Decreto Lei/77."
94. MHN, "Machel's Speech on Unjust Detentions in Re-education Camps," *Summary of World Broadcasts* (London), no. ME/6846, 6 October 1981, p. B/1. See also AHN, António Souto, "Reeducação e legalidade fabricam Homen Novo," *Notícias*, 29 August 1981.
95. "A reeducação é uma escola onde se forma o Homem Novo," *Notícias*, 24 November 1978. Frelimo leaders drew from the playbook of their favorite ideologue. In the commemoration of the CCP (Chinese Communist Party) victory in 1949, Chairman Mao said: "As for the members of the reactionary classes . . . so long as they do not rebel . . . land and work will be given to them as well in order to allow them to live and remold themselves through labor into new people. . . . Propaganda and educational work will be done among them too. . . . This may be called a 'policy of benevolence' if you like." Mao Tse-Tung, *Selected Works of Mao Tse-Tung* (Oxford: Pergamon Press, 1961), 4:419.
96. MHN, "Machel's Speech on Unjust Detentions."
97. MHN, "Machel's Speech on Unjust Detentions."
98. Hanlon, *Mozambique*, 249.
99. See Albie Sachs and Gita Honwana Welch, *Liberating the Law: Creating Popular Justice in Mozambique* (London: Zed Books, 1990).
100. "Constituição da República Popular de Moçambique," in Reis and Muiuane, *Datas e documentos*, 494–95.

101. See Rohit De, *A People's Constitution: The Everyday Life of Law in the Indian Republic* (Princeton, NJ: Princeton University Press, 2018).
102. AGGPN, DPSRN/MINT, "Comentários à proposta de lei."
103. AGGPN, DPSRN/MINT, "Comentários à proposta de lei."
104. AGGPN, DPSRN/MINT, "Comentários à proposta de lei."
105. AGGPN, DPSRN/MINT, "Comentários à proposta de lei," 5–6.
106. AGGPN, DPSRN/MINT, "Comentários à proposta de lei," 5–6.
107. See "Justiça popular em debate," *Tempo,* no. 413, 3 September 1978, 23–25. According to José Cabaço, when the Council of Ministers decided to pass the *lei do chamboco* (flogging law) in 1983, Teodato Hunguana was the only member who voted against it. Interview with author in Maputo, 25 February 2015. Yet, on the public stage, he never voiced any opposition to public floggings or even to the death penalty (which was amended to include black marketeering in 1983). See "O que é o crime? A posição do nosso país perante esta questão," *Tempo,* 19 October 1980, 11–14.

CHAPTER 3: "THESE MORAL DESERTERS MUST BE REEDUCATED"

Epigraph: "Rompamos definitivamente com a burguesia para consolidar o poder popular: Documento do Presidente Samora Machel no comício de 22 de Junho em Maputo," *Tempo,* 8 August 1982.

1. AGGPM, RPM, Assembleia Popular, "Linhas fundamentais do Plano Prospectivo Indicativo para 1981–1990," Maputo, Imprensa Nacional, 1981. For more details on PPI, see Carlos Nuno Castel-Branco, ed., *Moçambique: Perspectivas económicas* (Maputo: UEM/FFE, 1994); Anne M. Pitcher, *Transforming Mozambique: The Politics of Privatization, 1975–2000* (Cambridge: Cambridge University Press, 2002), 77.
2. AGGPM, RPM, Assembleia Popular, "Discurso de abertura e de encerramento da 8a Sessão," Maputo, Imprensa Nacional, Outubro 1981, p. 29.
3. For a nuanced description of the role of *cooperantes* in Mozambique, see Sarah LeFanu, *S Is for Samora: A Lexical Biography of Samora Machel and the Mozambican Dream* (Scottsville, South Africa: University of KwaZulu-Natal Press, 2012), 41–43.
4. For changes in Frelimo's diplomatic relations with China and the Soviet Union, see Steven Jackson, "China's Third World Foreign Policy: The Case of Angola and Mozambique, 1961–93," *China Quarterly,* no. 142 (June 1995): 401–22; Jeremy Friedman, "Soviet Policy in the Developing World and the Chinese Challenge in the 1960s," *Cold War History* 10, no. 2 (May 2010): 247–72; Natasha Telepneva, "Mediators of Liberation: Eastern Bloc Officials, Mozambican Diplomacy and the Origins of Soviet Support for FRELIMO, 1958–1965," *Journal of Southern African Studies* 43, no. 1 (January 2017): 67–81.
5. Luís de Brito, *A Frelimo, o Marxismo e a construção do estado nacional, 1962–1983* (Maputo: Instituto de Estudos Sociais e Económicos, 2019), 90–92; Pitcher, *Transforming Mozambique.*

6. Benedito Machava, "State Discourse on Internal Security and the Politics of Punishment in Post-independence Mozambique, 1975–1983," *Journal of Southern African Studies* 37, no. 3 (September 2011): 593–609.
7. See Jean Tartter, "Government and Politics," in *Mozambique: A Country Study,* ed. Harold Nelson (Washington, DC: American University, 1984), 201; Herbert Howe, "National Security," in Nelson, *Mozambique,* 277; Omar Ribeiro Thomaz, "Escravos sem dono: A experiência social dos campos de trabalho em Moçambique no período socialista," *Revista de antropologia* 51, no. 1 (2008): 191; Carlos Quembo, *Poder do poder: Operação Produção e a inveção dos "improdutivos" urbanos no Moçambique socialista, 1983–1988* (Maputo: Alcance, 2017).
8. "Na prática da Ofensiva pela legalidade libertamos muitas pessoas: Inspector de estado Raimundo Pachinuapa à Tempo," *Tempo,* no. 609, 13 June 1982. Although under severe pressure from the ruling party, the Catholic Church was one of the few nonstate entities that continued to be critical of Mozambique's public affairs. See Éric Morier-Genoud, *Catholicism and the Making of Politics in Central Mozambique* (Rochester, NY: University of Rochester Press, 2019).
9. "Na prática da Ofensiva."
10. MHN, "Inspection of re-education centres in Mozambique's Cabo Delgado Province," *Summary of World Broadcasts* (London), 19 October 1981; "Na prática da Ofensiva."
11. AGGPN, DPSRN, "Inquérito tipo B (desertores)," 1979; João Carlos Trindade, interview with author in Maputo, 10 September 2014.
12. See the December 26, 1979, special issue of *Tempo* entitled *Número especial dedicado à viagem presidencial à província do Niassa.*
13. MHN, António Souto, "Libertados 684 reeducandos: Medida de clemência ordenada pelo Presidente Samora em Cabo Delgado," *Notícias,* 28 September 1981.
14. "Na prática da Ofensiva."
15. AGGPM, "1a Reunião Nacional das Cidades e Bairros Comunais: Síntese do trabalho realizado nos bairros do grande Maputo," 24 February 1979, 3.
16. AGGPM, RPM, "1a Reunião Nacional das Cidades e Bairros Comunais: Síntese da resolução sobre a organização da Direcção Estatal das Cidades," Maputo, Imprensa Nacional, 1979.
17. AGGPM, "Síntese do trabalho realizado," 15.
18. A *Tempo* report in December 1980 revealed that more than eleven thousand tenants did not pay rent in Maputo, and many more occupied houses illegally. See "Maputo: Mais de 11 mil inquilinos não pagam renda de casa," *Tempo,* no. 530, 7 December 1980.
19. AGGPM, "1a Reunião Nacional das Cidades e Bairros Comunais: Discurso de abertura por sua exa. o ministro de estado na presidência," 27 February 1979, 12–13.
20. AGGPM, OMM, "1a Reunião da Comissão Coordenadora Nacional: Plano de trabalho para o 10 semestre," Manica, 13 October 1977, 8–11; AGGPM,

"Relatório do secretariado provincial a apresentar à 1a Conferência Provincial da OMM," Maputo, 21 November 1977, 3.

21. Samora Machel, "We Are Declaring War on the Enemy Within," in *Samora Machel: An African Revolutionary; Selected Speeches and Writings,* ed. Barry Munslow (London: Zed Books, 1985), 86–103.
22. "A ofensiva política e organizacional faz parte da nossa maneira de viver," *Notícias,* 28 July 1980.
23. See John Lewis, *Leadership in Communist China* (Ithaca, NY: Cornell University Press, 1963); Lili Wu, "The Dilemma of Charismatic Authority: Mao's Cultural Revolution in China" (PhD diss., University of Chicago, 2010); Charles Cell, *Revolution at Work: Mobilization Campaigns in China* (New York: Academic Press, 1977).
24. "A Ofensiva: O que é? Da campanha à metodologia permanente para o combate ao subdesenvolvimento," *A voz da revolução,* no. 71, August 1980, 15–21; "Legalidade e visitas presidenciais pontos altos da vida do país," *Notícias,* 19 December 1981.
25. "Em tribunal as pessoas detidas durante a Ofensiva," *Tempo,* no. 514, 17 August 1980; "O que é illegal não é nosso!," *Notícias,* 6 November 1981.
26. "Ofensiva política e organizational: 400 elementos expulsos em dois anos do Ministério da Segurança (SNASP)," *Tempo,* 20 February 1982.
27. Machel, "We Are Declaring War," 94.
28. Colin Darch and David Hedges, *Samora Machel: Retórica politica e independencia em Moçambique* (Salvador: Edufba, 2018).
29. Machel, "We Are Declaring War," 88.
30. "Consolidar Maputo como zona libertada," *Notícias,* 24 June 1982.
31. "Rompamos definitivamente com a burguesia."
32. Machel, "We Are Declaring War," 93; 101–2.
33. Machel, 102.
34. James Scott, *Seeing Like a State: How Certain Schemes to Improve the Human Condition Have Failed* (New Haven: Yale University Press, 1998).
35. The thirty medical doctors who remained in the country to take care of the health needs of twelve million people provide an example of the challenges that Frelimo faced. See Carol Barker, "Bringing Health Care to the People," in *A Difficult Road: The Transition to Socialism in Mozambique,* ed. John Saul (New York: Monthly Review Press, 1985), 323; Margaret Hall and Tom Young, *Confronting Leviathan: Mozambique since Independence* (London: Hurst, 1997), 57.
36. David Wield, "Mozambique: Late Colonialism and Early Problems of Transition," in *Revolutionary Socialist Development in the Third World,* ed. Gordon White (Lexington: University Press of Kentucky, 1983), 80; Barry Pinsky, "Territorial Dilemmas: Changing Urban Life," in Saul, *A Difficult Road,* 284.
37. Bridget O'Laughlin, "A questão agrária em Moçambique," *Estudos Moçambicanos,* no. 3 (1981): 9–32; Marc Wuyts, *Camponeses e economia rural em Moçambique* (Maputo: INLD, 1981); Helena Dolny, "The Challenge of

Agriculture," in Saul, *A Difficult Road,* 211–52; Carlos Nuno Castel-Branco, "Problemas estruturais do desenvolvimento Agrário," in Castel-Branco, *Moçambique,* 31–86.

38. AGGPM, RPM-CCR/DNE, "10 recenceamento geral da população: Projecções demográficas," vol. 10, 1980; AGGPM, RPM-CCR/DNE, "10 recenseamento geral da população de 1980: Informação pública," 1983, p. 6.
39. As Peter Gutkind pointed out in the foreword to Hillary Mitchell's study of urbanization in colonial Lourenço Marques, urbanization in Mozambique "was primarily a function of pressure on the rural areas to produce raw materials," and it was "stimulated by an escape from rural poverty," rather than industrialization. See Peter Gutkind, foreword to *Aspects of Urbanization and Age Structure in Lourenço Marques (Maputo), 1957,* by Hillary Flegg Mitchell (Lusaka: Institute for African Studies, 1975), viii.
40. David Wield, "Some Characteristics of the Mozambican Economy Particularly Relating to Industrialization" (mimeograph, Centro de Estudos Africanos, 1977); Maria Clara Mendes, *Maputo antes da independência: Geografia de uma cidade colonial* (Lisbon: Memórias do Instituto de Investigação Científica Tropical, 1985), 468–69.
41. Luís de Brito, "Dependência colonial e integração regional," *Estudos Moçambicanos,* no. 1 (1980): 23–32; Marc Wuyts, "Economia política do colonialismo em Moçambique," *Estudos Moçambicanos,* no. 1 (1980): 9–22; William Minter, *Apartheid's Contras: An Inquiry into the Roots of War in Angola and Mozambique* (Johannesburg: Wits University Press, 1994).
42. David Hedges, "O sul e o trabalho migratório," *Cadernos de história de Moçambique* (Tempo, 1982); Ruth First, *Black Gold: The Mozambican Miner, Proletarian and Peasant* (New York: St. Martin's Press, 1983), 55–56; Bertil Egerö, *Mozambique: A Dream Undone; The Political Economy of Democracy, 1975–84* (Uppsala: Nordiska Afrikainstitutet, 1987), 91.
43. Frelimo, *Relatório do Comité Central ao 3o Congresso: Documentos do 3o Congresso* (February 1977). See also Hall and Young, *Confronting Leviathan,* 104.
44. "República Popular de Moçambique: A 1a Ofensiva," *Tempo,* no. 252, 3 August 1975; "As fontes do sanguessuga," *Tempo,* 1 January 1978, 20–25.
45. See James Brennan, "Blood Enemies: Exploitation and Urban Citizenship in the Nationalist Political Thought of Tanzania, 1958–1975," *Journal of African History* 47, no. 3 (2006): 389–413; Andrew Ivaska, *Cultured States: Youth, Gender, and Modern Style in 1960s Dar es Salaam* (Durham, NC: Duke University Press, 2011).
46. Jeanne M. Penvenne, *African Workers and Colonial Racism: Mozambican Strategies and Struggles in Lourenço Marques, 1877–1962* (Portsmouth, NH: Heinemann, 1995); Malyn Newitt, *A History of Mozambique* (Bloomington: Indiana University Press, 1995). For similar examples elsewhere, see Keletso Atkins, *The Moon Is Dead! Give Us Our Money! The Cultural Origins of an African Work Ethic, Natal, South Africa, 1843–1900* (Portsmouth, NH: Heinemann, 1993).

47. This was a widespread assumption in many settler colonies, where colonial authorities spent much of their energy devising strategies and policies to prevent Africans from settling and claiming a place in urban areas. Just as the South African Native Urban Areas Act of 1923 represented an extreme measure to prevent African urbanization, other settler colonies pursued similar policies. See William Beinart, *Twentieth-Century South Africa* (Oxford: Oxford University Press, 2001), 126.
48. Jeanne M. Penvenne, "Here Everyone Walked with Fear: The Mozambican Labor System and the Workers of Lourenço Marques, 1945–1962," in *Struggle for the City: Migrant Labor, Capital, and the State in Urban Africa*, ed. Frederick Cooper (London: Sage, 1983), 131–66.
49. Mitchell, *Aspects of Urbanization*. Similar surveys were conducted in other cities in East Africa. See Aiden Southall and Peter Gutkind, *Townsmen in the Making: Kampala and Its Suburbs* (Kampala: EAISR, 1956); J. A. K. Leslie, *A Survey of Dar es Salaam* (London: Oxford University Press, 1963).
50. António Rita-Ferreira, *Os Africanos de Lourenço Marques* (Lourenço Marques: Instituto de Investigação Científica de Moçambique, 1968), 366.
51. See Krisno Nimpuno et al., *The Malhangalane Survey: A Study of an Unplanned Settlement in Maputo, 1976* (Gothenburg: Chalmers University of Technology, 1977).
52. Machel, "We Are Declaring War," 99.
53. AGGPM, Decisão no. 1/CM, "Confidencial: Plano de tarefas e prazos para a implementação pelo Conselho de Ministros e aparelho de estado da decisão de lançar a guerra ao inimigo interno," Maputo, 19 April 1980.
54. AGGPM, "Criação do Gabinete para o Levantamento da Situação dos Bairros da Cidade de Maputo: Tarefa 32," Maputo, 2 May 1980. As Joseph Hanlon commented in 1984, secrecy was a working method among Frelimo's top administrators and policymakers. *Mozambique: Revolution under Fire* (London: Zed Books, 1984), 194.
55. AGGPM, "Implementação pelo Conselho de Ministros da decisão de lançar a guerra ao inimigo interno: Cumprimento da Tarefa 31," Maputo, 9 May 1980.
56. Azarias Tivane, interview with author in Maputo, 13 January 2015.
57. Green belts (*zonas verdes*) were agricultural labor camps initially established in the riverine fertile lands near Maputo, but the term was also used to refer to labor camps in the far reaches of the country. AGGPM, "Plano de tarefas e prazos," 13.
58. AGGPM, GLSBCM (Gabinete para o Levantamento da Situação dos Bairros da Cidade de Maputo), "Reunião sobre o desenvolvimento dos trabalhos do Gabinete," Maputo, 2 June 1980.
59. Rita-Ferreira, *Os Africanos*, 154; Penvenne, *African Workers*. For similar examples of social control in colonial East Africa, see Andrew Burton, *African Underclass: Urbanization, Crime and Colonial Order in Dar es Salaam* (Oxford: James Currey, 2005).

60. "Que é cartão de trabalho?," *Tempo,* no. 394, 23 April 1978, 40–43.
61. "Cartão de trabalho obrigatório em 1982," *Notícias,* 23 December 1981.
62. MHN, "Controlemos o crescimento das nossas cidades: Comunicado do secretariado do Comité Central do partido Frelimo," *Notícias,* 14 June 1982; "Vai ser criado cartão de residente: Comunicado do Secretariado do CC do partido," *Notícias,* 14 June 1982.
63. MHN, Joseph Hanlon, "Maputo Imposes Pass Laws to Halt Rural Influx," *Guardian,* 15 June 1982.
64. MHN, "Operações selectivas: Dezenas de anti-sociais detidos em Maputo," *Notícias,* 31 May 1982.
65. MHN, Rogério Sitoe, "O bem que vem por mal: Avalancha de pedidos de bilhetes de identidade; Operação da PPM na origem," *Notícias,* 11 June 1982.
66. MHN, Bernardo Mavanga, "Quem tem direito ao cartão de residente: Direcção de Identificação Civil esclarece," *Notícias,* 14 August 1982; "Cartão de residente: Serviços de Identificação esclarecem dúvidas," *Notícias,* 28 August 1982.
67. MHN, "Cartão de residente em mais bairros," *Notícias,* 6 August 1982.
68. "As fontes do sanguessuga," 20–25.
69. AGGPM, Partido Frelimo, *A situação actual no nosso país: O que herdámos, a realidade que vivemos, o nosso futuro* (30 January 1982).
70. "Rompamos definitivamente com a burguesia"; "Contra os bandidos, armas nas mãos do povo," *Tempo,* 27 June 1982, 46–47.
71. MHN, "Na cidade de Maputo: Anunciado patrulhamento nos prédios residenciais," *Notícias,* 2 August 1982; "Quatro bairros de Maputo: Cadastrados e vadios nas mãos da polícia," *Notícias,* 5 August 1982.
72. "Lei dos crimes contra a segurança do povo e do estado popular," *Tempo,* no. 439, 4 March 1979, 25–33.
73. "Povo é constructor da paz," *Tempo,* 27 February 1983, 14–23.
74. José Cabaço, interview with author in Maputo, 25 February 2015.
75. "Lei sobre penas mais severas contra os inimigos da revolução," *Notícias,* 2 April 1983; see also AJN, Amnistia Internacional, "O uso da chicotada na República Popular de Moçambique," London, February 1984.
76. Hanlon, *Mozambique,* 246.
77. "Especuladores apresentados no Mercado do Xipamanine," *Notícias,* 21 January 1981.
78. "Candonga: Reeducação para 81 candongueiros," *Notícias,* 19 December 1981.
79. "O plano suplementar em apoio ao IV Congresso no sector da justiça," *Justiça popular,* no. 7 (1983): 4.
80. Fernando Manuel, "TMR: Contra-revolucionários condenados à morte," *Tempo,* no. 611, 27 June 1982; "TMR: Candongueiros e bandidos condenados à morte," *Tempo,* no. 652, 10 April 1983.
81. "Candongueiro e bandidos," 5–6.
82. "Justiça popular pune exemplarmente: Fuzilados seis bandidos no Hulene," *Tempo,* 17 April 1983, 8–9.

83. MHN, "No próximo Sábado em Maputo: Manifestação em apoio à lei da chicotada," *Notícias,* 7 April 1983.
84. Hanlon, *Mozambique,* 244.
85. Hanlon, 250.
86. AGGPM, "Criação do Gabinete."
87. "Directiva ministerial sobre evacuação das cidades," *Notícias,* 20 Jun. 1983.
88. "Directiva ministerial sobre evacuação."
89. Machel, "We Are Declaring War," 94.
90. AGGPN, MINT, "Gabinete do Ministro: Reunião do Comando Central Operativo com os representantes dos comandos provinciais," Maputo, 7 July 1983.
91. MHN, "Na cidade de Maputo: 'Operação Produção' acção permanente—decide Comando Operativo respectivo," *Notícias,* 23 September 1983.
92. AGGPN, MINT, "Gabinete do Ministro."
93. "Operação Produção: Primeiros voluntários avançam, iniciada fase compulsiva," *Tempo,* 10 July 1983, 13.
94. Gita Honwana, "Operação Produção: Actuação dos tribunais; Consolidação da justiça popular," *Justiça popular* nos. 8/9 (January/June 1984): 6.
95. Honwana, 6.
96. Hanlon, *Mozambique,* 248.
97. AGGPM, CO-OP/CPO de Maputo, "1o Seminário do Comando Provincial Operativo, documento final: Constatações havidas aquando da apresentação e discussão dos relatórios dos distritos sobre o trabalho desenvolvido no âmbito da Operação Produção," Maputo, 17 September 1983.
98. Honwana, "Operação Produção," 5.
99. MHN, "Na 'Operação Produção': Estão garantidos os direitos do cidadão," *Notícias,* 8 July 1983; Honwana, 10.
100. Honwana, 4.
101. Honwana, 4. See also Aase Gundersen, "Popular Justice in Mozambique: State Law and Folk Law," *Social & Legal Studies* 1, no. 2 (June 1992): 257–82.
102. AGGPM, CO-OP/CPO de Maputo, "1o Seminário do Comando Provincial Operativo: Intervenção," Namaacha, 9 September 1983.
103. AGGPM, CO-OP/CPO de Maputo, "Proposta de agenda para a realização do seminário da 'Operação Produção' na província de Maputo," September 1983.
104. AGGPM, CO-OP/CPO de Maputo, "Intervenção."
105. AGGPM, CO-OP/CPO de Maputo, "Constatações."
106. AGGPM, CO-OP/CPO de Maputo, "Proposta de agenda."
107. Honwana, "Operação Produção," 9.
108. MHN, "Fasificadores de documentos querem outros documentos," *Notícias,* 6 July 1983.
109. Honwana, "Operação Produção," 5.
110. MHN, "Operação Produção: Queria salvar o amigo e passou-lhe cartão de trabalho," *Notícias,* August 1983.

111. MHN, "Responsável de bairro acusado de desvirtuar 'Operação Produção,'" *Notícias,* 29 July 1983.
112. MHN, "Na 'Operação Produção': Tentativas de suborno neutralizados nas Mahotas e Bairro Central," *Notícias,* 21 July 1983; "Por ocupação illegal, representantes de ministérios no 'banco dos réus,'" *Notícias,* 27 August 1983.
113. Honwana, "Operação Produção," 6.

CHAPTER 4: VIGILANTE CITIZENSHIP AND THE POLITICS OF DENUNCIATION, 1974–1984

Epigraph: John Lonsdale, "Moral and Political Argument in Kenya," in *Ethnicity and Democracy in Africa,* ed. Bruce Berman, Dickson Eyoh, and Will Kymlicka (Oxford: James Currey, 2004), 76.

1. Margaret Hall and Tom Young, *Confronting Leviathan: Mozambique since Independence* (London: Hurst, 1997), 82.
2. Anne M. Pitcher, *Transforming Mozambique: The Politics of Privatization, 1975–2000* (Cambridge: Cambridge University Press, 2002), 11. See also Joel Migdal, *State in Society: Studying How States and Societies Transform and Constitute One Another* (Cambridge: Cambridge University Press, 2001).
3. See José Capela, *Moçambique pelo seu povo,* 3rd ed. (Porto: Afrontamento, 1974).
4. For an analysis of intimacy and denunciatory practices elsewhere, see Tobias Kelly and Sharika Thiranagama, "Introduction: Specters of Treason," in *Traitors: Suspicion, Intimacy, and the Ethics of State-Building,* ed. Sharika Thiranagama and Tobias Kelly (Philadelphia: University of Pennsylvania Press, 2009), 1–23.
5. See Svend Ranulf, *Moral Indignation and Middle-Class Psychology* (New York: Schocken Books, 1964).
6. For a sociological exploration of Mozambique's urban class structures, see Jason Sumich, *The Middle Class in Mozambique: The State and the Politics of Transformation* (Cambridge: Cambridge University Press, 2018).
7. For parallel examples, see Sheila Fitzpatrick and Robert Gellately, eds., *Accusatory Practices: Denunciation in Modern European History, 1789–1989* (Chicago: Chicago University Press, 1997); Orlando Figes, *The Whisperers: Private Life in Stalin's Russia* (New York: Metropolitan Books, 2007); Paul Corner, ed., *Popular Opinion in Totalitarian Regimes: Fascism, Nazism, Communism* (Oxford: Oxford University Press, 2009); Peter Kenez, *The Birth of the Propaganda State: Soviet Methods of Mass Mobilization, 1917–1929* (Cambridge: Cambridge University Press, 1985); Robert Gellately, *The Gestapo and German Society: Enforcing Racial Policy, 1933–1945* (Oxford: Clarendon, 1990); Daniel Goldhagen, *Hitler's Willing Executioners: Ordinary Germans and the Holocaust* (New York: Vintage Books, 1996); David Crew, ed., *Nazism and German Society* (New York: Routledge, 1994); Lynn White III, *Policies of Chaos: The Organizational Causes of Violence in China's Cultural Revolution* (Princeton, NJ: Princeton University Press, 1989); Michael Dutton, *Policing Chinese Politics: A History* (Durham, NC: Duke University Press, 2005).

8. Samuel Nguja, "Problemas da juventude: Namoro (1)," *Tempo,* 376, 18 December 1977.
9. Emídio Xavier Machiana, *A revista "Tempo" e a revolução Moçambicana* (Maputo: Promédia, 2002).
10. See, for example, Jacinto Manhasseia, "Problemas da juventude," *Tempo,* no. 384, 12 January 1978.
11. Alfredo Simango, "Problemas da juventude 1: Um Africano verdadeiro não beija nem abraça na rua," *Tempo,* no. 378, 1 January 1978, 3. There were a dozen follow-up letters in this debate, lasting up to 1979.
12. Stephen Ellis, "Writing Histories of Contemporary Africa," *Journal of African History* 43, no. 1 (2002): 3.
13. "Ao leitor," *Tempo,* 7 January 1979.
14. Albino Magaia, *A informação em Moçambique: A força da palavra* (Maputo: Notícias, 1994); Fatima Ribeiro and António Sopa, eds., *140 anos da imprensa em Moçambique* (Maputo: Associação Moçambicana de Língua Portuguesa, 1996); Maria Massingue, *A imprensa, o estado e a democracia* (Maputo: Promédia, 2000).
15. Fernando Lima, "Como encarar a prostituição," *Notícias,* 13 August 1976; Fernando Lima, interview with author in Maputo, 24 September 2014.
16. Machiana, *A revista "Tempo,"* 101.
17. Derek R. Peterson and Emma Hunter, "Print Cultures in Colonial Africa," in *African Print Cultures: Newspapers and Their Publics in the Twentieth Century,* ed. Derek R. Peterson, Emma Hunter, and Stephanie Newell (Ann Arbor: Michigan University Press, 2016), 7. For additional discussions of African print cultures, see Emma Hunter, *Political Thought and the Public Sphere in Tanzania: Freedom, Democracy and Citizenship in the Era of Decolonization* (Cambridge: Cambridge University Press, 2015); Jonathon Glassman, *War of Words, War of Stones: Racial Thought and Violence in Colonial Zanzibar* (Bloomington: Indiana University Press, 2011); and Karin Barber, *The Generation of Plays: Yoruba Popular Life in Theatre* (Bloomington: Indiana University Press, 2000).
18. Cumbane, "Preso por abraçar a namorada na rua," *Tempo,* no. 389, 19 March 1978.
19. "Indivíduos corruptos apresentados à população," *Notícias,* 18 May 1978.
20. "Não é a FRELIMO que obriga o uso da capulana," *Notícias,* 11 September 1974.
21. "Como age a reacção: Ataques a mulheres e roubos," *Tempo,* no. 212, 20 October 1974.
22. "Jovem de mini-saia agredida por desordeiros," *Notícias,* 25 October 1074.
23. See Audrey Wipper, "African Women, Fashion, and Scapegoating," *Canadian Journal of African Studies* 6, no. 2 (1972): 329–49; Andrew Ivaska, *Cultured States: Youth, Gender, and Modern Style in 1960s Dar es Salaam* (Durham, NC: Duke University Press, 2011); Doreen Kembabazi, "The State of Morality: Sexual, Reproductive and Sartorial Politics in Idi Amin's Uganda" (PhD diss., University of Michigan, 2020); Barbara Cooper, "The Politics of

Difference and Women's Associations in Niger: Of 'Prostitutes,' the Public, and Politics," *Signs* 20, no. 4 (1995): 851–82.

24. José Ortega y Gasset, *The Revolt of the Masses* (London: George Allen & Unwin, 1961).
25. José Craveirinha, "Povo contra mini-saia nos subúrbios," *Notícias da Beira,* 25 September 1974. See the rebuke of Craveirinha's claims by Bernardes Silva, "Ainda as mini-saias: Carta aberta ao Sr. José Craveirinha," *Notícias,* 13 October 1974.
26. Abílio Hauaniaca, "Vender o corpo por cem escudos," *Tempo,* no. 347, 29 May 1977.
27. José Walemo, "Vender o corpo por cem escudos," *Tempo,* no. 350, 19 June 1977; Manuel Luís, "Prostituição: Crítica a uma crítica," *Tempo,* no. 351, 26 June 1977; José da Silva, "Vender o corpo por cem escudos," *Tempo,* no. 354, 17 July 1977.
28. Luís, "Prostituição."
29. Francisco Nhaduco, Paulo Chachine, and Diamantino Paulino, "Carta aberta aos distribuidores das revistas imorais em geral," *Tempo,* no. 254, 17 August 1975.
30. During his 1975 "triumphal journey," Samora Machel condemned the dancing culture of the Portuguese and of those urbanities who inherited it. "They used to say that was the civilizing culture. In Mozambique that culture was never condemned as immoral. It's a culture that begins at 9 pm and ends at 4 in the morning," he told an audience in Vila Cabral (Lichinga). When he reached Inhambane, he asked his audience: "What is a ball? Is it a civilized dance when a man and a woman hold and kiss each other?" And he determined: "No more balls and mini-skirts here in Mozambique, because those are foreign and imported civilizations, decadent and corrupt civilizations." Samora Machel, as quoted by António Rita-Ferreira, "Moçambique post-25 de Abril: Causas do êxodo da população de origem Europeia e Asiática," *Moçambique: Cultura e história de um país* 8 (1988): 144.
31. Carlos Agostinho do Rosário, "Abaixo o baile," *Tempo,* no. 250, 20 July 1975.
32. "Não queremos bailes nem farras no nosso país," *Tempo,* no. 259, 21 September 1975; Gaspar Tomás, "Abaixo o baile," *Tempo,* no. 256, 31 August 1975.
33. The government recognized the economic difficulties. In early 1982, *Notícias* published an extensive resolution by Frelimo's Central Committee on the situation. See "Temos ainda muitas dificuldades mas temos forma de as resolver: Partido FRELIMO faz balanço e perspectiva o future da situação socio-económica de Mozambique," *Notícias,* 1 February 1982.
34. PRM, Boletim da República, 1 Série, Número 46, Decreto-Lei no 21/75, de 11 de Outubro, 1975; "Serviço Nacional de Segurança Popular (SNASP): Assegurar o processo revolucionário e consolidar a independência e unidade nacionais," *Tempo,* 261, 20 October 1975, 8–9.
35. Jacinto Veloso, *Memórias em voo rasante,* 4th ed. (Maputo: JV Editores, 2011), 108.

36. PRM, Decreto-Lei no 21/75. For a juridical interpretation of this decree, see João Carlos Trindade, "Rupturas e continuidades nos processos políticos e jurídicos," in *Conflito e transformação social: Uma paisagem das justiças em Moçambique,* vol. 1, ed. Boaventura de Sousa Santos and João Carlos Trindade (Porto: Afrontamento, 2003), 106; Benedito Machava, "State Discourse on Internal Security and the Politics of Punishment in Post-independence Mozambique, 1975–1983," *Journal of Southern African Studies* 37, no. 3 (September 2011): 601.
37. Howe, "National Security," 281.
38. Veloso, *Memórias em voo rasante,* 108.
39. Howe, "National Security," 281.
40. "Implantada a criação dos grupos de vigilância," *Tempo,* no. 404, 2 July 1978.
41. "Rezar . . . Sim, mas vigilantes," *Tempo,* 23 December 1984.
42. "Grupos de vigilância integram milhares de pessoas," *Tempo,* no. 410, 13 August 1978.
43. "Colocar o inimigo na defensiva passiva," *Tempo,* no. 460, 5 August 1979.
44. "50 aniversário do SNASP: Impermeabilidade contra o inimigo," *Tempo,* 19 October 1980.
45. Bertil Egerö, *Mozambique: A Dream Undone; The Political Economy of Democracy, 1975–84* (Uppsala: Nordiska Afrikainstitutet, 1987), 119.
46. Azarias Tivana, interview with author in Maxaquene, Maputo, 13 January 2015.
47. "50 Aniversário do SNASP: Grupos de vigilância, a segurança do povo," *Tempo,* no. 522, 12 October 1980. For a fictionalized depiction of these groups, see Mia Couto, "O apocalipse privado do tio Geguê," in *Cada homem é uma raça,* 3rd ed. (Lisbon: Caminho, 1990), 33; Suleiman Cassamo, "Teresa, tu vai mbunhar," in *O regresso do morto* (Lisbon: Caminho, 1997).
48. See Dalila Mateus, *A PIDE/DGS na guerra colonial, 1961–1974* (Lisbon: Terramar, 2004).
49. In fact, the party had to assure the public that the government was not reviving the infamous colonial secret police but was instead creating a "revolutionary" and popular service. See "Grupos de vigilância: As experiências do passado são uma fonte de inspiração," *Tempo,* no. 414, 10 September 1978.
50. "Grupos de vigilância: Aprovados os documentos que traçam objectivos e programas," *Tempo,* no. 421, 29 October 1978.
51. "Vigilância popular: Forças de defesa e segurança reúnem-se com as populações de Maputo," *Tempo,* no. 477, 2 December 1979.
52. "SNASP: Apelo a todos os cidadãos," *Tempo,* no. 378, 1 January 1978.
53. "Grupos de vigilância: Estudar a actuaçao inimiga," *Tempo,* no. 444, 15 April 1979; AGGPN, Conselho de Ministros, "Análise da situação política e social do país," July 1977; "Como age o inimigo? Análise política da situação económica e social do país em comunicado do Conselho de Ministros," *Tempo,* no. 355, 24 July 1977, 58–64. For an analysis of the pamphlet, see Peter Meyns, "Liberation Ideology and National Development Strategy in Mozambique," *Review of African Political Economy* no. 22 (October–December 1981): 42–64.

54. "Intensificar a vigilância para a defesa das nossas conquistas," *Tempo,* no. 446, 29 April 1979.
55. "Grupos de vigilância reúnem-se em Maputo," *Tempo,* no. 489, 24 February 1980.
56. "Enviar marginais para zonas verdes," *Notícias,* 4 June 1982.
57. "Enviar marginais para zonas verdes," *Notícias,* 8 Jun. 1982.
58. "Nos bairros Luís Cabral e Inhagóia: PPM estende rede de limpeza de marginais; 32 vadios e oito criminosos detidos," *Notícias,* 22 June 1982.
59. "Luís Cabral e Inhagóia."
60. "Luís Cabral e Inhagóia."
61. Jean Tartter, "Government and Politics," in *Mozambique: A Country Study,* ed. Harold Nelson (Washington, DC: American University, 1984), 199; "Justiça popular em debate," *Tempo,* no. 413, 3 September 1978.
62. Albie Sachs and Gita Honwana Welch, *Liberating the Law: Creating Popular Justice in Mozambique* (London: Zed Books, 1990), 55.
63. "Tribunais populares: Democracia na justiça," *Tempo,* 17 October 1982.
64. MHN, "Detidos dois cadastrados que se intitulavam do SNASP," *Notícias,* 24 April 1980. Mia Couto drew his inspiration from these "infiltrations" for the character Geguê in *Cada homem é uma raça.* See also "Milícias e abusos," *Tempo,* 26 August 1984.
65. MHN, "Jornal do povo: Reforcemos a vigilância popular," *Notícias,* 6 February 1980.
66. MHN, Jacinto Veloso, "Resultados da ofensiva no SNASP," *Notícias,* 22 February 1982; MHN, "Purificação de fileiras na segurança," *Notícias,* 22 February 1982; MHN, "Mozambique: Purge of security forces," *Africa,* no. 124, December 1981, 39.
67. AGGPM, "Administração do 20 bairro, ao gabinete do governador provincial: Confidencial," Maputo, 17 June 1978.
68. Aminda Smith, *Thought Reform and China's Dangerous Classes: Reeducation, Resistance, and the People* (New York: Rowman & Littlefield, 2013), 129.
69. On Xico Feio, see, among many others, Matias Mboa, *Memórias da luta clandestina* (Maputo: Marimbique, 2009), 127.
70. AGGPM, "Distrito de Maputo, administração do 20 bairro: Informação," Maputo, 6 March 1978.
71. "Segurança: Do povo, para o povo, com o povo," *Tempo,* 30 May 1982.
72. See Hall and Young, *Confronting Leviathan,* 81; Carlos Quembo, *Poder do poder: Operação Produção e a inveção dos "improdutivos" urbanos no Moçambique socialista, 1983–1988* (Maputo: Alcance, 2017).
73. Alfredo Langa, interview with author in Matama, 18 May 2015.
74. António Rita-Ferreira, *Os Africanos de Lourenço Marques* (Lourenço Marques: Instituto de Investigação Científica de Moçambique, 1968), 180. See also Krisno Nimpuno et al., *The Malhangalane Survey: A Study of an Unplanned Settlement in Maputo, 1976* (Gothenburg: Chalmers University of Technology, 1977), 159.

75. As the famous song "Katchasa" from Gêmeos Parruque goes, "Ai me lembro que politica era conversa perigosa" (I remember that politics was dangerous talk). On the Russians' strategy of avoiding the public gaze and scrutiny under Stalin, see Figes, *Whisperers.*
76. After 1979, when the South African regime took over the rebel group MNR (Mozambique National Resistance) from the Rhodesians and transformed it into a well-equipped anti-Frelimo guerrilla army, the already poor relationship between the two countries deteriorated completely. In January 1981, a South African special army brigade drove all the way to Matola and launched an attack on ANC (African National Congress) operatives, killing several of them, including some civilians. Frelimo was convinced that such an audacious operation could not have happened without the collaboration of Mozambican citizens who had provided intelligence about the exact location of the houses where ANC operatives lived. Therefore, any allegation of collusion with South Africans was a serious crime, punishable with death under the Law for Crimes Against the People and the People's State. See MHN, "Esmagaremos qualquer agressão: Discurso do camarada presidente na Praça da Independência," *Boletim da célula,* número especial, February 1981.
77. Carlos Sevene Matsinhe and Adelaide Matsolo, interview with author in Unango, 13 June 2015.
78. Alexandre Jorge, interview with author in Matama, 24 May 2015.
79. Alberto Malate, interview with author in Unango, 13 June 2015.
80. Adam Smith, *The Theory of Moral Sentiments* (London: A. Millar, 1759; repr., Oxford: Clarendon, 1979).
81. José Ngovene, interview with author in Unango, 25 June 2015.
82. Manuel Felix Cossa, interview with author in Lichinga, 13 May 2015.
83. Ananias Tivane, interview with author in Xai-Xai, 14 December 2014.
84. AGGPM, CPO de Maputo, "Seminário provincial: Síntese do 20 Grupo," Namaacha, 9 September 1983.
85. "Um caso exemplar," *Tempo,* 28 August 1983, 24–25.
86. "Bairro da Coop: Detectados casos de denúncias infundadas," *Notícias,* 18 July 1983.
87. Kathleen Sheldon, *Pounders of Grain: A History of Women, Work, and Politics in Mozambique* (Portsmouth, NH: Heinemann, 2002), 155.
88. "Sofala: Os passos que a 'Operação Produção' deu," *Tempo,* 6 November 1983, 31.
89. "Operação Produção: Uma missão histórica," *Tempo,* 14 August 1983, 14–19.
90. "Desempregados a caminho do futuro," *Tempo,* 21 August 1983, 22–24.
91. "Medidas para corrigir erros na 'Operação Produção': Postas em liberdade mulheres detidas irregularmente," *Notícias,* 14 July 1983.

CHAPTER 5: REEDUCATION CAMPS, AUSTERITY, AND THE CARCERAL REGIME

1. AJN, "Centro de reeducação de Msauíze: Transformar pelo trabalho marginais da sociedade colonial," *Notícias,* 18 August 1976.

2. See, for example, MHN, Marion Duncan, "Mozambique: Machel Reeducation Camps Teach a Tough Lesson," *To the Point,* 3 June 1977, 54; MHN, José Ramalho, "Alarm Spreads as Executions Continue," *To the Point,* 1 June 1979, 35; MHN, Jay Ross, "Mozambican Reeducation Camps Raise Rights Questions," *Washington Post,* 7 May 1980.
3. AJN, "Centro de reeducação de Msauíze."
4. Unlike the Russian Gulag or other similar internment camps—which remained terra incognita for the wider public and for scholars until former detainees produced memoirs or the so-called literature of survival—Mozambique's camps were open to outside visitors, so long as they procured appropriate authorization. From the reeducation program's beginning, diplomats, domestic and international journalists, filmmakers, and academics with close ties to Frelimo visited the camps; the only exception was the site at M'telela, which held political detainees. See "Centros de reeducação em Moçambique," *Tempo,* 26 March 1976; Alves Gomes, "O que hoje somos: Dois factos," *Tempo,* no. 454, 24 June 1979.
5. Harry West, *Kupilikula: Governance and the Invisible Realm in Mozambique* (Chicago: Chicago University Press, 2005), 176.
6. Laura Bear, *Navigating Austerity: Currents of Debt along a South Asian River* (Stanford: Stanford University Press, 2015), 1, 198.
7. See chapter 2.
8. AGGPN, DPSRN/MINT, "7a Sessão Ordinária do Conselho de Ministros de 9 de Julho de 1976, síntese XI-parte: Centros de reeducação," Maputo, 9 July 1976, 4.
9. AGGPM, MINT, Circular 6/GMI/976, "Assunto: Objectivos dos centros de reeducação," 5 January 1976.
10. AGGPN, DPSRN, No. 262/SR/76, "Relatório do mês de Abril de 1976," Lichinga, 28 May 1976.
11. Simeão Mazuze (a.k.a. Salimo Muhamed), interview with author in Matola, 20 November 2014; Felizardo Chaguala, interview with author in Matola, 4 December 2014.
12. MHN, Ross, "Mozambican Reeducation Camps."
13. João Carlos Trindade, interview with author in Maputo, 10 September 2014; Benedito Marrime, interview with author in Maputo, 9 December 2015.
14. AGGPN, MINT, "Boletim informativo no 5," Maputo, 31 May 1980.
15. Carlos Fumo, interview with author in Matola, 4 December 2014.
16. AGGPN, DPSRN, "Mês de Abril."
17. Simeão Mazuze (a.k.a. Salimo Muhamed), Felizardo Chaguala, and Ché Mafuiane, interview with author in Matola, 8 December 2014. For a literary description of the journey and its perils, see João Paulo Borges Coelho, *Campo de trânsito* (Maputo: Ndjira, 2010), 29.
18. Silva Santana, interview with author in Maputo, 18 January 2015.
19. Mazuze, interview; Chaguala, interview; Ché Mafuiane, interview with author in Maputo, 4 December 2014; Beto Tembe, interview with author in Maputo, 18 January 2015.

20. See Manuel Araújo, "As aldeias comunais e o seu papel na distribuição territorial da população rural na RPM," *Finisterra* 28, no. 36 (1983): 365–77; Adolfo Yanes Casal, "Le processus de socialization au Mozambique: Les villages comunaux" (PhD diss., University of Paris, 1987).
21. AGGPN, DPSRN/MINT, "1o Seminário Nacional de Reeducação, documento de apoio no. 2: Projecto de programa para os centros de reeducação," November 1976.
22. Mafuiane, interview.
23. "Niassa: Libertar a riqueza de uma terra fértil," *Tempo,* special issue, 26 December 1979, 56.
24. Edward Alpers, "Trade, State and Society among the Yao in the Nineteenth Century," *Journal of African History* 10, no. 3 (1969): 406; Gerhard Liesegang, "Guerras, terras e tipos de povoações: Sobre uma 'tradição urbanística' do norte de Moçambique no século XIX," *Revista internacional de estudos africanos,* no. 1 (1984): 169–84; Eduardo Medeiros, *História de Cabo Delgado e do Niassa, c. 1836–1929* (Maputo: Central Impressora, 1997), 81–124.
25. Carlos Serra, ed., *História de Moçambique,* 2nd ed. (Maputo: Livraria Universitária, 2000), 1:238.
26. AGGPM, RPM-CCR/DNE, "1o recenceamento geral da população: Projecções demográficas," vol. 10, 1980.
27. AGGPN, RPM, Conselho de Ministros, "8a Sessão Ordinária alargada aos senhores governadores, a questão da legalidade: Alguns aspectos inseridos no âmbito da aplicação da justiça, particularlemnte em Niassa," Maputo, 11 August 1981.
28. AGGPN, "Primeira reunião de administradores, comissários, políticos e grupos dinamizadores dos distritos da província do Niassa: Majune, 13a sessão," Lichinga, 21 May 1976.
29. José Pinto de Sá, "A história inédita dos 'centros de reeducação' em Moçambique: Os campos da vergonha," *Público magazine* 277 (June 1995), 23.
30. AGGPN, DPSRN, "Mês de Abril."
31. AGGPN, DPSRN, 249/SR/76, "Pedido de peças para viaturas ao ministério do interior," Lichinga, 25 May 1976.
32. AGGPN, DPSRN, SR/78, "Relatório referente ao mês de Maio de 1977," Lichinga, 31 May 1977.
33. AGGPN, DPSRN, SR/76, "Relatório referente ao mês de Agosto de 1976," Lichinga, 3 September 1976.
34. AGGPN, DPSRN, SR/78, "Relatório referente ao mês de Fereveiro, Março, e Abril de 1977" Lichinga, 30 April 1977.
35. AGGPN, DPSRN/MINT, "Documento de apoio."
36. AGGPN, DPSRN/MINT, "7a Sessão Ordinária."
37. The inclusion of constitutional law as a field of study in the training program for camp authorities might have stemmed from the legal debates around the reeducation bill (see chapter 2).
38. AGGPN, DPSRN/MINT, "Documento de apoio."

39. See João Paulo Borges Coelho and Paulino Macaringue, "Da paz negativa à paz positiva: Uma perspectiva histórica sobre o papel das forças armadas Moçambicanas num contexto de segurança em transformação," *Estudos Moçambicanos,* no. 20 (2002): 41–90.
40. AGGPN, DPSRN, "Mês de Fereveiro, Março, e Abril."
41. MHN, Ross, "Mozambican Reeducation Camps."
42. AGGPN, DPSRN, "Efectivo dos campos de reeducação: Relação dos responsáveis e pessoal em seriço nos campos de reeducação," Lichinga, n.d.
43. The Red Cats were detainees trusted with keeping watch of their fellow inmates, and they seem to have only existed in select camps, such as Sacudzo, Chaimite, and Bilibiza. Their name derives from the red badge that they wore. Chaguala, interview; Pinto de Sá, "A história inédita," 28.
44. Edmundo Tanasse, interview with author in Maputo, 5 June 2019; Pedro Comissário, interview with author in Maputo, 6 June 2019.
45. On the dangers of lions in northern Mozambique, see Paolo Israel, "The War on Lions: Witch-Hunts, Occult Idioms and Post-socialism in Northern Mozambique," *Journal of Southern African Studies* 35, no. 1 (March 2009): 155–74.
46. Ana Maria, interview with author in Matola-Kongoloti, 12 December 2014. For example, a walk from M'sawize to the nearest village of the same name in Mavago took two and a half hours. Escapees avoided open paths and ventured through the thick bush that covers much of Niassa. Under such circumstances, it took half a day to reach Mavago. Escaping to Lichinga on foot could take three to five exhausting days, during which time the escapee would need water, food, and shelter.
47. AGGPN, DPSRN, Mensagem No. 346/SR/76 do administrador de Majune ao GPN, Lichinga, 22 July 1976.
48. Manuela Nascimento, interview with author in Lichinga, 11 June 2015.
49. André Macovo (a.k.a. Picuane), interview with author in Maputo, 22 December 2014; Father Inácio, interview with author in Lichinga Diocese, 19 May 2015; Naíta Ussene, interview with author in Maputo, 17 February 2015.
50. Michel Foucault, *Discipline and Punish: The Birth of the Prison* (New York: Vintage, 1995), 200.
51. Chaguala, interview.
52. Comissário, interview.
53. AGGPN, DPSRN, "Mês de Maio."
54. AGGPN, DPSRN, "Mês de Abril."
55. AJN, "Centro de reeducação de Msauíze."
56. AGGPN, DPSRN, "Relação nominal de nacionais detidos arbitrariamente," Lichinga, 24 March 1978; AGGPN, DPSRN, "Relação nominal de nacionais que por terem sido detidos arbitrariamente se propõe o seu regress à procedência," Lichinga, 4 April 1978.
57. AGGPN, DPSRN, "Lista nominal de reeducados de M'sawize e Naisseco: Menores de 16 anos em Naisseco," Lichinga, 1978.
58. AGGPN, DPSRN, "Lista nominal de reeducados de M'sawize e Naisseco: Casos duvidosos em Naisseco," Lichinga, 1978.

59. AGGPN, DPSRN, No. 536/SR/77, "Relação nominal dos reeducandos existentes nos centros da reeducação desta província, maiores de 50 anos de idade," Lichinga, 30 August 1977.
60. AGGPN, DPSRN, "Casos duvidosos."
61. AGGPN, DPSRN, "Maiores de 50 anos."
62. AGGPN, DPSRN, "Nacionais detidos arbitrariamente."
63. AGGPN, DPSRN, "Menores de 16 anos."
64. AGGPN, DPSRN, "Maiores de 50 anos."
65. Joseph Hanlon estimated the amount of money illegally exported from Mozambique between 1975 and 1976 was 150 million pounds sterling. *Mozambique: Revolution under Fire* (London: Zed Books, 1984), 48.
66. AGGPN, DPSRN, "Casos duvidosos."
67. AGGPN, DPSRN, "Maiores de 50 anos."
68. AGGPN, DPSRN, "Maiores de 50 anos."
69. AGGPN, DPSRN, "Nacionais detidos arbitrariamente."
70. AGGPN, DPSRN, "Casos duvidosos."
71. AGGPN, DPSRN, "Menores de 16 anos."
72. AGGPN, DPSRN, "Maiores de 50 anos."
73. AGGPN, DPSRN, "Nacionais detidos arbitrariamente."
74. AGGPN, DPSRN, "Maiores de 50 anos."
75. AGGPN, DPSRN, "Maiores de 50 anos."
76. AGGPN, DPSRN, "Casos duvidosos."
77. AGGPN, DPSRN, "Regresso à procedência."
78. See Bertil Egerö, *Mozambique: A Dream Undone; The Political Economy of Democracy, 1975–84* (Uppsala: Nordiska Afrikainstitutet, 1987), 119; Margaret Hall and Tom Young, *Confronting Leviathan: Mozambique since Independence* (London: Hurst, 1997), 104.
79. CDSM, Documentos/Pasta SN, Correspondência de e para o president, n.d.
80. AGGPN, DPSRN, "Mês de Maio."
81. AGGPN, DPSRN, "Mês de Maio."
82. AGGPN, DPSRN, "Mês de Maio."
83. AGGPN, DPSRN, "Nacionais detidos arbitrariamente"; AGGPN, DPSRN, "Regresso à procedência."

CHAPTER 6: ABANDONMENT AND EVERYDAY LIFE IN REEDUCATION CAMPS, 1974–1982

1. Simeão Mazuze (a.k.a. Salimo Muhamed), interview with author in Matola, 20 November 2014.
2. On chamboco, see chapter 3.
3. Rufus Maculuve, personal communication with author, June 2018.
4. João Biehl, *Vita: Life in the Zone of Social Abandonment* (Berkeley: University of California Press, 2005), 2–3.
5. AGGPN, MINT, "Boletim informativo no 5," Maputo, 31 May 1980.
6. AJN, "Centro de reeducação de Msauíze: Transformar pelo trabalho marginais da sociedade colonial," *Notícias,* 18 August 1976.

7. José Pinto de Sá, "A história inédita dos 'centros de reeducação' em Moçambique: Os campos da vergonha," *Público magazine* 277 (June 1995); Ché Mafuiane, interview with author in Maputo, 4 December 2014.
8. Mafuiane, interview; Ana Maria, interview with author in Matola-Kongoloti, 12 December 2014.
9. Carlos Fumo, interview with author in Matola, 4 December 2014.
10. Felizardo Chaguala, interview with author in Matola, 4 December 2014.
11. João Paulo Borges Coelho, *Campo de trânsito* (Maputo: Ndjira, 2010), 46–49.
12. Simeão Mazuze (a.k.a. Salimo Muhamed), Ché Mafuiane, and Felizardo Chaguala, interview with author in Matola, 8 December 2014.
13. Fumo, interview.
14. Mafuiane, interview; Chaguala, interview.
15. Pinto de Sá, "A história inédita," 28; Mazuze, interview.
16. AGGPN, DPSRN, SR/78, "Relatório referente ao mês de Fereveiro, Março, e Abril de 1977," Lichinga, 30 April 1977.
17. AGGPN, MINT, "10 Seminário sobre Reeducação, documento de apoio no. 2: Projecto de programa para os centros de reeducação," November 1976, 3.
18. AGGPN, MINT, "Documento de apoio," 3–4.
19. See Bertil Egerö, *Mozambique: A Dream Undone; The Political Economy of Democracy, 1975–84* (Uppsala: Nordiska Afrikainstitutet, 1987).
20. AGGPN, DPSRN, "Mês de Fereveiro, Março, e Abril."
21. AGGPN, DPSRN, "Mês de Fereveiro, Março, e Abril."
22. AJN, "Centro de reeducação de Msauíze."
23. Ana Maria, interview.
24. Chaguala, interview.
25. "Trabalho da reeducação foi positivo—Constata II Seminário efectuado em Maputo," *Tempo,* 27 January 1980, 2.
26. AJN, "Centro de reeducação de Msauíze."
27. AGGPN, DPSRN, No. 262/SR/76, "Relatório do mês de Abril de 1976," Lichinga, 28 May 1976.
28. AGGPN, DPSRN, "Mês de Abril."
29. AGGPN, Departamento de Defesa Provincial, Serviços de Transmissões, Impresso de mensagem de Ilumba para DSR, Lichinga, 22 April 1976.
30. AGGPN, DPSRN, "Mês de Abril."
31. *Atlas de Moçambique* (Maputo: Editora Nacional de Moçambique, 2008), 25.
32. AGGPN, DPSRN, "Mês de Abril."
33. AJN, "Centro de reeducação de Msauíze"; Manuel Felix Cossa, interview with author in Lichinga, 13 May 2015.
34. AGGPN, Correspondência expedita 230.D.21.2, Médico chefe do Hospital Provincial do Niassa, Lichinga, 8 April 1981. These were the same maladies that affected the rural population of Niassa.
35. Senhora Felicitas, interview with author at Associação Progresso, Lichinga, 22 June 2015.
36. Mafuiane, interview.
37. AGGPN, DPSRN, "Mês de Abril."

38. Barker, "Health Care," 323.
39. Barker, 325; Joseph Hanlon, *Mozambique: Revolution under Fire* (London: Zed Books, 1984), 55.
40. Barker, 331.
41. AGGPN, Correspondência, Direcção Provincial de Saúde do Niassa, "Relatório anual relativo ao período 1 de Janeiro a 31 de Dezembro de 1980," Lichinga, December 1980, p. 10.
42. AGGPN, DPSRN, SR/76, "Relatório referente ao mês de Maio de 1976," Lichinga, 26 June 1976.
43. AGGPN, Correspondência, Mensagem urgente do centro de reeducação de Naisseco para o gabinete do governador, 21 April 1978.
44. In November 1976, for example, a helicopter rescued two sick detainees in M'telela. AGGPN, DPSRN, Mensagem do centro de reeducação de M'telela para o governador do Niassa, 24 November 1976.
45. AGGPN, Correspondência, Direcção Provincial de Saúde do Niassa, "Assunto: Situação de surto de sarampo no distrito de Mavago-informação," Lichinga, 11 November 1980.
46. AGGPN, Direcção Provincial de Saúde do Niassa, "Relatório anual," 5.
47. AJN, "Centro de reeducação de Msauíze." In some ways, life in Mozambique's reeducation camps resembled descriptions of the Soviet Gulag or similar internment camps elsewhere, where transactions based on the exchange of scarce goods, such as soap and clothing, for food were commonplace. Although it was forbidden, local peasants occasionally prowled around the camps with pieces of dried fish or grilled chicken, hoping to trade them for soap and clothing. Detainees often violated camp rules and ventured into nearby villages to trade their own provisions with local villagers. But most trade took place inside the camp among detainees. In M'sawize and Ilumba, cases of offering sex for a piece of bush meat from male guards were common. Ana Maria, interview.
48. Ana Maria, interview.
49. Pinto de Sá, "A história inédita," 28; Chaguala, interview.
50. Like most of TMR's sentences, Zequinho's was published in *Notícias* under his original name, José Júlio Domingos Pereira. I read his case after my interview with him. His memory was remarkably accurate. See "Comunicado do Tribunal Militar Revolucionário," *Notícias,* 18 June 1982.
51. See "Comunicado do Tribunal Militar Revolucionário."
52. José Júlio Pereira (a.k.a. Zequinho), interview with author in Maputo, 18 January 2015.
53. António Matusse, interview with author in Maputo, 14 January 2015.
54. AGGPN, DPSRN, Correspondência, "Direcção provincial do Niassa para o programa de desenvolvimento do Niassa (PDN)," Lichinga, 1 September 1981.
55. Ana Maria, interview.
56. José Capela, *O álcool na colonização do Sul do Save, 1860–1920* (Maputo: Edição do Autor, 1995).
57. Chaguala, interview.

58. Mazuze, Chaguala, and Mafuiane, interview.
59. Ana Maria and Ché Mafuiane, interview with author in Matola-Kongoloti, 12 December 2014.
60. Silva Santana, interview with author in Maputo, 18 January 2015. It is not surprising that the military neighborhood in Maputo, near the headquarters of Frelimo, was for many years the center of illicit trade in drugs. To this day, the area is popularly called Colombia, a name that draws inspiration from the Latin American drug cartels.
61. MHN, "Machel's Speech on Unjust Detentions in Re-education Camps," *Summary of World Broadcasts* (London), no. ME/6846, 6 October 1981, p. B/1.
62. AGGPN, DPSRN, "Mês de Maio"; AGGPN, DPSRN, No. 322/SR/76, "Relação das camaradas em estado de gravidez, campo de reeducação de M'sawize," Lichinga, 13 July 1976.
63. AGGPN, DPSRN, No. 514/SR/77, Lichinga, 16 August 1977.
64. Ana Maria, interview.
65. AGGPN, DPSRN, No. 458/SR/976, Lichinga, 22 September 1976.
66. AGGPN, Relatórios dos Distritos, "Síntese dos trabalhos da brigada do governo provincial durante a visita de trabalho efectuado ao distrito de Mavago," October 1981.
67. Ana Maria, interview.
68. This situation did not last long because the women's camp was closed sometime in 1979 or 1980.
69. AGGPN, DPSRN, "Mês de Abril."
70. AGGPN, DPSRN, No. 458/SR/976.
71. AGGPN, GPN, No. 986/SC/78, Requerimento de Mário Francisco, Lichinga, 9 June 1976.
72. AJN, "Centro de reeducação de Msauíze."
73. AGGPN, DPSRN, "Mês de Maio."
74. AGGPN, DPSRN, SR/76, "Relatório referente ao mês de Outubro de 1976," Lichinga, 16 November 1976.
75. AGGPN, DPSRN/SR, "Relação das crianças que se encontram nos campos com as suas mães," n.d.
76. Ana Maria, interview.
77. AGGPN, Direcção Provincial de Saúde do Niassa, "Relatório anual."
78. In Mozambique, women normally graduate to full motherhood upon the birth of their second child, when they are considered to be experienced enough to care for the baby without assistance from their mother, mother-in-law, or a close relative. See Henri Alexandre Junod, *The Life of a South African Tribe*, vol. 1, *The Social Life* (Neuchâtel: Imprimerie Attinger Freres, 1912), 188–89.
79. Ana Maria, interview.
80. AGGPN, Direcção Provincial de Saúde do Niassa, "Relatório anual," 6.
81. AGGPN, DPSRN, "Mês de Fereveiro, Março, e Abril."
82. CDSM, Pasta 2, Documentos da Frelimo, Frelimo, "II Conferência do Departamento de Educação e Cultura (DEC)," September 1970.

83. Frelimo, "Revolutionary Education," in *The African Liberation Reader: Documents of the National Liberation Movements,* ed. Aquino de Bragança and Immanuel Wallerstein (London: Zed Press, 1982), 3:194–95.
84. CDSM, Frelimo, "DEC: Recomendações."
85. Frelimo, "Poetry and the Revolution," in de Bragança and Wallerstein, *African Liberation Reader,* 3:179.
86. Paolo Israel, *In Step with the Times: Mapiko Masquerades of Mozambique* (Athens: Ohio University Press, 2014), 32, 151–53; Polly Savage, "Avenida Mao Tse-Tung (or How Artists Navigated the Mozambican Revolution)," in *Art, Global Maoism and the Chinese Cultural Revolution,* ed. Jacopo Galimberti et al. (Manchester: Manchester University Press, 2020), 249–68; Ariana Huhn, "Imposing Culture in Post-liberation Mozambique," in *Socialismes en Afrique,* ed. François Blum et al. (Paris: Editions de la Maison des Sciences de L'homme, 2021), 537–50.
87. Israel, *In Step with the Times,* 154.
88. Maria-Benedita Basto, *A guerra das escritas: Literatura, nação e teoria pós-colonial em Moçambique* (Lisbon: Vendaval, 2006), 176. For a complete list of palavras de ordem, see "Comunicado da FRELIMO: O comité político-militar aprovou as seguintes palavras de ordem para o III Congresso," *Notícias,* 30 December 1976.
89. Paolo Israel, "Utopia Live: Singing the Mozambican Struggle for National Liberation," *Kronos* 35, no. 1 (November 2009): 109.
90. Frelimo, "Revolutionary Education," 3:195.
91. AGGPN, DPSRN/MINT, "7a Sessão Ordinária do Conselho de Ministros de 9 de Julho de 1976, síntese XI-parte: Centros de reeducação," Maputo, 9 July 1976.
92. Mazuze, interview.
93. AGGPN, DPSRN, Centro de Reeducação de M'telela, "Poesia, *A luta armada,*" 12 September 1977.
94. But it was still possible to subvert the official cultural script, particularly in the free world. As Paolo Israel demonstrates in his brilliant study of the Makonde masquerades, cultural producers often appropriated party dictates to articulate their own cultural subjectivities and not necessarily the socialist and nationalist identity. Israel, *In Step with the Times.*
95. AGGPN, DPSRN, Centro de Reeducação de M'telela, "Poesia, *O meu poema,*" 12 September 1977.
96. Curiously, the initial script for the film was written by Licínio Azevedo, who produced the first feature film on reeducation camps, *Virgem Margarida.* On *O tempo dos leopardos,* see Guido Convents, *Os Moçambicanos perante o cinema e o audiovisual: Uma história político-cultural do Moçambique colonial até à Republica de Moçambique, 1896–2010* (Maputo: Dokanema, 2011), 491–96.
97. Mafuiane credited Mazuze for his artistic career, who introduced him to music and acting at Chaimite in Cabo Delgado. Mafuiane, interview.
98. The only record of a musical instrument, an acoustic guitar, appears in 1983. The guitar was an offer by President Machel to a talented musician

in M'sawize, two years after the president made the promise. AGGPN, DDAC/138/GAB, 11 April 1983.

99. AGGPN, DPSRN, SR/76, "Mês de Agosto."
100. Ana Maria and Ché Mafuiane, interview with author in Matola-Kongoloti, 12 December 2014.
101. AHM, António Souto, "Reeducação e legalidade fabricam Homem Novo," *Notícias,* 29 Aug. 1981.
102. André Macovo (a.k.a. Picuane) and Ché Mafuiane, interview with author in Maputo, 22 December 2014.
103. See chapter 1. See also José Moiane, "O direito e a justiça nas zonas libertadas," *Justiça popular,* nos. 8/9 (January/June 1984): 11–14.
104. Macovo, interview.
105. Pereira, interview.
106. Mazuze, interview; Macovo and Mafuiane, interview; Pereira, interview.
107. Mazuze, interview.
108. Pereira, interview.
109. Macovo, interview.
110. Mazuze, interview.
111. MHN, International Commission of Jurists, "Mozambique's Re-education Camps," *Review of the International Commission of Jurists,* no. 27 (December 1981): 14–15.
112. MHN, International Commission of Jurists, 14–15; MHN, Russell Kay, "The Da Costa File, Part 1: Why Is This Man Hiding His Face?," *SCOPE,* 11 February 1983.
113. João Carlos Trindade, interview with the author in Maputo, 10 September 2014.
114. Dalmazia Colombo, "Ntelela: Campo di sterminio," *Missione in directa,* March 1996.
115. Inácio, interview.
116. The execution of Simango and company was in gross contrast with President Machel's statement at the close of the Nachingwea trial, in which he declared that the traitors would not be killed but reeducated and then reintegrated in rural villages. Some scholars have suggested that the executions were carried out because of Frelimo's fear that Renamo would free the detainees and then recruit them to lead the rebel movement. For details on how they were killed, and the possible rationale behind the operation, see João Cabrita, *Mozambique: The Tortuous Road to Democracy* (New York: Palgrave, 2000), 100–103; Barnabé Ncomo, *Uria Simango: Um homem, uma causa* (Maputo: Edições Novafrica, 2004).
117. Colombo, "Ntelela"; Cuinica, interview.
118. Inácio, interview; Cuinica, interview.
119. Cuinica, interview.
120. Trindade, interview.
121. Everyone I interviewed in Niassa told me about this case.

122. AGGPN, DPSRN, "Mês de Abril."
123. See Cabrita, *Mozambique,* 100–103.
124. Giorgio Agamben, *Homo Sacer: Sovereign Power and Bare Life,* trans. Daniel Heller-Roazen (Stanford: Stanford University Press, 1998).
125. AGGPN, MINT-SR, Documentos Dispersos 1976–1984, Circular 44-GSREED-978, Maputo, 11 April 1978.
126. AGGPN, DPSRN, Documentos Dispersos, 1976–1977, Lichinga.
127. These estimated numbers might include all other camps and will only be confirmed when more postcolonial archives become available, particularly the archives from MINT's extinct National Directorate of Reeducation Service.
128. AGGPN, Documentos Dispersos 1976–1984, SISTREP da Base Central para GPN, 24 August 1976.
129. AGGPN, DPSRN, Mensagem No. 361/SR/76 do Camp de Reeducação de Ilumba, 30 July de 1976.
130. AGGPN, DPSRN, No. 494/SR/77, Lichinga, 16 August 1977.
131. AGGPN, "Mês de Maio."
132. AGGPN, DPSRN, Mensagem No. 735/SR/977, confidencial, do Centro de Reeducação de Chiputo ao GPN, 21 November 1977.
133. AGGPN, DPSRN, Mensagem No. 418/SR/76 ao MINT-SR, Lichinga, 4 September 1976. In this report, Francisco Taibo wrote: "Quase todos os Campos de Reeducação apresentam nos problemas de fugas de marginais e em contrapartida propôe a necessidade de duas bicicletas para cada campo, para fins de perseguição em caminhos que não dão acesso às viaturas."
134. AGGPN, DPSRN, Mensagem No. 281/SR/76, do Campo de Reeducação de M'telela, 10 June 1976.
135. AGGPN, DPSRN, Serviços Técnicos de Mensagem, urgente, do Campo de Reeducação de M'telela, 10 June 1976.
136. AGGPN, Rede Privativa de Radiocomunicações, Mensagem expedida no. 175/A/16/GAB/76 para ADM Mecula, 10 June 1976.
137. Tzvetan Todorov, *Facing the Extreme,* cited in Anne Applebaum, *Gulag: A History* (New York: Anchor Books, 2003), 340.
138. Applebaum, 343.
139. AGGPN, DPSRN/SR, "Lista nominal de cidadãos reeducandos dos campos de Naisseco e M'sawize," n.d.
140. AGGPN, MINT-SR, Circular 44-GSREED-978.
141. AGGPN, MINT-SR, Circular 44-GSREED-978.
142. AGGPN, DPSRN, Mensagem No. 344/SR/79 ao GPN: Informação, Lichinga, 13 June 1979.
143. AGGPN, GPN, Mensagem 77/A/16/GAB/77 para ADM, Mandimba, 5 February 1977.
144. Dipesh Chakrabarty, "History and the Politics of Recognition," in *Manifestos for History,* ed. Keith Jenkins, Sue Morgan, and Alun Munslow (London: Routledge, 2007).

CHAPTER 7: WRETCHEDNESS AND SURVIVAL DURING OPERAÇÃO PRODUÇÃO AND THE CIVIL WAR, 1983–1989

1. António Jorge is a pseudonym for a person who did not want his real name or identity to be revealed.
2. AGGPM, RPM, Assembleia Popular, "Linhas fundamentais do Plano Prospectivo Indicativo para 1981–1990," Maputo, Imprensa Nacional, 1981, p. 17.
3. "A batalha contra o subdesenvolvimento produzirá heróis do trabalho," *Tempo,* 26 December 1979, 52.
4. AGGPM, "Direcção provincial de apoio e controlo: Comissão de reintegração social, 1981–1987."
5. "A batalha contra o subdesenvolvimento," 51.
6. "A batalha contra o subdesenvolvimento," 53.
7. MHN, "Niassa: Unango não é um sonho," *Tempo,* no. 549, 19 April 1981.
8. MHN, "Familiares de ex-reeducandos brevemente no Niassa," *Notícias,* 17 December 1981.
9. Francisco Cuinica, interview with author in Lichinga, 26 June 2015.
10. "Com grande emoção e alegria: Ex-reeducandos no Niassa recebem as suas famílias," *Notícias,* 18 August 1980; "Nos ex-centros de reeducação: Trezentos lares reconstruidos no Niassa," *Notícias,* 11 June 1982.
11. AGGPN, Empresa Agrícola de Unango, "Relatório: Balanço da Campanha 82–83," Unango, 10 February 1984; MHN, "Programa do Niassa começa a dar frutos: Boa campanha agrícola em M'sawize e Unango," *Notícias,* 15 June 1982.
12. MHN, António Souto, "Libertados 684 reeducandos: Medida de clemência ordenada pelo Presidente Samora em Cabo Delgado," *Notícias,* 28 September 1981; André Macovo (a.k.a. Picuane) and Ché Mafuiane, interview with author in Maputo, 22 December 2014.
13. "A batalha contra o subdesenvolvimento," 51.
14. Silvestre Mulhanga, interview with author in Unango, 13 June 2015; Ché Mafuiane, interview with author in Maputo, 4 December 2014.
15. AGGPN, Conselho Municipal da Cidade de Unango, "Análise dos trabalhos realizados no plano, 1982/83."
16. Merle Bowen, *The State against the Peasantry: Rural Struggles in Colonial and Postcolonial Mozambique* (Charlottesville: University of Virginia Press, 2000), 54.
17. Joseph Hanlon, *Mozambique: Revolution under Fire* (London: Zed Books, 1984), 100–120; Carlos Nuno Castel-Branco, "Problemas estruturais do desenvolvimento Agrário," in *Moçambique: Perspectivas económicas,* ed. Carlos Nuno Castel-Branco (Maputo: Universidade Eduardo Mondlane em associação com Fundação Friedrich Ebert, 1994), 54–58.
18. AGGPN, E. A. Matama, Relatórios, Caetano de Oliveira Massaka para ministro da agricultura, 28 May 1984.
19. AGGPN, E. A. Matama, Relatórios, Memorandum à consideração do governador do Niassa, 19 May 1983.
20. AGGPN, E. A. Matama, Relatórios, Relatório de 1989.

21. "Para o centro de reeducação só se vai depois de julgado e condenado," *Notícias*, 4 January 1985.
22. AGGPN, PRM, "Balanço historial do desenvolvimento do trabalho policial no Niassa," Lichinga, 18 January 1988.
23. Rui Zunguza, "Niassa: Que integração para os ex-improdutivos?," *Tempo*, 1 July 1984, 12.
24. AGGPN, OP, Mensagem 106/GPN/C/6 para Tenente General Armando Guebuza ministro do interior, de Coronel Sérgio Vieira, governador de Niassa: Relâmpago, 3 September 1983.
25. MHN, "Prepara-se 2a fase da 'Operação Produção' em Sofala," *Notícias*, 9 August 1983.
26. AGGPN, OP, Mensagem 301/GAB/SC/C/5 para Tenente General Armando Guebuza ministro do interior, de Coronel Sérgio Vieira, governador de Niassa: Relâmpago, 6 July 1983.
27. Every city in Mozambique had a trade fair for the exhibition of local economic activities. Today, FEN is the largest informal market in Lichinga and the city's red-light district.
28. Francisco Cuinica, interview with author in Lichinga, 26 June 2015.
29. Celina Nhantumbo, interview with author in Lichinga, 13 May 2015.
30. Manuela Nascimento, interview with author in Lichinga, 11 June 2015.
31. Cuinica, interview.
32. AGGPN, OP, Mensagem 278/GPN/C/15 para ministro dos correios e telecomunicações, de Coronel Sérgio Vieira, governador de Niassa: M. urgente, 11 July 1983.
33. AGGPN, OP, Mensagem para Guebuza de Vieira, 3 September 1983.
34. AGGPN, "Encerramento do ano económico: Balanço," Lichinga, 7 May 1985. For the exchange rate, see Hanlon, *Mozambique*, 280.
35. Between December 20, 1975, and July 1976, the DPSRN received 3,695,676 escudos ($111,990.20) for camp maintenance. See AGGPN, DPSRN, "Gratificação abonada mensalmente aos funcionários em serviço na secretaria provincial em Lichinga enquanto não for definida a sua situação," Lichinga, 14 August 1977; AGGPN, "Direcção provincial de finanças do Niassa, Lichinga," 27 August 1979.
36. AGGPN, "Encerramento do ano económico."
37. Zunguza, "Niassa: Que integração," 16.
38. Manuel Jumba, interview with author in Lichinga, 18 June 2015; Ngovene, interview; Cacilda Sithole, interview with author in Unango, 6 June 2015.
39. Ngovene, interview.
40. See Castel-Branco, "Problemas estruturais"; Helena Dolny, "The Challenge of Agriculture," in *A Difficult Road: The Transition to Socialism in Mozambique*, ed. John Saul (New York: Monthly Review Press, 1985), 211–52.
41. Zunguza, "Niassa: Que integração," 16.
42. Zunguza, 14.
43. Zunguza, 15.

44. Zunguza, 14.
45. Zunguza, 19.
46. MHN, "Operação Produção: Passados os primeiros momentos, improdutivos tentam regressar à cidade," *Notícias*, September 1983.
47. Zunguza, "Niassa: Que integração," 17.
48. José Júlio Pereira (a.k.a. Zequinho), interview with author in Maputo, 18 January 2015. Zequinho might have added the number of those relocated inside the camp and those who were scattered nearby. His number should be taken as an estimate—and an after-the-fact recollection informed by a traumatic experience.
49. Jumba, interview.
50. Jumba, interview; C. Sithole, interview; Nascimento, interview.
51. AGGPN, OP, "Programa de tarefas e prazos da III Sessão Ordinária," 28 May 1985.
52. "Directiva ministerial sobre evacuação das cidades," *Notícias*, 20 June 1983.
53. William Finnegan, *A Complicated War: The Harrowing of Mozambique* (Berkeley: University of California Press, 1992). The literature on Mozambique's civil war is vast. For an overview, see David Robinson, "Curse on the Land: A History of the Mozambican Civil War" (PhD diss., University of Western Australia, 2006); Alice Dinerman, *Revolution, Counter-revolution and Revisionism in Postcolonial Africa: The Case of Mozambique, 1975–1994* (London: Routledge, 2006); Éric Morier-Genoud, Michel Cahen, and Domingos do Rosário, eds., *The War Within: New Perspectives on the Civil War in Mozambique, 1976–1992* (Suffolk, UK: James Currey, 2018).
54. Sérgio Chichava, "The Anti-Frelimo Movements and the War in Zambezia," in Morier-Genoud, Cahen, and do Rosário, *War Within*, 17–45.
55. Ken Flower, *Serving Secretly: An Intelligence Chief on Record* (London: John Murray, 1987).
56. João Cabrita, *Mozambique: The Tortuous Road to Democracy* (New York: Palgrave, 2000), 147.
57. Hermínio Morais, interview with author in Maputo, 24 May 2019.
58. Juliano Cumbane, interview with author in Maputo, 10 June 2019.
59. Cabrita, *Mozambique*, 147.
60. Cumbane, interview.
61. Cabrita, *Mozambique*, 148.
62. Edmundo Tanasse, interview with author in Maputo, 5 June 2019.
63. Felizardo Chaguala, interview with author in Matola, 4 December 2014.
64. Beto Tembe, interview with author in Maputo, 18 January 2015.
65. Cabrita, *Mozambique*, 154–57.
66. Artur Carlos, interview with author in Maputo, 24 May 2019.
67. Cumbane, interview.
68. Cabrita, *Mozambique*, 219.
69. Morais, interview.

70. Ngovene, interview. He narrated the same story to Carlos Quembo, *Poder do poder: Operação Produção e a inveção dos "improdutivos" urbanos no Moçambique socialista, 1983–1988* (Maputo: Alcance, 2017), 86.
71. Robert Gersony, cited in Margaret Hall and Tom Young, *Confronting Leviathan: Mozambique since Independence* (London: Hurst, 1997), 167.
72. Hall and Young, 167.
73. AGGPN, "Síntese da visita do governador de Niassa à Empresa Agrícola de Unango," 24 July 1984.
74. Morais, interview.
75. C. Nhantumbo, interview; C. Sithole, interview; Celina Nhambe, interview with author in Unango, 6 June 2015; Herbert Sithole, interview with author in Unango, 6 June 2015.
76. AGGPN, "Síntese da visita do governador."
77. Cuinica, interview.
78. Paulino Nhantumbo, interview with author in Lichinga, 7 May 2015; Alfredo Langa, interview with author in Matama, 18 May 2015.
79. AGGPN, Ministério da Segurança–Serviço Central de Cifras, Joaquim Chissano, ministro dos negócios estrangeiros para governador de Niassa, 18 December 1984.
80. AGGPN, "Projecto: Campanha de combate a fome na cidade de Lichinga," 8 August 1987.
81. AGGPN, Distrito de Sanga, Relatório, 2 May 1986.
82. AGGPN, Gabinete do Director, Comunicação 230/DPCN/GD, 14 July 1989.
83. AGGPN, Província do Niassa, Mensagem expedita 41/SCDFN/86, 2 October 1986.
84. AGGPN, Distrito de Sanga, Relatório.
85. AGGPN, Gabinete do Governador, 40/GAB/E/48, Lichinga, 19 January 1989.
86. Alex Vines, *Renamo: Terrorism in Mozambique* (Bloomington: Indiana University Press, 1991), 1.
87. Robinson, "Curse on the Land," 338.
88. Carlos Sevene and Adelaide Matsolo, interview with author in Unango, 13 June 2015.

EPILOGUE

1. See the debate in Barry Munslow, "Mozambique and the Death of Machel," *Third World Quarterly* 10, no. 1 (January 1988): 23–36; Paul Fauvet and Marcelo Mosse, *Carlos Cardoso: Telling the Truth in Mozambique* (Cape Town: Double Storey, 2003); João Cabrita, *A morte de Samora Machel* (Maputo: Novafrica, 2005); Daniel Douek, "New Light on the Samora Machel Assassination: 'I Realized That It Was No Accident,'" *Third World Quarterly* 38, no. 9 (May 2017): 2045–65.
2. See MHN, Ananias Benjamim Sigaúque, "Melhorar Operação Produção," *Domingo,* 6 July 1986.

3. AJN, Salomão Moiana, "Intervenção resolve problemas de ex-reeducandos em Nampula," *Notícias,* 10 June 1986.
4. MHN, Foreign Broadcast Information Service, "Government Halts Controversial Labor Program," no. FBIS-AFR-88-090, 10 May 1988, 3–4.
5. John Saul, "Mozambique: The Failure of Socialism?," *Transformation* 14 (1991): 100–10.
6. Anne M. Pitcher, *Transforming Mozambique: The Politics of Privatization, 1975–2000* (Cambridge: Cambridge University Press, 2002), 239–40.
7. See Anne M. Pitcher, "Forgetting from Above and Memory from Below: Strategies of Legitimation and Struggle in Post-socialist Mozambique," *Africa: Journal of the International African Institute* 76, no. 1 (2006): 88–112; Victor Igreja, "Memories as Weapons: The Politics of Peace and Silence in Post–Civil War Mozambique," *Journal of Southern African Studies* 34, no. 3 (September 2008): 539–56.
8. MHN, "Frelimo acknowledges error," *Indian Ocean Newsletter,* no. 332, 14 May 1988, 4.
9. Elísio Macamo and Dieter Neubert, "The Politics of Negative Peace: Mozambique in the Aftermath of the Rome Cease-Fire Agreement," *Portuguese Literary & Cultural Studies,* no. 10 (Spring 2003): 23–47; see also Anders Nilsson, *Peace in Our Time: Towards a Holistic Understanding of World Society Conflicts* (Gothenburg: Padrigu, 1999).
10. Éric Morier-Genoud, *Catholicism and the Making of Politics in Central Mozambique* (Rochester, NY: University of Rochester Press, 2019), 148–68.
11. Emílio Etelvino (director of Caritas in Niassa), interview with author in Lichinga, 25 May 2015; Manuela Nascimento (former director of Caritas in Niassa), interview with author in Lichinga, 11 June 2015.
12. MHN, Rogério Sitoe, "(Ex)improdutivos: O regresso às famílias cerca de 5 anos depois," *Notícias,* 15 December 1988.
13. Celina Nhantumbo, interview with author in Lichinga, 13 May 2015; Cacilda Sithole, interview with author in Unango, 6 June 2015; Alfredo Langa, interview with author in Matama, 18 May 2015.
14. Nascimento, interview.
15. Sebastião Manhique, interview with author in Lichinga, 12 May 2015.
16. José Ngovene, interview with author in Unango, 25 June 2015.

Bibliography

ARCHIVES IN MOZAMBIQUE

Maputo Province

Arquivo da Revista Tempo (ART)
Arquivo do Gabinete do Governador da Província de Maputo (AGGPM)
Arquivo do Jornal Notícias (AJN)
Arquivo do Tribunal Supremo (ATS)
Arquivo Histórico de Moçambique (AHM)
Arquivo Municipal de Maputo (AMM)
Centro de Documentação Samora Machel (CDSM)
Departamento de Documentação do Ministério da Administração Estatal (DDMAE)

Niassa Province

Arquivo do Gabinete do Governador da Província de Niassa (AGGPN)
Cáritas Diocesanas, Delegação Provincial de Niassa (CDDPN)
Departamento Provincial de Finanças de Niassa (DPDN)
Empresa Agrícola de Matama (EAM)

ONLINE ARCHIVES

Center of Research Libraries (CRL)
Mozambique History Net, mozambiquehistory.net (MHN)

NEWSPAPERS, MAGAZINES, AND BLOGS

A capital (Lisbon, 1974)
A tribuna (Lourenço Marques, 1974–77)
A voz da revolução (Dar es Salaam and Maputo, 1965–84)
Boletim de informação (Dar es Salaam, 1964)
Chicago Sun-Times (Chicago, 1974)

Daily News (Dar es Salaam, 1974–75)
DW África (http://www.dw.com/pt/, 2012)
Guardian (London, 1982)
International Herald Tribune (Paris, 1979)
Justiça popular (Maputo, 1983–84)
Media Fax (Maputo, 2010)
Missione in directa (Rome, 1996)
Moçambique para todos (http://macua.blogs.com/)
Notícias (Maputo, 1974–90)
Notícias da Beira (Beira, 1974–75)
O africano (Lourenço Marques, 1908–18)
O brado africano (Lourenço Marques, 1918–66)
O clamor africano (Lourenço Marques, 1932)
Público magazine (Lisbon, 1995)
Savana (Maputo, 2009)
SCOPE (Johannesburg, 1983)
Tempo (Maputo, 1974–90)
Washington Post (Washington, DC, 1980)

FILMS AND MUSIC

Azevedo, Licínio. *A última prostituta.* Maputo: Ebano Multimédia, 1999. Compact disc.

——. *Virgin Margarida.* Maputo: Ebano Multimédia, 2012. Compact disc.

Bertels, Ike, and Wim Lourier. *Mozambique, or Treatment for Traitors.* Netherlands: 1983. Compact disc.

Muhamed, Salimo. "Bilibiza." Single. Released by Radio Moçambique. N.d.

Nachingwea. Maputo: Instituto Nacional de Audiovisual e Cinema, n.d. Compact disc.

Parruque, Gêmeos. "Katchasa." On *Papai Nyankhadle.* Produced by Radio Moçambique. Released 1993.

INTERVIEWS

Maputo and Matola

Alves Gomes, Maputo, 28 June 2019
Ana Maria, Matola-Kongoloti, 12 December 2014
Ana Maria and Ché Mafuiane, Matola-Kongoloti, 12 December 2014
André Macovo (a.k.a. Picuane), Maputo, 22 December 2014
André Macovo (a.k.a. Picuane) and Ché Mafuiane, Maputo, 22 December 2014
António Matusse, Maputo, 14 January 2015
Artur Carlos, Maputo, 25 May 2019
Aurélio Le Bon, Maputo, 4 September 2014
Azarias Tivana, Maputo, 13 January 2015
Barnabé Ncomo, Matola, 27 November 2015

Benedito Marrime, Maputo, 9 December 2015
Beto Tembe, Maputo, 18 January 2015.
Carlos Fumo, Matola, 4 December 2014.
Ché Mafuiane, Maputo, 4 December 2014
Edmundo Tanasse, Maputo, 5 June 2019
Felizardo Chaguala, Matola, 4 December 2014
Fernando Lima, Maputo, 24 September 2014
Gonçalves Fernando, Maputo, 17 February 2015
Group interview of Simeão Mazuze (a.k.a. Salimo Muhamed), Ché Mafuiane, and Felizardo Chaguala, Matola, 8 December 2014
Hermínio Morais, Maputo, 24 May 2019
Isabel Casimiro, Maputo, 26 November 2014
João Carlos Trindade, Maputo, 10 September 2014
João de Sousa, Maputo, 18 November 2014
José Júlio Pereira (a.k.a. Zequinho), Maputo, 18 January 2015
José Cabaço, Maputo, 25 February 2015
Juliano Cumbane, Maputo, 10 June 2019
Leontina Tauzene, Matola, 25 October 2014
Mia Couto, Maputo, 23 February 2015
Moisés Sengulane, Maputo, Caritas, 13 January 2015
Naíta Ussene, Maputo, 17 February 2015
Pastora Felicidade Xirindza, Matola, 16 March 2015
Pastor Agriga Djive, Maputo, 11 March 2015
Pastor Isaías Funzamo, Maputo, 11 March 2015
Pastor Jonas Ngomane, Maputo, 12 March 2015
Pedro Comissário, Maputo, 6 June 2019
Reginaldo Cumbane, Maputo, 19 June 2019
Rosália Nhantumbo, Maputo, 14 April 2014
Silva Santana, Maputo, 18 January 2015
Simeão Mazuze (a.k.a. Salimo Muhamed), 20 November 2014
Teresa Cruz e Silva, Maputo, 4 March 2015
Teresinha da Silva, Maputo, 22 April 2015
Tony Craveirinha, Matola, 22 February 2015
Vicente Mulungo, Maputo, 5 June 2019

Xai-Xai

Fernanda Mazuze, Xai-Xai, 23 June 2019
Group interview of Francisco Muchave, Ananias Tivane, and Zefanias Mangue, Xai-Xai, 12 December 2014

Niassa

African Century employee (anonymous), Matama, 18 May 2015
Alberto Malate, Unango, 13 June 2015

Alexandre Jorge, Matama, 24 May 2015.
Alfredo Langa, Matama, 18 May 2015
Cacilda Sithole, Unango, 6 June 2015
Carlos Sevene and Adelaide Matsolo, Unango, 13 June 2015
Celina Nhambe, Unango, 6 June 2015
Celina Nhantumbo, Lichinga, 13 May 2015
Cristina Mabusa, Unango, 13 June 2015
Etelvino Emílio Carlos, Cáritas Lichinga, 25 May 2015
Father Inácio, Lichinga Diocese, 19 May 2015
Fátima Mula, Lichinga, 13 May 2015
Francisco Cuinica, Lichinga, 26 June 2015
Group interview of Operação Produção ex-deportees, Matama, 24 May 2015
Group interview of Operação Produção ex-deportees, Unango, 13 June 2015
Group interview of Operação Produção ex-deportees, Unango, 25 June 2015
Group interview of Universidade Lúrio students, Unango, 30 May 2015
Herbert Sithole, Unango, 6 June 2015
José Ngovene, Unango, 25 June 2015
Manuela Nascimento, Lichinga, 11 June 2015
Manuel Felix Cossa, Lichinga, 13 May 2015
Manuel Jumba, Lichinga, 18 June 2015
Paulino Nhantumbo, Lichinga, 7 May 2015
Sebastião Manhique, Lichinga, 12 May 2015
Senhora Felicitas, Associação Progresso, Lichinga, 22 June 2015
Silvestre Mulhanga, Unango, 13 June 2015
Virgílio Sabuni, Lichinga, 19 May 2015
Wazimbo Félix Bengala, Lichinga, 25 May 2015

Portugal

Constantino Reis, Leiria, 15 August 2013

Eswatini

João Cabrita, Mbabane, 28 November 2014

Netherlands

Ike Bertels, Amsterdam, 7 November 2012

BOOKS, ARTICLES, AND MANUSCRIPTS

Abrahamsson, Hans, and Anders Nilsson. *Moçambique em transição: Um estudo da história do desenvolvimento durante o período 1974–1992.* Gothenburg/Maputo: Gothenburg University Centro de Estudos Estratégicos e Internacionais–Instituto Superior de Relações Internacionais, 1994.

Adam, Yussuf. *Escapar aos dentes do crocodilo e cair na boca do leopardo: Trajectória de Moçambique pós-colonial.* Maputo: Promédia, 2006.

Adler, H. G. "Ideas toward a Sociology of the Concentration Camp." *American Journal of Sociology* 63, no. 5 (March 1958): 513–22.

Agamben, Giorgio. *Homo Sacer: Sovereign Power and Bare Life.* Translated by Daniel Heller-Roazen. Stanford: Stanford University Press, 1998.

———. *State of Exception.* Translated by Kevin Attell. Chicago: University of Chicago Press, 2005.

Aho, James. *This Thing of Darkness: A Sociology of the Enemy.* Seattle: University of Washington Press, 1994.

Akyeampong, Emmanuel. "African Socialism: Or the Search for an Indigenous Model of Economic Development?" *Economic History of Developing Regions* 33, no. 1 (January 2018): 69–87.

Alexander, Jocelyn. "Dissent Perspectives on Zimbabwe's Post-independence War." *Africa* 68, no. 2 (1998): 151–82.

———. "Nationalism and Self-Government in Rhodesian Detention: Gonakudzingwa, 1964–1974." *Journal of Southern African Studies* 37, no. 3 (September 2011): 551–69.

Alexander, Jocelyn, and Gary Kynoch. "Introduction: Histories and Legacies of Punishment in Southern Africa." *Journal of Southern African Studies* 37, no. 3 (September 2011): 395–413.

Alexander, Jocelyn, and JoAnn McGregor. "African Soldiers in the USSR: Oral Histories of ZAPU Intelligence Cadres' Soviet Training, 1964–1979." *Journal of Southern African Studies* 43, no 1 (January 2017): 49–66.

Alexander, Jocelyn, JoAnn McGregor, and Blessing-Miles Tendi. "The Transnational Histories of Southern African Liberation Movements: An Introduction." *Journal of Southern African Studies* 43, no. 1 (January 2017): 1–12.

Alexander, Michelle. *The New Jim Crow: Mass Incarceration in the Age of Colorblindness.* New York: New Press, 2010.

Allina, Eric. *Slavery by Any Other Name: African Life under Company Rule in Mozambique.* Charlottesville: University of Virginia Press, 2012.

Allman, Jean. "Phantoms of the Archive: Kwame Nkrumah, a Nazi Pilot Named Hanna, and the Contingencies of Postcolonial History-Writing." *American Historical Review* 118, no. 1 (February 2013): 104–29.

Alpers, Edward. "Trade, State and Society among the Yao in the Nineteenth Century." *Journal of African History* 10, no. 3 (1969): 405–20.

Amaral, Ilídio. "Beira: Cidade e porto do Índico." *Finisterra* 6, no. 7 (1969): 76–92.

Ankersmit, Frank. "Manifesto for an Analytical Political History." In *Manifestos for History,* edited by Keith Jenkins, Sue Morgan, and Alun Munslow, 179–96. London: Routledge.

Applebaum, Anne. *Gulag: A History.* New York: Anchor Books, 2003.

Araújo, Manuel. "As aldeias comunais e o seu papel na distribuição territorial da população rural na RPM." *Finisterra* 28, no. 36 (1983): 365–77.

Arendt, Hannah. *The Origins of Totalitarianism.* San Diego: Harvest Book, 1985.

Arnfred, Signe. *Sexuality and Gender Politics in Mozambique: Rethinking Gender in Africa.* Woodbridge, UK: James Curry, 2011.

Askew, Kelly. "African Socialism." *Oxford Bibliographies Online*. Last modified February 22, 2018. https://doi.org/10.1093/obo/9780199846733-0200.

Atkins, Keletso. *The Moon Is Dead! Give Us Our Money! The Cultural Origins of an African Work Ethic, Natal, South Africa, 1843–1900*. Portsmouth, NH: Heinemann, 1993.

Atlas de Moçambique. Maputo: Editora Nacional de Moçambique, 2008.

Bailey, Martin. "Tanzania and China." *African Affairs* 74, no. 294 (January 1975): 39–50.

Barber, Karin. *The Anthropology of Texts, Persons and Publics: Oral and Written Culture in Africa and Beyond*. Cambridge: Cambridge University Press, 2007.

———. *The Generation of Plays: Yoruba Popular Life in Theatre*. Bloomington: Indiana University Press, 2000.

Barker, Carol. "Bringing Health Care to the People." In *A Difficult Road: The Transition to Socialism in Mozambique*, edited by John Saul, 316–46. New York: Monthly Review Press, 1985.

Basto, Maria-Benedita. *A guerra das escritas: Literatura, nação e teoria póscolonial em Moçambique*. Lisbon: Vendaval, 2006.

———. "The Writings of the National Anthem in Independent Mozambique: Fictions of the Subject-People." *Kronos* 39, no. 1 (November 2013): 185–203.

Bayart, Jean-François. "Africa in the World: A History of Extraversion." *African Affairs* 99, no. 395 (April 2000): 217–67.

———. *The State in Africa: The Politics of the Belly*. 2nd ed. Cambridge, UK: Polity Press, 2009.

Bear, Laura. *Navigating Austerity: Currents of Debt along a South Asian River*. Stanford: Stanford University Press, 2015.

Beinart, William. *Twentieth-Century South Africa*. Oxford: Oxford University Press, 2001.

Bernault, Florence, ed. *A History of Prison and Confinement in Africa*. Portsmouth, NH: Heinemann, 2003.

———. "The Shadow of Rule: Colonial Power and Modern Punishment in Africa." In *Cultures of Confinement: A History of the Prison in Africa, Asia, and Latin America*, edited by Frank Dikötter and Ian Brown, 55–94. Ithaca, NY: Cornell University Press, 2007.

Biehl, João. *Vita: Life in the Zone of Social Abandonment*. Berkeley: University of California Press, 2005.

Block, Marc. *The Historian's Craft*. New York: Vintage Books, 1953.

Bonnell, Victoria. *Iconography of Power: Soviet Political Posters under Lenin and Stalin*. Berkeley: University of California Press, 1997.

Borges Coelho, João Paulo. *Campo de trânsito*. Maputo: Ndjira, 2010.

———. *Crónica da rua 513.2*. Lisbon: Caminho, 2006.

———. "Da violência colonial ordenada à ordem pós-colonial violenta: Sobre um legado das guerras coloniais nas ex-colónias Portuguesas." *Lusotopie*, no. 10 (2003): 175–93.

———. "Politics and Contemporary History of Mozambique: A Set of Epistemological Notes." *Kronos* 39, no. 1 (November 2013): 20–31.

———. "Protected Villages and Communal Villages in the Mozambican Province of Tete (1968–1982): A History of State Resettlement Policies, Development and War." PhD. diss., University of Bradford, 1993.
———. "State Resettlement Policies in Post-colonial Rural Mozambique: The Impact of the Communal Village Programme on Tete Province, 1977–1982." *Journal of Southern African Studies* 21, no. 1 (March 1998): 61–91.
———. "Um itinerário histórico da Moçambicanidade." In *Portugal na viragem do século: Língua Portuguesa, a herança comum,* edited by Fernando Rosas and Maria Rollo, 87–126. Lisbon: Assitio & Alvim, 1998.
Borges Coelho, João Paulo, and Paulino Macaringue. "Da paz negativa à paz positiva: Uma perspectiva histórica sobre o papel das forças armadas Moçambicanas num contexto de segurança em transformação." *Estudos Moçambicanos,* no. 20 (2002): 41–90.
Bowen, Merle. *The State against the Peasantry: Rural Struggles in Colonial and Postcolonial Mozambique.* Charlottesville: University of Virginia Press, 2000.
Boyer, Paul. *Urban Masses and Moral Order in America, 1820–1920.* Cambridge, MA: Harvard University Press, 1978.
Bragança, Aquino de. "O Marxismo de Samora." *Três continentes* 3 (September 1980): 43–50.
Bragança, Aquino de, and Jacques Depelchin. "Da idealização da FRELIMO à compreensão da história de Moçambique." *Estudos Moçambicanos,* no. 5/6 (1986): 29–52.
———. "From the Idealization of Frelimo to the Understanding of the Recent History of Mozambique." *African Journal of Political Economy,* no. 1 (1986): 162–80.
Bragança, Aquino de, and Immanuel Wallerstein, eds. *The African Liberation Reader: Documents of the National Liberation Movements.* 3 vols. London: Zed Press, 1982.
Braga-Pinto, César, and Fátima Mendonça. *João Albasini e as luzes de Nwandzengele: Jornalismo e política em Moçambique, 1908–1922.* Maputo: Alcance Editores, 2014.
Branch, Daniel. "Imprisonment and Colonialism in Kenya, c. 1930–1952: Escaping the Carceral Archipelago." *International Journal of African Historical Studies* 38, no. 2 (2005): 239–65.
Brennan, James. "Blood Enemies: Exploitation and Urban Citizenship in the Nationalist Political Thought of Tanzania, 1958–1975." *Journal of African History* 47, no. 3 (2006): 389–413.
———. *Taifa: Making Nation and Race in Urban Tanzania.* Athens: Ohio University Press, 2012.
Brito, Luís de. *A Frelimo, o Marxismo e a construção do estado nacional, 1962–1983.* Maputo: Instituto de Estudos Sociais e Económicos, 2019.
———. "Dependência colonial e integração regional." *Estudos Moçambicanos,* no. 1 (1980): 23–32.
———. "Le FRELIMO et la construction de l'etat national au Mozambique." PhD diss., Université de Paris 8, 1991.

———. "Une relecture nécessaire: La genèse du parti-état Frelimo." *Politique Africaine,* no. 29 (1988): 15–27.

Brito, Luís de, João Paulo Borges Coelho, and José Negrão. "História da luta armada de libertação." Unpublished manuscript, 1985.

Bruce-Lockhart, Katherine. *Carceral Afterlives: Prisons, Detention, and Punishment in Postcolonial Uganda.* Athens: Ohio University Press, 2022.

Bukenya, A. S. Preface to *The Arusha Declaration and Christian Socialism,* vii–ix. Dar es Salaam: Tanzania Publishing House, 1969.

Buntman, Fran. *Robben Island and Prisoner Resistance to Apartheid.* Cambridge: Cambridge University Press, 2003.

Burges, Thomas. "To Differentiate Rice from Grass: Youth Labor Camps in Revolutionary Zanzibar." In *Generations Past: Youth in East African History,* edited by Andrew Burton and Hélène Charton-Bigot, 221–36. Athens: Ohio University Press, 2010.

Burton, Andrew. *African Underclass: Urbanization, Crime and Colonial Order in Dar es Salaam.* Oxford: James Currey, 2005.

———. "The Haven of Peace Purged: Tackling the Undesirable and Unproductive Poor in Dar es Salaam, ca. 1950–1980s." *International Journal of African Historical Studies* 40, no. 1 (2007): 119–51.

Burton, Andrew, and Hélène Charton-Bigot, eds. *Generations Past: Youth in East African History.* Athens: Ohio University Press, 2010.

Buur, Lars. "Xiconhoca: Mozambique's Ubiquitous Post-independence Traitor." In *Traitors: Suspicion, Intimacy, and the Ethics of State-Building,* edited by Sharika Thiranagama and Tobias Kelly, 24–47. Philadelphia: University of Pennsylvania Press, 2009.

Byrne, Jeffrey. *Mecca of Revolution: Algeria, Decolonization, and the Third World Order.* New York: Oxford University Press, 2016.

Cabaço, José. *À sombra da utopia: Quando eu era nós.* Maputo: Fundação Fernando Leite Couto, 2021.

———. *Moçambique: Identidades, colonialismo e libertação.* Maputo: Marimbique, 2010.

———. "O Homem Novo: Breve itinerário de um projecto." In *Samora: Homem do povo,* edited by António Sopa, 137–46. Maputo: Meguezo, 2001.

Cabrita, João. *A morte de Samora Machel.* Maputo: Novafrica, 2005.

———. *Mozambique: The Tortuous Road to Democracy.* New York: Palgrave, 2000.

Caden, Michel. "Check on Socialism: What Check? What Socialism?" *Review of African Political Economy,* no. 57 (July 1993): 46–59.

———. *Mozambique: La révolution implosée; Etudes sur 12 ans d'indepéndance (1975–1987).* Paris: Editions L'Harmattan, 1987.

Callaci, Emily. *Street Archives and City Life: Popular Intellectuals in Postcolonial Tanzania.* Durham, NC: Duke University Press, 2017.

Camara, Mohamed. *His Master's Voice: Mass Communication and Single Party Politics in Guinea under Sékou Touré.* Trenton, NJ: Africa World Press, 2005.

Cann, John. *Counterinsurgency in Africa: The Portuguese Way of War, 1961–1974.* Westport, CT: Greenwood Press, 1998.

Capela, José. *Moçambique pelo seu povo*. 3rd ed. Porto: Afrontamento, 1974.

———. *O álcool na colonização do Sul do Save, 1860–1920*. Maputo: Edição do Autor, 1995.

———. *O vinho para o preto. Notas e textos sobre a exportação do vinho para África*. Porto: Centro de Estudos Africanos, 2009. First published 1973 by Afrontamento (Porto).

Cardoso, Ribeiro. *O fim do império*. Alfragide: Caminho, 2011.

Casal, Adolfo Yanes. "Les processus de socialization au Mozambique: Les villages comunaux." PhD diss., University of Paris, 1987.

Casimiro, Isabel. "Movimento associativo como foco de nacionalismo: O movimento estudantil—NESAM e AMM." In *Os outros da descolonização: Ensaios sobre o colonialismo tardio em Moçambique*, edited by Cláudia Castelo, Omar Ribeiro Thomaz, Sebastião Nascimento, and Teresa Cruz e Silva, 117–34. Lisbon: Imprensa de Ciências Sociais, 2012.

Cassamo, Suleiman. *O regresso do morto*. Lisbon: Caminho, 1997.

Castel-Branco, Carlos Nuno, ed. *Moçambique: Perspectivas económicas*. Maputo: Universidade Eduardo Mondlane em associação com Fundação Friedrich Ebert, 1994.

Caulfield, Sueann. *In Defense of Honor: Sexual Morality, Modernity, and Nation in Early Twentieth-Century Brazil*. Durham, NC: Duke University Press, 2000.

Cell, Charles. *Revolution at Work: Mobilization Campaigns in China*. New York: Academic Press, 1977.

Centro de Estudos Africanos. *Cotton Production in Mozambique: A Survey, 1939–1979*. Maputo: Universidade Eduardo Mondlane, 1981.

———. *Sumário preparado a pedido da Direcção Nacional de Habitação para ser utilazado noa preparação prévia do seminário sobre as aldeias comunais de 1979–1980*. Maputo: Universidade Eduardo Mondlane, 1979.

Chabal, Patrick. *Power in Africa: An Essay in Political Interpretation*. New York: St. Martin's Press, 1992.

Chabal, Patrick, and Jean-Pascal Daloz. *Africa Works: Disorder as Political Instrument*. Oxford: James Currey, 1999.

Chakrabarty, Dipesh. "History and the Politics of Recognition." In *Manifestos for History*, edited by Keith Jenkins, Sue Morgan, and Alun Munslow, 77–87. London: Routledge, 2007.

Cheng, Yinghong. *Creating the "New Man": From Enlightenment Ideals to Socialist Realities*. Honolulu: University of Hawai'i Press, 2009.

Chichava, Sérgio. "The Anti-Frelimo Movements and the War in Zambezia." In *The War Within: New Perspectives on the Civil War in Mozambique, 1976–1992*, edited by Éric Morier-Genoud, Michel Cahen, and Domingos do Rosário, 17–45. Suffolk, UK: James Currey, 2018.

Chissano, Joaquim. *Vidas, lugares e tempos*. Maputo: Texto Editores, 2010.

Christie, Ian. *Samora Machel: Uma biografia*. Maputo: Ndjira, 1996.

Churchich, Nicholas. *Marxism and Morality: A Critical Examination of Marxist Ethics*. Cambridge, UK: James Clarke, 1994.

Clerc, André Daniel. *Chitlangou: Son of a Chief.* Westport, CT: Negro University Press, 1971.

Collins, Carole. "Mozambique: Dynamizing the People." *Issue: A Journal of Opinion* 8, no. 1 (Spring 1978): 12–16.

Comaroff, Jean, and John Comaroff. *Of Revelation and Revolution.* Vol. 1, *Christianity, Colonialism, and Consciousness in South Africa.* Chicago: University of Chicago Press, 1991.

Convents, Guido. *Os Moçambicanos perante o cinema e o audiovisual: Uma história político-cultural do Moçambique colonial até à Republica de Moçambique (1896–2010).* Maputo: Dokanema, 2011.

Cooper, Barbara. "The Politics of Difference and Women's Associations in Niger: Of 'Prostitutes,' the Public, and Politics." *Signs* 20, no. 4 (1995): 851–82.

Cooper, Frederick. *Africa since 1940: The Past of the Present.* 2nd ed. Cambridge: Cambridge University Press, 2019.

——, ed. *Struggle for the City: Migrant Labor, Capital, and the State in Urban Africa.* London: Sage, 1983.

Corner, Paul, ed. *Popular Opinion in Totalitarian Regimes: Fascism, Nazism, Communism.* Oxford: Oxford University Press, 2009.

Couto, Fernando. *Moçambique 1974: O fim do império e o nasciemento da nação.* Alfragide: Caminho, 2011.

Couto, Mia. *Cada homem é uma raça.* 3rd ed. Lisbon: Caminho, 1990.

Cravinho, João. "Modernizing Mozambique: Frelimo Ideology and the Frelimo State." PhD diss., Oxford University, 1995.

Crew, David, ed. *Nazism and German Society.* New York: Routledge, 1994.

Cruz e Silva, Teresa. "Identity and Political Consciousness in Southern Mozambique, 1930–1974: Two Presbyterian Biographies Contextualized." *Journal of Southern African Studies* 24, no. 1 (March 1998): 223–36.

——. *Protestant Churches and the Formation of Political Consciousness in Southern Mozambique (1930–1974).* Basel: P. Schlettwein, 2001.

Darch, Colin. "As publicações da FRELIMO: Um estudo preliminar." *Estudos Moçambicanos,* no. 2 (1981): 105–20.

Darch, Colin, and David Hedges. "'Não temos a possibilidade de herdar nada de Portugal': As raízes do exclusivismo e vanguardismo político em Moçambique, 1969–1977." In *Territórios da língua Portuguesa: Culturas, sociedades, politicas; Anais do IV Congresso Luso-Africano-Brasileiro de Ciências Sociais, Rio de Janeiro, 1 a 5 de Setembro de 1996,* edited by Glaucia V. Boas, 135–49. Rio de Janeiro: UFRJ-IFICS, 1998.

——. "Political Rhetoric in the Transition to Mozambican Independence: Samora Machel in Beira, June 1975." *Kronos* 39, no. 1 (November 2014): 32–65.

——. *Samora Machel: Retórica política e independência em Moçambique.* Salvador: Edufba, 2018.

Davis, Angela. *Are Prisons Obsolete?* New York: Seven Stories, 2003.

De, Rohit. *A People's Constitution: The Everyday Life of Law in the Indian Republic.* Princeton, NJ: Princeton University Press, 2018.

Del Toro, Carlos. *Cuba: Towards the New Man.* Chamber of Commerce of the Republic of Cuba, 1969.

Derluguian, Georgi. "The Social Origins of Good and Bad Governance: Re-interpreting the 1968 Schism in FRELIMO." In *Sure Road? Nationalisms in Angola, Guinea Bissau, and Mozambique,* edited by Éric Morier-Genoud, 79–101. Leiden: Brill, 2012.

Dikötter, Frank. *Crime, Punishment, and the Prison in Modern China.* New York: Columbia University Press, 2002.

Dikötter, Frank, and Ian Brown, eds. *Cultures of Confinement: A History of the Prison in Africa, Asia, and Latin America.* Ithaca, NY: Cornell University Press, 2007.

Dinerman, Alice. *Revolution, Counter-revolution and Revisionism in Postcolonial Africa: The Case of Mozambique, 1975–1994.* London: Routledge, 2006.

Doan, Van Toai, and David Chanoff. *The Vietnamese Gulag.* New York: Simon & Schuster, 1986.

Dolny, Helena. "The Challenge of Agriculture." In *A Difficult Road: The Transition to Socialism in Mozambique,* edited by John Saul, 211–52. New York: Monthly Review Press, 1985.

Donham, Donald. *Marxist Modern: An Ethnographic History of the Ethiopian Revolution.* Oxford: James Currey, 1999.

Douek, Daniel. "New Light on the Samora Machel Assassination: 'I Realized That It Was No Accident.'" *Third World Quarterly* 38, no. 9 (May 2017): 2045–65.

Douglas, Mary. *Purity and Danger: An Analysis of Concepts of Pollution and Taboo.* London: Routledge Classics, 2002.

Dutton, Michael. *Policing Chinese Politics: A History.* Durham, NC: Duke University Press, 2005.

Egerö, Bertil. *Mozambique, A Dream Undone: The Political Economy of Democracy, 1975–1984.* Uppsala: Nordiska Afrikainstitutet, 1987.

———. *Moçambique: Os primeiros dez anos de construção da democracia.* Maputo: AHM, 1992.

Ellis, Stephen. "Writing Histories of Contemporary Africa." *Journal of African History* 43, no. 1 (2002): 1–26.

Fanon, Frantz. *A Dying Colonialism.* New York: Grove Press, 1965.

———. *The Wretched of the Earth.* New York: Grove Press, 2004.

Farge, Arlette. *The Allure of the Archives.* New Haven: Yale University Press, 2013.

Faris, Robert. *Liberating Mission in Mozambique: Faith and Revolution in the Life of Eduardo Mondlane.* Eugene, OR: Pickwick, 2014.

Fassin, Didier. *The Will to Punish.* New York: Oxford University Press, 2018.

Fauvet, Paul, and Marcelo Mosse. *Carlos Cardoso: Telling the Truth in Mozambique.* Cape Town: Double Storey, 2003.

Figes, Orlando. *The Whisperers: Private Life in Stalin's Russia.* New York: Metropolitan Books, 2007.

Filipe, Eléusio. "Where Are the Mozambican Musicians? Music, Marrabenta, and National Identity in Lourenço Marques, Mozambique, 1950s–1975." PhD diss., University of Minnesota, 2012.

Finnegan, William. *A Complicated War: The Harrowing of Mozambique.* Berkeley: University of California Press, 1992.

First, Ruth. *Black Gold: The Mozambican Miner, Proletarian and Peasant.* New York: St. Martin's Press, 1983.

Fitzpatrick, Sheila. "Signals from Below: Soviet Letters of Denunciation of the 1930s." In *Accusatory Practices: Denunciation in Modern European History, 1789–1989,* edited by Sheila Fitzpatrick and Robert Gellately, 85–120. Chicago: Chicago University Press, 1997.

Fitzpatrick, Sheila, and Robert Gellately, eds. *Accusatory Practices: Denunciation in Modern European History, 1789–1989.* Chicago: Chicago University Press, 1997.

Flower, Ken. *Serving Secretly: An Intelligence Chief on Record.* London: John Murray, 1987.

Frelimo. *Defender a pátria, eliminar a fome: Tarefa de todos os Moçambicanos.* Maputo: Collecção 4o Congresso, 1983.

———. *Relatório do Comité Central ao 3o Congresso: Documentos do 3o Congresso.* Maputo, Fevereiro 1977.

Friedland, William, and Carl Rosberg, eds. *African Socialism.* Stanford: Stanford University Press, 1964.

Friedman, Jeremy. *Ripe for Revolution: Building Socialism in the Third World.* Cambridge, MA: Harvard University Press, 2021.

———. "Soviet Policy in the Developing World and the Chinese Challenge in the 1960s." *Cold War History* 10, no. 2 (May 2010): 247–72.

Foucault, Michel. *Discipline and Punish: The Birth of the Prison.* New York: Vintage, 1995.

———. "Governmentality." In *The Anthropology of the State: A Reader,* edited by Aradhana Sharma and Akhil Gupta, 131–43. Oxford: Blackwell, 2006.

———. *The Punitive Society: Lectures at the Collège de France, 1972–1973.* New York: Picador, 2018.

Geffray, Christian. *La cause des armes au Mozambique: Anthropologie d'une guerre civile.* Paris: Karthala, 1990.

Gellately, Robert. *The Gestapo and German Society: Enforcing Racial Policy, 1933–1945.* Oxford: Clarendon, 1990.

Gentile, Emilio. *Politics as Religion.* Princeton, NJ: Princeton University Press, 2006.

Getachew, Adom. *Worldmaking after Empire: The Rise and Fall of Self-Determination.* Princeton, NJ: Princeton University Press, 2020.

Giddens, Anthony. *Émile Durkheim.* New York: Penguin, 1978.

Glassman, Jonathon. *War of Words, War of Stones: Racial Thought and Violence in Colonial Zanzibar.* Bloomington: Indiana University Press, 2011.

Goldhagen, Daniel. *Hitler's Willing Executioners: Ordinary Germans and the Holocaust.* New York: Vintage Books, 1996.

Goldman, Wendy. *Inventing the Enemy: Denunciation and Terror in Stalin's Russia.* Cambridge: Cambridge University Press, 2011.

Gundersen, Aase. "Popular Justice in Mozambique: State Law and Folk Law." *Social & Legal Studies* 1, no. 2 (June 1992): 257–82.

Gupta, Pamela. *Portuguese Decolonization in the Indian Ocean World: History and Ethnography.* London: Bloomsbury, 2018.

Halfin, Igal. *From Darkness to Light: Class, Consciousness, and Salvation in Revolutionary Russia.* Pittsburgh: University of Pittsburgh Press, 2000.

———. *Intimate Enemies: Demonizing the Bolshevik Opposition, 1918–1928.* Pittsburgh: University of Pittsburgh Press, 2007.

Hall, Margaret, and Tom Young. *Confronting Leviathan: Mozambique since Independence.* London: Hurst, 1997.

Hanlon, Joseph. *Mozambique: Revolution under Fire.* London: Zed Books, 1984.

Harries, Patrick. *Butterflies and Barbarians: Swiss Missionaries and Systems of Knowledge in South-East Africa.* Oxford: James Currey, 2007.

Harsch, Ernest. "African States in Social and Historical Context." *Sociological Forum* 12, no. 4 (December 1997): 671–79.

Harvey, A. D. "Counter-coup in Lourenço Marques: September 1974." *International Journal of African Historical Studies* 39, no. 3 (2006): 487–98.

Hedges, David, ed. *História de Moçambique.* Vol. 2, *Moçambique no auge do colonialismo, 1930–1961.* Maputo: Universidade Eduardo Mondlane, 1999.

———. "O sul e o trabalho migratório." *Cadernos de história de Moçambique.* Tempo, 1982.

Helgesson, Alf. "Church, State and People in Mozambique: An Historical Study with Special Emphasis on Methodist Developments in the Inhambane Region." PhD diss., University of Uppsala, 1994.

Hinton, Elizabeth. *From the War on Poverty to the War on Crime: The Making of Mass Incarceration in America.* Cambridge, MA: Harvard University Press, 2016.

Ho Wei-yang. *Communist China's Policy in Africa.* Scholarly Book Translation Series. Annapolis: Research and Microfilms Publications, 1967. Originally published in *Aussenpolitik (Foreign Policy)* 2, no. 3 (March 1961): 162–68.

Hodgson, Dorothy, and Sheryl McCurdy, eds. *"Wicked" Women and the Reconfiguration of Gender in Africa.* Portsmouth, NH: Heinemann, 2001.

Hoile, David. *Mozambique: A Nation in Crisis.* London: Claridge, 1989.

Holston, James, ed. *Cities and Citizenship.* Durham, NC: Duke University Press, 1999.

Honwana, Raúl Bernardo. *The Life History of Raúl Honwana: An Inside View of Mozambique from Colonialism to Independence, 1905–1975.* Edited by Allen F. Isaacman. Boulder, CO: Lynne Rienner, 1988.

———. *Memórias.* Maputo: Marimbique, 2010.

Howe, Herbert. "National Security." In *Mozambique: A Country Study,* edited by Harold Nelson, 241–84. Washington, DC: American University, 1984.

Huhn, Ariana. "Imposing Culture in Post-liberation Mozambique." In *Socialismes en Afrique,* edited by François Blum, Héloïse Kiriakou, Martin Mourre, Maria-Benedita Basto, Pierre Guidi, Céline Pauthier, Ophélie Rillon, Alexis

Roy, and Elena Vezzadini, 537–50. Paris: Editions de la Maison des Sciences de L'homme, 2021.

Hunter, Emma. *Political Thought and the Public Sphere in Tanzania: Freedom, Democracy and Citizenship in the Era of Decolonization.* Cambridge: Cambridge University Press, 2015.

Hutchison, Alan. *China's African Revolution.* Boulder, CO: Westview, 1976.

Igreja, Victor. "FRELIMO's Political Rule through Violence and Memory in Postcolonial Mozambique." *Journal of Southern African Studies* 36, no. 4 (December 2010): 781–99.

———. "Memories as Weapons: The Politics of Peace and Silence in Post–Civil War Mozambique." *Journal of Southern African Studies* 34, no. 3 (September 2008): 539–56.

———. "Politics of Memory, Decentralisation and Recentralization in Mozambique." *Journal of Southern African Studies* 39, no. 2 (June 2013): 313–35.

Igreja Presbiteriana de Moçambique. *Buku dra jaha: O livro do rapaz.* Maputo: Momento, 1991.

Isaacman, Allen F. *A Luta Continua: Creating New Society in Mozambique.* New York: Foundation of State University of New York, 1978.

———. "Colonial Mozambique, an Inside View: The Life History of Raúl Honwana." *Cahiers d'etudes africaines* 28, no. 109 (1988): 59–88.

———. *Cotton Is the Mother of Poverty: Peasants, Work, and Rural Struggle in Colonial Mozambique, 1938–1961.* Portsmouth, NH: Heinemann, 1996.

Isaacman, Allen F., and Barbara S. Isaacman. *Mozambique: From Colonialism to Revolution, 1900–1982.* Boulder, CO: Westview, 1983.

———. *Mozambique's Samora Machel: A Life Cut Short.* Athens: Ohio University Press, 2020.

Isaacman, Barbara S., and June Stephen. *A mulher Moçambicana no processo de libertação.* Maputo: Instituto Nacional do Libro e do Disco, 1982.

Israel, Paolo. *In Step with the Times: Mapiko Masquerades of Mozambique.* Athens: Ohio University Press, 2014.

———. "Utopia Live: Singing the Mozambican Struggle for National Liberation." *Kronos* 35, no. 1 (November 2009): 98–141.

———. "The War on Lions: Witch-Hunts, Occult Idioms and Post-socialism in Northern Mozambique." *Journal of Southern African Studies* 35, no. 1 (March 2009): 155–74.

Ivanova, Galina. *Labor Camp Socialism: The Gulag in the Soviet Totalitarian System.* New York: M. E. Sharpe, 2000.

Ivaska, Andrew. *Cultured States: Youth, Gender, and Modern Style in 1960s Dar es Salaam.* Durham, NC: Duke University Press, 2011.

Jackson, Steven. "China's Third World Foreign Policy: The Case of Angola and Mozambique, 1961–93." *China Quarterly*, no. 142 (June 1995): 401–22.

José, Alexandrino, and Paula Maria Meneses, eds. *Moçambique 16 anos de historiografia: Focos, problemas, metodologias, desafios para a década de 90.* Maputo: Notícias, 1991.

Jubber, Ken. "The Persecution of Jehovah's Witnesses in Southern Africa." *Social Compass* 24, no. 1 (February 1977): 121–34.

Junod, Henri Alexandre. *The Life of a South African Tribe*. Vol. 1, *The Social Life*. Neuchâtel: Imprimerie Attinger Freres, 1912.

Kaldis, Byron, ed. *Encyclopedia of Philosophy and the Social Sciences*. Thousand Oaks, CA: SAGE, 2013.

Kapuscinski, Ryszard. *Another Day of Life*. New York: Penguin, 1988.

Karlström, Michael. "On the Aesthetics and Dialogics of Power in the Postcolony." *Africa* 73, no. 1 (February 2003): 57–76.

Keiser, Daniel. "'Makers of Bonds and Ties': Transnational Socialisation and National Liberation in Mozambique." *Journal of Southern African Studies* 43, no. 1 (January 2017): 29–48.

Keller, Edmond, and Donald Rothchild, eds. *Afro-Marxist Regimes: Ideology and Public Policy*. Boulder, CO: Lynne Rienner, 1987.

Kelly, Tobias, and Sharika Thiranagama. "Introduction: Specters of Treason." In *Traitors: Suspicion, Intimacy, and the Ethics of State-Building*, edited by Sharika Thiranagama and Tobias Kelly, 1–23. Philadelphia: University of Pennsylvania Press, 2009.

Kenez, Peter. *The Birth of the Propaganda State: Soviet Methods of Mass Mobilization, 1917–1929*. Cambridge: Cambridge University Press, 1985.

Kissinger, Henry. *Leadership: Six Studies in World Strategy*. London: Penguin, 2022.

Kleimann, Arthur, Veena Daas, and Margaret Lock, eds. *Social Suffering*. Berkeley: University of California Press, 1997.

Konate, Dior. *Prison Architecture and Punishment in Colonial Senegal*. Lanham: Lexington Books, 2018.

Kornai, János. *Economics of Shortage*. Vol. A. Amsterdam: North-Holland, 1980.

Kruks, Sonia. "From Nationalism to Marxism: The Ideological History of FRELIMO, 1962–1977." In *Studies in Power and Class in Africa*, edited by Irving Leonard Markowitz, 237–56. Englewood Cliffs, NJ: Prentice-Hall, 1977.

Lal, Priya. *African Socialism in Postcolonial Tanzania: Between the Village and the World*. Cambridge: Cambridge University Press, 2015.

Landau, Paul. *Spear: Mandela and the Revolutionaries*. Athens: Ohio University Press, 2022.

Lavoie, John. "The University Student and Nation-Building in Modern Africa." In *The Arusha Declaration and Christian Socialism*, 11–28. Dar es Salaam: Tanzania Publishing House, 1969.

Lawrence, Benjamin, Emily Osborn, and Richard Roberts, eds. *Intermediaries, Interpreters, and Clerks: African Employees in the Making of Colonial Africa*. Madison: University of Wisconsin Press, 2006.

Le Bon, Aurélio. *Mafalala 1974: Memórias do 7 de Setembro, a grande operação*. Maputo: Movimento Editora, 2015.

Lees, Andrew. *Cities, Sin, and Social Reform in Imperial Germany*. Ann Arbor: University of Michigan Press, 2002.

———. *Cities Perceived: Urban Life and Society in European and American Thought, 1820–1940.* New York: Columbia University Press, 1985.

LeFanu, Sarah. *S Is for Samora: A Lexical Biography of Samora Machel and the Mozambican Dream.* Scottsville, South Africa: University of KwaZulu-Natal Press, 2012.

Leslie, J. A. K. *A Survey of Dar es Salaam.* London: Oxford University Press, 1963.

Lewis, John. *Leadership in Communist China.* Ithaca, NY: Cornell University Press, 1963.

Liesegang, Gerhard. "Guerras, terras e tipos de povoações: Sobre uma 'tradição urbanística' do norte de Moçambique no século XIX." *Revista internacional de estudos africanos,* no. 1 (1984): 169–84.

———. "Samora Moisés Machel: Os anos de formação, 1933–1963." In *Samora: Homem do povo,* edited by António Sopa, 23–36. Maputo: Meguezo, 2001.

Lifton, Robert J. *Thought Reform and the Psychology of Totalism: A Study of "Brainwashing" in China.* New York: W. W. Norton, 1961.

Lonsdale, John, "Moral and Political Argument in Kenya." In *Ethnicity and Democracy in Africa,* edited by Bruce Berman, Dickson Eyoh, and Will Kymlicka, 73–95. Oxford: James Currey, 2004.

———. "Threads and Patches: Moral and Political Argument in Kenya." In *State, Power, and New Political Actors in Postcolonial Africa,* edited by Alessandro Triulzi and M. Cristina Ercolessi, 27–52. Milan: Fondazione Giangiacomo Feltrinelli, 2004.

———. "Writing Competitive Patriotisms in Eastern Africa." In *Recasting the Past: History Writing and Political Work in Modern Africa,* edited by Derek R. Peterson and Giacomo Macola, 251–67. Athens: Ohio University Press, 2009.

Ludtke, Alf. "Introduction: What Is the History of Everyday Life and Who Are Its Practitioners?" In *The History of Everyday Life,* edited by Alf Ludtke, 3–40. Princeton, NJ: Princeton University Press, 1995.

Lukes, Steven. *Marxism and Morality.* Oxford: Clarendon, 1983.

Macamo, Elísio. "Power, Conflict and Citizenship: Mozambique's Contemporary Struggles." *Citizenship Studies* 21, no. 2 (January 2017): 196–209.

Macamo, Elísio, and Dieter Neubert. "The Politics of Negative Peace: Mozambique in the Aftermath of the Rome Cease-Fire Agreement." *Portuguese Literary & Cultural Studies* no. 10 (Spring 2003): 23–47.

Machava, Benedito. "Galo amanheceu em Lourenço Marques: O 7 de Setembro e o verso da descolonização em Moçambique." *Revista crítica de ciências sociais,* no. 106 (May 2015): 53–84.

———. "Reeducation Camps, Austerity, and the Carceral Regime in Socialist Mozambique (1974–79)." *Journal of African History* 60, no. 3 (November 2019): 429–55.

———. "Reeducation Camps and the Messianic Ethos of Mozambique's Socialism." In *Socialismes en Afrique,* edited by François Blum, Héloïse Kiriakou, Martin Mourre, Maria-Benedita Basto, Pierre Guidi, Céline Pauthier, Ophélie Rillon, Alexis Roy, and Elena Vezzadini, 319–56. Paris: Editions de la Maison des Sciences de L'homme, 2021.

———. "State Discourse on Internal Security and the Politics of Punishment in Post-independence Mozambique, 1975–1983." *Journal of Southern African Studies* 37, no. 3 (September 2011): 593–609.

Machava, Benedito, and Euclides Gonçalves. "The Dead Archive: Governance and Institutional Memory in Independent Mozambique." *Africa* 91, no. 4 (August 2021): 553–74.

Machel, Samora. *The Enemy Within.* Maputo: Department of Information & Propaganda, 1982.

———. "FRELIMO's Tasks in the Struggle Ahead." In *Mozambique: Revolution or Reaction?* Oakland, CA: LSM Information Center, 1975.

———. *Mozambique: Sowing the Seeds of Revolution.* London: CFMAG, 1974.

Machiana, Emídio Xavier. *A revista "Tempo" e a revolução Moçambicana.* Maputo: Promédia, 2002.

MacQueen, Norrie. *The Decolonization of Portuguese Africa: Metropolitan Revolution and the Dissolution of Empire.* London: Longman, 1997.

Magaia, Albino. *A informação em Moçambique: A força da palavra.* Maputo: Notícias, 1994.

Mandela, Nelson. *Long Walk to Freedom.* Boston: Little, Brown, 1994.

Manghezi, Nadja. *O meu coração está nas mãos de um negro: Uma história da vida de Janet Mondlane.* 2nd ed. Maputo: Livraria Universitária, 2001.

Mao Tse-Tung. *Obras escolhidas de Mao Tse-Tung.* Vol. 1. Beijing: Edições em Línguas Estrangeiras, 1971.

———. *Selected Works of Mao Tse-Tung.* Vol. 4. Oxford: Pergamon Press, 1961.

Marcum, John. *Conceiving Mozambique.* New York: Palgrave Macmillan, 2018.

Markakis, John, and Michael Waller, eds. *Military Marxist Regimes in Africa.* London: Frank Cass, 1986.

Marshal, Judith. "Making Education Revolutionary." In *A Difficult Road: The Transition to Socialism in Mozambique,* edited by John Saul, 155–210. New York: Monthly Review Press, 1985.

Martin, David, and Phillis Johnson, eds. *Destructive Engagement: South Africa at War.* Harare: Zimbabwe Publishing House, 1986.

Martins, Hélder. "Samora na luta armada (1965–1968)." In *Samora: Homem do povo,* edited by António Sopa, 99–115. Maputo: Meguezo, 2001.

Massingue, Maria. *A imprensa, o estado e a democracia.* Maputo: Promédia, 2000.

Mateus, Dalila. *A PIDE/DGS na guerra colonial, 1961–1974.* Lisbon: Terramar, 2004.

Matsinhe, Cristiano. "Biografias e heróis no imaginário nacionalista Moçambicano." In *Moçambique: Ensaios,* edited by Peter Fry, 181–223. Rio de Janeiro: Editora Universidade Federal do Rio de Janeiro, 2001.

Mbembe, Achille. *On the Postcolony.* Berkeley: University of California Press, 2001.

Mboa, Matias. *Memórias da luta clandestina.* Maputo: Marimbique, 2009.

McGovern, Mike. *Unmasking the State: Making Guinea Modern.* Chicago: University of Chicago Press, 2013.

Medeiros, Eduardo. *História de Cabo Delgado e do Niassa, c. 1836–1929.* Maputo: Central Impressora, 1997.

Meert, Abigail. "From Students to Soldiers: Radical Politics and the Ugandan Exile Community in Dar es Salaam, 1967–1979." Paper presented at the African History and Anthropology Workshop, University of Michigan, Ann Arbor, MI, November 28, 2023.

Mendes, Maria Clara. *Maputo antes da independência: Geografia de uma cidade colonial.* Lisbon: Memórias do Instituto de Investigação Científica Tropical, 1985.

Mendonça, Fátima. "Dos confrontos ideológicos na imprensa em Moçambique." In *Os outros da descolonização: Ensaios sobre o colonialismo tardio em Moçambique,* edited by Cláudia Castelo, Omar Ribeiro Thomaz, Sebastião Nascimento, and Teresa Cruz e Silva, 193–220. Lisbon: ICS, 2012.

Meneses, Maria Paula. "Xiconhoca, o Inimigo: Narrativas de violência sobre a construção da nação em Moçambique." *Revista crítica de ciências sociais,* no. 106 (May 2015): 9–52.

Meyns, Peter. "Liberation Ideology and National Development Strategy in Mozambique." *Review of African Political Economy,* no. 22 (October–December 1981): 42–64.

Migdal, Joel. *State in Society: Studying How States and Societies Transform and Constitute One Another.* Cambridge: Cambridge University Press, 2001.

Miller, Robert. "Elite Formation in Africa: Class, Culture and Coherence." *Journal of Modern African Studies* 12, no. 4 (December 1974): 521–42.

Ministério da Educação e Cultura. *O Homen Novo.* Maputo: MEC, 1977.

Mitchel, William J. T. *Iconology: Image, Text, Ideology.* Chicago: University of Chicago Press, 1986.

Mitchell, Hillary Flegg. *Aspects of Urbanization and Age Structure in Lourenço Marques (Maputo), 1957.* Lusaka: Institute for African Studies, 1975.

Mittleman, James. "State Power in Mozambique." *Issue: A Journal of Opinion* 8, no. 1 (Spring 1978): 4–11.

Moiane, José. "O direito e a justiça nas zonas libertadas." *Justiça popular,* nos. 8/9 (January/June 1984): 11–14.

Mokoena, Hlonipha. "'The Hardness of the Times and the Dearness of All the Necessaries of Life': Class and Consumption in Bilingual Nineteenth-Century Newspapers." *Social History* 45, no. 4 (October 2020): 453–75.

Mondlane, Eduardo. *The Struggle for Mozambique.* London: Zed Press, 1983.

Moore, Barrington. *Moral Purity and Persecution in History.* Princeton, NJ: Princeton University Press, 2000.

Moreira, José. *Os assimilados, João Albasini e as eleições, 1900–1922.* Maputo: AHM, 1997.

Morgenthaler, Elisabeth. *Catecismo da Juventude: Tidyondzo ta Mintlawa.* Johannesburg: Central Mission Press, 1956.

Morier-Genoud, Éric. *Catholicism and the Making of Politics in Central Mozambique, 1940–1986.* Rochester, NY: University of Rochester Press, 2019.

Morier-Genoud, Éric, Michel Cahen, and Domingos do Rosário, eds. *The War Within: New Perspectives on the Civil War in Mozambique, 1976–1992*. Suffolk, UK: James Currey, 2018.

Morris, Norval, and David Rothman, eds. *The Oxford History of the Prison: The Practice of Punishment in Western Society*. Oxford: Oxford University Press, 1998.

Morton, David. *Age of Concrete: Housing and the Shape of Aspiration in the Capital of Mozambique*. Athens: Ohio University Press, 2019.

Mosca, João. *A experência socialista em Moçambique*. Lisbon: Instituto Jean Piaget, 1999.

Mosse, Marcelo. "Os últimos dias de Samora." In *Samora: Homem do povo*, edited by António Sopa, 179–89. Maputo: Meguezo, 2001.

Muhlhahn, Klaus. "The Concentration Camp in Global Historical Perspective." *History Compass* 8, no. 6 (June 2010): 543–61.

———. "'Remembering a Bitter Past': The Trauma of China's Labor Camps, 1949–1978." *History and Memory* 16, no. 2 (October 2004): 108–39.

Munguambe, Clinarete. "Nationalism and Exile in an Age of Solidarity: Frelimo-ZANU Relations in Mozambique (1975–1980)." *Journal of Southern African Studies* 43, no. 1 (January 2017): 161–78.

Munochiveyi, Munyaradzi. *Prisoners of Rhodesia: Inmates and Detainees in the Struggle for Zimbabwean Liberation, 1960–1980*. New York: Palgrave Macmillan, 2014.

Munslow, Barry, ed. *Africa: Problems in the Transition to Socialism*. London: Zed Books, 1986.

———. "Mozambique and the Death of Machel." *Third World Quarterly* 10, no. 1 (January 1988): 23–36.

———. *Mozambique: The Revolution and Its Origins*. London: Longman, 1983.

———, ed. *Samora Machel: An African Revolutionary; Selected Speeches and Writings*. London, Zed Books, 1985.

Muravchik, Joshua. *Heaven on Earth: The Rise and Fall of Socialism*. San Francisco: Encounter Books, 2002.

Mussanhane, Ana Bouene. *Protagonistas da luta de libertação nacional*. Maputo: Marimbique, 2012.

Ncomo, Barnabé. *Uria Simango: Um homem, uma causa*. Maputo: Edições Novafrica, 2004.

Ndelana, Lopes T. *Da udenamo a Frelimo e a diplomacia Moçambicana*. Maputo: Marimbique, 2012.

Neier, Aryeh. "Confining Dissent: The Political Prison." In *The Oxford History of the Prison: The Practice of Punishment in Western Society*, edited by Norval Morris and David Rothman, 350–80. Oxford: Oxford University Press, 1998.

Newitt, Malyn. *História de Moçambique*. Lisbon: Europa-America, 2012.

———. *A History of Mozambique*. Bloomington: Indiana University Press, 1995.

———. *A Short History of Mozambique*. Oxford: Oxford University Press, 2017.

Nielsen, Kai. *Marxism and the Moral Point of View: Morality, Ideology, and Historical Materialism.* London: Westview, 1989.

Nilsson, Anders. *Peace in Our Time: Towards a Holistic Understanding of World Society Conflicts.* Gothenburg: Padrigu, 1999.

Nimpuno, Krisno, Ingemar Sävors, Lars Buur, Ruth Näslund, Nea Lavén, Björn Brandberg, Zounkata Tuina, and Hans Tollin. *The Malhangalane Survey: A Study of an Unplanned Settlement in Maputo, 1976.* Gothenburg: Chalmers University of Technology, 1977.

Nyerere, Julius. "African Socialism: Ujamaa in Practice." *Black Scholar* 2, no. 6 (February 1971): 2–7.

———. *Freedom and Unity.* Dar es Salaam: Oxford University Press, 1967.

———. *On Socialism.* Dar es Salaam: Oxford University Press, 1969.

O'Brien, Patricia. "The Prison on the Continent: Europe, 1865–1965." In *The Oxford History of the Prison: The Practice of Punishment in Western Society,* edited by Norval Morris and David Rothman, 178–201. Oxford: Oxford University Press, 1998.

O'Laughlin, Bridget. "From Basic Needs to Safety-Nets: The Rise and Fall of Urban Food-rationing in Mozambique." *European Journal of Development Research* 8, no. 1 (June 1996): 200–23.

Opello, Walter. "Pluralism and Elite Conflict in an Independence Movement: FRELIMO in the 1960s." *Journal of Southern African Studies* 2, no. 1 (October 1975): 66–82.

Organização da Mulher Moçambicana. *Documentos da 2a Conferência da Organização da Mulher Moçambicana: Maputo, 10 a 17 de Novembro de 1976.* Maputo: Imprensa Moçambicana, 1977.

Ortega y Gasset, José. *The Revolt of the Masses.* London: George Allen & Unwin, 1961.

Ossemane, H. "Xiconhoca—o Inimigo e o processo de criação do Homem Novo." Licentiatura diss., Universidade Eduardo Mondlane, 2003.

Ottaway, Marina, and David Ottaway. *Afrocommunism.* 2nd ed. New York: Africana Press, 1986.

Panzer, Michael. "Building a Revolutionary Constituency: Mozambican Refugees and the Development of the FRELIMO Proto-state, 1964–1968." *Social Dynamics* 39, no. 1 (March 2013): 5–23.

———. "A Nation in Name, a State in Exile: The FRELIMO Proto-state, Youth, Gender, and the Liberation of Mozambique, 1962–1975." PhD diss., State University of New York, 2013.

———. "The Pedagogy of Revolution: Youth, Generational Conflict, and Education in the Development of Mozambican Nationalism and the State, 1962–1970." *Journal of Southern African Studies* 35, no. 4 (December 2009): 803–20.

Paterman, Carole. *The Disorder of Women: Feminism and Political Theory.* Stanford: Stanford University Press, 1989.

Penvenne, Jeanne M. *African Workers and Colonial Racism: Mozambican Strategies for Survival in Lourenço Marques, Mozambique 1877–1962.* Portsmouth, NH: Heinemann, 1995.

———. “Here Everyone Walked with Fear: The Mozambican Labor System and the Workers of Lourenço Marques, 1945–1962.” In *Struggle for the City: Migrant Labor, Capital, and the State in Urban Africa,* edited by Frederick Cooper, 131–66. London: Sage, 1983.

———. “João dos Santos Albasini (1876–1922): The Contradictions of Politics and Identity in Colonial Mozambique.” *Journal of African History* 37, no. 3 (1996): 419–64.

———. “We Are All Portuguese! Challenging the Political Economy of Assimilation: Lourenço Marques, 1870–1933.” In *The Creation of Tribalism in Southern Africa,* edited by Leroy Vail, 255–88. London: James Currey, 1989.

———. *Women, Migration and the Cashew Economy in Southern Mozambique, 1945–1975.* Rochester, NY: James Currey, 2015.

Peterson, Derek R. “Conversion and the Alignments of Colonial Culture.” *Social Sciences and Missions* 24, no. 2–3 (January 2011): 207–32.

———. *Ethnic Patriotism and the East African Revival: A History of Dissent, c. 1935–1972.* Cambridge: Cambridge University Press, 2012.

———. “The Intellectual Lives of Mau Mau Detainees.” *Journal of African History* 49, no. 1 (2008): 73–91.

Peterson, Derek R., Emma Hunter, and Stephanie Newell, eds. *African Print Cultures: Newspapers and Their Publics in the Twentieth Century.* Ann Arbor: University of Michigan Press, 2016.

Peterson, Derek R., and Edgar Taylor. “Rethinking the State in Idi Amin’s Uganda: The Politics of Exhortation.” *Journal of Eastern African Studies* 7, no. 1 (2013): 58–82.

Pinsky, Barry. “Territorial Dilemmas: Changing Urban Life.” In *A Difficult Road: The Transition to Socialism in Mozambique,* edited by John Saul, 279–315. New York: Monthly Review Press, 1985.

Pinto de Sá, José. “A história inédita dos ‘centros de reeducação’ em Moçambique: Os campos da vergonha.” *Público magazine* 277 (June 1995).

Pitcher, Anne M. “Forgetting from Above and Memory from Below: Strategies of Legitimation and Struggle in Post-socialist Mozambique.” *Africa: Journal of the International African Institute* 76, no. 1 (2006): 88–112.

———. *Transforming Mozambique: The Politics of Privatization, 1975–2000.* Cambridge: Cambridge University Press, 2002.

Pitcher, Anne M., and Kelly Askew. “African Socialisms and Postsocialisms.” *Africa: Journal of the International African Institute* 76, no. 1 (2006): 1–14.

Potekhin, I. I. *The Stalinist Theory of Colonial Revolution and the National Liberation Movement in Tropical and South Africa.* Scholarly Book Translation Series. Annapolis: Research and Microfilms Publications, 1967. Originally published in *Sovetskaya etnografiya,* no. 1 (April 1950): 24–40.

Purdeková, Andrea. *Making Ubumwe: Power, State and Camps in Rwanda’s Unity-Building Project.* New York: Berghahn, 2015.

Quembo, Carlos. *Poder do poder: Operação Produção e a inveção dos “improdutivos” urbanos no Moçambique socialista (1983–1988).* Maputo: Alcance, 2017.

Raikes, Philip. "Food Policy and Production in Mozambique since Independence." *Review of African Political Economy*, no. 29 (July 1984): 95–107.

Ranger, Terence. "Nationalist Historiography, Patriotic History and the History of the Nation: The Struggle over the Past in Zimbabwe." *Journal of Southern African Studies* 30, no. 2 (June 2004): 215–34.

Ranulf, Svend. *Moral Indignation and Middle-Class Psychology*. New York: Schocken Books, 1964.

Reis, João, and Armando Pedro Muiuane, eds. *Datas e documentos da história da FRELIMO*. Lourenço Marques: Imprensa Nacional, 1975.

Ribeiro, Fatima, and António Sopa, eds. *140 anos da imprensa em Moçambique*. Maputo: AMOLP, 1996.

Ricardo, Paulino. "A Missão Suiça e a educação não formal nas comunidades Ronga, 1930–1960: O caso das Mintlawa." Licenciatura diss., Universidade Eduardo Mondlane, 2006.

Riegel, Klaus-Georg. "Marxism-Leninism as a Political Religion." *Totalitarian Movements and Political Religions* 6, no. 1 (June 2005): 97–126.

Rita-Ferreira, António. "Moçambique post-25 de Abril: Causas do êxodo da população de origem Europeia e Asiática." *Moçambique: Cultura e história de um País* 8 (1988): 122–69.

———. "O problema das bebidas Africanas: Breve análise." *Notícias*, May 5, 1975.

———. *Os Africanos de Lourenço Marques*. Lourenço Marques: Instituto de Investigação Científica de Moçambique, 1968.

———. *Povos de Moçambique: História e cultura*. Porto: Afrontamento, 1975.

Robinson, David Alexander. "Curse on the Land: A History of the Mozambican Civil War." PhD diss., University of Western Australia, 2006.

Rocha, Aurélio. *Associativismo e nativismo em Moçambique: Contribuição para o estudo das origens do nacionalismo Moçambicano*. Maputo: Texto Editores, 2006.

———. "Moçambique e a república: Colonialismo, interesses locais, e a ideia de autonomia." In *Moçambique: Relações históricas regionais e com países da CPLP*, edited by Augusto Nascimento, Aurélio Rocha, and Eugénia Rodrigues, 109–53. Maputo: Alcance, 2011.

Ros, Enrique. *La UMAP: El Gulag Castrista*. Miami, FL: Ediciones Universal, 2004.

Rosberg, Carl, and Thomas Callaghy, eds. *Socialism in Sub-Saharan Africa: A New Assessment*. Berkeley: University of California Press, 1979.

Sachs, Albie, and Gita Honwana Welch. *Liberating the Law: Creating Popular Justice in Mozambique*. London: Zed Books, 1990.

Santana, Jacimara Sousa. *Mulheres Africanas de Moçambique na revista "Tempo" (1975–1985)*. Itajaí: Casa Aberda, 2014.

Saul, John, ed. *A Difficult Road: The Transition to Socialism in Mozambique*. New York: Monthly Review Press, 1985.

———. "Eduardo Mondlane and the Rise and Fall of Mozambican Socialism." *Review of African Political Economy* 32, no. 104/105 (June–September 2005): 309–15.

———. "Mozambique: The Failure of Socialism?" *Transformation* 14 (1991): 100–110.

Savage, Polly. "Avenida Mao Tse-Tung (or How Artists Navigated the Mozambican Revolution)." In *Art, Global Maoism and the Chinese Cultural Revolution,* edited by Jacopo Galimberti, Noemi de Haro García, and Victoria H. F. Scott, 249–68. Manchester: Manchester University Press, 2020.

Saymour, James, and Richard Anderson. *New Ghosts, Old Ghosts: Prisons and Labor Reform Camps in China.* New York: M. E. Sharpe, 1998.

Schoenfeld, Heather. *Building the Prison State: Race and the Politics of Mass Incarceration.* Chicago: University of Chicago Press, 2018.

Schram, Stuart. *The Thought of Mao Tse-Tung.* Cambridge: Cambridge University Press, 1989.

Scott, James. *Seeing Like a State: How Certain Schemes to Improve the Human Condition Have Failed.* New Haven: Yale University Press, 1998.

Scruton, Roger. *The Palgrave Macmillan Dictionary of Political Thought.* 3rd ed. New York: Palgrave Macmillan, 2007.

Senghor, Léopold. *On African Socialism.* New York: Frederick A. Praeger, 1964.

Serra, Carlos, ed. *História de Moçambique.* Vol. 1. 2nd ed. Maputo: Livraria Universitária, 2000.

Sheldon, Kathleen. *Pounders of Grain: A History of Women, Work, and Politics in Mozambique.* Portsmouth, NH: Heinemann, 2002.

Shore, Herbert. "Mondlane, Machel and Mozambique: From Rebellion to Revolution." *Africa Today* 21, no. 1 (Winter 1974): 3–12.

———. "Resistance and Revolution in the Life of Eduardo Mondlane." In *The Struggle for Mozambique,* by Eduardo Mondlane, xiii–xxxi. London: Zed Press, 1983.

Shubin, Vladimir. *The Hot "Cold War": The USSR in Southern Africa.* London: Pluto Press, 2008.

Siliya, Carlos, ed. *Samora Machel na memória do povo e do mundo: Discursos.* Vol. 1. Maputo: CPHLLN, 2011.

Silva, Calane da. *Xicandarinha na lenha do mundo.* Maputo: AEMO, 1987.

Slovo, Joe. "Shared Values: Socialism and Religion." *African Communist* (1994): 46–49.

Smith, Adam. *The Theory of Moral Sentiments.* Oxford: Clarendon, 1979. First published by A. Millar, 1759 (London).

Smith, Aminda. *Thought Reform and China's Dangerous Classes: Reeducation, Resistance, and the People.* New York: Rowman & Littlefield, 2013.

Sopa, António. *A alegria é uma coisa rara: Subsídios para a história da música popular urbana em Lourenço Marques (1920–1975).* Maputo: Marimbique, 2014.

———, ed. *Samora: Homem do povo.* Maputo: Meguezo, 2001.

Southall, Aiden, and Peter Gutkind. *Townsmen in the Making: Kampala and Its Suburbs.* Kampala: EAISR, 1956.

Stoler, Ann Laura. *Carnal Knowledge and Imperial Power: Race and the Intimate in Colonial Rule.* Berkeley: University of California Press, 2002.

———. "Matters of Intimacy as Matters of State: A Response." *Journal of American History* 88, no. 3 (December 2001): 893–97.

Strauss, Julia. "Morality, Coercion and State Building by Campaign in the Early PRC: Regime Consolidation and After, 1949–1956." *China Quarterly*, no. 188 (December 2006): 891–912.

Strayer, Joseph. Introduction to *The Historian's Craft*, by Marc Block, vii–xii. New York: Vintage Books, 1953.

Sumich, Jason. "Elites and Modernity in Mozambique." PhD diss., London School of Economics, 2005.

———. *The Middle Class in Mozambique: The State and the Politics of Transformation*. Cambridge: Cambridge University Press, 2018.

Tahbaz, Joseph. "Demystifying las UMAP: The Politics of Sugar, Gender, and Religion in 1960s Cuba." *Delaware Review of Latin American Studies* 14, no. 2 (December 2013).

Tartter, Jean. "Government and Politics." In *Mozambique: A Country Study*, edited by Harold Nelson, 181–239. Washington, DC: American University, 1984.

Taylor, Edgar. "Risk and Labour in the Archives: Archival Futures from Uganda." *Africa* 91, no. 4 (August 2021): 532–52.

Telepneva, Natasha. *Cold War Liberation: The Soviet Union and the Collapse of the Portuguese Empire in Africa, 1961–1975*. Chapel Hill: University of North Carolina Press, 2022.

———. "Mediators of Liberation: Eastern Bloc Officials, Mozambican Diplomacy and the Origins of Soviet Support for FRELIMO, 1958–1965." *Journal of Southern African Studies* 43, no. 1 (January 2017): 67–81.

Tembe, Joel das Neves, ed. *História da luta armada de libertação*. Vol. 1. Maputo: Ministério dos Combatentes, 2014.

Thiranagama, Sharika, and Tobias Kelly, eds. *Traitors: Suspicion, Intimacy, and the Ethics of State-Building*. Philadelphia: University of Pennsylvania Press, 2009.

Thomaz, Omar Ribeiro. "Escravos sem dono: A experiência social dos campos de trabalho em Moçambique no período socialista." *Revista de antropologia* 51, no. 1 (2008): 177–214.

Thompson, Drew. *Filtering Histories: The Photographic Bureaucracy in Mozambique, 1960 to Recent Times*. Ann Arbor: University of Michigan Press, 2021.

Timóteo, Adelino. *Os últimos dias de Uria Simango*. Maputo: Edição do Autor, 2017.

Todorov, Tzvetan. "Communist Camps and Their Aftermath." *Representations* 49 (Winter 1995): 120–32.

Touré, Ahmed Sékou. *Afrika and Imperialism*. Newark, NJ: Jihad Publishing, 1973.

———. "Revolution and Religion." *African Democratic Revolution* 144 (March 1980).

Trindade, João Carlos. "Rupturas e continuidades nos processos políticos e jurídicos." In *Conflito e transformação social: Uma paisagem das justiças em Moçambique*, vol. 1, edited by Boaventura de Sousa Santos and João Carlos Trindade, 97–127. Porto: Afrontamento, 2003.

Trouillot, Michel-Rolph. *Silencing the Past: Power and the Production of History.* Boston: Beacon Press, 1995.

Turner, Denys. *Marxism and Christianity.* Oxford: Blackwell, 1983.

Tutashinda, N. *As manifestações da 'autenticidade' Africana.* Lisbon: Cadernos Ulmero, 1978.

Urdang, Stephanie. *And Still They Dance: Women, War, and the Struggle for Change in Mozambique.* London: Monthly Review Press, 1989.

van Butselaar, Jan. *Africanos, missionários e colonialistas: As origens da Igreja Presbiteriana de Moçambique (Missão Suiça), 1880–1896.* Lausanne: Département Missionnaire des Eglises Protestantes de la Suisse Romande, 1987.

van de Walle, Nicolas. *African Economies and the Politics of Permanent Crisis.* Cambridge: Cambridge University Press, 2001.

Veloso, Jacinto. *Memórias em voo rasante.* 4th ed. Maputo: JV Editores, 2011.

Vieira, Sérgio. *Participei, por isso testemunho.* Maputo: Ndjira, 2010.

Vines, Alex. *Renamo: Terrorism in Mozambique.* Bloomington: Indiana University Press, 1991.

Viola, Lynne. *The Unknown Gulag: The Lost World of Stalin's Special Settlements.* New York: Oxford University Press, 2007.

Voegelin, Erich. *Political Religions.* Translated by T. J. DiNapoli and E. S. Easterly III. New York: Edwin Mellen Press, 1986. Originally published as *Die politischen Religionen.* Vienna: Bermann-Fischer, 1938.

Vu, Tran Tri. *Lost Years: My 1,632 Days in Vietnamese Reeducation Camps.* Berkeley: University of California Press, 1988.

Walkowitz, Judith. *City of Dreadful Delight: Narratives of Sexual Danger in Late-Victorian London.* Chicago: Chicago University Press, 1992.

Walzer, Michael. *The Revolution of the Saints: A Study in the Origins of Radical Politics.* Cambridge, MA: Harvard University Press, 1965.

Weber, Max. *The Protestant Ethic and the Spirit of Capitalism.* New York: Charles Scribner's Sons, 1976.

West, Harry. *Kupilikula: Governance and the Invisible Realm in Mozambique.* Chicago: Chicago University Press, 2005.

Westad, Odd Arne. *The Global Cold War: Third World Interventions and the Making of Our Times.* Cambridge: Cambridge University Press, 2005.

Westerlund, David. "Christianity and Socialism in Tanzania, 1967–1977." *Journal of Religion in Africa* 11, no. 1 (1980): 30–55.

White, Luise. *The Comforts of Home: Prostitution in Colonial Nairobi.* Chicago: University of Chicago Press, 1990.

———. "Students, ZAPU, and Special Branch in Francistown, 1964–1972." *Journal of Southern African Studies* 40, no. 6 (December 2014): 1289–303.

White, Luise, and Miles Larmer. "Introduction: Mobile Soldiers and the Un-national Liberation of Southern Africa." *Journal of Southern African Studies* 40, no. 6 (December 2014): 1271–74.

White, Lynn, III. *Policies of Chaos: The Organizational Causes of Violence in China's Cultural Revolution.* Princeton, NJ: Princeton University Press, 1989.

Whyte, Martin King. *Small Groups and Political Rituals in China.* Berkeley: University of California Press, 1974.

Wield, David. "Mozambique: Late Colonialism and Early Problems of Transition." In *Revolutionary Socialist Development in the Third World,* edited by Gordon White, 75–113. Lexington: University Press of Kentucky, 1983.

———. "Some Characteristics of the Mozambican Economy Particularly Relating to Industrialization." Mimeograph, Centro de Estudos Africanos, 1977.

Wilson, Elizabeth. *The Sphinx in the City: Urban Life, the Control of Disorder, and Women.* Berkeley: University of California Press, 1991.

Wipper, Audrey. "African Women, Fashion, and Scapegoating." *Canadian Journal of African Studies* 6, no. 2 (1972): 329–49.

Wu, Lili. "The Dilemma of Charismatic Authority: Mao's Cultural Revolution in China." PhD diss., University of Chicago, 2010.

Wuyts, Marc. *Camponeses e economia rural em Moçambique.* Maputo: INLD, 1981.

———. "Economia política do colonialismo em Moçambique." *Estudos Moçambicanos,* no. 1 (1980): 9–22.

Young, Crawford. *Ideology and Development in Africa.* New Haven: Yale University Press, 1982.

Zamparoni, Valdemir. "Entre Narros e Mulungos: Colonialismo e paisagem social em Lourenço Marques c. 1890–1940." PhD diss., Universidade de São Paulo, 1998.

———. "Frugalidade, moralidade, e respeito: A política do assimilacionismo em Moçambique, c. 1890–1930." X Congresso Internacional da Associação Latino-Americana de Estudos Afro-asiáticos, Rio de Janeiro, Brasil, 2000. https://aladaainternacional.com/wp-content/uploads/Frugalidade-moralidade-e-respeito.pdf.

Žižek, Slavoj. *For They Know Not What They Do: Enjoyment as a Political Factor.* London: Verso, 1991.

Index

Numbers in *italics* indicate pages with illustrations.